LUTHER'S WORKS

VOLUME 40

Church and Ministry

II

EDITED BY

CONRAD BERGENDOFF

GENERAL EDITOR

HELMUT T. LEHMANN

FORTRESS PRESS / PHILADELPHIA

Library of Congress Catalog Card Number 55–9893

ISBN 0–8006–0340–0

Printed in the United States of America   *1-340*

GENERAL EDITORS'
PREFACE

The first editions of Luther's collected works appeared in the sixteenth century, and so did the first efforts to make him "speak English." In America serious attempts in these directions were made for the first time in the nineteenth century. The Saint Louis edition of Luther was the first endeavor on American soil to publish a collected edition of his works, and the Henkel Press in New Market, Virginia, was the first to publish some of Luther's writings in an English translation. During the first decade of the twentieth century, J. N. Lenker produced translations of Luther's sermons and commentaries in thirteen volumes. A few years later the first of the six volumes in the Philadelphia (or Holman) edition of the *Works of Martin Luther* appeared. But a growing recognition of the need for more of Luther's works in English has resulted in this American edition of Luther's works.

The edition is intended primarily for the reader whose knowledge of late medieval Latin and sixteenth-century German is too small to permit him to work with Luther in the original languages. Those who can will continue to read Luther in his original words as these have been assembled in the monumental Weimar edition (*D. Martin Luthers Werke.* Kritische Gesamtausgabe; Weimar, 1883-   ). Its texts and helps have formed a basis for this edition, though in certain places we have felt constrained to depart from its readings and findings. We have tried throughout to translate Luther as he thought translating should be done. That is, we have striven for faithfulness on the basis of the best lexicographical materials available. But where literal accuracy and clarity have conflicted, it is clarity that we have preferred, so that sometimes paraphrase seemed more faithful than literal fidelity. We have proceeded in a similar way in the matter of Bible versions, translating Luther's translations. Where this could be done by the use of an

existing English version—King James, Douay, or Revised Standard—
we have done so. Where it could not, we have supplied our own.
To indicate this in each specific instance would have been pedantic;
to adopt a uniform procedure would have been artificial—especially
in view of Luther's own inconsistency in this regard. In each
volume the translator will be responsible primarily for matters of
text and language, while the responsibility of the editor will extend
principally to the historical and theological matters reflected in the
introductions and notes.

Although the edition as planned will include fifty-five volumes,
Luther's writings are not being translated in their entirety. Nor
should they be. As he was the first to insist, much of what he wrote
and said was not that important. Thus the edition is a selection of
works that have proved their importance for the faith, life, and
history of the Christian church. The first thirty volumes contain
Luther's expositions of various biblical books, while the remaining
volumes include what are usually called his "Reformation writings"
and other occasional pieces. The final volume of the set will be an
index volume; in addition to an index of quotations, proper names,
and topics, and a list of corrections and changes, it will contain a
glossary of many of the technical terms that recur in Luther's works
and that cannot be defined each time they appear. Obviously
Luther cannot be forced into any neat set of rubrics. He can
provide his reader with bits of autobiography or with political
observations as he expounds a psalm, and he can speak tenderly
about the meaning of the faith in the midst of polemics against his
opponents. It is the hope of publishers, editors, and translators that
through this edition the message of Luther's faith will speak more
clearly to the modern church.

J.P.
H.T.L.

CONTENTS

ABBREVIATIONS

C. R. — *Corpus Reformatorum,* edited by C. G. Bretschneider and H. E. Bindseil (Halle, 1834-1860).

CL — *Luthers Werke in Auswahl,* edited by Otto Clemen *et al.* (Bonn, 1912-1933; Berlin, 1955-1956).

EA — *D. Martin Luthers sämmtliche Werke* (Frankfurt and Erlangen, 1826-1857).

LW — American edition of *Luther's Works* (Philadelphia and St. Louis, 1955-)

MA[3] — *Martin Luther.* Ausgewählte Werke (Munchen, 1948-).

Migne — *Patrologiae, Series Latina,* 221 vols. in 222 (Paris, 1844-1904), J. P. Migne, editor.

PE — *Works of Martin Luther* (Philadelphia, 1915-1943).

St. L. — *D. Martin Luthers sämmtliche Schriften,* edited by Johann Georg Walch. Edited and published in modern German, 23 vols. in 25 (St. Louis, 1880-1910).

WA — *D. Martin Luthers Werke.* Kritische Gesamtausgabe (Weimar, 1883-).

WA, Br — *D. Martin Luthers Werke.* Briefwechsel (Weimar, 1930-1948).

WA, TR — *D. Martin Luthers Werke.* Tischreden (Weimar, 1912-1921).

WA, DB — *D. Martin Luthers Werke.* Deutsche Bibel (Weimar, 1906-).

INTRODUCTION TO VOLUME 40

The documents included in this volume date from the decade 1523-1532. They may be said to be the result of the revolutionary statements which inaugurated the Reformation, especially the works of 1517-1520 when the great issues were identified, and the pattern of the controversy between old and new was drawn. The germinal power was in the theses of 1517, but the implications were made clearer in *The Freedom of a Christian, The Babylonian Captivity of the Church* and *The Address to the Christian Nobility of the German Nation.* But as men pondered the meaning of a Reformation in the life of church and society they saw how great the effect would be on old institutions and beliefs. And not least the Reformers themselves began to sense that the next step would lead either to a more radical change or to an attempt to conserve the heritage of the past in re-ordering the newly created conditions.

It will be evident from a reading of this volume that Luther found himself confronted not only by papal opposition but by dissensions in the ranks of those who, for one reason or another, had followed him up to this point. The situation became increasingly confused. Some felt Luther had not gone far enough and even accused him of having retreated in the direction of Rome. Others had used Luther to strengthen their own attack on political or economic conditions, and were not interested in his confining the struggle to religious questions. Surrounded by foes of many kinds, Luther had to marshal his best efforts to establish a clear path on which the reformation of the church could proceed. It is in this period that he came to greater clarity on what the church of Jesus Christ should be, and developed his position over against both the church of Rome and the groups who went on to more radical interpretations of the nature of the church in the world.

For at the heart of the controversy lay the questions of the meaning of the church and the form of its organization. The force of his attack on the papacy is the measure of Luther's conviction that the Roman church was not exercising the function of the true church of Christ. This clearly emerges in the treatise, *The Keys*. All the elaborate organization of the hierarchy is beside the point. All the pomp and prestige and power of Rome represent a caricature of the church. For the purpose of the church is to convict men of sin and to effect the forgiveness of sin through the preaching of the gospel. This central task had been neglected by a ministry which considered other aims more essential and left this function to a lower order of clergy who knew little of what they were doing. What were commonly considered marks of a great and powerful church were to Luther an abomination, because these other, outward, things only obscured the one necessary task—the preaching of the forgiveness of sins through faith in the work of the Savior.

How far Luther was prepared to go in discarding the time-honored organization of the church is seen in the letter to the Bohemian Christians. He had reason to believe that the followers of John Huss would join forces with himself, and give up a very questionable method of obtaining an ordained ministry. Luther envisioned the possibility of small groups of Christians obtaining a minister by selection from their own midst. Supporters of the most advanced type of congregationalism can find confirmation of their views in this letter. But it should be remembered that the situation in Bohemia was highly abnormal and that Luther's suggestion is confined to an emergency. He advocated no such solution for Germany. The statement does clearly prove that apostolic succession in the Roman sense, or the doctrine of an indelible character in ordination, meant nothing to Luther, and that there may be times when a small band of Christians must establish a ministry based on nothing but the right of a congregation to elect those who shall preach the Word to it. The foundation of the ministry is in the Word and in the sacrament of baptism, not in age-old traditions, or the vote of a majority.

But if so much freedom is given a community of Christians what bounds are set on the kind of ministry churches may elect? Events soon happened which made some recoil from the proclamation of freedom for individual and congregation. While still at the Wartburg Luther had had to return to Wittenberg to control the emotions of those who expressed their faith in the destruction of the old—images, shrines, altars. The Reformation let loose a multitude of long-pent-up forces which sought to get rid of the old order of society as well as of the church. The extreme found expression in Thomas Münzer and his followers. Luther forcibly indicated that this was not the way to go in the *Letter to the Princes of Saxony* in which the authorities were urged, in the name of order and peace, to suppress this rebellious spirit.

A more subtle antagonist appeared in Karlstadt and in the movement characterized by spiritualist aspects. Here in fact began one of the great divisions in Protestantism. Luther dealt with the issue briefly in the *Letter to the Christians at Strassburg* and more fully in *Against the Heavenly Prophets*. In the course of his thinking he was drawn more and more to the Word as the final authority. He recognized the freedom of the soul from earthly ordinances of the papacy, but it is not an absolute freedom. The error of Rome was not in preaching obedience but in making a human organization the object of obedience. Man is bound to obey the Word of God, and the errors of the enthusiasts, or *Schwaermer,* were in setting themselves up as authorities, claiming to hear heavenly voices within themselves. These were a delusion to Luther who maintained that no doctrine could be established unless it has a clear and definite basis in Scripture. The enthusiasts confused the inward and the outward, and denied an external authority, thereby making them dependent on subjective feelings. For Luther, the Word of God was the authority in all matters of faith and no form of spiritualizing could supersede it.

It was not accidental that the sacraments became burning points in the controversy. For the enthusiasts made inner experiences the substance of Christianity, while Luther could never get away from an element of obedience, imposed by the Word. When Christ said, "This is my body," Luther bowed before the truth that Christ was in the bread and wine, though, as he said, his nature would the rather incline him to deny what his reason could not fathom. No amount of sophistry could move him, and the position he took against Karlstadt was the same that he held against Zwingli. Reason had to accommodate itself to the Word, and not the Word to reason. All other matters were secondary—matters of organization, aids to worship, and religious customs. Christ was present in the church through his Word and that must be believed and followed.

Likewise when the sacrament of baptism was challenged because it could not be proved that infants had faith, Luther countered that it is not sure that they do not have faith, but that in any case the sacrament does not rest on the faith either of the child or of the adult but on the command of Christ which the church must obey. He ridiculed the notion that the Anabaptist could be any more sure of faith on his second than on his first baptism, and he saw the temptation of making rebaptism a work of righteousness. But the grace of God is so complete that it excludes all possibility of man grounding his confidence in any possession of his own, be it a work of his hands or a work of his spirit.

Defending himself, both on the right against the papacy, and on the left against foes in his own following, Luther set himself to the constructive task of rebuilding the church on the basis of the Word. The congregations which had accepted reformation found themselves without pastors or supervision. Public worship had to be brought into line with the proclamation of the Word. Schools had to be maintained and some kind of discipline exercised. These were crucial years and years full of disappointment. But the Reformer proved himself equal to the challenge. He laid down the principles of worship in 1523, in the *Formula Missae*, and in 1526, in the *Deutsche Messe*. Through preaching and writing and counselling he constructed the outline of the faith of the church in the catechism. He turned, in lieu of other help, to the princes and pleaded with them to act as protectors of the church. Together with Melanchthon and others he sketched the organization of an evangelical church in the *Instructions for the Visitors of Parish Pastors*, who were to go from place to place and order the life of Christian communities. Out of all these and other experiences gradually emerged the church of the Reformation.

In general much of the old was retained. As Luther remarked in the treatise, *Concerning Rebaptism*, customs which were traditional should not be done away with because they were traditional, but on the grounds of being opposed to the Word of God. This principle was followed in the congregations. The Ten Commandments were to be observed as the law of God and enforced by the secular authorities to whom Christians were subject. Baptism should be administered to infants as hitherto, the sacrament of the altar should be safeguarded by diligent pastors. The church year was to continue with a proper celebration of the holidays. Christian freedom was to be interpreted not as freedom from all ordinances, religious or secular, but as freedom to live the life of the Spirit in a perilous world. In all changes from the old to the new the Christian was to seek to exemplify the Word and obey its authority.

Lacking episcopal supervision, the parishes were to be supervised by superintendents who would exercise the essential functions of a bishop, namely, to see to it that the Word was preached and the sacraments administered—the real work of the church. The need of the moment as well as the custom from the past led Luther to depend on the secular authorities for help in establishing the superintendencies and enforcing their regulations. The vast property of the medieval church, both in parish churches and monastic establishments, fell to the secular power in the changes of the Reformation, and Luther reminded the princes that they owed an obligation to give financial aid to the new order in preaching and teaching. With his conviction that the form of church organization was secondary Luther's dependency on the temporal powers was no more fundamental or essential than any other form. It was the only method available under the circumstances and should be replaced when it was possible for the churches to exercise greater independency. The goal of evangelical preaching and a Christian conduct should be served by any form of organization and such forms were to be judged by their success in reaching the goal.

The doctrine of the ministry which Luther held has to be deduced from his many statements on what the ministry should not be, as well as from his definition of the purpose of the church. All the inherited trappings of the medieval ministry were to be tested by the Word. Every spiritualistic interpretation was likewise subject to the Word. The essential element was the activity of the pastor in proclaiming and applying the Word in his parish. Luther insisted on order, and this included the propriety of a public call. The congregation was not to have men foisted on it, and no man should be pastor without being called. This conviction underlies the vehemence of Luther's attack on clandestine preachers who sneak around covertly undermining order and bringing the gospel into disrepute. How to provide a sufficient number of properly educated and supervised pastors was a problem that required a longer time for solution than Luther's lifetime. But Luther did live long enough to imprint on the evangelical churches a new conception of the nature and function of a Christian ministry.

In fact the great accomplishment of Luther in the realm of the doctrine of church and ministry was the redefinition of what the church is and what its pastors and laymen are to be. His was an age where church and state were closely tied together. One of the consequences of his work was the clearer differentiation between them and this was finally to lead, in some areas, to a separation. With such arrangements Luther was not greatly concerned. He was concerned that the church be re-established on scriptural grounds and that its ministry be recalled to proper functions. What was to be purged from the old—the old mass, old customs, old beliefs, and old structure—depended on a new sense of the meaning of the Word and its creative power in individual and community. Luther fought through to a clarity in standards by which all the activity of the church was to be judged. He wanted first things first—other things would follow in time.

The documents of this volume date from 1523—two years after the Diet of Worms, to 1532—two years after the Diet of Augsburg. At the former date the old was breaking up and the effects of the hammer blows of the preceding years were beginning to show. By the latter date a great constructive work had been accomplished so that the evangelical churches were able to give an account of their faith at Augsburg and to distinguish themselves from those who drew other conclusions from the Reformation. Instead of a traditional organization dependent on a hierarchy with its summit in Rome a new church life was growing up based on the preaching of a Word which had its roots in the obscure existence of men and women of faith in every Christian community. That the removal of spiritual domination by Rome had its perils Luther well knew. Nor did he altogether deny the right of others to preach differently from himself. His appeal to the authorities was to suppress men who were preaching insurrection. They might be allowed to preach heresy—that was involved in the new order. But Luther believed that the preaching of the Word would hold its own and, if not hindered by ecclesiastical or secular government, would establish itself among the people. Everything depended on the Word and the sacraments. These constituted the church and determined both the work of the universal priesthood of believers and the special functions of a selected ministry. What the Word was, what it contained and how it was to be interpreted—that was the chief concern of Luther, and his answers have permanently affected the structure and spirit of the Christian church.

C. B.

LUTHER'S WORKS

VOLUME 40

CONCERNING THE MINISTRY

1523

Translated by Conrad Bergendoff

INTRODUCTION

This treatise was written by Luther in 1523 to the Bohemian Christians, and addressed to the Senate in Prague. The circumstances attending its origin throw light on the nature of the contents.

Ever since the days of Huss the Bohemians had withstood Rome. Their insistence on receiving the sacrament in both kinds had given them the name Utraquists, and because the pope refused to sanction their position they had been in schism with Rome for a century. But they still held to most of the teachings of the Roman church and counted ordination as one of the sacraments. Since the pope refused them an archbishop, the archbishopric of Prague was vacant from 1421-1560, and a consistory with elected administrators ruled the churches. In order that the churches might have properly ordained pastors, candidates who had received instruction were sent to Italy where Italian bishops, mainly Venetian, ordained them, on the understanding they would administer communion at home only in one kind. On their return to Bohemia the newly ordained clergymen had to renounce this vow before the consistory if they wanted to serve a parish. It was clearly a subterfuge, but it enabled the Bohemians to keep up the semblance of having a regular ministry.

Luther had hoped that with their independent traditions the Bohemians would become his allies in the contest with Rome. In 1522 he had written to one of the Bohemian nobles, Graf Schlick, whose estates were on the border of Germany, urging the leaders of the nation to remain true to their Hussite heritage. In 1523, probably during the summer, a Bohemian clergyman, Gallus Cahera, appeared in Wittenberg. Cahera was a contentious and ambitious person. He led Luther to believe that Bohemia was inclining to the German reformer, and would be influenced by his words. Luther later complained that he was driven by Cahera to write and advise the Bohemians what to do in their difficult situation. He wrote this treatise and in it reproached them for their compromising with Rome. He showed the right of the congregations to elect their own

5

pastors, when the superiors were not interested in the Word. He advised the Bohemians to have nothing to do with foreign bishops whose ordination they could accept only with a bad conscience.

Cahera returned to Prague and seemed to enjoy success with his backing by Luther. He became administrator in Prague, and wanted the Bohemians to go farther in their reformation. But when he detected this was an unpopular move, he swung around to the Roman position and joined in the denunciation of the new measures as a German, and foreign innovation. The friends of Luther were deposed, and the Utraquists again sought agreement with Rome. What had seemed in the summer of 1523 to be a dawn of an evangelical day in Bohemia had turned by the summer of 1524 into a day of bitter disappointment for Luther. For in the former year Cahera had painted a bright picture for Luther; in the latter, the pastor of the Bethlehem Church of Prague was a refugee in Wittenberg. In 1525 the Bohemians openly declared their hostility to the conception of the ministry Luther had described in his treatise.

The Latin work was published late in 1523. It was immediately translated by Paul Speratus who had been a pastor in Moravia and was now in Wittenberg, where he was to enrich the Reformation by his contribution to hymnody.

The Latin text of the translation appears in WA 12, 169-195. The German translation, prepared by Speratus, appears in St. L. 10, 1548ff.

CONCERNING THE MINISTRY

To the Illustrious Senate and People of Prague,
from Martin Luther, Preacher at Wittenberg.
Grace and peace from God our Father and Jesus Christ our Lord.

Often and by many correspondents I have been asked to write to you, honored sirs, concerning the calling and ordination of a pastor of the church. Now at last the law of love will not allow me to decline any longer. Though I know it is beyond my ability, and that I have more duties at home than one man can be equal to, yet your situation and need are such that love must be undaunted, assured that it can do all things by His power who works in love. What I have, therefore, I give you, but with the understanding that each and all of you may use his own judgment. For my ministry does not allow me to go beyond what someone else asks. I am not an authority on something new. I only give my counsel and encouragement. But the Lord, who initiated and gave you the desire to ask and seek my advice, will fulfil and accomplish what you seek and intend, in full and rich measure to the praise of his grace and gospel. To Him be glory forever and ever.

A Warning

To begin with I freely confess that in this book I will disappoint all who may hope that I will endorse or amend the rite and custom hitherto prevailing of priestly tonsure and anointing. Such religion, or superstition, I will allow them to enjoy, however common, traditional, or vaunted it may be. We are interested in the pure and true course, prescribed in holy Scripture, and are little concerned about usage or what the fathers have said or done in this matter. We have already sufficiently made clear that herein we neither ought, should, nor would be bound by human traditions, however sacred and highly regarded, but clearly exercise our reason and

7

Christian liberty, as it is written, "All things are yours, whether Peter or Paul, but you are Christ's" [I Cor. 3:22, 23].

An Exhortation Against Receiving Papal Ordination

But before we come to our manner of appointment, that is, the Christian form, it is proper and fair to consider the papal consecrations (as they call them) and to expose publicly the abomination[1] of their order, so that its "iniquity may be found out and hated" [Ps. 36:2] and those who yet adhere closely to it may the more easily be persuaded to desist therefrom. And to begin with minor factors we would first present the reasons why you in Bohemia have been distressed in a special way, more than other peoples.

When Satan got the upper hand and the bishops and priests (as they are called) deserted the Bohemian kingdom, leaving it devastated and isolated, the Roman bishops laid on you the hard and dire necessity of sending your clerics annually to Italy to purchase papal ordination. For your neighboring bishops would not at all condescend to ordain them, since they considered you obstinate heretics. And what inconvenience and danger this need has caused you! I pass over what you have had to endure in body and goods, your exhaustion by such toil of journey, and by expense among strangers, even enemies, and the diseases, evil customs, and ruined conscience with which you return, in order to govern yourselves. A cause of greater misery is the fact that the pacts and dishonest circumstances force you to purchase ordination from your tyrant and his executioners, the bishops, through a violation of conscience, so that not a single one of you can ever rejoice in good conscience that you have entered the sheep-fold by the door [John 10:1]. Always and alone to be afflicted with such pastors as have entered in some other way than through the door is the greatest hardship.

For this reason, unfortunately, an opportunity is given a scamp, or apostate, or such as no other part of the world would tolerate, to enter into your ministry. Indeed this plight of yours has given rise to a proverb, namely, that one who has earned the noose or the wheel among the Germans qualifies as priest among the Bohemians.

---

[1] Literally, "execramentum," a play on "sacramentum."

So Bohemia has had to harbor eminent scoundrels, ignorant pastors, even rapacious wolves. Meanwhile, what concern has it been of the Holy Father in Rome in what ways the Bohemians were destroyed? He has looked on it as a great concession to purchase through such favors freedom and license for these pests and beasts to attack you. For though he was in a position to spare you these pests, yet the love of money prevails and in his mercy he sells his consecrations to heretics and to his enemies.

Hence arise the chaos and Babylonian confusion in your celebrated kingdom. Since you must have a ministry but have no means of correcting abuses, each one teaches what he wishes, one preaches this, another that, some deceive the people with the assumed title of priest, some purchase parishes, others force their way in, a successor upsets the work of his predecessor. In the absence of any form or basis of a valid ministry, we see noble Bohemia transformed into a Babylonia described by Isaiah, in which satyrs dance, and howling creatures and sorceresses answer each other [Isa. 13:21, 22]. What wonder, then, if in this confusion the people of Bohemia become nothing but schismatics, and no certain basis of faith or life exists, and the ministry seems to be one of perdition?

These atrocious and cruel conditions ought in all justice compel us, with one accord, to rid all Bohemia of these monsters. Clearly if misfortune and need are so great that they can secure ministers in no other way [than by subterfuge], I would confidently advise that you have no ministers at all. For it would be safer and more wholesome for the father of the household to read the gospel and, since the universal custom and use allows it to the laity, to baptize those who are born in his home, and so to govern himself and his according to the doctrine of Christ, even if throughout life they did not dare or could not receive the Eucharist. For the Eucharist is not so necessary that salvation depends on it. The gospel and baptism are sufficient, since faith alone justifies and love alone lives rightly.

Surely if in this way two, three, or ten homes, or a whole city, or several cities agreed thus among themselves to live in faith and love by the use of the gospel in the home, and even if no ordained man, shorn or anointed, ever came to them or in any other way was placed over them as minister to administer the Eucharist and other sacraments, Christ without a doubt would be in their midst and

9

would own them as his church. Christ would not only not condemn, but surely would reward a pious and Christian abstinence from all the other sacraments when these would be offered by impious and sacrilegious men. For He himself said "One thing only is necessary" [Luke 10:42], the Word of God, in which man has his life. For if he lives in the Word and has the Word, he is able to forego all else in order to avoid the teachings and ministries of impious men. And what would it avail to have all other things, but not the Word by which one lives? The mercenary papists who have intruded themselves ply their trade of consecrations, so that while the sacraments are here the Word does not exist in Bohemia. That is, they deprive you of essentials and lord it over you in nonessentials.

The father in the home, on the other hand, can provide his own with the necessities through the Word and in pious humility do without the nonessentials as long as he is in captivity. In this regard we follow the custom and law of the Jewish captives who were not able to be in Jerusalem or to make offering there. Upheld in their faith alone by the Word of God they passed their lives among enemies while yearning for Jerusalem. So in this case the head of the household suffering under the tyranny of the pope would act most appropriately and safely if while longing for the Eucharist, which he neither would dare nor could receive, in the meantime zealously and faithfully propagated faith in his home through the Word of God until God on high in his mercy either brought the captivity to an end or sent a true minister of the Word. So, I hold, it is better to have none than to have a minister who is guilty of sacrilege, impiety, and crime, and comes as a thief and robber only to kill and destroy [John 10:10].

But now, thanks be to God, this condition is grievous and inevitable only in the case of the weak and over-scrupulous. The others who have faith and know the truth, possess full freedom and means to drive away unworthy ministers and to call and appoint only such worthy and devout men as they choose. For by a pretty invention, of which only the man of sin is capable [II Thess. 2:3], the papal theory perpetuates its ministry through an *indelible character* and safeguards it against removal by any kind of wrong-doing. In this way the pope establishes his tyranny and confirms the commission of sin with impunity while no freedom is given to

10

choose better men and we are forced to endure evil men. But of this we shall speak a little later. Now that we have directed attention to your suffering of evils in Bohemia and urged you to forego papal ordinations I add a general reason to arouse you and all the world to abstain from the stench and apostasy of these offensive and abominable ordinations.

For the time being I will concede the papal ordinations whereby those whom they call priests are anointed and appointed by the authority of the bishop alone without any consent or election by the people over whom they are to be placed. Yet, since they are a people of God it is due them that no one be set over them without their election, and the bishop ought to confirm no one whom they did not know and approve of as suitable. But now those who are ordained are mostly without certain call and no one knows whose minister he is to be. Consequently the majority are ordained only, as they say, to benefices, in order to offer mass only, and the people have no idea whom the bishop anoints as their pastor. Yet, I say, I am willing to overlook this grievous error in papal ordinations, for a time.

Everyone who loves Christ ought to shudder before this situation and rather endure any suffering than to be ordained by the papists since everything in those ordinations is done and performed in greatest perverseness and impiety. Were they not performed in blindness and senselessness they might seem to be a deliberate mockery in the face of God. Ordination indeed was first instituted on the authority of Scripture, and according to the example and decrees of the Apostle, in order to provide the people with ministers of the Word. The public ministry of the Word, I hold, by which the mysteries of God are made known, ought to be established by holy ordination as the highest and greatest of the functions of the church, on which the whole power of the church depends, since the church is nothing without the Word and everything in it exists by virtue of the Word alone. But my papists do not even dream of this in their ordinations. What is it they do?

In the first place they have been struck by blindness so that they do not even recognize what the Word or what the ministry of the Word is. This is especially true of the bishops who do the ordaining. How then is it possible for them to provide ministers of the Word by their ordinations? In place of ministers of the Word they only ordain priestly functionaries who offer up masses and hear confessions. For this is what the bishop means by giving the chalice into the hands of the candidate and giving him the power of consecrating, and sacrificing for the living and the dead. This indeed is a power that angels never could glory in, nor could the virgin mother of God possess it, but they have it though they be more impure than seducers and thieves. And thus in a most holy mysterious manner the bishop breathes in their ears and makes them father confessors, saying, "Receive the Holy Spirit." [2] Such is this most glorious power of consecration and absolution.

You would say that I exaggerate and lie if I claimed you could find one person ordained in their manner who dared assert that by such ordination he was commanded to communicate the mysteries of Christ and teach the gospel and rule the church which he obtained with his own blood [Acts 20:28]. Clearly no one ever hears this nor thinks that it concerns him. The chalice of course he accepts and thinks that all his ordination means is that he is permitted to consecrate and sacrifice Christ in the mass, and to hear confessions. Indeed he is concerned about his title to a benefice so as to feed his stomach, but otherwise he considers nothing at all beyond the sacrifice of masses—thus all the obligations of ordination are fulfilled. Whoever performs this, he is an ordained priest of the church and no one but him has this power. Anointing by the fingers and the tonsure of the head bear witness of this fact.

As to the call of a parish, or of a magistrate, to the ministry of the Word, this is considered by them as a rather recent and certainly incomparably minor obligation, compared to their sacred order and character. Their pastors and bishops and their high officials do not think they should be bothered by this kind of work, but turn it over to the lowest, meanest, vilest, and most ignorant. It is by far the meanest and most inexpert task, since communicating the mysteries of God and tending souls is of course an office lacking *indelible character* or the sacrament of ordination. But to consecrate Christ and sacrifice him, that implies *character*, that truly evidences a sacramental order.

---

[2] Cf. *The Ceremonies of Ordination to the Priesthood* (Chicago: Loyola University Press, 1917).

12

The wrath of God hovers over these ridiculous masks of bishops, not only because they despise the Word of God and replace it by the office of sacrifice, but also because they turn away from life-giving baptism, by which men are made alive and sanctified as reasonable souls unto eternal life. For they look on this sacrament as altogether unworthy and alien to their gem-studded mitres and golden mantles. But they consider it indeed fitting to baptize, not souls, but stones, altars, bells, dead and inanimate objects, as receptive of baptism as they themselves are of truth. So great is their madness and foolishness that you would faint from laughter were you not to regard with seriousness a bishop who toys with such things. But if you were to regard this in spirit as blasphemy you might explode in indignation.

If any are to be denied the name of priests, then above all those anointed by papal ordinations should be rejected. From the foregoing it is sufficiently clear that the papal bishops could in no way act as if they were ordaining to the ministry of the Word, but only to the sacrifice of masses and the hearing of confessions. For they are not able to act otherwise than as they really intend to act, namely, they are not concerned about the office of teaching, but confer the power of sacrificing and of hearing confession of sins. Consequently there is nothing else those ordained can obtain. Since it is most certain that the mass is not a sacrifice, therefore, their confession, which they would make compulsory, is nothing, and both are but a human and sacrilegious invention and falsehood. It clearly follows that their sacred ordinations make no one a priest or minister in the eyes of God, but only confer a certain mask of falsehood and vanity so that they offer where there is no sacrifice, and grant absolution where there is no accusation. It is as if some actor laughed and gesticulated in an empty theater.

Such are the things which ought justly to move not only you in Bohemia but all pious hearts everywhere to tolerate anything rather than to be sullied by these sacrilegious ordinations. And they who already have been ordained should grieve that they thus have been misled through masks of falsehood. For if these ever rightly celebrated the mass or fulfilled the ministry of the church, it certainly was not by virtue of a sacred ordination, which is mere falsehood and derision of God, but by virtue of the faith and spirit

13

of the church which has had to tolerate these masks in place of a true ministry. But now that the situation has been forced into the light, God is no longer to be mocked and derided, and we should flee these masks of falsehood as the most terrible pests of the soul and the most shameful disgrace of the church of God.

But he who came into the ministry through these masks, let him carry on, assume the office and administer it in a pure and worthy manner. Rejecting the office of sacrificing the mass, let him teach the Word of God and govern the church. This he can do while inwardly condemning and hating the anointing and the whole form of ordination by which he came into the office. For it is not necessary to leave the place of the ministry though you may have reached it by wrong and impious methods, as long as the mind has mended its ways and the method has been condemned.

Further, if these feigned priests and masquerading bishops plied their ordinations and sacrifices, either in a spirit of amusement or of seriousness, so as not directly to oppose the gospel, and at least would leave us Christ inviolate in his kingdom, maybe their arrogance would be the less reprehensible and their temerity might be tolerated. But now their madness and senselessness is such that Christ must be denied and altogether rejected so that their sacrifices and offices might survive. I have abundantly showed this elsewhere but it will not hurt to repeat some of it here.

The gospel and all of Scripture present Christ as the high priest, who alone and once for all by offering himself has taken away the sins of all men and accomplished their sanctification for all eternity. For once and for all he entered into the holy place through his own blood, thus securing an eternal redemption [Heb. 9:12, 28; 10:12, 14]. Thus no other sacrifice remains for our sins than his, and, by putting our trust altogether in it, we are saved from sin without any merits or works of our own. Of this sacrifice and offering he has instituted a perpetual remembrance in that he intends to have it proclaimed in the sacrament of the altar and thereby have faith in it strengthened. But how can this be accomplished in the abomination of the papal ordinations?

But now as if his unique sacrifice were not enough, or as if he had not obtained an eternal redemption, they daily offer body and

14

blood in innumerable places throughout the world. By this sacrifice they promise a remission of sins not eternal, but which is repeated every day. This abomination goes beyond all reason. What else is this than honoring the sacrifice of Christ in name only but in fact wholly rejecting and destroying it? For how is it possible that I should at the same time believe that I have eternal forgiveness of sins by the sacrifice of Christ and yet by a sacrifice repeated daily seek remission again and again? For if I believe that Christ offered once for all, has won for me perpetual forgiveness of sins, I cannot seek forgiveness anew by some other sacrifice. For if I seek forgiveness by a daily sacrifice there is no room for a faith that the unique sacrifice of Christ has taken away all my sins forever.

You see, thus, with what frightful perversity these sacrifices in the name of Christ completely deprive us of Christ and his kingdom and in his place give us their own work, their sacrifice, their invention, just as Christ predicted that the abomination would stand in the holy place [Matt. 24:15]. Here the words of Christ hold true in mighty fashion: "Many will come in my name, saying 'I am the Christ'" [Matt. 24:5]. But are not these counterfeiting Christ who by their daily repeated sacrifices in so many thousands of places promise that which Christ alone by his sacrifice once for all effected? Is not this to remove faith from the rock of truth which is in Christ and to build on the sand of human falsehood?

We see, then, what kind of priests are created by papal ordinations—not indeed priests of God, but priests of Satan, such as trample down Christ and destroy his sacrifice, who in truth do business in his name but teach faith in their own sacrifices. So it is no longer a question of whether one should seek or receive holy orders from the papists, but it is a definite conclusion that no one confers holy orders and makes priests less than those under the papal dominion. A semblance, indeed, of ordination and of making priests is magnificently present but it behooves the king of semblance to grant nothing but semblance so as to guarantee his abominations. Therefore, our conscience and faith impel us, under penalty of God's anathema, to guard against their ordination. Indeed consideration of our salvation necessarily compels us to abstain from their disgraceful and damnable ordinations. Woe to those then who knowingly and sagaciously consecrate themselves to this adversary of God and this Baal Peor.[3]

These reasons surely ought to influence you Bohemians more than any other people. For not only is it as impious for you as for others in the sight of God to seek and receive ordinations from your foe, but also in the sight of men, for it was this foe that burnt John Huss[4] and Jerome of Prague[5] and many others, slandering your name. It is the same foe that wants always to extinguish you, who brands you as hateful heretic endlessly and in every way throughout the earth. You have had to withstand his plagueful attacks with the shedding of blood. Yet he has not repented of the bloody tyranny of his disgraceful acts, nor recanted of any victim innocently condemned to bloody death, nor restored the sacrilegiously stolen name of Christian. It does not grieve him that so much German blood has been spilled against you, in vain and to the ruin of souls, because of his profane tyranny. Indeed so obstinate is he in brow and neck that even today he would like to see both yourselves and ourselves perish altogether and so not even the least spark of light remain to the honor of Christ.

To this date he holds under his futile and invalid ban King George and his family at Münsterberg,[6] an eminent dukedom of Bohemia, and likewise many others. But it is well that the man of perdition be revealed [II Thess. 2:3ff.] of whom Peter foretold that he would place kings and rulers under his curse without fear [II Pet. 2:10; Jude 8]. We have, though, another bishop, who can bless where this one curses as it is written, "Let them curse, but do thou bless" [Ps. 109:28]. The ban of the pope on King George and the duchy of Münsterberg, and those who have suffered the same always will be and now are in the condition described by Solomon in Proverbs, "Like a sparrow in its flitting, like a swallow in its flying, a curse that is causeless does not alight" [Prov. 26:2]. But it

---

[3] An idol of Moab which Israel, by the counsel of Balaam to the Midianites, was enticed to worship [Num. 25:3f.].

[4] John Huss, reformer of Bohemia, was burned at the stake at Constance, June 6, 1415. Cf. *The Leipzig Debate, LW* 31, p. 307.

[5] Jerome of Prague, friend and follower of Huss, was likewise burned at the stake at Constance, May 30, 1416.

[6] Pius II put George Podiebrad under the ban of excommunication in 1464 and Paul II deprived him of his kingdom in 1466. The Bohemian insistence on receiving communion in both bread and wine resulted in excommunication.

will always be a cause of unusual glory before God that King George and his family more than other kings and princes of the earth have been cursed by an abusive see and by the son of cursing.

Will you then continue, people of Bohemia, needlessly to receive impious and hateful ordinations from so cruel and blood-thirsty and implacable a foe of yours or have anything to do with one who curses you and is an abomination before God and men? For if you do so, are you not in fact agreeing with and justifying one who condemns you? Are you not then condemning all the glorious resistance you have offered him and compromising yourselves? Do you not dishonor the pious blood of John Huss, innocently shed, and confess his death was deserved, as long as you kiss the hands of him who slew him and prostrate yourselves before the feet of him who spurns you and tortures you with unending shame?

How much better it would be if you separated yourselves so far from him that, if it were possible, you would not smell the foul odor of his name. When Paul commands us to avoid the fornicator and drunkard [Rom. 13:12, 13; Eph. 5:3f., 18], how much more all who confess Christ ought to avoid this most recent abomination which refuses to be controlled or corrected and lays waste on all sides!

Allow me, then, good sirs, first to plead with you, though your conscience and fear of God ought to impel you if you are unwilling, henceforth neither to seek nor receive ordinations from this son of perdition, even if he offers them. Much less ought you to receive anyone ordained by him, who comes to you with the name and mark of the beast [Rev. 19:20]. For unless we made this a first requirement, we would toil in vain, and in vain would seek ways in which to help you. Your far-famed resistance, truly a happy secession from Satan's rule, would then be only a semblance and pretense. For how can one enjoy far-spread fame for having rejected the papal yoke and yet admit no one to guide consciences other than the murderers and thieves who are a part of the tyranny one has cast off? Will not all the world conclude that all that you obtained for so much blood, so many perils, and by so great a disgrace of your Christian name, even suffering the name of heretics, was the title of rejectors of papal tyranny, while in fact you have

17

reintroduced his tyranny over you? In that respect we stupid Germans suffer simple tyranny, inasmuch as we endure that which the name implies, without having the title of rejectors of the pope. We cannot comfort ourselves with false glory, that is, deriving peculiar satisfaction from attributing to the infamous tyrant what is our own mockery.

But, someone says, "What method of appointing ministers shall we adopt? Necessity knows no law. We do not have priests and we cannot do without them." Were this so, it would have been wiser to realize this, and so to feel, speak, and remark, before leaving the papacy. Or now, certainly, when liberty is gone, you should return quickly to the name of servitude from which you departed rather than to enjoy the title only of an asserted freedom, and to feed on empty air in a captivity doubly hard to bear. It remains therefore to face the issue squarely. Either we must learn how to provide ourselves with presbyters apart from papal tyranny, or if we are not willing to do so (though it is possible) we must give ourselves into captivity, resigned and willingly, and with full knowledge and purpose enter the service of the king of perdition, which the merciful Christ our Lord and Master prevent. Amen.

A Priest is not identical with Presbyter or Minister—
for one is born to be priest, one becomes a minister.

And here above all constancy in faith is required if through the power of the divine Word we are to rid ourselves of a widespread and long-standing offense, namely, that men call those priests who are so only through human error, and that they undertake to defend with unyielding obstinacy those whom the bishops have shorn and anointed. For by this deceptive name Satan has fraudulently found entrance and wreaks ruin on all sides with unbelievable madness. Taking seven spirits worse than himself he takes possession of the court and dwells there in peace [Luke 11:21, 26], so that no one has any other conception of the word priest than that monstrosity of shaving and anointing introduced by human brashness and superstition. You will not triumph over this scandalous condition unless with closed eyes you disregard

18

usage, tradition, and great numbers, and with open ears heed only the Word of God.

First, regard as an unmovable rock that the New Testament knows of no priest who is or can be anointed externally. If there are such, they are imitators and idols. There is neither example nor command nor a simple word in Gospels or Epistles of the apostles in support of this vanity. They are established and brought in only by the kind of human invention of which Jeroboam once was guilty in Israel's history [I Kings 12:32f.]. For a priest, especially in the New Testament, was not made but was born. He was created, not ordained. He was born not indeed of flesh, but through a birth of the Spirit, by water and Spirit in the washing of regeneration [John 3:6f.; Titus 3:5f.]. Indeed, all Christians are priests, and all priests are Christians. Worthy of anathema is any assertion that a priest is anything else than a Christian. For such an assertion has no support in the Word of God and is based only on human opinions, on ancient usage, or on the opinions of the majority, any one of which is ineffectual to establish an article of faith without sacrilege and offense, as I have sufficiently shown elsewhere.

The scriptures of God, by which our consciences should be formed and confirmed as over against the shorn and the anointed and which hold that the Christians and they alone are priests, assert, "You are a priest forever after the order of Melchizedek" [Ps. 110:4]. Christ himself was neither shorn nor anointed with oil in order to become a priest. Therefore, it is not enough for anyone who follows Christ to be anointed in order to become a priest. But it is necessary that he have something far different and, possessing this, he needs no oil or tonsure. It is obvious that these pseudo-ordainers—the bishops—blaspheme and err in holding that their anointing and ordinations are so necessary that without them no one can be a priest, however holy he be, be he Christ himself. On the other hand they hold that such ceremonies make a priest even if the person be a worse character than Nero[7] or Ashurbanipal.[8]

What else do they accomplish than a denial that Christ is a

---

[7] Nero, Roman emperor from A.D. 54-68, during whose reign the first known persecution of Christians outside of Palestine occurred.
[8] Ashurbanipal was the king of Assyria from 668-626 B.C.

priest among his Christians? For in carrying on their hateful office they make no one a priest until he denies that he was a priest before. Thus in the very act of making him a priest they in fact remove him from his priesthood, so that before God their ordination is a mockery, but also a veritable and serious degradation. For to say, "I am ordained a priest," is only to confess, "I was not, and am not now a priest." It is just as great an abomination as when the monks vow obedience to "Evangelical Counsels," [9] and at the same time deny the commandments of God.

Furthermore, I shall also prove this conclusion to be trust-worthy: Christ is a priest, therefore Christians are priests, as Psalm 22 [:23] states: "I will tell of thy name to my brethren." Again, "God, your God, has anointed you with the oil of gladness above your fellows" [Ps. 45:8]. That we are his brethren is true only because of the new birth. Wherefore we are priests, as he is Priest, sons as he is Son, kings as he is King. For he makes us to sit with him in heavenly places, as companions and co-heirs with him, in whom and with whom all things are given us. And many similar expressions indicate our oneness with Christ—one loaf, one cup, one body, members of his body, one flesh, bone of his bone, and we are told we have all things in common with him [Rom. 8:32; Gal. 3:28; I Cor. 10:17; Eph. 4:4; 5:30].

So it follows naturally that Christ has been made the first priest of the New Testament without shaving, without anointing, and so without any of their "character" or all the masquerade of episcopal ordination. He made all his apostles and his disciples priests, but through no such masks. So this mask of ordination is unnecessary. And if you have it, it is not enough in order to be a priest. Other-wise, you would have to confess that neither Christ nor the apostles were priests. You see how right I am saying that no one is less a priest than those today ordained as priests. For everything is left out by which Christ and his apostles were made priests, and only those things included which Christ and the apostles did without when they were made priests, and which make no priests. It is a lie

---

[9] Evangelical Counsels, also described as Counsels of Perfection, are three in number: poverty, chastity, and obedience. Intended chiefly for members of religious and monastic orders, fulfilment of their requirements leads to a higher perfection than is demanded of Christians generally.

which comes from their own brains when they maintain, "Thus you are created a priest, otherwise not." This is as much as to say, "Christ was not shaved or anointed by us, therefore he is no priest."

But let us go on and show from the priestly offices (as they call them) that all Christians are priests in equal degree. For such passages as, "You are a royal priesthood" (I Pet. 2 [:9]) and, "Thou has made them a kingdom and priests" (Rev. 5 [:10]), I have sufficiently treated in other books.[10] Mostly the functions of a priest are these: to teach, to preach and proclaim the Word of God, to baptize, to consecrate or administer the Eucharist, to bind and loose sins, to pray for others, to sacrifice, and to judge of all doctrine and spirits. Certainly these are splendid and royal duties. But the first and foremost of all on which everything else depends, is the teaching of the Word of God. For we teach with the Word, we consecrate with the Word, we bind and absolve sins by the Word, we baptize with the Word, we sacrifice with the Word, we judge all things by the Word. Therefore when we grant the Word to anyone, we cannot deny anything to him pertaining to the exercise of his priesthood. This Word is the same for all, as Isaiah says, "All your sons shall be taught by the Lord" [Isa. 54:13]. They are taught by the Lord, who hear and learn from the Father, as Christ explains in John 6 [:45]. And hearing is through the Word of Christ (Rom. 10 [:17]) in order that the praise of Ps. 149 [:9] may be realized: "This is glory for all his faithful ones." For whom? "Let the high praises of God be in their throats and two-edged swords in their hands, to wreak vengeance on the nations and chastisement on the peoples, to bind their kings with chains and their nobles with fetters of iron, to execute on them the judgment written" [Ps. 149:6f.].

The first office, that of the ministry of the Word, therefore, is common to all Christians. This is clear, from what I have already said, and from I Pet. 2 [:9], "You are a royal priesthood that you may declare the wonderful deeds of him who called you out of darkness into his marvelous light." I ask, who are these who are called out of darkness into marvelous light? Is it only the shorn and anointed masks? Is it not all Christians? And Peter not only

---

[10] Cf. *An Address to the Christian Nobility. . . .* WA 6, 407ff.; PE 2, 66ff.; *Ein Widerspruch D. Luthers Seines Irrtums erzwungen durch den hochgelehrtesten Herrn Hieronymus Emser, Vikar zu Meissen.* WA 8, 247ff.

21

gives them the right, but the command, to declare the wonderful deeds of God, which certainly is nothing else than to preach the Word of God. But some[11] imagine a twofold priesthood, one spiritual and common to all, the other external and limited, and say that Peter here speaks of the spiritual one. But what is the function of this limited and external office? Is it not to declare the wonderful deeds of God? But this Peter enjoins on the spiritual and universal priesthood. In truth these blasphemers have another, external, ministry in which they declare, not the wonderful deeds of God, but their own and the pope's impious deeds. So, as there is no other proclamation in the ministry of the Word than that which is common to all, that of the wonderful deed of God, so there is no other priesthood than that which is spiritual and universal, as Peter here defines it.

Christ proves the same thing according to the account in Matthew, Mark, and Luke, where he says to all at the Last Supper: "Do this in remembrance of me" [Luke 22:19; I Cor. 11:24]. For this he did not say only to the shorn and anointed, else only the shorn and anointed could receive the body and blood of the Lord. Even this remembrance is nothing else than a preaching of the Word, as Paul explains in I Cor. [11:26], "For as often as you eat this bread and drink the cup, you proclaim the Lord's death until he comes." To proclaim the death of the Lord is to declare the wonderful deeds of God who called us from darkness into marvelous light. Here, thus, is nothing of the dreams of impious men who find herein that the apostles were made priests, that is, ordained with their masks. Christ here enjoined the same ministry of the Word on them all equally. All of them are given the right and command to hold the Lord in remembrance, so that God may be praised and glorified in his marvelous deeds. He means that we should remember him not by offering masses in hidden corners or by enforced meditations, but by a public ministry of the Word, for the salvation of those who hear.

Paul confirms this in I Cor. 14 [:26] as he speaks not to the shorn or to a few, but to the whole church and each individual Christian: "Each one of you has a hymn, a lesson, a revelation, a

---

[11] For example, Jerome Emser. WA 8, 247.

tongue or an interpretation." And further on: "For you can all prophesy one by one, so that all may learn and all be encouraged" [I Cor. 14:31]. For say, what is meant by "each one of you"? And by "all"? Can this mean only the shorn? These passages very strongly and clearly corroborate that the ministry of the Word is the highest office in the church, that it is unique and belongs to all who are Christians, not only by right but by command. Indeed it is not a priesthood if it is not unique and common to all. Nothing can prevail against these divine thunderings, be it numberless fathers, innumerable councils, the custom of ages, or a majority of all the world. For these are but as straws by which the shorn masqueraders strive to establish their priesthood.

The second function, to baptize, they themselves have by usage allowed in cases of necessity even to ordinary women, so that it is hardly regarded any more as a sacramental function. Whether they wish or not we deduce from their own logic that all Christians, and they alone, even women, are priests, without tonsure and episcopal "character." For in baptizing we proffer the life-giving Word of God, which renews souls and redeems from death and sins. To baptize is incomparably greater than to consecrate bread and wine, for it is the greatest office in the church—the proclamation of the Word of God. So when women baptize, they exercise the function of priesthood legitimately, and do it not as a private act, but as a part of the public ministry of the church which belongs only to the priesthood.

The stupidity and senselessness of the papists here sufficiently reveals itself. For they permit the ministry of baptism to all, and yet consider the priesthood as their own property and baptism as impossible without their priests. They themselves have established it as the first sacrament and have permitted no one but priests to administer sacraments. But one sacrament cannot be of greater rank than another, since all are founded on the same Word of God. But their own blindness has deceived them, so that they do not see the majesty of the Word of God reigning in baptism. For if they had a right sense of values they would discern that no dignity, be it of priest, or bishop, or even of the pope, can compare with that which they attribute to the ministry of the Word. Small indeed appears the name of priest, or bishop, or pope as over against the name of minister of the Word of God, a Word that lives and remains forever, powerful and able to do all things.

There is something ridiculous about this conferring of orders. For the episcopal dignity is not a sacrament nor has it a "character." Yet it gives a priestly dignity and power supposedly above all others. Though the episcopal authority ranks as the highest since it grants the ordination and "character" of a priest, it is at the same time inferior since it is not itself an order or in possession of a peculiar "character." So the lesser bestows what is greater. And since it proved necessary to dress up this absurdity they created this fictitious distinction between dignity and power. What else was possible once the imprudent lie got started, but to continue to vacillate? Wherefore Christ predicted how all things in the papal realm would be guided by no consistent reason but overleap the bounds of common sense. So it is not surprising that they concede the priestly sacrament of baptism to all, yet lay claim to exclusive possession of the priesthood.

The third function is to consecrate or to administer the sacred bread and wine. Here those in the order of the shorn vaunt themselves and set themselves up as rulers of a power given neither to angels nor the virgin mother. Unmoved by their senselessness we hold that this function, too, like the priesthood, belongs to all, and this we assert, not on our own authority, but that of Christ who at the Last Supper said, "Do this in remembrance of me" [Luke 22:19; I Cor. 11:24]. This is the word by means of which the shorn papists claim they can make priests and give them the authority to consecrate. But Christ spoke this word to all those then present and to those who in the future would be at the table, to eat this bread and drink this cup. So it follows that what is given here is given to all. Those who oppose this have no foundation on which to stand, except the fathers, the councils, tradition, and that strongest article of their faith, namely, "We are many and thus we hold: therefore it is true."

A further witness is the word of Paul in I Cor. 11 [:23], "For I received from the Lord what I also delivered to you," etc. Here Paul addresses all the Corinthians, making each of them, as he himself was, consecrators. But in this case so great a beam is in the eyes of the papists [Matt. 7:3] that they do not see the majesty of

24

the Word of God, but only stand in awe before the transubstantiation of the bread. Yet I ask you, what is this splendid power of consecration, compared to the power of baptizing and of proclaiming the Word? A woman can baptize and administer the Word of life, by which sin is taken away, eternal death abolished, the prince of the world cast out, heaven bestowed; in short by which the divine majesty pours itself forth through all the soul. Meanwhile this miracle-working priest changes the nature of the bread, but by no other or greater word or power, and it has no other effect than that it increases his awe and admiration before his own dignity and power. Is not this to make an elephant out of a fly? What wonder workers! In despising the power of the Word they make marvelous their own power.

Furthermore we note how seldom the Evangelists and Apostles make mention of the Eucharist, a fact that has led many to wish they had said more about it. On the other hand they ceaselessly emphasize, even to the point of weariness, the ministry of the Word. It is as if the Spirit had foreseen these coming abuses and errors of the shorn ones which would turn the heart from the Word of power and truth to that futile change of bread and wine, all through life clinging to these outward appearances while rejecting the marvelous light into which we have been called. If then that which is greatest, namely, Word and baptism, is conferred on all, then it can rightly be maintained that the lesser, the power to consecrate, is also so conferred, even if there be no direct authority of Scripture. Just as Christ proclaimed, "Is not life more than food, and the body more than clothing?" [Matt. 6:25], implying, if God gives the greater how much more would he give the lesser?

The fourth function consists in binding and loosing from sin. Not only have they appropriated this function arrogantly to themselves, but from it drawn the conclusion boastfully that to them alone is given the power of establishing laws. For "to bind," they claim, means to make laws, to prohibit, and to command. It becomes indeed a binding of consciences, though falsely and deceitfully, for they bind when there is no reason for it, as in the case of prohibition of marriage and of certain foods, though both have the sanction of God's creation. To absolve, again, among them means to take money for making dispensations in regard to their stipulations and false laws, so that they deceitfully forgive what they have falsely imposed on consciences. They make use of the office of binding and loosing also in confessions and excommunications, though this practice is invalid in law and an abuse to be condemned.

By this theft and impious embezzlement they have brought it about that the office of the keys, or of binding and loosing, is never less used than among themselves. They never employ the keys to open or close heaven to consciences, but they do use them to regulate the money pouches of all the earth. But this office of the keys belongs to all of us who are Christians, as I have so often proved and shown in my books against the pope.[12] For the word of Christ in Matt. 18 [:15] is addressed not only to the Apostles, but, certainly, to all the brethren: "If your brother sins against you, go and tell him his fault . . . if he listens to you, you have gained your brother." And, further on, "If he refuses to listen even to the church, let him be to you as a Gentile and a tax collector. Truly I say to you, whatever you bind on earth shall be bound in heaven, and whatever you loose on earth shall be loosed in heaven" [Matt. 18:17, 18].

We need pay no attention to the bogey man of these masqueraders when they distinguish between the power of the keys and the use of the keys, a distinction based on no Scripture but on their own recklessness alone. As usual they beg the question. For when it is incumbent on them to show that they have a power different from that given the whole church, they rush on as if this were already demonstrated, and then go on to this fictitious distinction that the power of the keys belongs to the church, their use, however, to the bishops. This is trifling, and the argument has nothing to support it. Christ gives both the power and the use of the keys to each Christian, when he says, "Let him be to you as a Gentile" [Matt. 18:17]. For who is this "you" to whom Christ refers when he says, "Let him be to you"? The pope? Indeed, he refers to each

---

[12] Cf. *Resolutio Lutheriana super propositione sua decima tertia de potestate papae* (*Lutheran Declaration Concerning the Thirteenth Thesis on the Power of the Pope*) (1519), WA 2, 189ff.; 248f.; 716. *Von dem Papsttum zu Rom Wider den hochberühmten Romanisten zu Leipzig* (*Concerning the Papacy at Rome in Opposition to the Celebrated Romanist at Leipzig*) (1520), WA 6, 309ff.

and every Christian. And in saying, "Let him be to you," he gives not only the authority, but also commands its use and exercise. For what else does the phrase, "Let him be to you as a Gentile," mean than to have nothing to do with him, to have no fellowship with him. This truly is to excommunicate, to bind, and to close the door of.heaven.

This is confirmed by what follows: "Whatever you bind . . . shall be bound." Who are those addressed? Are they not all Christians? Is it not the church? If here the giving of the keys to the church means not the use but only the authority, we would by the same source claim that its use has never been given to anyone, even to Peter (Matt. 16 [:19]). For clearly the words of Christ are everywhere the same when he bestows the office of binding and loosing. If in one place or with reference to one person they signify a conferring of authority, they signify a conferring of authority everywhere. If they signify the conferring of the use in one place, they signify the conferring of the use everywhere. For the words of God are everywhere the same and we are not permitted to give them one meaning in one place and another meaning elsewhere, though these masks make bold to ridicule the mysteries of God with their fictions.

So the lies of men are of no avail. The keys belong to the whole church and to each of its members, both as regards their authority and their various uses. Otherwise we do violence to the words of Christ, in which he speaks to all without qualification or limitation: "Let him be to you," and "You will have gained your brother," and "Whatever you," etc. And the words which were spoken alone to Peter, "I will give you the keys of the kingdom of heaven," here find their confirmation. This word also, "If two of you agree on earth," and "Where two are gathered in my name there am I in the midst of them" [Matt. 18:19, 20]. In all of these declarations we find established the fullest authority and the most immediate exercise of the right to bind and to absolve. Were this not true we would be denying to Christ himself the right and use of the keys as he dwells among even a couple of his disciples. But this indeed I have abundantly elaborated elsewhere.

As we have declared already, the ministry of the Word belongs to all. To bind and to loose clearly is nothing else than to proclaim and to apply the gospel. For what is it to loose, if not to announce the forgiveness of sins before God? What is it to bind, except to withdraw the gospel and to declare the retention of sins? Whether they want to or not [they must concede][13] that the keys are an exercise of the ministry of the Word and belong to all Christians.

Yet what is the use of struggling to secure this office for us who know Christ? It is clear enough that among the papists the knowledge of Christ, faith, and the gospel are altogether unknown, and at present even damned. When faith is lacking and Christ is ignored, it is impossible to see what is and is not sin before God. For the blindness of unbelief forces them to call evil good and good evil, and to lose their way altogether. If we do not know the difference between sin and good works we cannot loose or bind. So if we want to speak and feel as followers of Christ, we must hold that the papists and the shorn sacrificers, as long as they persist in their contention, cannot possess the function of binding and loosing or even be priests, much less be the only ones who have this office or who confer it on anyone by their ordinations. What will you bind when you do not know what should be bound? So their blindness leads them on in their fury. They close heaven and open hell to themselves and theirs. By their binding they despise the gospel and by their loosing they exalt their own traditions. They have lost both the authority and the use of the keys by their perverse and impious abuse.

The fifth function is to sacrifice. This is the crown of glory of the drunkards of Ephraim [Isa. 28:1]. By this they have separated themselves from us and stupified the whole earth. Supporting themselves only by foolish and absurd lies they have made a sacrifice out of a sacrament. Of this I have already spoken, so I can pass over it briefly. We call as witness the writings of the New Testament, to which we appeal in opposing Satan, and assert that in the New Testament there is no sacrifice except the one which is common to all, namely the one described in Rom. 12 [:1], where Paul teaches us to present our bodies as a sacrifice, just as Christ sacrificed his body for us on the cross. In this sacrifice he includes

---

[13] Apparently this phrase was interpolated later on the basis of the insertion of *so erhalten wir* at this point in the translation of Paul Speratus.

the offering of praise and thanksgiving. Peter likewise commands in I Pet. 2 [:5] that we offer spiritual sacrifices acceptable to God through Jesus Christ, that is, ourselves, not gold or animals.

Therefore that which they boast of as a singular sacrifice is indeed a singular sacrifice of a singular priesthood, but of a kind in which no Christian could or should in any way wish to be a participant. He should, on the contrary, denounce such participation as idolatry and a most blasphemous abuse and pray to be as far removed as possible from a part in it, however ancient and universal they allege it to be. For he does not less err who errs along with many others, nor will he burn less who burns with many. So be firm and unmoved on this point: in the church there is only this sacrifice, namely, our body. For today no other sacrifice is possible than that which is sacrificed and perfected by the Word of God, and since the Word (as we said) is common to all, the sacrifice too must be one pertaining to all.

Now since there can be only spiritual sacrifices in the church, as Peter says, that is, such as are in spirit and in truth, they can be offered only by one who is spiritual, that is, by a Christian who has the Spirit of Christ. But the papists enjoy their own fabrication and quibble that their sacrifice can be performed even by those who are criminals, and in no sense spiritual. They think that their sacrifices effect grace by the doing of the act of sacrifice itself and and not by the person doing it (*opere operati, non operantis*). They are led to defend such abominable sacrilege by arguing that God regarded favorably the sacrifice of Cain even if he did not so regard Cain as a person. Defending their own sacrifices they say that a sacrifice is an external work, even if offered by one who is damned and unacceptable. But in the church nothing at all counts unless the person first be acceptable, as Abel was, and he was in God's favor not by sacrifice, but by faith and spirit. So they must confess that since their sacrificing priests to a large extent are not spiritual, and that they are not sacrificing priests in the church unless they are spiritual, their sacrifice clearly is not one that belongs to the church but to the realm of human falsehood.

The sixth function is to pray for others. How horribly and shamelessly these masks have deceived the world and made a sort of fictitious synagogue out of the true church is a grievous story.

29

For Christ gave the Lord's Prayer to all his Christians. By this alone we are sufficiently able to prove and confirm that the priesthood is one and the same to all, whereas the papal priesthood is a falsehood devised outside the church of God and through mere effrontery brought into the church. To pray for others is to go between and make intercession of God, which is befitting Christ only and all his brethren. Though the papists earnestly desire that those be called priests who pray for lay Christians, they but worship a Dagon[14] and a god of their stomachs. But since we are commanded to pray for all certainly all are equally commanded to function as priests.

It is hard to know whether these masks have been unwilling to test the power and function of this Lord's Prayer through ignorance or through arrogance. For they too preach that it is given to all, and yet they have arrogated the function or priesthood of prayer to themselves alone, depriving others of it. For what does it mean to say, "We alone are priests, you are lay," except, "We alone are Christians and can pray. You are Gentiles who cannot pray but can be aided by our prayers"? And to say, "You also ought to pray, not only we," does this not mean, "You too are priests and brethren of Christ, able to stand for others in the presence of God"?

Just indeed are the judgments of God on these shameful intercessors! Behold, they want to be regarded as the only ones who pray for the people. But by a marvelous counsel of God they are turned into a kind of imaginary picture of intercessors, so that this iniquity which they thought would deceive God and men is made to deceive only themselves. For who really prays in all this great number of chapters, monasteries, and benefices? The words of prayer indeed roll over their lips, and they think they have the musical instruments of David [Neh. 12:36; Amos 6:5], but as Amos says, God himself rejects the noise of their songs [Amos 5:23], and avers, "This people . . . honor me with their lips, while their hearts are far from me" [Isa. 29:13; Matt. 15:8].

So you will find many of them who for forty years or all through their lives have rolled off their lips the sacred words of prayer, but never for a moment have really offered a single prayer

---

[14] The national god of the Philistines whose most famous temples were at Gaza and Ashdod. I Sam. 5:2ff.

before God. And such perverse persons are supposed to be worthy of the name of priests. For them we are to provide such massive churches, such outlays and revenues, and to them we are to subordinate kingdoms of all the world and even the true priests and intercessors before God, namely the Christians, for whom they were to pray. Yet God would not consider them worthy of comparison even with the heathen, who hope to be heard for the sake of their many words [Matt. 6:7]. But these indeed do not even mean or hope to be heard, nor do they carry on their barrage of incessant words in order to be heard, but that they may honor God with their lips and by this show win the dues of the multitudes to fatten their stomachs. By the pope's authority, though, they are the priests of God, priests indeed of Satan, who is the god of this age, and they pray for us, to bring the judgment of the true God on us.

But let us listen to Christ, the Judge and Arbiter in this case: "God is spirit, and those who worship him must worship in spirit and truth . . . for such the Father seeks to worship him [John 4:23, 24], that is, not such as pray on this mountain or in Jerusalem. Since this final and sovereign judgment prevails we maintain our position confidently, and assured by divine authority we adjudge that the pope and his minions have indeed a singular priesthood and singular office of intercession for all Christians, but instead of a genuine priesthood and intercession theirs is a masquerade and a counterfeit priesthood and intercession. Furthermore, only Christians and all those who cry in spirit, "Abba, Father" [Rom. 8:15], are genuine in their prayer and they alone are priests.

The seventh and last function is to judge and pass on doctrines. Clearly it is not without good reason that the mask priests and counterfeit Christians have claimed this office for themselves. For they could foresee that if they allowed all to have this function they could not monopolize any of the aforementioned privileges. If you could deprive the hearers of this function, what would not a teacher be able and dare to do, even surpassing Satan himself if he could? On the other hand if the hearers are permitted, even bidden to exercise this function, what would a teacher be able or try to do even if he were greater than an angel in heaven? If this is granted, Paul could not only correct Peter, but even pronounce anathema

31

on angels from heaven [Gal. 2:14; 1:8]. With what fear and trembling bishops and councils would have spoken and issued decrees, if the judgment of hearers would have had to be regarded when decisions were made with respect to priesthood, to the office of teaching, of baptizing, of consecrating, of sacrificing, of binding, of prayer, of judging doctrine. Indeed, there never would have been a universal papacy if this right of judgment had prevailed. They took good counsel when they monopolized this office!

But they have succeeded and prevailed until, as Daniel says, the indignation is accomplished [Dan. 11:36]. But now we see the light of the advent of the Savior and the destruction of this lawless one begins, for the spirit of His voice stays the adversary who has exalted himself against every worship of God [II Thess. 2:8; 2:4]. Now the word of Christ in John 10 [:27, 5] applies: "My sheep hear my voice. They do not know the voice of strangers," and in Matt. 7 [:15], "Beware of false prophets," and Matt. 16 [:6; Luke 12:1], "Beware of the leaven of the Pharisees," which is hypocrisy, and in Matt. 23 [:2f.], "The scribes and the Pharisees sit on Moses' seat; so practice and observe whatever they tell you, but not what they do." By these and many similar passages of the gospel, even all of Scripture, we are admonished not to believe false teachers. What else does this mean than that each of us shall have regard for his own salvation and be sure of Him in whom he believes and whom he follows? Each is a most free judge of all who teach him, if he himself is inwardly taught of God, as John 6 [:45] says. For you will not be damned or saved by the teaching of another, be it true or false, but by your faith alone. Anyone may teach as he pleases, but what you believe is your responsibility whether it result in your peril or your benefit.

But Paul has bound this strong man in his own place and taken away his armor [Luke 11:22] when he said, "If a revelation is made to another sitting by, let the first be silent" [I Cor. 14:30], and again, "The spirits of prophets are subject to prophets" [I Cor. 14:32]. Also, "You can all prophesy, one by one" [I Cor. 14:31]. What sense is there to this drunken prattle of the pope and his papists, though handed down over many generations: "We command, we earnestly direct, the Church of Rome is Mistress of the churches and the articles of faith"? All right, let her sit and teach and be a mistress,

32

yet here she is commanded to be silent, if a revelation is made to one sitting by. Not only she, but each of us, one by one, may prophesy, says Paul, a master and corrector even of Peter when he acted insincerely [Gal. 2:14ff.]. How much more ought we not then confidently judge the church of Rome in its insincerity and feigned authority. We are not to be judged by this church lest we imperil our own salvation and be found to deny Christ.

How attractive this wisdom of the masks appear, by which they horribly contradict themselves while they oppose God and all that belongs to God! We believe that they believe, at least we see them professing and boasting that they are the leaders and shepherds of the Christian people. But I believe they will also be forced to confess that a Christian is one who has the Holy Spirit, and who as Christ says, is taught all things by the Spirit [John 14:26]. And John writes, "His anointing teaches you about everything" [I John 2:27], that is, to put it briefly, a Christian is so certain about what he ought and ought not believe that he will even die, or at least be prepared to die, for it. Now I ask you, what effrontery it is of the papists to vaunt themselves and say: "The laity ought to believe us and not themselves"? What is this but to assert: "We admit that Christians have the Holy Spirit by which they know with certainty what is to be believed and what not to be believed; yet, because the Holy Spirit is inferior to ourselves, and we are much more learned than the Spirit, therefore they ought to subject themselves to us and heed us"?

By this reasoning they have wanted to set themselves up as masters with power to teach however they please and without respect to the judgment of any one else. Once this was granted them they could easily usurp all authority of God or man and obviously become gods. But we have this word: "For you have one Master, Christ. You are all brethren" [Matt. 23:8, 10]. We have then altogether the same rights. For if we have in common the name of brethren, then one cannot be especially superior to the other or enjoy more of heritage or authority than the other in spiritual matters, of which we now are speaking. So not only do we have the right to recover this function of judging doctrine, as well as all the other functions we have mentioned, but unless we recover it we are denying Christ as a brother. For here we are

33

dealing not with a matter that is optional or permissible, but with a command and a necessity. Condemned is he who recognizes the tyranny of the pope, but blessed is he who rejects it in a pious apostasy.

It is of the common rights of Christians that we have been speaking. For since we have proved all of these things to be the common property of all Christians, no one individual can arise by his own authority and arrogate to himself alone what belongs to all. Lay hold then of this right and exercise it, where there is no one else who has the same rights. But the community rights demand that one, or as many as the community chooses, shall be chosen or approved who, in the name of all with these rights, shall perform these functions publicly. Otherwise, there might be shameful confusion among the people of God, and a kind of Babylon in the church, where everything should be done in order, as the Apostle teaches [I Cor. 14:40]. For it is one thing to exercise a right publicly; another to use it in time of emergency. Publicly one may not exercise a right without consent of the whole body or of the church. In time of emergency each may use it as he deems best.

Now let us approach the papist priests and ask them to show us if their priesthood has other functions than these. If they have others theirs is not a Christian priesthood. If they have what we have described theirs is not a peculiar priesthood. So we judge, regardless of their contention, that either they have no other priesthood than that which the laity possesses, or they have a priesthood of Satan. For Christ teaches us to judge all trees by their fruits [Matt. 7:17f.]. We have seen what the fruits of our common priesthood are. So let them either show us other fruits than these or admit that they are not priests. For a difference in public or in private use of the kind of fruits does not prove that it is a different function or priesthood, but means only another function and another use of the same priesthood. As for shaving, anointing and a long cloak being signs of their peculiar priesthood we are willing to let them boast of these mean things, for we know it would be quite easy to shave, anoint, and clothe in a long robe even a pig or a block of wood.

Here we take our stand: There is no other Word of God than that which is given all Christians to proclaim. There is no other baptism than the one which any Christian can bestow. There is no other remembrance of the Lord's Supper than that which any Christian can observe and which Christ has instituted. There is no other kind of sin than that which any Christian can bind or loose. There is no other sacrifice than of the body of every Christian. No one but a Christian can pray. No one but a Christian may judge of doctrine. These make the priestly and royal office. Let therefore the papists either prove other functions of the priesthood or let them resign their own. Shaving, anointing, putting on of vestments, and other rites arising out of human superstition, do not convince us otherwise, even were they given by angels from heaven. Much less are we affected by the arguments of ancient use, the opinion of the majority, or of the authority which has been recognized.

On this account I think it follows that we neither can nor ought to give the name priest to those who are in charge of Word and sacrament among the people. The reason they have been called priests is either because of the custom of heathen people or as a vestige of the Jewish nation. The result is greatly injurious to the church. According to the New Testament Scriptures better names would be ministers, deacons, bishops, stewards, presbyters (a name often used and indicating the older members). For thus Paul writes in I Cor. 4 [:1], "This is how one should regard us, as servants of Christ and stewards of the mysteries of God." He does not say, "as priests of Christ," because he knew that the name and office of priest belonged to all. Paul's frequent use of the word "stewardship" or "household," "ministry," "minister," "servant," "one serving the gospel," etc., emphasizes that it is not the estate, or order, or any authority or dignity that he wants to uphold, but only the office and the function. The authority and the dignity of the priesthood resided in the community of believers.

In this view of the ministry, the so-called "indelible character" vanishes and the perpetuity of the office is shown to be fictitious. A minister may be deposed if he proves unfaithful. On the other hand he is to be permitted in the ministry as long as he is competent and has the favor of the church as a whole, just as in civil matters any administrator is treated as an equal among his brethren. In fact a spiritual minister is more readily removable than any civil administrator, since if he is unfaithful he should be less tolerable than a civil officer. The latter can be harmful only in matters of this life, whereas the former can be destructive of eternal possessions. Therefore, it is a privilege of the other brethren to excommunicate such a one and substitute someone else.

Such is the firm and dependable foundation of Scripture, if we are to believe the Word of God. Over against it we see the deplorable need of Bohemia, which hitherto has been reduced almost to a beggar's condition and forced to endure a tonsured priesthood and the most unworthy of those. In this Word we see more clearly and surely than by any light or assurance whence priests or ministers of the Word are to be sought, namely, from the flock of Christ alone, and nowhere else. We have clearly shown that to each one is given the right of ministering in the Word, and indeed that he is commanded to do so if he sees that teachers are lacking or if those in office are not teaching correctly, as Paul affirmed in I Cor. 14 [28ff.], so that the power of God might be proclaimed by us all. How much more, then, does not a certain community as a whole have both right and command to commit by common vote such an office to one or more, to be exercised in its stead. With the approval of the community these might then delegate the office to others.

Thus Paul writes in II Tim. 2 [:2]: "These things entrust to faithful men who will be able to teach others." Here Paul rejects all the show of tonsure and anointing and ordaining and only requires that they be able to teach, and to them alone he wants to entrust the Word. If the office of teaching be entrusted to anyone, then everything accomplished by the Word in the church is entrusted, that is, the office of baptizing, consecrating, binding, loosing, praying, and judging doctrine. Inasmuch as the office of preaching the gospel is the greatest of all and certainly is apostolic, it becomes the foundation for all other functions, which are built upon it, such as the offices of teachers, prophets, governing [the church], speaking with tongues, the gifts of healing and helping, as Paul directs in I Cor. 12 [:28]. Even Christ chiefly proclaimed the gospel, as the highest function of his office, and did not baptize [John 4:2]. Paul, too, gloried in the fact that he was sent not to baptize [I Cor. 1:17], as to a secondary office, but to the primary office of preaching the gospel.

This procedure is forced upon us by necessity and is commended by the common understanding of faith. For since the church owes its birth to the Word, is nourished, aided and strengthened by it, it is obvious that it cannot be without the Word. If it is without the Word it ceases to be a church. A Christian, thus, is born to the ministry of the Word in baptism, and if papal bishops are unwilling to bestow the ministry of the Word except on such as destroy the Word of God and ruin the church, then it but remains eithef to let the church perish without the Word or to let those who come together cast their ballots and elect one or as many as are needed of those who are capable. By prayer and the laying on of hands let them commend and certify these to the whole assembly, and recognize and honor them as lawful bishops and ministers of the Word, believing beyond a shadow of doubt that this has been done and accomplished by God. For in this way the common agreement of the faithful, those who believe and confess the gospel, is realized and expressed.

If the aforementioned arguments are not conclusive, it ought to be sufficient to admonish and affirm what Christ said in Matt. 18 [:19, 20], "If two of you agree upon earth about anything they ask, it will be done for them by my Father in heaven. For where two or three are gathered in my name, there am I in the midst of them." If then the agreement of three or two in the name of the Lord makes all things possible, and Christ endorses as his own the things they do, how much more may we not believe that it has happened or can happen with his approval and guidance when we come together in his name, pray together, and elect bishops and ministers of the Word from among ourselves. Even before such election we have been born and called into such a ministry through baptism.

If we ask for an example, there is one in Acts 18 [:24ff.], where we read of Apollos who came to Ephesus without call or ordination, and taught fervently, powerfully confuting the Jews. By what right, I ask, did he exercise the ministry of the Word except by the general right common to all Christians, as described in I Cor. 14 [:30], "If a revelation is made to another sitting by, let the first be silent," and in I Pet. 2 [:9], "That you might declare his wonderful deeds"? This man was afterward even made an apostle without the formality of ordination, and not only functioned in the ministry of the Word but also proved himself useful in many ways to those who had already come to faith. In the same way any Christian should feel obligated to act, if he saw the need and was competent to fill it, even without a call from the community. How much more then should he do so if he is asked and called by the brethren who are his equals, or by the whole community?

Another example is provided by Stephen and Philip, who were ordained only to the service at the tables [Acts 6:5, 6]. Yet the one wrought signs and wonders among the people, disputed with members of the synagogue and refuted the council of the Jews with the word of the Spirit [Acts 6:8ff.], and the other converted Samaritans and travelled to Azotus and Caesarea [Acts 8:5ff., 40]. By what right and authority, I ask? Certainly they were not asked or called by anyone, but they did it on their own initiative and by reason of a common law, since the door was open to them, and they saw the need of a people who were ignorant and deprived of the Word. How much more readily they would have done it had they been asked or called by anyone or by the community? And the eunuch converted by Philip [Acts 8:36], whom we may reasonably believe remained a Christian, undoubtedly taught the Word of God to many, since he had the command to make known the wonderful deeds of God who called him from darkness into his marvelous light [I Pet. 2:9]. From his word resulted the faith of many, since the Word of God does not return in vain [Isa. 55:11]. From faith sprang a church, and the church through the Word received and exercised a ministry of baptizing and teaching, and of all the other functions enumerated above. All these things a eunuch accomplished through no other right than that inherent in baptism and faith, especially in places lacking any other ministers.

It remains only, dear sirs, that you be clothed in an unyielding faith, a faith which needs to be courageous, if you would advise your Bohemia well. We write these things to those who believe. Unbelievers will not comprehend what we say. To them it makes no difference whether they have bishops or not, since they are neither Christians nor a church of God. They are not persuaded by ever so clear Scriptures or examples, but are persuaded by superficial masks such as tonsure, anointing, and vestments, which are based on no Scripture or example, but approved only by the use of centuries and of multitudes. To such things the devout Christian pays no attention. He needs only attend to the substance which is the Word of God, and, full of faith, believe that he can do and attain all that he knows is promised therein.

They object and say, "A new thing and unprecedented, so to elect and create bishops." I answer, it is the most ancient custom, following the example of the Apostles and their disciples, but abolished and destroyed by the contrary examples and pestilential teachings of the papists. Therefore we had much rather labor to drive out this more recent kind of plague and recover an earlier kind of health. Yet, even if it were a most recent innovation, if the Word of God here enlightens and commands us, and the need of souls compels it, then the novelty of the thing ought not at all to affect us, but the majesty of the Word. For, I ask, is it not new things that faith effects? Was not this kind of a ministry new in the days of the Apostles? Was it not a new thing when Abraham offered his son? Was it not a new thing for the children of Israel to pass through the sea? Will it not be a new thing for me to go through death to life? In all these things it is the Word of God, not the novelty, that we regard. If we should stop at the novelty of a thing, we would never be able to believe anything in the Word of God.

Believe the Word of God, therefore, my brethren, and the novelty of your own example will not affect you. For if novelty means anything why does it not mean something that you Bohemians alone have withstood the pope and dared everything in the spirit of John Huss? Was that not a novelty, not only unprecedented but contrary to what the whole earth has been used to, even to this day, and you were then not as clear as to the support of Scripture as in this case? If then, alone, you dared and attempted to assert and defend rights in danger of destruction and extinction when the peril of souls was not so present or so great, why now should you not attempt, assert and defend rights being destroyed when you are supported by so many shields and arms of the arsenal of David? [Song of Sol. 4:4]. There is the further consideration of such a pressing danger to souls and of a wretched captivity on the one hand, and of the challenge of liberty, with right and justice, on the other. If there is some difficulty in this new situation it will be eased after a period of trial. Certainly it will be much easier than what you had to endure because of your defection from papal tyranny. That is, if you dare in the Lord to do this, and the Lord will be with you.

Act in this way: first beseech God with prayers, both individually and in common. For this is a great undertaking, and the magnitude of it, rather than its novelty, impresses me. I don't want you to attempt anything by your own powers or wisdom, but to approach the matter in humility, with fear and trembling, lamenting and confessing that your own sins have brought on this misery and captivity. Before the seat of propitiation and the throne of grace [Heb. 4:16], namely, Jesus Christ, the bishop of our souls [I Pet. 2:25], bring your supplications and prayers that he might send his Spirit into your hearts. For he works with you, or rather, works in you both to will and to do [Phil. 2:13]. For if this thing is to be begun auspiciously and to continue successfully, it is necessary that there be in you the divine strength which, as Peter testifies, God supplies [I Pet. 4:11].

When you have so prayed, have no doubt that he to whom you have prayed is faithful and will give what you ask, opening to him who knocks and granting to him who seeks [Matt. 7:8]. Thus you may be assured that you are not pushing this matter, but being pushed in it. Then call and come together freely, as many as have been touched in heart by God to think and judge as you do. Proceed in the name of the Lord to elect one or more whom you desire, and who appear to be worthy and able. Then let those who are leaders among you lay hands upon them, and certify and commend them to the people and the church or community. In this way let them become your bishops, ministers, or pastors. Amen. The qualifications of those to be elected are fully described by Paul, in Tit. 1 [:6ff.], and I Tim. 3 [:2ff.].

It is not necessary, I think, to put this form of election immediately into practice in the Diet of Bohemia as a whole. But if individual cities adopt it for themselves the example of one will soon be followed by another. The Diet might well consider whether this form should be adopted by all of Bohemia, or if one part might accept, and another part postpone decision or even reject it altogether. For none should be forced to believe. We must give freedom and honor to the Holy Spirit that he may move wherever he will. We cannot hope that these things will be acceptable to all, especially right away. The fact that not all agree should not affect you—rather you ought be moved to the venture when many do not agree with you. It is enough if at first a few set the example. After the use has been established and in the course of time the whole people will be challenged to follow their example. As the venture succeeds, with the help of the Lord, and many cities adopt this method of electing their bishops, then these bishops may wish to come together and elect one or more from their number to be their superiors, who would serve them and hold visitations among them, as Peter visited the churches, according to the account in the Book of Acts [Acts 8:14ff.; 9:32ff.]. Then Bohemia would return again to its rightful and evangelical archbishopric, which would be rich, not in large income and much authority, but in many ministers and visitations of the churches.

But if you are altogether too weak to dare attempt this free and apostolic way of establishing a ministry, I suppose we must endure your weakness and permit you to go on accepting those ordained by papal bishops, such as your Gallus.[15] Use these, instead of the papal bishops, to call and elect and ordain such as they think capable and you will endure, according to the foregoing and to the teaching of Paul. For in Paul's view he is certainly a bishop who takes the lead in the preaching of the Word. Such is your Gallus though he is not resplendent in bishop's mitre and staff and other pride and pomp, which are only meant to amaze the stupid crowd. Let it be thus until you grow up and fully know what is the power of the Word of God. Clearly we cannot advise you in any other way at this time. For it is not possible for you to accept papal ordination and those ordained by it without sin and disobedience, and therefore without the risk of the destruction of souls.

If you are troubled and anxious as to whether or not you are truly a church of God, I would say to you, that a church is not known by customs but by the Word. In I Cor. 14 [:24, 25], Paul says that if an unbeliever comes into the church and finds those

---

[15] Gallus Cahera. Cf. Introduction, p. 32.

disclosing the secrets of his heart, he will fall on his face and declare that God is really present there. Of this you can be sure, that the Word of God and knowledge of Christ are richly present among you. And wherever the Word of God and knowledge of Christ are, they are not in vain, however deficient those who have the Word may be in external customs. The church indeed is weak because of its sins. But its fault is not in the Word. It sins indeed, but it does not deny or ignore the Word. We may not, therefore, reject those who accept and confess the Word, even though they do not shine in any splendid sanctity, as long as they do not persist in manifest sins. There is then no reason for you to doubt that the church of God is among you, even if there are only ten or six who have the Word. What such would do, along with others who do not yet have the Word but who would give their consent, certainly may be considered the work of Christ if they act, as we have said, in humility and in the spirit of prayer.

Finally, that which I fear will be the most formidable hindrance to this plan, namely, that in this matter as in every one that is of God, we must reckon with a cross. For Satan is neither asleep nor unaware of what we propose, and he will not be slow in his opposition. He is the prince of this world and knows our thoughts, even as we know his. But I speak of this cross because the powers of the world and the princes of the nations in their power will not permit you to attempt these plans. Indeed they will try to stop you before you really decide how to begin. Not only is Satan a prince, but a god of this age, and he so works in the heart of the unbelievers that clearly there can be no hope of achieving your plans with peace and outward tranquillity. Rather, when the tumult becomes greatest and the tempest strongest and the vessel is overwhelmed by waves, you will think that it will surely sink.

What else can I say to this than what Peter said, "We must obey God rather than man"? [Acts 5:29]. For when it has been established that the matter is holy and pleasing to God, as indeed this is, it is necessary to take one's stand as on a rock, not regarding the towering waves and threatening winds or the onrushing waters. This only should be regarded, that peace and quiet, grace and honor belong to them who know and do the things of God. Christ in fact sends this fire on earth and arouses this terrible Behemoth, not

42

because he is harsh, but in order to teach us that any success we have is not the result of our infirmity but of his power, lest we boast or exalt ourselves above the grace of God. We ourselves are silent in our despair, and as Scripture everywhere admonishes, we allow Him to fight for us. Despite our weakness he overcomes every force and power, and while we are silent he quiets the movement of the wide sea and its waves. So Scripture says, "In quietness and in trust shall be your strength" [Isa. 30:15], and again, "I have given him a bitter struggle in order that he may overcome" [Wisd. of Sol. 10:12].

Most of all you ought be impelled to go on when you see the resistance of powers and princes, strengthened as by a very sure argument that your enterprise is of God and that God himself, whose word you hear, will be with you. For if this counsel were of the world, the world would not only allow, but also would love, what is its own [John 15:19]. But now since it is not of this world, but God put it in your heart through his Word, therefore the world not only will not allow it, but will even hate and persecute it. "But be of good cheer, he has overcome the world" [John 16:33]. And, "He who is in you is greater than he who is in the world" [I John 4:4], even if things be so overturned by tumult and dissension that, to the unbelieving, heaven itself threatens to fall. But our rock is undisturbed by thundering and lightning,[16] and fears no darkening skies or stormy clouds.[17] It does not tremble before contending winds and roaring tempests, but is sure of itself and confidently awaits clear skies.

Wherefore, "Fear not, Judah and Jerusalem, but stand still, and see the victory of the Lord on your behalf . . . go out against them, and the Lord will be with you" [II Chron. 20:17]. For it is not something new or strange if the prince of this world rages when he sees his kingdom threatened. What else can he do? He would prefer to possess his palace in peace [Luke 11:21], but when he sees that he cannot do this, he tries that which is his final weapon, namely rage and force. "Like a roaring lion he prowls around, seeking someone to devour" [I Pet. 5:8]. Since God has

---

[16] Juvenal *Satires*, xiii, 223.
[17] Virgil, *Aeneid* i, 53.

forewarned us to recognize what kind of character he has, can we ever expect him to be different, and should we not the more bravely resist him, in faith? Stand fast then, good sirs, and go forth with the Word of God, armed with the invincible and all-powerful sword of the Spirit. For either you must attempt this way in brave faith, or else desist altogether. "For we are not contending against flesh and blood, but against the spiritual hosts of wickedness in the heavenly places" [Eph. 6:12].

I have spoken thus (since it was necessary) about the method of establishing a ministry of the church, in my simplicity, satisfied if I have furnished occasion to others more able and learned and apt in speech to think and express themselves. For not all are competent in everything. "There are varieties of service but the same Lord" [I Cor. 12:5, 6], who works not in one alone, but in all, not as we want, but as he wills.

As to the reform of the mass and the arranging of the worship of God as well as to other functions of the ecclesiastical ministry either others may speak or I myself may say something some other time. A person who is commissioned as a minister of the gospel ought, however, to be able to conduct himself successfully in these matters, if he follows the teaching of Him by whom he was anointed. Now it is enough if by prayer and devotion we obtain from God such a ministry and if we are worthy, when we obtain it, to keep it and to rejoice in it.

LETTER TO THE PRINCES OF SAXONY CONCERNING THE REBELLIOUS SPIRIT

1524

Translated by Conrad Bergendoff

INTRODUCTION

Thomas Münzer was a pastor in Zwickau when the teaching of Luther influenced a group in this town to go far beyond the intentions of the Reformer. The Middle Ages had known of many tendencies toward a radicalism which opposed all authority, whether in church or state. Some of these based themselves on direct revelation from God, and were opposed to a special ministry and to the sacraments. Neither the organized church nor the Bible were superior in authority to the commands the advocates of this kind of mystical religion felt within themselves.

Such were the ideas of a fanatical group in Zwickau who came to be known as the Zwickau prophets. It included Nicholas Storch, a weaver; Marcus Stübner, a Wittenberg student; and Martin Cellarius, a theologian. Münzer became their leader. When the authorities suppressed the movement in Zwickau in 1521 some took refuge in Wittenberg. Münzer went eastward, was for a while among the Taborites in Bohemia, and around Easter time in 1523 settled at Allstedt where he was given the position of pastor, though without the knowledge or consent of the Elector.

With Allstedt as a center, Münzer soon affected the whole area by his revolutionary doctrines. The ungodly were to be eliminated and the elect would establish a kingdom of Christ on earth. The political rulers came under severe criticism, and the people understood the implications of their preachers that the civil rulers must yield to the heavenly directives. They understood too the fiery denunciation of the papal shrines and the images in the churches. In March, 1524, a shrine dedicated to the Virgin was burned near Allstedt. Münzer grew bolder in his denunciation of the authorities, and called for an elimination of the enemies of God, in the spirit of the Old Testament account of the Jewish massacre of their enemies.

As early as the summer of 1523 Luther warned against Münzer.[*]

---

[*] Letter to Spalatin, August 3, 1523. *Luther's Correspondence and Other Contemporary Letters*, trans. by Preserved Smith and C. M. Jacobs, II, 193.

He followed the developments in Allstedt with apprehension. Finally he could restrain himself no longer, and probably in July, 1524, wrote the letter to the princes. He did not ask for the suppression of Münzer's preaching because it conflicted with his own. He appealed to the rulers to act before the incendiary suggestions of this preacher led to civil rebellion and open revolt. He felt free to counsel the princes that it was their duty to maintain peace and order, which were threatened by the fanatical mob gathering around Münzer.

In the summer of 1524 the princes became convinced that the disturbance might lead to rebellion, and they summoned the leaders before them. The Allstedt council and Münzer were examined in Weimar at the beginning of August. To escape the impending verdict, Münzer fled to Mühlhausen, where later in the year he gained leadership over the city. He became a central figure in the Peasants' Revolt and suffered death in May, 1525, when that revolt was crushed.

The letter of Luther to his princes was directed primarily against Münzer. But he was suspicious of Karlstadt and detected a relationship between the two. Karlstadt and his followers, however, rejected this implication, and argued with the rulers that they had nothing to do with the Allstedt party. The reader nonetheless will find much in common between this letter against Münzer and Luther's answer to Karlstadt in *Against the Heavenly Prophets in the Matter of Images and Sacraments*.

The translation follows the German text in WA 15, 210-221, which is the text of the letter as it was printed in the first Wittenberg edition, 1524.

LETTER TO THE
PRINCES OF SAXONY
CONCERNING
THE REBELLIOUS SPIRIT

To the Illustrious and Noble Princes and Lords Frederick, Elector of the Roman Empire, and John, Duke of Saxony, Count of Thuringia and Margrave of Meissen, my most gracious Lords.

Grace and peace in Christ Jesus our Savior. Fortune would have it that whenever the holy Word of God blossoms forth Satan opposes it with all his might by employing, first of all, the fist and outrageous force. When this method proves unsuccessful, he attacks it with evil tongues and false spirits and teachings. What he cannot quench with force he suppresses with deceit and falsehood. So he did in the beginning, when the gospel first came into the world, attacking it violently through the Jews and Gentiles, shedding much blood and creating many martyrs in Christendom. When this method of attack failed, he thrust forth false prophets and erring spirits, filling the world with heretics and sects right down to the time of the pope, who (as befits the last and greatest Antichrist) has overthrown Christendom with nought but sects and heresy.

So we may recognize the Word of God for what it is, things must go on as they always have. The pope, the Emperor, kings and princes lay hold on the Word with violence, and in madness would suppress, damn, blaspheme, and persecute it, without recognizing it or giving it a hearing. But the verdict stands and our arrogance was crushed long ago as Ps. 2 [:1, 2, 4] points out, "Why do the nations conspire, and the peoples plot in vain? The kings of the earth set themselves, and the rulers take counsel together, against the Lord

49

and his anointed. . . . He who sits in the heavens laughs: the Lord has them in derision. Then he will speak to them in his wrath, and terrify them in his fury." This, too, will assuredly be the fate of our raging rulers who want it that way. For they will neither see nor listen. God has so blinded and hardened them that they rush on to their ruin. They have had warning enough.

Satan sees this and knows right well that such raving finally accomplishes nothing. In fact, he beholds and finds that (as is the nature of the Word of God) the more it is suppressed, the farther it spreads and grows. Since he now comes at us with false spirits and sects, we must take stock of our situation so as not to be led astray. For it must be as Paul says to the Corinthians, "There must be factions among you in order that those who have stood the test among you may be recognized" [I Cor. 11:19]. Accordingly, after Satan has been driven out and for several years has wandered around in waterless places, seeking rest but finding none [Matt. 12:43], he has settled down in your Grace's principality and made himself a nest at Allstedt, thinking he can fight against us while enjoying our peace, protection, and security. For the principality of Duke George, lying next to us, is too kind and gentle in the treatment of this kind of an undaunted and invincible spirit (as they boast), thus making it impossible for them to put their overbearing behavior and arrogance to a test. Though so far no one has touched them either with fist or mouth or pen he cries out horribly, complaining he must suffer much. They dream that they must bear a heavy cross. With such frivolity and without cause this devil has to lie, though he cannot conceal himself.

I am especially glad that none of ours start a disturbance of this kind. They themselves boast that they do not belong to us, and have learned and received nothing from us. They come from heaven, and hear God himself speaking to them as to angels. What is taught at Wittenberg concerning faith and love and the cross of Christ is an unimportant thing. "You yourself must hear the voice of God," they say, "and experience the work of God in you and feel how much your talents weigh. The Bible means nothing. It is Bible—Booble—Babel," etc. Were we to say such things of them their cross and sufferings would seem more precious than the sufferings of Christ, and be more highly esteemed and praised, too. In this manner the poor spirit is eager to suffer and boast of his cross. But he will not suffer anyone to cast a bit of doubt or counsel caution as to his heavenly voice and work of God. Without considering that I have never read or heard of a more arrogant, imperious holy spirit (if such there be) he wants to enforce faith in an immediate and dictatorial manner.

But there is neither time nor space to judge their doctrines now. Twice before I have fully considered and criticized them.[1] If it becomes necessary God willing I can and will deal with them again. I have written this letter to Your Princely Graces because I heard and also gathered from their writings that this same spirit will not let the matter rest with words. Intending to resort to violence and the use of force against the authorities he will instigate revolt without delay. Here Satan lets us catch a glimpse of the knave that's giving too much away. What would this spirit attempt if he gained the following of a mob?

I have already heard earlier from the spirit himself here in Wittenberg,[2] that he thinks it necessary to use the sword to carry out his undertaking. At that time I had a hunch that they would go so far as to overthrow civil authority and make themselves lords of the world. Yet before Pilate Christ rejected such an aim, saying that His kingdom is not of this world [John 18:36]. He also taught his disciples not to be as the rulers of the world [Matt. 20:25].

Though I realize full well that Your Princely Graces will know how to deal in this matter better than I can advise, yet I am in duty bound to do my part and respectfully to pray and exhort you to look into this matter carefully. Your obligation and duty to maintain order requires you to guard against such mischief and to prevent rebellion. Your Graces know very well that your power and earthly authority are given you by God in that you have been bidden to preserve the peace and to punish the wrongdoer, as Paul teaches, Rom. 13 [:4]. Therefore your Graces should not sleep nor be idle. For God will want and require an answer if the power of the sword

---

[1] Probably a reference to the *Eight Wittenberg Lenten Sermons* (1522), WA 10[III], 1-64; PE 2, 391-425, and the treatise *On Both Kinds in the Sacrament* (1522), WA 10[II], 11-41.
[2] Luther refers to his conversations with Marcus Stübner, Martin Cellarius, and Nicholas Storch in 1522.

is carelessly used or regarded. Nor would your Graces be able to give account to the people or the world if you tolerated and endured violence and rebellion.

If, however, they attempt to justify themselves (as they usually do with big words) by saying that the Spirit impels them to achieve their goal by resorting to force, I would reply: First, it must be an evil spirit which has no other fruits than the destruction of churches and cloisters and the burning of images. The worst rascals on earth can do this, especially if they feel secure and are unopposed. It would be more impressive if the spirit at Allstedt would go to Dresden, or Berlin, or Ingolstadt to riot against cloisters and burn images. Secondly, their boasting about the Spirit means nothing, for we have the word of St. John that we should "test the spirits to see whether they are of God" [I John 4:1]. This spirit surely has not been tested, but rages about and creates a furor with his wantonness. Were he good he would first allow himself to be tested and judged, in humility, as the Spirit of Christ does.

It would be a fine fruit of the spirit, allowing us to judge him, if he didn't so seek to crawl into corners and shun the light, but came into the open before his enemies and opponents, make a clean breast of things, and give an account of his actions. But the spirit of Allstedt avoids this as the devil avoids the cross. In his hiding place he uses the most fearless language as though he were full of three holy spirits. Such unseemly boasting reveals clearly what kind of a spirit he is. In his book[3] he offers to appear before a harmless assembly, and stake his life and soul upon it, but he will not appear and give answer for himself in a closed session before two or three.

Tell me, who is this bold and defiant holy spirit who confines himself so closely that he will not appear except before a harmless assembly or give answer in closed session or before two or three persons? What kind of a spirit is this that is afraid of two or three and will not appear in an assembly that might imperil him? I can tell you. He smells the roast. He has been once or twice in my cloister at Wittenberg and had his nose punched. So he doesn't like the soup, and doesn't want to appear except in company with his own who will applaud his bombast. If I (who have no

---

[3] Thomas Münzer's *Protestation,* etc. 1524.

52

spirit and hear no heavenly voice) had spoken such words against the papists, how they would have shouted "Victory," and stopped my mouth!

I cannot boast or brag myself with such lofty words. I, poor miserable man, did not initiate my undertaking with such self-confidence, but with much trembling and fear, (as St. Paul confessed even of himself in I Cor. [2:3], though he too could have boasted somewhat of a heavenly voice). How humbly I at first attacked the pope, how I besought him, how I implored him, as my first writings prove! Nevertheless in the poverty of my spirit, I accomplished such things as this world-consuming spirit has never attempted. Rather he has hitherto avoided and fled from foes, as a knight and gentleman, and even seriously boasted of this aversion as befitting his character of knight and gentleman.

At Leipzig[4] I had to take my stand in debate before a very threatening assembly. I had to appear at Augsburg[5] without safe-conduct before my worst enemy. At Worms[6] I had to appear before the Emperor and the whole realm, though I already knew well that my safe-conduct was worthless, and all kinds of strange wiles and deceit were directed at me. Weak and poor though I was there, yet this was the disposition of my heart: If I had known that as many devils as there were tiles on the roofs at Worms took aim at me, I would still have entered the city on horseback, and this, even though I had never heard of a heavenly voice, or of God's talents and works, or of the Allstedt spirit. I had to take my stand in closed groups of one, two, or three, and meet them wherever and whenever they decided. My poor and troubled spirit has had to stand unshielded as a flower in the field, without being able to choose time, person, place, manner, or degree. I had to be ready and willing to give every man an answer, as St. Peter admonishes [I Pet. 3:15].

But this spirit, who is as high above us as the sun is above the earth, and hardly regards us as worms, chooses for himself only harmless and friendly judges and examiners, of whom he can be

---

[4] Luther disputed with Eck at Leipzig in 1519. Cf. *LW* 31, 307.
[5] Luther appeared before Cajetan, the papal legate, in Augsburg in 1518. Cf. *LW* 31, 253.
[6] The reference is to the Diet of Worms, 1521.

sure. He refuses to meet two or three in a selected place, and give an account of himself. He feels suspicious, and wants to frighten us with big words. Very well, we can do only what Christ enables us to do. If he forsakes us, we will be frightened by so much as a rustling leaf. If he upholds us, this spirit will become well aware of his high boasting. If it is necessary, I hereby offer your Graces to make public what took place between this spirit and myself in my quarters. From it your Graces and all the world can discern and realize how deceitful a devil this spirit is, and yet a poor devil at that. I have been, and still am, opposed by one who is more cunning. Not the spirits who boast and bluster with proud words accomplish something, but those who sneak around secretly and do damage, before one knows of it.

I have had to say these things so that your Graces might not shrink from this spirit or delay in giving his people strict orders to cease from their violence, the destruction of monasteries and churches and the burning of saints' images. If they want to prove their spirit, let them do it in a becoming manner, and first submit to an examination, either by us or by the papists. For (God be praised) they consider us worse than the papists. Yet they enjoy and use the fruits of our victory, such as marrying, and discarding the papal laws, though they have done no battle for it and risked no bloodshed to attain it. But I have had to attain it for them and, until now, at the risk of my body and my life. I have to boast a little, even as St. Paul [II Cor. 11:16ff.], though it is foolish for me to do so. I would rather refrain from it, if it were not for these deceiving spirits.

If, as is their custom, they claim that their spirit is too high and ours too meager for their cause to be judged by us, then I answer: St. Peter was well aware that his spirit and the spirit of all Christians was superior to that of the Jews and the heathen, yet he commanded that we should be ready and willing to give everyone an answer in a gentle and reverent spirit [I Pet. 3:15f.]. Christ too was aware that his spirit was higher than that of the Jews, yet he submitted himself and offered to be judged by them, saying, "Which of you convicts me of sin?" [John 8:46]. And to Annas he said, "If I have spoken wrongly, bear witness to the wrong"

[John 18:23], etc. I know and am assured, by the grace of God, that I am more learned in the Scriptures than all the sophists and papists. But so far God has saved me from pride, and will preserve me, so that I shall never refuse to give answer, or listen to the most insignificant Jew or heathen, or whoever it may be.

How is it that they permit their case to be stated in writing, when they are unwilling to submit to two or three examiners or to a hostile assembly? Do they really think that their literature will be read only by friendly gatherings and not come into the hands of two or three individuals? Indeed, I am amazed how they have forgotten their spirit. Now they want to teach the people orally and in writing, though they still boast that each one must hear the voice of God for himself; yet they ridicule us who teach the Word of God orally and in written form, which they claim is of no value. They have a much higher and more precious office than the Apostles and Prophets and Christ himself. These all taught the Word of God orally or in writing, and said nothing about the heavenly voice of God which we are supposed to hear. This giddy spirit juggles so that he is unaware of his own contradictions.

But I am sure that we who have and acknowledge the gospel, even though we be poor sinners, have the right spirit, or as Paul says, "the first fruits of the Spirit" [Rom. 8:23], even if now we do not have the fulness of the Spirit. There is none other than this one Spirit who apportions his gifts in a wonderful way. For we know what faith is, and love, and the cross; and we can learn no greater thing on earth than faith and love. Hence we can know and judge what doctrine is true or not true, and whether it is in accordance with the faith or not. Hence we recognize and judge this spirit as having as his purpose the invalidating of the Scriptures and the oral Word of God, and doing away with the sacrament of the altar and of baptism. He would force us into a spirit wherein we should tempt God with our own works and free will, and take over his work, while we set time, place, and measure for God when he wants to deal with us. Their writings exhibit such grievous arrogance that they explicitly write in opposition to the Gospel of St. Mark, claiming that St. Mark has mistakenly written of baptism in his last chapter [Mark 16:15]. They don't dare so

55

to speak of St. John, and in the words, "Unless one is born of the water and of the spirit" (John 3 [:5]), they interpret water, I know not how, but reject completely the bodily baptism in water.

The Spirit is not without fruits. Since their spirit is so much higher than ours I should like to know if their fruits, too, are higher than ours. Indeed their spirit must bear other and better fruits than ours, since it is better and higher. We teach and confess that our Spirit, whom we preach and proclaim, produces the kinds of fruit described by St. Paul in Gal. 5 [:22], such as, "love, joy, peace, patience, kindness, goodness, faithfulness, gentleness, self-control." And as he says in Rom. 8 [:13], he "puts to death the deeds of the body," and in Gal. 5 [:24], "with Christ he crucifies the old Adam with his passions." In brief, the fruit of our spirit is the fulfillment of God's Ten Commandments. Surely the spirit of Allstedt, which doesn't want to be inferior to ours, must produce something higher than love and faith, peace, patience, etc. (though St. Paul in I Cor. 13 [:13] tells us that love is the greatest fruit of all). He must accomplish much more than God has commanded. But I should like to know what this is, especially since we know that the Spirit won for us by Christ is given for this purpose alone, that we should fulfil the commandments of God, as Paul says in Rom. 8 [:4].

They claim that we do not live as we teach, and do not have the Spirit that produces such fruits. I would allow them to make this claim, for then we could plainly discern that it is not a good spirit that speaks through them. We ourselves confess (and need no heavenly voice and lofty spirit to tell us) that we regrettably do not do everything we ought to do. In fact, St. Paul tells us in Gal. 5 [:17] that it will never be different, as long as flesh and spirit are on earth together, and opposed to each other. I do not perceive any particular fruit of the Allstedtian spirit, except that he wants to do violence and destroy wood and stone. Love, peace, patience, goodness, gentleness, have been very little in evidence so far. It doesn't want its fruits to be that common. By the grace of God I can, however, point to much fruit of the Spirit on our part. If it is a question of boasting, I, the least and most sinful person, am willing to set myself alone over against all the fruits of all the spirits of Allstedt, no matter how greatly he criticizes my life.

It is not a fruit of the Spirit to criticize a doctrine by the imperfect life of the teacher. For the Holy Spirit criticizes false doctrine while bearing with those who are weak in faith and life, as Paul teaches in Rom. 14 [:1ff.] and 15 [:1] and everywhere else. I am not so much offended by the unfruitfulness of the spirit of Allstedt as I am by his lying and his attempt to establish other doctrines. I would have paid little attention to the papists, if only they would teach correctly. Their evil life would not cause much harm. When this spirit goes so far as to be offended at our sickly life and makes this a ground for boldly judging our doctrine, he has shown sufficiently his true character. For the Spirit of Christ condemns no one who teaches rightly, but bears with and supports and helps those who live rightly. He does not despise weak sinners, as this Pharisaical spirit does.

As far as doctrine is concerned, time will tell. For the present, your Graces ought not to stand in the way of the ministry of the Word. Let them preach as confidently and boldly as they are able and against whomever they wish. For, as I have said, there must be sects, and the Word of God must be under arms and fight. Therefore the followers of the Word are called an "army" (Ps. 68 [:12]), and Christ is designated as a "commander" [Josh. 5:14], in the Prophets [Mic. 5:1; cf. Matt. 2:6; Heb. 2:10]. If their spirit is genuine, he will not be afraid of us and will stand his ground. If our spirit is genuine, he, again, will not fear either it or anyone else. Let the spirits collide and fight it out. If meanwhile some are led astray, all right, such is war. Where there is battle and bloodshed, some must fall and some are wounded. Whoever fights honorably will be crowned.

But when they want to do more than fight with the Word, and begin to destroy and use force, then your Graces must intervene, whether it be ourselves or they who are guilty, and banish them from the country. You can say, "We are willing to endure and permit you to fight with the Word, in order that the true doctrine may prevail. But don't use your fist, for that is our business, else get yourselves out of the country." For we who are engaged in the ministry of the Word are not allowed to use force. Ours is a spiritual conflict in which we wrest hearts and souls from the devil.

It is written in Dan. [8:25] that the Antichrist shall be vanquished without human hand. And in Isa. 2 [11:4] we read that in his realm Christ will "smite the earth with the rod of his mouth, and with the breath of his lips." Our calling is to preach and to suffer, not to strike and defend ourselves with the fist. Christ and his apostles destroyed no churches and broke no images. They won hearts with the Word of God, then churches and images fell of themselves.

We should do likewise. First liberate hearts from cloisters and monastic orders. If this is done, shrines and cloisters will be empty, and temporal rulers can dispose of them as they see fit. Why should we worry about wood and stone, when hearts are no longer attached to them? Look at what I have done. I have never disturbed a stone, broken a thing, or set fire to a cloister. Yet, because of my word, the monasteries are now empty in many places, some of which are even in the hands of princes who are opposed to the gospel. Had I done as these prophets and carried on with violence, hearts in all the world would still be in captivity, while I in some place would have crumpled stone or wood. Of what use would this have been? You may gain fame and honor in that way, but certainly you do not thus win any soul's salvation. Some would say that without force I have done more damage to the pope than a mighty king could do. But these prophets want badly to do something bigger and better. They are not able to do it, so they fail to free souls and attack wood and stone. This is the wonderfully new work of the lofty spirit.

Probably they will object on the ground that the law of Moses commanded the Jews to destroy idols and tear down their altars. I answer: They themselves know well that from the beginning God has performed many kinds of work through one kind of Word and faith and by various saints. The Epistle to the Hebrews makes this clear and tells us that we should follow the faith of these saints [Heb. 13:7]. We cannot imitate all the deeds of the saints. At that time the Jews had a particular command of God enjoining them to destroy altars and images. We in our time do not have such a command. Abraham had a particular command of God to offer his son [Gen. 22:2]. But people who were to follow his example and sacrifice their children would do wrong. We are not commanded

58

to imitate all the various deeds, else we should have to be circumcised and follow all Jewish customs.

Indeed, if we Christians justified our damaging of churches and our violence by Jewish examples, then it would follow that we are bound to put all non-Christians to death. For the Jews were as strictly bidden to put to death Canaanites and Amorites [Exod. 23:23] as they were to destroy images. But all the Allstedtian spirit would gain by this would be the shedding of blood. All who did not hear his heavenly voice would be put to the sword by him, so that the people of God might be free of offenses which are far greater among living non-Christians than images of wood and stone. Furthermore, this command was given to the Jews as a people who had been miraculously saved by God and in a special sense were his people, and who acted through the authority of civil government. It was not a self-appointed mob. But this spirit has still to prove that he is of God's people by a single miracle. Following the behavior of a mob, he sets himself up as if he alone were God's people, and carries on without the command of God or the civil authority ordained by God. Yet he wants us to believe in his spirit.

The doing away with offense must take place through the Word of God. For even if all outward offense were destroyed and done away with, it would be to no avail as long as hearts are not brought from unbelief to the right faith. For an unbelieving heart always finds cause for new offense. When the Jews destroyed one idol they set up ten others instead. Therefore in the New Testament we must adopt the right way to drive out the devil and all offense, namely, by the Word of God. When we redeem the heart, the devil and all his pomp and power will assuredly fall of themselves.

So I will close for this time. I have hurriedly entreated your Graces to deal seriously with such disturbance and extravagances, so that in this matter we act only according to the Word of God, as is fitting for Christians. Only thus can we eliminate the causes of sedition, to which the mob is otherwise all too much inclined. For they are not Christians who want to go beyond the Word and to use violence, but are not ready to suffer much else, even if they boast of being full and overfull with ten holy spirits. The mercy of God eternally strengthen and preserve your Graces. Your Graces' obedient, Martin Luther

LETTER
TO THE CHRISTIANS
AT STRASSBURG
IN OPPOSITION TO THE
FANATIC SPIRIT

1524

Translated by Conrad Bergendoff

INTRODUCTION

When Karlstadt was expelled from Saxony at the end of summer in 1524 he visited Strassburg, probably in October, and as soon as his writings were printed in Switzerland they quickly found their way to this city. The differences between Luther and Karlstadt gave rise to questioning and uncertainty among the preachers and people of Strassburg. In November the evangelical preachers, probably under the leadership of Bucer, wrote a formal letter to Luther, describing their difficulties and seeking help. They wanted Luther to give a dispassionate statement concerning the presence of Christ in the sacrament of the altar, the validity of infant baptism, and the use of images in worship. Evidently Karlstadt had won adherents and in order to quiet disturbances the preachers wanted biblical confirmation of Luther's position against Karlstadt.

Luther had meanwhile obtained copies of the eight books which Karlstadt had written and had printed despite the censor's prohibition. He found these so contradictory to his own teachings that he did not attempt to give the Strassburg preachers a detailed refutation. Instead he promised to treat fully of these differences in a longer work, which came from his pen under the title of *Against the Heavenly Prophets*. For the moment he only wanted the Strassburgers to realize the errors of Karlstadt, and to counsel them to hold to the Word. Dissensions would of course arise, but they were meant to drive Christians closer to the Word. Luther was confident that his teachings were based on the Word, while Karlstadt was pursuing notions born of his own fancy.

The Strassburgers wrote to Zwingli at the same time that they asked Luther's guidance. Zwingli's reply came earlier, and seems to have won greater favor than Luther's, especially in the matter of the interpretation of the sacrament of the altar.

Luther's reply was sent from Wittenberg about December 17. In February of 1525 a printed edition of the letter was circulating in Strassburg. The text of the translation is that of a Wittenberg edition which is the basis of the text in WA 15, 391-397.

LETTER
TO THE CHRISTIANS
AT STRASSBURG
IN OPPOSITION TO THE
FANATIC SPIRIT

by Martin Luther

Martin Luther, humble churchman and evangelist at Wittenberg, to the very beloved friends of God, all the Christians at Strassburg.

Grace and peace from God our Father and the Lord Jesus Christ.

Dear sirs and brethren. I greatly rejoice and thank God the Father of mercy for the riches of his grace bestowed upon you, in that he has called you into his wonderful light and let you come into the participation of all the treasures of his Son, Jesus Christ. Now through his salutary Word you can recognize and acknowledge with joyful hearts the true Father, who has redeemed us from the iron furnace of Egyptian sin and death and brought us into the broad, secure, free and veritable Promised Land.

See to it that you do not forget what you previously were, lest you appropriate to yourselves this great grace and mercy without gratitude, as some already have done and fallen again under God's wrath. Remain steadfast, exercise yourselves and increase daily in this knowledge and grace of Jesus Christ (for such is the right road to salvation which will not deceive you). Make it an aim to be of one mind and show brotherly love to each other by your deeds. Thereby your faith will prove itself true, instead of being false, worthless, and idle, and the enemy which has been expelled will not return to find the house empty and swept clean and enter with seven evil spirits, so that the last condition will be worse than the first [Luke 11:26].

If on this account you are reviled or persecuted, you are blessed. If they have called the lord of the house Beelzebub, how much more will they do to the children of the household [Matt. 10:24, 25]. A servant is not to fare better than his master. And what does it matter if pitiful men who like smoke vanish away [Cf. Ps. 37:20] revile you, if you can be assured that myriads of angels in heaven as well as God himself rejoice over you, and with all creatures render thanks and praise for you? All of which your faith and good conscience in the Holy Spirit experience and testify, if indeed you rightly believe and have Christ so that he truly lives and reigns in you. For these sufferings only serve to enrich and foster our blessedness.

But it is perilous when dissension, sects, and errors arise among Christians, for these deprive consciences of such a comforting knowledge, lead to error, and unconsciously turn the spirit from inward grace toward external things and works. Such was the work of false apostles and, after them, of many different kinds of heretics and now, finally, of the pope. It is of greatest importance that we be on our guard. For if our gospel is the true gospel, as I am convinced and have no doubt that it is, then it must naturally follow that it will be attacked, persecuted, and tested from both sides. On the left the opponents will show open contempt and hate, on the right our own will be guilty of dissension and party spirit. "For," says Paul, "there must be factions among you in order that those who have stood the test among you may be recognized" [I Cor. 11:19]. Christ finds not only Caiaphas among his enemies, but also Judas among his friends.

Knowing this, we must be equipped and armed as people who surely must expect at any moment to meet both kinds of attack. We cannot be at all surprised or frightened if dissension arises among us. Instead we must confidently say to ourselves, "So it will and must be," and pray God to be with us and keep us on the right path. For, as Moses said, God tests us to know whether or not we depend on him with all our heart [Deut. 8:2; 13:3]. This I say because I have learned how new prophets are appearing in various regions, and, as some of you have written to me, because Dr. Karlstadt has started disturbance among you with his fanaticism in the matter of the sacrament, images,[1] and baptism. This he has also done elsewhere, and he blames me for his banishment.

Now my very dear friends, I am not your pastor. No one has to believe me. Each one is responsible for himself. I can warn every one, I can thwart no one. I hope, too, that you have hitherto learned to know me through my writings so that you would admit that in regard to the gospel, the grace of Christ, the law, faith, love, the cross, human ordinances, our stand toward the papacy, monasticism, and the mass, and the articles of faith which a Christian should know, I have written with such clarity and certainty that I am blameless. Nor, I hope, would you deny that, though I am an unworthy instrument of God, he has helped many through me.

Not a single one of these items has been properly treated by Dr. Karlstadt, for he has not the ability, as I now can see from his writings. Truly, I never imagined, and at the same time was shocked, to see how deeply he still clings to his errors. As I see his course, he pounces on outward things with such violence, as though the whole strength of the Christian enterprise consisted in the destruction of images, the overthrow of the sacrament [of the Lord's Supper] and the hindering of baptism. He would like with such smoke and mist to obscure altogether the sun and light of the gospel and the main articles of Christianity, so that the world might forget everything that we have hitherto taught. Yet he does not come forward to show what in fact is the nature of a true Christian. For it is a mean art, of which any rascal is capable, to destroy images, deny the sacrament, and decry baptism. This never makes any one a Christian. I must say that he is a coarse devil who hurts me but little.

My sincere counsel and warning is that you be circumspect and hold to the single question, what makes a person a Christian? Do not on any account allow any other question or other art to enjoy equal importance. When anyone proposes anything ask him at once, "Friend, will this make one a Christian or not?" If not, it cannot be a matter of major importance which requires earnest

---

[1] Karlstadt had not caused a disturbance in the matter of images in Strassburg. Cf. WA 15, 381f.

consideration. If someone is too weak to do this, let him go slowly and wait until he sees what we or others have to say about it. I have hitherto treated fairly and fully of the chief articles of faith. Whoever claims otherwise cannot be a good spirit. I hope that I do no one harm also in the external matters on which these prophets harp so much.

I confess that if Dr. Karlstadt, or anyone else, could have convinced me five years ago that only bread and wine were in the sacrament he would have done me a great service. At that time I suffered such severe conflicts and inner strife and torment that I would gladly have been delivered from them. I realized that at this point I could best resist the papacy. There were two who then wrote me,[2] with much more skill than Dr. Karlstadt has, and who did not torture the Word with their own preconceived notions. But I am a captive and cannot free myself. The text is too powerfully present, and will not allow itself to be torn from its meaning by mere verbiage.

Even if someone in these days might try more persuasively to prove that only bread and wine are present, it would not be necessary that he attack me in bitter spirit—which I, unfortunately, am altogether inclined to do, if I assess the nature of the old Adam in me correctly. But the way Dr. Karlstadt carries on in this question affects me so little that my position is only fortified the more by him. If I had not previously been of this opinion, such loose, lame, empty talk, set forth on the basis of his own reason and idiosyncrasy without scriptural foundation, would lead me to believe first of all that his opinions amount to nothing. This I hope every one will see, as I give my answer. It is hard for me to believe that he can be serious; if so, God must have hardened his heart and blinded him. For if he were in earnest, he would not have thrown in so many ridiculous passages by wilfully manipulating the Greek and Hebrew languages which, as every one well knows, he has not forgotten to do.

I might well endure his uproar against images, since my writings have done more to overthrow images than he ever will do

---

[2] Probably a reference to letters from Cornelius Hoen of the Netherlands, and Franz Kolb of Wertheim, though these were written in 1521 and 1524, respectively.

with his storming and fanaticism. But I will not endure any one inciting and driving Christians to works of this kind, as if one cannot be a Christian without their performance. Nor can we tolerate anyone imprisoning Christian freedom by laws and laying a snare for consciences. For we know that no work can make a Christian, and that such external matters as the use of images and the keeping of the Sabbath are, in the New Testament, as optional as all other ceremonies enjoined by the Law. Paul says, "We know that 'an idol has no real existence'" [I Cor. 8:4]. If so, why then should the Christian conscience be ensnared and tortured on account of something that has no reality? If it has no existence, let it be of no account, whether it falls or stands, as Paul also says about circumcision [I Cor. 7:19]. But of this we will treat further in our answer.

He blames me for his banishment, and I could endure this if it were true. But this too I will answer in full, if God will. But I am glad that he is out of our land, and I wish he were not among you. It would have been advisable for him to refrain from such an accusation. For I am afraid that clearing myself will mean a severe accusation of him. Beware of the false prophet, whoever can—this is my advice, for no good will come from him. When I met him at Jena[3] he almost convinced me, through a writing of his, not to confuse his spirit with the rebellious and murderous spirit of the Allstedtians. But when, on the order of the prince, I visited his Christians at Orlamünde, I soon found what kind of seed he had sown. I was glad that I wasn't driven out with stones and filth, though some of his people gave me this benediction, "Get out in the name of a thousand devils, and break your neck before you are out of the city." This they have of course covered up beautifully in the book[4] they have published about the event. If the ass had horns, that is, if I were prince of Saxony, Dr. Karlstadt would not be banished, unless I had been prevailed upon. Under no circumstances ought he to scorn the indulgence of the princes.

---

[3] Luther met Karlstadt personally in Jena on August 21, 1524, at which time Karlstadt objected to being identified with the rebellious spirit of Thomas Münzer. Cf. WA 15, 335.

[4] *Der von orlemund schrifft an die zu Alstedt, wie man Christlich fechten soll.* Cf. WA 15, 395.

But I pray, dear friends, that you might be wiser than we, even though we have become foolish and have written about our actions. I realize well enough that the devil is only seeking opportunities to have us write and read about ourselves, whether we be pious or wicked, so that the main subject of Christ be passed over in silence and the people be made to gape at novelties. Let each one keep his mind on the straight road, for we need all eternity to learn fully about such matters as law, gospel, faith, the kingdom of Christ, Christian liberty, love, patience, and human ordinances. If meanwhile you aren't destroying images, you will not be guilty of sin. Yes, even if you don't receive the sacrament, you can yet be saved through the Word and faith. The devil has as his main purpose to turn our eyes in this perilous night away from our lamp and lead us off our path by his flying brands and flames.

Ask your evangelists, my dear sirs and brothers, to turn you away from Luther and Karlstadt and direct you always to Christ, but not, as Karlstadt does, only to the work of Christ, wherein Christ is held up as an example,[5] which is the least important aspect of Christ, and which makes him comparable to other saints. But turn to Christ as to a gift of God or, as Paul says, the power of God, and God's wisdom, righteousness, redemption, and sanctification, given to us. For such matters these prophets have little sympathy, taste, or understanding. Instead they juggle with their "living voice from heaven," their "laying off the material," "sprinkling," "mortification,"[6] and similar high-sounding words, which they themselves never understood. They make for confused, disturbed, anxious consciences, and want people to be amazed at their great skill, but meanwhile Christ is forgotten.

Dear brethren, pray that God the Father may keep us from falling into temptation, and may strengthen us according to his unfathomable mercy, preserve us and complete the work he has begun in us. For we have the comfort of being admonished to pray for this through Christ our Savior. This is an advantage we have over these prophets. For I know and am certain that they have never prayed to God the Father or sought him in initiating their

---

[5] Cf. *Against the Heavenly Prophets*, pp. 84-101.
[6] *Ibid.*, p. 117.

70

movement; nor do they have a sufficiently good conscience to dare to implore him for a blessed completion. As they began their enterprise in arrogance, so they rush forward recklessly in search of vain honor until at last they end in disgrace. The grace of God be with you all. Amen.

AGAINST THE
HEAVENLY PROPHETS
IN THE MATTER OF
IMAGES AND SACRAMENTS

1525

Part I — Translated by Bernhard Erling

Part II — Translated by Conrad Bergendoff

INTRODUCTION

This treatise is Luther's reply to a former colleague who had disagreed with him and gone in a direction which threatened the doctrines of the Lutheran Reformation. While there is occasionally a glimpse of the former friendship between the two men, the earnestness of Luther in defending his position leads him to speak sharply of Karlstadt and his companions, "the heavenly prophets." It is, however, not a personal attack, but a thorough attempt to show how subjective and unbiblical the "spiritualists" are.

Andreas Bodenstein von Karlstadt was probably a couple of years older than Luther (born *ca.* 1480). After studies at Erfurt and Cologne he came to Wittenberg, where he was made a doctor in 1510. A student of Thomas Aquinas, he had at first opposed Luther, but later, through his interest in Augustine, he became his advocate, and debated against Eck at Leipzig. In 1520 he broke with the papal church, and in 1521 aided Christian II in reforming the Danish church. While Luther was at the Wartburg, Karlstadt became a leader of the movement in Wittenberg to demolish everything connected with the Roman mass, and to do away with all traditional forms, images, vestments, and the like. This provoked excesses and Luther returned to preach against the destructive mob.*

Karlstadt became pastor at Orlamünde, in the neighborhood of Wittenberg, in 1523. He was not in sympathy with the revolutionary tendencies of Thomas Münzer, but he and his followers were associated in the minds of many with the mysticism and agitations of the "Allstedtians" (Münzer was pastor at Allstedt). Luther sought to win Karlstadt back at a conference in Jena, August 22, 1524. The effort was fruitless, and because of the incendiary character of his preaching Karlstadt was expelled from Saxony, in 1524. He went to southern Germany, and eventually became a professor in Basel.

At Jena Luther had challenged Karlstadt to state his views publicly and in writing, and as a token of this invitation Luther

---

* Cf. Luther's *Eight Wittenberg Sermons*, PE 2, 387ff.

gave him a gold coin. Karlstadt accepted the challenge and began a series of treatises on the Lord's Supper.† After his expulsion his tone became sharper toward Luther. In all, eight tracts were prepared—five on the Lord's Supper, one on consideration for weak consciences, one on the nature of faith and unbelief, one in opposition to infant baptism.

Thus it was largely on the question of the sacraments that Karlstadt opposed Luther and found himself in Zwingli's camp. For a disciple of Karlstadt brought the tracts to Zurich where they were read by the Anabaptist leaders, and to Basel where they were secretly printed. Late in 1524, the tract on baptism was confiscated, and the printer imprisoned. The remaining tracts were circulated, along with a statement of Karlstadt on his expulsion, and led to Zwingli's statement on the Lord's Supper and the consequent controversy between Zwingli and Luther on this issue.

Concern was felt in Strassburg over the controversy between Luther and Karlstadt even before the appearance of the tracts. When these appeared seven Strassburg preachers, Wolfgang Capito and Martin Bucer among them, addressed a letter to Luther (November 23, 1524) asking for his counsel.‡ Not many liked Karlstadt's manner but there was sympathy for his interpretation of the sacament. Luther answered with a *"Letter to the Christians at Strassburg in Opposition to the Fanatic Spirit,"* in December, 1524.§ When the printed tracts came to Luther's attention he realized how widespread the opinions of Karlstadt were, and how related they were to those of Zwingli and other antagonists. He felt the necessity of a comprehensive refutation, and began his *Against the Heavenly Prophets.* The work expanded and Luther decided to divide it into two parts. The first was ready by the end of December, 1524, the second a month later in January, 1525.

Even Melanchthon complained over the violence of Luther's style. The book only hardened the opponents in their stand, but it was probably an effective bar to the further spread of Zwinglian doctrine among Luther's own followers. Its composition also

---

† Cf. *St. L.* 20, 92ff.; 2306ff.; 2312ff., *et. al.*
‡ *WA Br* 3, 381ff.
§ *WA* 15, 391ff. Preserved Smith and C. M. Jacobs, *Luther's Correspondence and Other Contemporary Letters* (Philadelphia: 1918), II, 274ff. Cf. *LW* 31, 61.

clarified in Luther's own thinking some of the fundamental doctrines with which he was struggling. The primacy of the Word of God as a basis for all doctrines caused him to repel the mysticism which underlay Karlstadt's subjective notions. He saw distinctly the role of faith and reason in the matter of authority, and foresaw that Karlstadt's ideas would end in denial of Christian faith altogether. We may regret the tone of the treatise and its blunt language, but we may not forget that the contest concerned crucial issues of the Reformation. It was not a question of Luther's or Karlstadt's opinions of each other, but a question of the unshakeable basis on which the Reformation could withstand attacks from both Rome and Zurich and thus hope to provide for future generations a firm foundation of faith.

The translation follows that of a German Wittenberg text of 1525 as given in WA 18:62-125, 134-214.

AGAINST THE
HEAVENLY PROPHETS
IN THE MATTER OF
IMAGES AND SACRAMENTS

PART I

In the name of God and our dear Lord Jesus Christ. There has been a change in the weather. I had almost relaxed and thought the matter was finished;[1] but then it suddenly arises anew and it is for me as the wise man says: "When man finishes, he must begin again" [Sirach 18:6].

Doctor Andreas Karlstadt has deserted us, and on top of that has become our worst enemy. May Christ grant that we be not alarmed, and give us his mind and courage, that we may not err and despair before the Satan who here pretends to vindicate the sacrament, but has much else in mind. For since he has not thus far been able to suppress with violence the whole doctrine of the gospel, he seeks to destroy it with cunning interpretation of Scripture.

Now I have foretold it, and my prophesying will become true (I'm afraid), that God will visit our ingratitude and permit the truth to be cast down, as Daniel says (Dan. 8:[12]). Because we persecute and do not accept the truth, we must again have vain error and false spirits and prophets. These have already been with us to some extent for three years,[2] though thus far hindered by his grace. Otherwise they would long ago have wrought havoc in our ranks. Whether he will keep this disturbance in check any longer,

---

[1] Cf. p. 75, par. 2.
[2] An allusion to the disturbance caused by the Zwickau prophets in 1521.

79

I do not know, since no one cares, no one prays for it, and all are without fear, as though the devil were sleeping who, however, goes about as a furious lion [I Pet. 5:8]. Although I hope restraint will not be lacking as long as I live. Therefore I personally, as long as I live, will resist insofar as God helps me, and help wherever possible. And this is my earnest, sincere warning and admonition:

First, that each one with complete earnestness pray God for a right understanding and for his holy, pure Word. In view of the fact that under such a mighty prince and god of this world—the devil—it is not within our power to preserve either the faith or God's Word, there must be divine power which protects it, as Psalm 12 well prays and says [Ps. 12:6-8], "The promises of the Lord are promises that are pure, purified seven times. Do thou, O Lord, protect us, guard us ever from this generation. On every side the wicked prowl, as vileness is exalted among the sons of men." If we boast that we have God's word and do not take care as to how we are to keep it, it is soon lost.

Second, we, too, ought to do our part and not close our eyes, but be on our guard. For God nonetheless always holds his grace firmly over the world, so that he permits no false prophets to attempt anything except something external, such as works and subtle minute discoveries about external things. No one concerns himself with faith and a good conscience before God, but only with what glitters and shines before reason and the world. Just as the Arians[3] apparently put up a good case in the court of reason, when they alleged that God was only one person, the Father, while the Son and the Holy Spirit were not true God.

Likewise, it was easy and pleasant for the Jews and Pelagians[4] to believe that works without grace made one pious; and under the papacy it was said in an attractive way that the free will also contributes something toward grace. So, since it is in accord with reason, it sounds altogether pleasant to say that there is simply bread and wine in the sacrament. Who cannot believe that? If one

---

[3] Arians derived their name from Arius (d. 336) whose views were condemned by the Council of Nicaea in 325.
[4] Pelagians derived their name from Pelagius (ca. 360-418) whose views were attacked by St. Jerome and St. Augustine and condemned by the Council of Ephesus in 431.

only today would grant to the Jews that Christ was simply a man, I think it would be easy to convert them.

So our concern here should now be that we keep these two teachings far apart from each other: the one that teaches of the main articles, to govern the conscience in the spirit before God; the other, which teaches of things external or works. For more depends on the teaching of faith and a good conscience than on the teaching of good works. When works are lacking, help and counsel are at hand so that one can produce them if the teaching of faith remains firm and pure. But if the teaching of faith is placed in the background and works are put forward, then nothing can be good and there is neither counsel nor help. Then works lead to vain glory and seem to people to be something great, while God's glory disappears.

So it is with these honor-seeking prophets who do nothing but break images, destroy churches, manhandle the sacrament, and seek a new kind of mortification, that is, a self-chosen putting to death of the flesh. Thus far they have not set aright the conscience, which is nonetheless most important and most necessary in the Christian teaching, as has been said.

And if they had now altogether succeeded so that there were no more images, no churches remained, no one in the whole world held that the flesh and blood of Christ were in the sacrament and all went about in gray peasant garb,[5] what would be accomplished thereby? What did they expect to achieve by pressing, straining, and pursuing this course of action? Would they therewith have become Christian? Where would faith and love be? Should they come later? Why should they not have precedence? Fame, vain glory and a new monkery would well thereby be achieved, as happens in all works, but the conscience would in no way be helped. Thus such false spirits do not care where faith or love are to be found, just as the pope does not care but presses on if only he can make sure of the works belonging to his obedience and laws. And when they do occur, still nothing has occurred.

Since Dr. Karlstadt pursues the same way and in so many books

---

[5] In answer to Luther's reproach, Karlstadt said: "Of what harm is my common dress since I do not give occasion with my gray garb for suspecting a false kind of holiness as Doctor Luther does with his monk's cowl." WA 18, 64.

does not even teach what faith and love are[6] (yes, they speak derisively and disdainfully of us on this account, as though it were a minor doctrine), but stresses and emphasizes external works, let everyone be warned of him. Everyone should know that he has a perverted spirit that thinks only of murdering the conscience with laws, sin, and works, so that thereby nothing is set aright, even if everything happened that he professes in all his books, and with mouth and heart. Even rascals are able to do and teach all that he urges. Therefore something higher must be there to absolve and comfort the conscience. This is the Holy Spirit, who is not acquired through breaking images or any other works, but only through the gospel and faith.

Now in order that we do not open our mouths too wide and marvel at the skill of these false spirits, and thereby abandon the main articles, and thus deceitfully be led off the track (for thereby the devil succeeds through these prophets), I will here briefly recount these articles of the Christian faith to which everyone is above all things to pay attention and hold fast.

The first is the law of God, which is to be preached so that one thereby reveals and teaches how to recognize sin (Rom. 3 [:20] and 7 [:7]), as we have often shown in our writings. However, these prophets do not understand this correctly, for this means a truly spiritual preaching of the law, as Paul says in Rom. 7 [:14], and a right use of the law, as he says in I Tim. 1 [:8].

Secondly, when now sin is recognized and the law is so preached that the conscience is alarmed and humbled before God's wrath, we are then to preach the comforting word of the gospel and the forgiveness of sins, so that the conscience again may be comforted and established in the grace of God, etc.

Christ himself teaches these two articles in such an order (Luke 24 [:47]). One must preach repentance and the forgiveness of sins in his name. "And the Spirit (he says in John [16:8]) will convince the world of sin and of righteousness and of judgment." You do not find either of these two articles in this one or any other of the false prophets. They also do not understand them, and yet these are the most important and necessary articles.

---

[6] Karlstadt had written a treatise on the subject (on the two great commandments of love to God and to one's neighbor) but Luther seems not to have seen it.

Now the third is judgment, the work of putting to death the old man, as in Romans 5, 6, and 7. Here works are concerned, and also suffering and affliction, as we through our own discipline and fasting, watching, labor, etc., or through other persecution and disgrace put to death our flesh. This putting to death is also not handled correctly by these false prophets. For they do not accept what God gives them, but what they themselves choose. They wear gray garb, would be as peasants, and carry on with similar foolish nonsense.[7]

In the fourth place, such works of love toward the neighbor should flow forth in meekness, patience, kindness, teaching, aid, and counsel, spiritually and bodily, free and for nothing, as Christ has dealt with us.

In the fifth and last place, we ought to proclaim the law and its works, not for the Christians, but for the crude and unbelieving. For among Christians we must use the law spiritually, as is said above, to reveal sin. But among the crude masses, on Mr. Everyman, we must use it bodily and roughly, so that they know what works of the law they are to do and what works ought to be left undone. Thus they are compelled by sword and law to be outwardly pious, much in the manner in which we control wild animals with chains and pens, so that external peace will exist among the people. To this end temporal authority is ordained, which God would have us honor and fear (Rom. 13 [:1]; I Pet. 3) [I Pet. 2:13, 17].

However, we must see to it that we retain Christian freedom and do not force such laws and works on the Christian conscience, as if one through them were upright or a sinner. Here question are in order concerning the place which images, foods, clothing, places, persons, and all such external things, etc., ought to have. Whoever does not teach according to this order certainly does not teach correctly. From which you now see that Dr. Karlstadt and his spirits replace the highest with the lowest, the best with the least, the first with the last. Yet he would be considered the greatest spirit of all, he who has devoured the Holy Spirit feathers and all.[8]

Therefore I beg every Christian who observes how we bicker in this matter to remember that we are not dealing with important

---

[7] Cf. p. 81, n. 5.
[8] An allusion to the dove, symbol of the Holy Spirit.

things, but with the most trivial ones. Bear in mind that the devil is eager to spruce up such minor matters, thereby drawing the attention of the people so that the truly important matters are neglected, as long as they gape in his direction. From this each one should recognize how false and evil the spirit of Dr. Karlstadt is, who, not content to ignore and be silent concerning the great and significant articles, so inflates the least significant ones as if the salvation of the world depended more on them than on Christ himself. Also, he compels us to turn from the great important articles to minor ones, so that we with him lose time and are in danger of forgetting the main articles. Let this be the first fruit by which one is able to know this tree [Matt. 7:16-20].

So that the books, however, will not become too many, I will answer all of his with this one book. And since I have not yet written anything especially about images,[9] this shall be the first. For while it pleases him to begin this work recklessly, he sought afterwards to mend himself and cover the shame with fig leaves.

On the Destruction of Images

I approached the task of destroying images by first tearing them out of the heart through God's Word and making them worthless and despised. This indeed took place before Dr. Karlstadt ever dreamed of destroying images. For when they are no longer in the heart, they can do no harm when seen with the eyes. But Dr. Karlstadt, who pays no attention to matters of the heart, has reversed the order by removing them from sight and leaving them in the heart. For he does not preach faith, nor can he preach it; unfortunately, only now do I see that. Which of these two forms of destroying images is best, I will let each man judge for himself.

For where the heart is instructed that one pleases God alone through faith, and that in the matter of images nothing that is pleasing to him takes place, but is a fruitless service and effort, the people themselves willingly drop it, despise images, and have none made. But where one neglects such instruction and forces the

[9] Cf., however, the third of Luther's *Eight Wittenberg Sermons*, PE 2, p. 401ff., and his *Letter to the Christians in Strassburg in Opposition to the Fanatic Spirit.* Cf. especially Luther's explanation of the first commandment in his *Large Catechism* (1529) in H. E. Jacobs' *Book of Concord* (Philadelphia: 1911), p. 391ff.; WA 30[I], 132ff.

issue, it follows that those blaspheme who do not understand and who act only because of the coercion of the law and not with a free conscience. Their idea that they can please God with works becomes a real idol and a false assurance in the heart. Such legalism results in putting away outward images while filling the heart with idols.

I say this so that every one may see the kind of a spirit that is lodged in Karlstadt. He blames me for protecting images contrary to God's Word, though he knows that I seek to tear them out of the hearts of all and want them despised and destroyed. It is only that I do not approve of his wanton violence and impetuosity. If the Holy Spirit were here, he would not lie as knowingly and unashamedly as that, but would say, "Yes, dear Luther, I am well pleased that you so utterly destroy images in the heart. Thereby it will be all the easier for me to destroy them before the eyes, and I accept your service as necessary to this end." Now I am supposed to be acting contrary to God's Word, and protecting images, I who do destroy images outwardly and inwardly. And I am not to say that he acts contrary to God's Word, he who only smashes them in pieces outwardly, while he permits idols to remain in the heart and sets up others alongside them, namely false confidence and pride in works.

Furthermore, I have allowed and not forbidden the outward removal of images, so long as this takes place without rioting and uproar and is done by the proper authorities. In the world it is considered foolish to conceal the true reason for a good venture[10] out of fear that it may fail. However, when Karlstadt disregards my spiritual and orderly putting away of images and makes me out to be only a "protector of images," this is an example of his holy and prophetic art, though I only resisted his factious, violent, and fanatical spirit. Now since the evil spirit sits so firmly in his mind I am less inclined than ever to yield to obstinacy and wrong. I will first discuss images according to the law of Moses, and then according to the gospel. And I say at the outset that according to the law of Moses no other images are forbidden than an image of God which one worships. A crucifix, on the other hand, or any

---

[10] Karlstadt had taunted Luther as to his reason for going slowly in the matter of destroying images.

other holy image is not forbidden. Heigh now! you breakers of images, I defy you to prove the opposite!

In proof of this I cite the first commandment (Exod. 20 [:3]): "You shall have no other gods before me." Immediately, following this text, the meaning of having other gods is made plain in the words: "You shall not make yourself a graven image, or any likeness . . ." [Exod. 20:4]. This is said of the same gods, etc. And although these spirits cling to the little word "make" and stubbornly insist, "Make, make is something else than to worship," yet they must admit that this commandment basically speaks of nothing else than of the glory of God. It must certainly be "made" if it is to be worshiped, and unmade if it is not to be worshiped. It is not valid, however, to pick out one word and keep repeating it. One must consider the meaning of the whole text in its context. Then one sees that it speaks of images of God which are not to be worshiped. No one will be able to prove anything else. From subsequent words in the same chapter [Exod. 20:23], "You shall not make gods of silver to be with me, nor shall you make for yourselves gods of gold," it follows that "make" certainly refers to such gods.

For this saying, "You shall have no other gods," is the central thought, the standard, and the end in accordance with which all the words which follow are to be interpreted, connected, and judged. For this passage points out and expresses the meaning of this commandment, namely, that there are to be no other gods. Therefore the words "make," "images," "serve," etc., and whatever else follows, are to be understood in no other sense than that neither gods nor idolatry are to develop therefrom. Even as the words, "I am your God" [Exod. 20:2], are the standard and end for all that may be said about the worship and service of God. And it would be foolish if I sought to conclude from this something that had nothing to do with the divine or the service of God, such as building houses, plowing, etc. No conclusion can be drawn from the words, "You shall have no other gods," other than that which refers to idolatry. Where however images or statues are made without idolatry, then such making of them is not forbidden, for the central saying, "You shall have no other gods," remains intact.

If they do not want to apply "make" to images of God, as the text requires, then I will also say that worship is not forbidden (since we are clinging so strictly to the letter). For in the first commandment nothing is said about worship. I might say, "Don't make images yourself. Let others make them. But you are not forbidden to worship them." If they, however, from other passages connect "make" with "worship," which is not done in this text, then in all fairness I may connect in the same text "make" with the gods, as the text clearly states. Thus we have no example of punishment being inflicted on account of images and altars, but it has followed on account of worship. We read thus that Moses' brazen serpent remained [Num. 21:8] until Hezekiah destroyed it solely because it had been worshiped [II Kings 18:4].

Concerning this I have a powerful passage in Lev. 26 [:1], "I am the Lord your God. You shall make for yourselves no idols and erect no graven image or pillar, and you shall not set up a figured stone in your land, to bow down to them." How is this? Here I think the interpretation is sufficiently clear. It is because of worship that idols and figured stones are forbidden. It is without doubt so that they will not be worshiped, and where they are not worshiped they might well be set up and made. What would be the need otherwise of referring to bowing down? Therefore the "making" in the first commandment must refer to worshiping and to no more. So also in Deut. 4 [:15f.], where he forbids the making of images, the passage speaks clearly of worship.

We have also an example of this in the Old Testament. For Joshua (Josh. 24 [:26]) set up a cairn at Shechem under an oak as a testimony, etc., even though above in Lev. 26 [:1] the setting up of such cairns was as strictly forbidden as the images. However, because it was a stone of testimony, and not for worship, he did not do this against the commandment. Thereafter also Samuel (I Sam. 7 [:12]) set up a stone and called it Stone of Help. This was also forbidden, as has been said, but because no worship but only remembrance was intended, he did not sin.

However, above all this, Joshua (Josh. 22:21f.), according to which the tribes of Reuben, Gad, and Manasseh built a large altar by the Jordan, so that all Israel became alarmed and with deep concern sent messengers to them, as though the altar had been set up contrary to God's command, which indeed was forbidden at that time. But see how they excused themselves. The altar remained when they heard that it was not for worship or sacrifice, but to be a witness. If, however, it had been incorrect to make an altar, and God's commandment had been strictly applied to making, they would have reduced the altar to ashes. Otherwise they would not have escaped sin, as they said they would. Now the making of altars is as strictly forbidden as the making of images. If one then can make and set up altars and special stones, so that God's commandment is not trespassed because worship is absent, then my image breakers must also let me keep, wear, and look at a crucifix or a Madonna, yes, even an idol's image, in full accord with the strictest Mosaic law, as long as I do not worship them, but only have them as memorials.

Now I wonder what these Jewish saints, who hold so strictly to the law of Moses and rage against images, do about the images on coins and jewelry? For I hear they have much money and jewelry. In Joachimsthal[11] St. Joachim[12] is minted on coins. It would be my advice that one should rescue these great saints from sin, taking from them the guilders and the silver coins and goblets. For though they may be opposed to images, it is to be feared that they have not "put away all selfish desire" nor advanced in their "concentration," "adoration," and "sprinkling" [13] to the point where they are of themselves able to cast away these treasures.[14] Human nature is probably still so weak that even the living voice from heaven is not strong enough for the task. To accomplish it, good strong apprentices are needed, who otherwise wouldn't have much to fritter away.

This breaking of images has also another weakness in that they themselves do it in a disorderly way, and do not proceed with proper authority. As when their prophets stand, crying and arousing the masses, saying: heigh, hew, rip, rend, smash, dash, stab, strike, run, throw, hit the idols in the mouth! If you see a crucifix, spit in

---

[11] A city, well known for its silver mines, located in northwestern Bohemia. Karlstadt spent some time in Joachimsthal and gained support for his ideas among its leading citizens. Cf. Hermann Barge, *Andreas Bodenstein von Karlstadt* (Leipzig, 1905), I, 200ff.

[12] The husband of St. Anne, father of Jesus' mother, according to later tradition.

[13] Terms employed by the Karlstadt group akin to medieval mysticism. Karlstadt spoke of a sevenfold "sprinkling," analogous to the sprinkling in the tabernacle.

[14] Karlstadt was accused of having too strong a desire for money, a suspicion which proved to be true when he sought by various tactics to retain his income from the cathedral church in Wittenberg and the parish in Orlamünde.

its face, etc. This is to do away with images in a Karlstadtian manner, to make the masses mad and foolish, and secretly to accustom them to revolution. Those who rush into this thing think they are now great saints, and become proud and impudent beyond all measure. When one looks at the matter more closely, one finds it is a work of the law which has taken place without the Spirit and faith. Yet it makes for pride of heart, as though they by such works had gained a special status before God. Actually this means teaching works and the free will all over again.

We read however in Moses (Exod. 18 [:20ff.]) that he appointed chiefs, magistrates, and temporal authority before he gave the law, and in many places he teaches: One is to try, judge, and punish in all cases with justice, witnesses, and in an orderly way. Otherwise, why have judges and sovereigns in the land? Karlstadt always skips over this matter altogether too easily. What Moses commands Karlstadt applies to the disorderly masses and teaches them to break into this field in disorder like pigs. This certainly is and must be called a seditious and rebellious spirit, which despises authority and itself behaves wantonly as though it were lord in the land and above the law. Where one permits the masses without authority to break images, one must also permit anyone to proceed to kill adulterers, murderers, the disobedient, etc. For God commanded the people of Israel to kill these just as much as to put away images. Oh, what sort of business and government that would turn out to be! Therefore, though I have not said that Dr. Karlstadt is a murderous prophet,[15] yet he has a rebellious, murderous, seditious spirit in him, which, if given an opportunity, would assert itself.

For this reason we always read in the Old Testament, where images or idols were put away, that this was done not by the masses but by the authorities, just as Jacob buried the idols of his household [Gen. 35:4]. Thus Gideon pulled down the altar of Baal when he was called by God to be a chief [Judg. 6:27]. Thus Jehu the king (not the masses) demolished Ahab's Baal [II Kings

---

[15] In conversation with Luther in the Black Bear Inn at Jena, Karlstadt complained that Luther had called him "a murderous prophet" from the pulpit in Jena and so lumped him together with Thomas Münzer of Allstedt. For a report of the conversation between Luther and Karlstadt at Jena, cf. WA 15, 335ff. For a detailed discussion of the legal aspects of Karlstadt's relation to his government, cf. MA' 4, 366ff.

10:26ff.]. So did Hezekiah also with the bronze serpent [II Kings 18:4]. Josiah did the same with the altars at Bethel [II Kings 23:15]. From this one sees clearly, that where God tells the community to do something and speaks to the people, he does not want it done by the masses without the authorities, but through the authorities with the people. Moreover, he requires this so that the dog does not learn to eat leather on the leash, that is, lest accustomed to rebellion in connection with the images, the people also rebel against the authorities. Talk of the devil and his imps appear.

Now that we are under our princes, lords, and emperors, we must outwardly obey their laws instead of the laws of Moses. We should therefore be calm and humbly petition them to put away such images. Where they will not do so we nonetheless have God's word meanwhile, whereby they may be put out of the heart, until they are forcibly put away outwardly by those properly authorized. However, when these prophets hear this, they call it papistic and fawning[16] before princes. That they, on the other hand, arouse the disorderly masses and make them rebellious, that is not to fawn. Thus we will not be cleared of fawning until we teach the masses to kill the princes and the lords. However, if I am a papist or one who fawns before princes, of that the pope and the princes themselves should be more honest witnesses than this lying spirit, who here speaks. For he well knows that the contrary is known to the whole world.

Let this be said about images strictly according to the law of Moses. The meaning is not that I wish to defend images, as has been sufficiently indicated. Rather murderous spirits are not to be permitted to create sins and problems of conscience where none exist, and murder souls without necessity. For although the matter of images is a minor, external thing, when one seeks to burden the conscience with sin through it, as through the law of God, it becomes the most important of all. For it destroys faith, profanes the blood of Christ, blasphemes the gospel, and sets all that Christ has won for us at nought, so that this Karlstadtian abomination is no less effective in destroying the kingdom of Christ and a good conscience, than the papacy has become with its prohibitions regarding food

---

[16] Münzer, not Karlstadt, originated this taunt.

90

and marriage, and all else that was free and without sin. For eating and drinking are also minor, external things. Yet to ensnare the conscience with laws in these matters is death for the soul.

From this let every man note which of us two is the more Christian. I would release and free consciences and the souls from sin, which is a truly spiritual and evangelical pastoral function, while Karlstadt seeks to capture them with laws and burden them with sin without good cause. And yet he does this not with the law of God, but with his own conceit and mischief, so that he is not only far from the gospel, but also not even a Mosaic teacher. And yet he continually praises the "Word of God, the Word of God," just as if it were therefore to become God's Word as soon as one could say the Word of God. Usually those who make great ado in praising God's Word do not have much to back them up, as unfortunately we have previously experienced under our papistic tyrants.

However to speak evangelically of images, I say and declare that no one is obligated to break violently images even of God, but everything is free, and one does not sin if he does not break them with violence. One is obligated, however, to destroy them with the Word of God, that is, not with the law in a Karlstadtian manner, but with the gospel. This means to instruct and enlighten the conscience that it is idolatry to worship them, or to trust in them, since one is to trust alone in Christ. Beyond this let the external matters take their course. God grant that they may be destroyed, become dilapidated, or that they remain. It is all the same and makes no difference, just as when the poison has been removed from a snake.

Now I say this to keep the conscience free from mischievous laws and fictitious sins, and not because I would defend images. Nor would I condemn those who have destroyed them, especially those who destroy divine and idolatrous images. But images for memorial and witness, such as crucifixes and images of saints, are to be tolerated. This is shown above to be the case even in the Mosaic law. And they are not only to be tolerated, but for the sake of the memorial and the witness they are praiseworthy and honorable, as the witness stones of Joshua [Josh. 24:26] and of Samuel (I Sam. 7 [:12]).

The destruction and demolishing of images at Eichen, in

91

Grimmetal, and Birnbaum,[17] or places to which pilgrimages are made for the adoration of images (for such are truly idolatrous images and the devil's hospices), is praiseworthy and good. However to teach that those who do not demolish them are therefore sinners is to go too far and to require more than is necessary of Christians who do enough when they fight and struggle against images with God's Word.

If you say, however: Yes, but while they remain, some will be offended by them and attracted to them, I answer: What can I do about that, I who as a Christian have no power on earth? Appoint a preacher who will instruct the people against them, or arrange to have them removed in an orderly way, not with tumult and riots.

Now then, let us get to the bottom of it all and say that these teachers of sin and Mosaic prophets are not to confuse us with Moses. We don't want to see or hear Moses. How do you like that, my dear rebels? We say further, that all such Mosaic teachers deny the gospel, banish Christ, and annul the whole New Testament. I now speak as a Christian for Christians. For Moses is given to the Jewish people alone, and does not concern us Gentiles and Christians. We have our gospel and New Testament. If they can prove from them that images must be put away, we will gladly follow them. If they, however, through Moses would make us Jews, we will not endure it.

What do you think? What will become of this? It will become evident that these factious spirits understand nothing in the Scriptures, neither Moses nor Christ, and neither seek nor find anything therein but their own dreams. And our basis for this assertion is from St. Paul (I Tim. 1 [:9]), "The law is not laid down for the just" (which a Christian is). And Peter (Acts 15 [:10-11]), "Now therefore why do you make trial of God by putting a yoke upon the neck of the disciples which neither our fathers nor we have been able to bear? But we believe that we shall be saved through the grace of the Lord Jesus, just as they will." With this saying (as Paul with his) Peter abrogates for the Christian the whole of Moses with all his laws.

Yes, you say, that is perhaps true with respect to the ceremonial

---

[17] Three towns in the vicinity of Leipzig.

and the judicial law, that is, what Moses teaches about the external order of worship or of government. But the decalogue, that is, the Ten Commandments, are not abrogated. There is nothing of ceremonial and judicial law in them. I answer: I know very well that this is an old and common distinction, but it is not an intelligent one. For out of the Ten Commandments flow and depend all the other commandments and the whole of Moses.

Because he would be God alone and have no other gods, etc., he has instituted so many different ceremonies or acts of worship. Through these he has interpreted the first commandment and taught how it is to be kept. To promote obedience to parents, and unwilling to tolerate adultery, murder, stealing, or false witness, he has given the judicial law or external government so that such commandments will be understood and carried out.

Thus it is not true that there is no ceremonial or judicial law in the Ten Commandments. Such laws are in the decalogue, depend on it, and belong there. And to indicate this God himself has expressly introduced two ceremonial laws, namely, concerning images and the sabbath. We can show that these two parts are ceremonial laws which are also each in its way abrogated in the New Testament, so that one may see how Dr. Karlstadt deals about as wisely in his book with the sabbath as with images. For St. Paul (Col. 2 [:16-17]), speaks frankly and clearly, "Therefore let no one pass judgment on you in questions of food and drink or with regard to a festival or a new moon or a sabbath. These are only a shadow of what is to come." Here Paul expressly abrogates the sabbath and calls it a shadow now past since the body, which is Christ himself, is come.

Also, Gal. 4 [:10-11], "You observe days, and months, and seasons, and years! I am afraid I have labored over you in vain." Here Paul calls it lost labor to observe days and seasons, among which is also the sabbath. Isaiah has also prophesied this (Isa. 66 [:23]), "From new moon to new moon, and from sabbath to sabbath," that is, there shall be a daily sabbath in the New Testament, with no difference as to time.

We must be grateful to Paul and Isaiah, that they so long ago freed us from the factious spirits. Otherwise we should have to sit through the sabbath day with "head in hand" awaiting the heavenly voice, as they would delude us. Yes, if Karlstadt were to write more about the sabbath, even Sunday would have to give way, and the sabbath, that is, Saturday, would be celebrated. He would truly make us Jews in all things, so that we also would have to be circumcised, etc.

For it is true, and no one can deny it, that whoever keeps the law of Moses as a law of Moses, or deems it necessary to keep it, must regard the keeping of all laws as necessary, as St. Paul (Gal. 5 [:3]) concludes and says, "Every man who receives circumcision—he is bound to keep the whole law." Therefore also, whoever destroys images, or observes the sabbath (that is, whoever teaches that it must be kept), he also must let himself be circumcised and keep the whole Mosaic law. In time (where one leaves room for these spirits) they would surely be compelled to do, teach, and observe this. However, by God's grace they now do even as St. Paul says (Gal. 6 [:13]), "For even those who receive circumcision do not themselves keep the law, but they desire to have you circumcised that they may glory in your flesh." Thus the image breakers themselves do not keep the law. For just as they fail to keep all the other laws, so also they destroy images unspiritually, as a work, so that they lose Christ, the fulfilment of the law, and seek only that they may attain a glory in us, as if they had taught something excellent and masterful.

The reference to images in the first commandment is also a temporal ceremony. St. Paul concludes and says among other things (I Cor. 7 [I Cor. 8:4]): "We know that 'an idol has no real existence.'" Just as he says of circumcision (I Cor. 7 [:19]), "Circumcision is nothing," that is, it is a matter of freedom and does not bind the conscience, just as he himself throughout that section speaks of freedom. However, let St. Paul and all the angels be defied, in that they call something nothing or a matter of freedom, which God so strictly commands. So the fanatics allege. But one is not to consider God's commandment as useless or as nothing, as Moses says in Deuteronomy, for it does concern life.

He points out especially that "an idol is nothing in the world" [I Cor. 8:4] in relation to external matters. In relation to God idols are no joke. Such idols in the heart are false righteousness, glory in works, unbelief, and anything else that takes the place of Christ in the heart in the form of unbelief. As if he were to say, the Jews avoid the external idols in the world, but before God their hearts are full of idols. He also says of them (Rom. 2 [:22]), "You who abhor idols, do you rob temples?" With these words he interprets in fine fashion the first commandment, which states: "You shall have no other gods before me" [Exod. 20:3], as if saying, "In relation to yourself or the world idols are nothing, but in relation to me, that is, in the heart, you may not worship or trust in them."

Since St. Paul declares that in all these three points the Corinthians have freedom, and would have these regarded as nothing, namely, idols, idol's temples and food offered to idols, all three of which are strictly prohibited in the first commandment and those following from it, it is indeed clear and proven forcefully enough that the reference to images in the first commandment is to a temporal ceremony, which has been abrogated in the New Testament. For just as I may with good conscience eat and drink that which has been offered to idols, and sit and dwell in an idol's temple [I Cor. 8:7-10], as St. Paul teaches, so I may also put up with idols and let them be, as things which neither make any difference nor hinder my conscience and faith.

Not only a teaching of St. Paul, the prophet Elisha (II Kings 5 [:18-19]) has also proven its truth with an admirable example in the Old Testament. According to Moses and also against Moses (as our rebellious spirits would understand Moses) he permitted Naaman, the Syrian commander, to worship the true God in the temple of Rimmon, the idol of Syria. Now if the first commandment were to be kept with Karlstadtian strictness, Naaman should not have done such a thing, nor should the prophet have permitted it. For it is, of course, strictly forbidden to go into an idol's temple and worship before an idol while at the same time worshiping the true God. God strictly forbids the Jews to construct altars, images, or holy places for the purpose of serving and worshiping him without his command. Even more strictly does he forbid them to serve and worship him in the presence of other gods. From this example one can see again that in the Old Testament also, true idols can do no harm as long as one worships while they are around, and only the true God is worshiped from the heart. Yet our enthusiasts would ensnare us who are free Christians and tie us

95

down so rigidly that we should not be able to put up with any idols without committing sin.

If, however, these destroyers of images will not show us any mercy, we beg them at least to be merciful to our Lord Jesus Christ and not to spit on him and say, as they do to us, "Phooey on you, you servant of idols!" For the three evangelists, Matthew [22:19ff.], Mark [12:15ff.], and Luke [20:24ff.] write that he took a coin from the Pharisees upon which was a likeness of Caesar, and asked whose likeness it was and said it should be given to Caesar. If all kinds of images had been forbidden, the Jews should not have given any to him, nor possessed any, much less should Christ have accepted it and allowed this to be unrebuked, especially since it was the image of a heathen. He must also have sinned when, according to Matt. 17 [:27], he asked Peter to take a tax shekel out of the fish's mouth and pay the tax for him. For he must have had to create the same image and the shekel in that very place and placed it in the fish's mouth. I presume also that the gold which the three holy kings offered to Christ [Matt. 2:11] was also coined with images, as is the custom in all lands. The same thing is true of the two hundred denarii (John 6 [:17]) with which the disciples wanted to buy bread. Yes, also all the fathers and the saints are guilty insofar as they have used money.

Now we do not request more than that one permit us to regard a crucifix or a saint's image as a witness, for remembrance, as a sign as that image of Caesar was. Should it not be as possible for us without sin to have a crucifix or an image of Mary, as it was for the Jews and Christ himself to have an image of Caesar who, pagan and now dead, belonged to the devil?[18] Indeed the Caesar had coined his image to glorify himself. However, we seek neither to receive nor give honor in this matter, and are yet so strongly condemned, while Christ's possession of such an abominable and shameful image remains uncondemned.

Would you here say, "You don't mean that the first commandment has been abrogated, for, after all, one ought to have a God? Furthermore, one ought not commit adultery, kill, steal?" Answer: I have spoken of the Mosaic law as laws of Moses. For to have a

---

[18] Roman Caesars belonged to the devil because they made themselves gods and persecuted Christians.

God is not alone a Mosaic law, but also a natural law, as St. Paul says (Rom. 1 [:20]), that the heathen know of the deity, that there is a God. This is also evidenced by the fact that they have set up gods and arranged forms of divine service, which would have been impossible if they had neither known or thought about God. For God has shown it to them in the things that have been made, etc. (Rom. 1 [:19-20]). Is it therefore surprising to find that the heathen have missed the true God and worshiped idols in the place of God? The Jews also erred and worshiped idols instead of God, even though they had the law of Moses. And they who have the gospel of Christ still misapprehend the Lord Christ.

Thus, "Thou shalt not kill, commit adultery, steal, etc.," are not Mosaic laws only, but also the natural law written in each man's heart, as St. Paul teaches (Rom. 2 [:15]). Also Christ himself (Matt. 7 [:12]) includes all of the law and the prophets in this natural law, "So whatever you wish that men would do to you, do so to them; for this is the law and the prophets." Paul does the same thing in Rom. 13 [:9], where he sums up all the commandments of Moses in the love which also the natural law teaches in the words, "Love your neighbor as yourself." Otherwise, were it not naturally written in the heart, one would have to teach and preach the law for a long time before it became the concern of conscience. The heart must also find and feel the law in itself. Otherwise it would become a matter of conscience for no one. However, the devil so blinds and possesses hearts, that they do not always feel this law. Therefore one must preach the law and impress it on the minds of people till God assists and enlightens them, so that they feel in their hearts what the Word says.

Where then the Mosaic law and the natural law are one, there the law remains and is not abrogated externally, but only through faith spiritually, which is nothing else than the fulfilling of the law (Rom. 3 [:31]). This is not the place to speak about that, and elsewhere enough has been said about it.[19] Therefore Moses' legislation about images and the sabbath, and what else goes beyond the natural law, since it is not supported by the natural law, is free, null and void, and is specifically given to the Jewish people

---

[19] Cf. *De votis monasticis (Concerning Monastic Vows)* WA 8, 573ff.

alone. It is as when an emperor or a king makes special laws and ordinances in his territory, as the *Sachsenspiegel*[20] in Saxony, and yet common natural laws such as to honor parents, not to kill, not to commit adultery, to serve God, etc., prevail and remain in all lands. Therefore one is to let Moses be the *Sachsenspiegel* of the Jews and not to confuse us gentiles with it, just as the *Sachsenspiegel* is not observed in France, though the natural law there is in agreement with it.

Why does one then keep and teach the Ten Commandments? Answer: Because the natural laws were never so orderly and well written as by Moses. Therefore it is reasonable to follow the example of Moses. And I wish that we would accept even more of Moses in worldly matters, such as the laws about the bill of divorce [Deut. 24:1], the sabbath year [Lev. 25:2-7], the year of jubilee,[21] tithes, and the like. Through such laws the world would be better governed than now with its practices in usury, trade, and marriage. This occurs whenever a land follows examples from laws of other lands, as the Romans took the Twelve Tables from the Greeks.[22]

It is not necessary to observe the sabbath or Sunday because of Moses' commandment. Nature also shows and teaches that one must now and then rest a day, so that man and beast may be refreshed. This natural reason Moses also recognized in his sabbath law, for he places the sabbath under man, as also Christ does (Matt. 12 [:1ff.] and Mark 3 [:2ff.]). For where it is kept for the sake of rest alone, it is clear that he who does not need rest may break the sabbath and rest on some other day, as nature allows. The sabbath is also to be kept for the purpose of preaching and hearing the Word of God.

There are, besides this, much better things in Moses,[23] namely

---

[20] Written by Eike von Repgow, knight and juryman, the *Sachsenspiegel* (early thirteenth century) contains economic and social laws obtaining in and around Magdeburg and Halberstadt. Although fourteen of its articles were condemned by Gregory XI in 1374 the book remained influential in the codification of German law until the middle of the nineteenth century.

[21] Cf. Lev. 25:8ff. The year of jubilee did not become established practice among the Jews.

[22] According to Livy iii. 31, the Romans sent three legates to Athens prior to their formulation of laws to copy the laws of Solon and to acquaint themselves with the laws and customs of other Greek city states. Cf. *WA* 18, 81.

[23] Luther has in mind the first five books of the Bible which are referred to in his German Bible as books of Moses.

the prophecy and promise of the coming of Christ, as St. Paul says (Rom. 3 [:21]). Also, Moses tells us about the creation of the world, the origin of marriage, and many precious examples of faith, love, and all virtues. In the writings of Moses we also find examples of unbelief and vice, from which one can learn to know God's grace and wrath. All are written not only for the sake of the Jews, but for the gentiles as well. Much in these writings speaks of unbelievers and gentiles, so that all such parts serve as examples to teach the whole world. However, the law of Moses concerns only the Jews, and such gentiles as have willingly submitted to it and accepted it. They are called proselytes. So St. Paul says in Rom. 9 [:4] that the Jews have been given the law, the covenant, and the promise. Psalm 147 [:19-20] says, "He declares his word to Jacob, his statutes and ordinances to Israel. He has not dealt thus with any other nation; they do not know his ordinances," etc.

I have myself seen and heard the iconoclasts read out of my German Bible. I know that they have it and read out of it, as one can easily determine from the words they use. Now there are a great many pictures in those books, both of God, the angels, men and animals, especially in the Revelation of John and in Moses and Joshua. So now we would kindly beg them to permit us to do what they themselves do. Pictures contained in these books we would paint on walls for the sake of remembrance and better understanding, since they do no more harm on walls than in books. It is to be sure better to paint pictures on walls of how God created the world, how Noah built the ark, and whatever other good stories there may be, than to paint shameless worldly things. Yes, would to God that I could persuade the rich and the mighty that they would permit the whole Bible to be painted on houses, on the inside and outside, so that all can see it. That would be a Christian work.

Of this I am certain, that God desires to have his works heard and read, especially the passion of our Lord. But it is impossible for me to hear and bear it in mind without forming mental images of it in my heart. For whether I will or not, when I hear of Christ, an image of a man hanging on a cross takes form in my heart, just as the reflection of my face naturally appears in the water when I look into it. If it is not a sin but good to have the image of Christ in my heart, why should it be a sin to have it in my eyes? This is especially true since the heart is more important than the eyes, and should be less stained by sin because it is the true abode and dwelling place of God.

However, I must cease lest I hereby give occasion to the image-breakers never to read the Bible, or to burn it, and after that to tear the heart out of the body, because they are so opposed to images. I only referred to the use of the Bible to show what happens when reason wants to be wise and gain the upper hand in understanding God's Word and works. Also I wanted to show what lies behind Dr. Karlstadt's brash boast that he has God's Word and must suffer so much on its account. Indeed, the devil, too, must suffer on account of it—not that he uses it rightly, but rather perverts it and thereby increases his wickedness and lies, as Dr. Karlstadt also does due to the same vexation.

And if I had time, I would like to satisfy my desire against Satan and before the whole world stuff down his throat again the saying which he wrings out of the Scripture in such nonsensical fashion in Karlstadt's little book, so that he would have to be ashamed. For I have really caught Karlstadt at so vulnerable a point, it seems like a miracle of God to me that he can make a fool of the devil. However, I have other things to do. Whoever will not be instructed by this argument, let him go and break images his whole life long! I cannot be blamed.

In conclusion I must give an example of what I am saying to see whether Dr. Karlstadt might learn a bit himself and be ashamed that he teaches his disciples so well. When I was in Orlamünde and discussed images with the good people there, and showed from the text that all the sayings from Moses that were brought forward dealt with idolatrous images which one worshiped, a man stepped forward who wanted to be the most wise among them and said to me, "Do you hear? I would like to address you as 'you.' [24] Are you a Christian?" I said, "Address me as you will." He would just as soon have struck me. He was so full of Karlstadt's

---

[24] The reference is to the distinction in German between the polite *ihr* (thou) and the familiar *du* (you).

spirit that the others could not make him keep silent. So he continued and said, "If you will not follow Moses, you must nevertheless endure the gospel. You have shoved the gospel under the bench. No, no! It must come forth and not remain under the bench."

I said, "What then does the gospel say?" He said, "Jesus says in the gospel (I don't know where, though my brethren know it) that the bride must take off her nightgown and be naked, if she is to sleep with the bridegroom. Therefore one must break all the images, so that we are free and cleansed of what is created." So far the words of our conversation.

What was I to do? I had come among Karlstadt's followers and then I learned that breaking images meant that a bride should take off her nightgown, and that this was to be found in the gospel. Such words, and words about shoving the gospel under the bench, he had heard from his master. Perhaps Karlstadt had blamed me with hiding the gospel under the bench, while he was the man who was to draw it forth. Such idle pride had brought the man into all misfortune, and had pushed him out of the light into such darkness, that he gave as a reason for breaking images, that a bride should take off her nightgown. Just as if they thereby were rid of created things in the heart, in that they madly destroy images. What though, if the bride and bridegroom were so chaste that they kept nightgown and robe on? It would certainly not hinder them much if they otherwise had desire for each other.

But so it goes, when one brings the disorderly masses into the picture. Due to great fulness of the spirit they forget civil discipline and manners, and no longer fear and respect anyone but themselves alone. This appeals to Dr. Karlstadt. These are all pretty preliminaries to riot and rebellion, so that one fears neither order nor authority. Let this be enough about images. I think it has been adequately proven that Dr. Karlstadt does not understand Moses at all. He peddles his own dreams as the Word of God and thinks less of orderly authority than he does of the disorderly masses. Whether this be conducive to obedience or to rebellion, I leave to each one to determine for himself.

With Respect to the Complaint of Dr. Karlstadt, That He Has Been Expelled from Saxony[25]

Thus far we have seen what kind of a Word of God Dr. Karlstadt has, for the sake of which he exalts himself and makes himself a holy martyr. Now let us see the work of God, for the sake of which, as he boasts, he suffers such great persecution. Although I would rather that he had kept silent and not compelled me to deal with his aversion. However, since he has also attacked the princes of Saxony, in that he has not even refrained from inveighing against the motto which they in all honor wear upon their sleeves, (so meanly does the bitter resentment in his heart seek occasion to bring infamy on people), I must, insofar as I have knowledge of the matter, defend the honor of my gracious lords. For the princes of Saxony have certainly deserved better of Dr. Karlstadt than that he should leave with such thanks, as he well knows. Well now, on with it and we shall see.

First, may I say this, that I have had no dealings with the elector of Saxony about Karlstadt. For that matter I have in my whole life never spoken one word with this prince, nor heard him speak, nor have I even seen his face, except once in Worms before the emperor [April 18, 1521] when I was being examined for the second time. It is to be sure true that I have often communicated with him in writing through Master Spalatin and especially insisted that the Allstedtian spirit be suppressed.[26] However I accomplished nothing, so that I was also much annoyed with the elector, until this spirit voluntarily fled, unexpelled. For this reason Karlstadt should rightly have spared such princes and become better acquainted with the matter before he cried out to the world in his slanderous booklet.[27] Also it is not right, much less Christian, even if it were true that he was driven out by the elector, to gain revenge in this way with libel. One should first humbly have asked the reason and set forth what was right, and thereafter suffered in

---

[25] In his little book, *Von dem alten und neuen Testament* (March 16, 1525), Karlstadt maintained he had been expelled from Saxony contrary to imperial law and was being persecuted without having been given a hearing. *St. L.* 20, 288.
[26] Cf. *Luther's Correspondence and other Contemporary Letters.* Trans. and ed. by Preserved Smith and C. M. Jacobs (Philadelphia, 1918), II, 222; and Ernst Ludwig Enders, *Dr. Martin Luther's Briefwechsel* (Stuttgart, 1893), V, 23.
[27] A reference to Karlstadt's pamphlet on his expulsion from Saxony.

silence. It could not be expected of me, who am made out to be simply flesh,[28] which unfortunately I also am. But the high spirit of Karlstadt cannot do wrong nor err. He is the right itself.

I have spoken about it with my young lord, Duke John Frederick[29] (that I admit) and pointed out Dr. Karlstadt's wantonness and arrogance. However since "the spirit" burns with such blinding intensity, I will here recount the reasons, some of which, indeed, are not known to the princes of Saxony, why I am happy that Dr. Karlstadt is out of the country. And insofar as my entreaties are effectual, he shall not again return, and would again have to leave were he to be found here, unless he become another Andrew,[30] which God grant. If God wills, I will fawn before no princes.[31] But much less will I suffer that the rebellious and the disobedient among the masses are to be led to despise temporal authority.

And my humble admonition and request to all princes, lords, and authorities is first, as I previously have also written against the Allstedtian spirit,[32] that they will assiduously see to it that preachers who do not teach peacefully, but attract to themselves the mobs and on their own responsibility wantonly break images and destroy churches behind the backs of the authorities, forthwith be exiled. Or they should deal with them so that they refrain from such action. Not that I thereby would hinder God's Word, but I would put a limit and bounds to the wantonness of mischievous enthusiasts and factious spirits, which the temporal authority is obligated to do. Above all, however, Dr. Karlstadt with his gang must be stopped, for he is obdurate and will not be instructed, but goes on justifying and defending his factiousness.

And this is my basis and reason: We have noted above how Dr. Karlstadt and image-breakers of his kind do not interpret Moses' commandment as referring to the constituted authority, as

---

[28] An allusion to Thomas Münzer's polemical writing, *Hoch verursachte Schutzrede . . . wider das sanft lebende Fleisch zu Wittenberg.*
[29] Duke John Frederick, son of John the Constant (1503-1554), later became elector of Saxony (1532-1547).
[30] A play on Karlstadt's name, Andreas. In the German "another Andrew" is "*ein ander Andres.*"
[31] Cf. p. 90.
[32] Cf. Luther's letter to the Elector Frederick and Duke John of Saxony (Wittenberg, July, 1524). *Luther's Correspondence, op. cit.,* II, 245; *WA Br* 15, 219.

is proper, but to the disorderly populace. That is certainly not the right spirit and attitude. For, as I have said, where the populace has the right and power to carry out a divine commandment, then one must thereafter give in and permit them to carry out all the commandments.[33] Consequently, whoever arrives on the scene first must put to death murderers, adulterers, thieves, and punish rogues. And thereby justice, jurisdiction, dominion, and all authority would fall apart. Matters would take their course in accordance with the proverb: Give a rogue an inch and he takes a mile. For why do we have sovereigns? Why do they carry the sword, if the masses are to rush in blindly and straighten things out themselves?

After that, such disorder will gain in momentum, and the masses will have to kill all of the wicked. For Moses, when he commands the people to destroy images (Deut. 7 [:16]), also commands them to destroy without mercy those who had such images in the land of Canaan. For this killing is just as strictly commanded as the destruction of images, which commandment these factious spirits so obstinately introduce and emphasize. Moses, however, commanded this of a people that had Joshua as chief and many magistrates and, besides, was a law-abiding people. Moreover the commandment did not apply to all of the wicked, but only to the heathen Canaanites, who through God's judgment were given over to death because of their wickedness, as the text clearly indicates. For he exempted the Edomites, Moabites, and Ammonites, though they also were wicked. Thus this work of God took place through regular governmental authority, and affected those whom God himself, not men, had publicly judged and condemned to death.

Since our murderous spirits apply Moses' commandment to the masses, and do not have God's judgment over the wicked, but themselves judge that those who have images are wicked and worthy of death, they will be compelled by such a commandment to engage in rebellion, in murdering and killing, as works which God has commanded them to do. Let the Allstedtian spirit be an example, who already had progressed from images to people, and who publicly called for rebellion and murder contrary to all authority. How could he act otherwise? For so he must teach. Since he had

---

[33] Cf. p. 90.

invited the devil to be his sponsor up to this point so that the masses without due process were to destroy images, as enjoined by God's commandment, then he had to continue and press the auxiliary commandment, which follows from it, and commands the people to murder. If I were to destroy images in the same sense as they, I, too, would be compelled to follow through and command people to be murdered. For the commandment stands there pressing its claim. Dear lords, the devil does not care about image breaking. He only wants to get his foot in the door so that he can cause shedding of blood and murder in the world.

But, you say, Dr. Karlstadt does not want to kill. That one can see from the letters which those of Orlamünde wrote to the Allstedtians.[34] Answer: I also believed it! But I believe it no longer. I no longer ask what Dr. Karlstadt says or does. He has not hit the truth for the first time. Of the spirit which they have and which impels them, I say that it is not good and is bent on murder and rebellion. Although he bows and scrapes because he sees that he is in a tight spot, I shall clearly show that what I have said is so. God forbid, but suppose Dr. Karlstadt won a large following, which he thought he could assemble on the Saale,[35] and the German Bible alone was read, and Mr. Everybody began to hold this commandment (about killing the wicked) under his own nose, in what direction would Dr. Karlstadt go? How would he control the situation? Even if he had never intended to consent to something like that, he would have to follow through. The crowds would mutiny and cry and shout as obstinately, "God's Word, God's Word, God's Word is there. We must do it!" As he now cries against images, "God's Word, God's Word!" My dear lords, Mr. Everybody is not to be toyed with. Therefore God would have authorities so that there might be order in the world.

If it were really true, and I could believe, that Dr. Karlstadt does not intend murder or rebellion, I would still have to say that he has a rebellious and murderous spirit, like the one at Allstedt, as long as he continues with wanton image breaking and draws the unruly rabble to himself. I well see that he neither strikes nor stabs,

---

[34] Luther refers to the letter of those in Orlamünde in which they renounced the spirit and actions of Thomas Münzer and his followers in Allstedt.
[35] The Saale River flows through Orlamünde.

but since he carries the murderous weapon and does not put it aside, I do not trust him. He could be waiting for time and place, and then do what I fear. By the murderous weapon I mean the false interpretation and understanding of the law of Moses. Through it the devil comes and the masses are aroused to boldness and arrogance.

You say, however, Oh, he won't be that obstinate. He is willing to be instructed and desist from such things. Who? Dr. Karlstadt? To be sure, he can say the words very well, and blare forth in writings that he wants to be instructed and would listen to a superior. If he's in earnest, I'm happy. But when has he ever yielded or listened? How often has not Philip [Melanchthon][36] admonished him at Wittenberg that he should not rave so about Moses, images, the mass, and confession? And when I came back and preached[37] against his image breaking and celebration of the mass, why did he not then desist and listen? Also, when Dr. Justus Jonas and Master Dietrich of Bila mediated between us,[38] how politely did he yield and permit himself to be instructed? He even summoned the Last Judgment upon me on account of the fanatic mass, which he at that time (Heaven help me!) as if with the great Holy Spirit had arranged, yet which he now himself condemns and changes.

Also, at Jena in the inn,[39] when we talked of the matter, and he sought to defend his cause most strongly, he turned to me, snapped his fingers and said, "You are nothing to me." If he doesn't respect me, whom among us will he then respect? Or why should I then continue to admonish? I think he nevertheless considers me one of the most learned at Wittenberg. And yet he tells me to my

---

[36] On February 5, 1522, Melanchthon stated in a letter to Hugold von Einsiedeln, "I have appealed also to Dr. Karlstadt to be more moderate, but I cannot stem the tide. . . . A reformation is in progress. May it redound to the glory of God. . . ." CR 1, 546.

[37] The eight sermons preached during Lent, 1522, in Wittenberg. Cf. p. 75.

[38] Justus Jonas was professor and dean of the cathedral at Wittenberg and one of Luther's staunchest friends. Dietrich of Bila was a friend of Karlstadt, to whom Karlstadt dedicated one of his treatises of 1523, indicating he was then in Joachimsthal. WA 18, 89, note 4.

[39] Cf. p. 75. The incident reported here is not included in the source referred to in footnote †, p. 76.

face that I am nothing to him, and then pretends that he seeks to be instructed.

Also, he freely writes back and forth across the land and considers us at poor Wittenberg as nothing at all compared to him. And now most recently we are called papists and cousins of the Antichrist. Also, at Orlamünde, when Master Wolfgang Stein,[40] the court preacher, bade Dr. Karlstadt most kindly and gently to yield, he screwed up his mouth and gave him such an answer as though he were prince in the land. Yet Master Wolfgang was there as a representative of the prince, whom he should have obeyed as soon as he was asked. This is the way he thinks one is to honor authority, indeed as if it were the rabble. Many more are the tricks of his nimble mind.

This I am recounting in order to show that Dr. Karlstadt's offer to be instructed is pure falsehood. Thereby he would only use forbearance and a good appearance as a smoke screen for his obdurate mind, and so dishonor both princes and myself. Also it is not proper to preach and teach in divine things and then immediately thereafter want to ask whether it is right. Then either the teaching must be wrong or the question hypocritical. But if he is really in earnest, well then, let him desist from his fanaticism. I have previously dealt quite extensively with the matter of images, so that he may understand how he is in error. Let him be instructed and separate himself from the heavenly prophets.[41] All will simply be forgotten and I will do for him and grant him all that I am able. I will gladly have him as friend if he will. If he will not, then I must leave it in God's hands.[42]

In much the same manner he has offered to dispute[43] but complains he has not been permitted to do so. Dear God, how can a man so publicly speak against his conscience! Should he have been refused permission to dispute by me or anyone else? Yet both

---

[40] Stein was court preacher at Weimar and had been sent by his prince to accompany Luther to Jena and Orlamünde on Luther's visit there in 1524. WA 15, 326.

[41] Luther has Thomas Münzer and his followers in mind.

[42] In a letter dated December 23, 1524, the text of which has been lost, Luther offered to meet Karlstadt in order to effect a reconciliation. Cf. WA 18, 49.

[43] Karlstadt had expressed his willingness to engage in a disputation in letters to Duke John (August 14, and September, 1524) and in the discussion with Luther at Jena.

princes and the university, with so much writing and issuing of summons, have not been able to get him to come back to Wittenberg, where he should attend to his preaching, lectures, and disputations, as he was obligated and bound to do. He added the stipulation that he must have safe conduct. Just as if he would be insecure at Wittenberg, where he held office and position, and where he was welcome. Who would hurt him? These are nothing but empty words to put up a good front. It may be that his conscience had made him afraid, as the wicked are wont to be afraid where there is no cause for fear, in that he at Orlamünde had fallen upon and seized what was the prerogative and right of the reigning prince. That, too, was not necessary.

If I were a prince, and paid a salary to a professor to lecture and to preach in my city or territory, and he without my knowledge and consent went elsewhere and wantonly took possession of what was rightfully due me and I meanwhile ordered him officially and through the university to resume his duties, but he, nevertheless, did what he pleased on my salary and my property, and later wrote me a letter and asked for safe conduct to dispute in my city, whereto I had already ordered him and he was obligated to come, what should I answer, since he so completely took me for a fool? And if I now did not answer, and he subsequently circulated an insulting letter against me, as though I had not been willing to permit him to dispute or be heard, what should I think? I would secretly think: He is a rascal. Not that I thereby call Dr. Karlstadt a rascal. But I indicate what in such a case might occur to a reigning prince as an individual.

However this man lacked nothing except that his princes were too indulgent. One could well have found princes, who, had he undertaken such tricks in their territories with such mischief and arrogance would have put him and his gang to the sword, and probably that would not have been just. Therefore I would advise Dr. Karlstadt not to insult the princes and to thank them that they have so graciously let him off, so that they be not compelled at last to deal with him more severely according to his merits.

Nor is this the least of all reasons why he trails along with the heavenly prophets from which, as is known, comes the Allstedtian spirit. From them he learns, to them he cleaves. They secretly smuggle error into the land and gather stealthily on the Saale,[44] where they plan to nest. The feeble devil will go nowhere but to our place, where already through the gospel we have created opportunity and security, and seeks only to defile and destroy our nest, as the cuckoo does with the hedge sparrow. These same prophets claim that they speak with God, and God with them, and are called to preach, and yet none of them dares come forth and appear openly, but they lay their eggs secretly and pour their poison into Dr. Karlstadt. He then promotes it with tongue and pen. But when he could not do this at Wittenberg, he began on the Saale.

These prophets teach and hold also that they are going to reform Christendom and establish it anew in this manner. They must slaughter all princes and the wicked, so that they become lords on earth and live only among saints. Such and much else I myself have heard from them. Dr. Karlstadt knows also that these are fanatics and murderous spirits and that such calamity has originated with them, which should be warning enough. Yet he does not avoid them. And I am to believe that he would not bring about murder and rebellion? Also when I reproached him about this in Jena,[45] he himself admitted it and moreover defended it, saying, why should he not hold to them in that which they say rightly? Why then does he not also hold to us or to the papists, where we are in the right. Or is nothing right with us, or with the papists? No, against these prophets he can neither preach nor write, but against us there must be preaching, writing, and raging.

Supposing there were in Dr. Karlstadt such a spirit and he were an honorable man by ordinary standards, if he found such people in his prince's territory, he should be the first to shun them and separate himself from them and bluntly renounce them, that they desist from such prophesying, otherwise he would have to write against them, as I have done against the Allstedtian spirit.[46] For since they are prepared and bent upon slaughter and murder, they can come from nowhere else than from the devil himself, even

---

[44] Cf. p. 40, n. 2.
[45] Cf. WA 15, 339.
[46] *Wider den neuen Abgott und alten Teufel, der zu Meihsen soll erhoben werden.* WA 15, 199ff.

though they knew all arts and letters. For the devil also well knows the Bible and letters together with other arts.

Isn't it annoying that the masses now and again are made so arrogant and restless by such spirits, before it becomes known to the princes, so that as soon as they hear a preacher who teaches them to be peaceful and obedient to government, they immediately call him a toad eater and a fawner before princes[47] and point their fingers at him? Who, however, says: "Strike dead, give no one anything, and be free Christians, you are the true people, etc.," he is a true evangelical preacher. These take the nightgown off the bride at Orlamünde[48] and the trousers off the bridegroom at Naschhausen.[49] They do not hide the gospel under the bench, and yet they teach not at all who Christ is, or what should be known about him.

If then a prince found Dr. Karlstadt of such a kind that he held to the factious and murderous spirits, thereby making the subjects arrogant and restless, and if he furthermore sought to justify and defend himself, would it not be time that the prince said to him: "If you're the trouble maker, get out of here before I have to speak to you in some other way?" For what good can be expected when such prophets remain in the land, in which the seed already shows itself so powerful? He dare not here object that he has not been admonished before this, and that he has not known, that there has been no love for him. Who could admonish, when they deal so secretly, until they have spread the poison all around so that no one could know what they were doing. Have they not been admonished sufficiently and publicly through my writing against the Allstedt spirit? How graciously have they allowed themselves to be instructed? Also, have they not known that I have judged the spirit of these prophets as the devil's spirit? How has it helped, other than that they are more hardened than ever, with secret cunning have planned to resist me?

Yes, why have they themselves shown so little love, and so busily worked against us behind our backs in their hiding place, written against us in several territories, and in the pulpit pulled

[47] Cf. p. 90.
[48] Cf. p. 101.
[49] Suburb of Orlamünde.

no one to pieces but the Wittenbergers, and yet they have thus far not shown us our error? Wittenberg has done it, on that the spirit feasts. Otherwise all's well in the world. And this is done under the protection of our princes, yes, under our name and sponsorship. But take care, you evil and wrathful spirits. It is still true that Wittenberg is too big a bite for you, and God may ordain that in swallowing you may choke to death on it.[50] We know Satan, and if sometimes we doze off as men, it will do you no good, for he does not slumber nor sleep, who protects and watches over us [Ps. 121:4]. We commit ourselves to him.

Dr. Karlstadt has brought this trouble and misfortune upon himself, in my opinion, inasmuch as he carries on his enterprise without call[51] while wilfully leaving his own calling. For he has forced himself upon Orlamünde as a wolf. For this reason it was impossible for him to do any good there. He was appointed to Wittenberg on a royally endowed income, as an archdeacon, to preach God's Word, lecture and dispute.[52] God had sent him there, and he agreed to discharge his responsibilities. He did serve for a time, usefully and with honor, and was liked and cherished. He cannot say it was otherwise. He received more advancement from the elector than many others, until the murderous prophets came and made the man wild and restless, so that he wanted to learn something better and more unusual than God teaches in the Bible.

Then he wantonly left and went to Orlamünde, without the knowledge and consent of either the prince or the university. He drove out the pastor who by order of the prince and university privilege was placed there, and personally took over the parish.[53] What do you think of a stunt like that? Does it contribute to quiet obedience to authority, or to insolent rebellion among the masses? The spirit of which I speak peered forth, for the very same spirit which swallows such a little strap would also very likely venture

---

[50] Probably a reference to Korah's rebellion, Num. 16:32-33.

[51] I.e., without a call by the proper authorities in church and state.

[52] Karlstadt was appointed archdeacon of All Saints' Church, Wittenberg, in 1510, and as such enjoyed the income of the parish at Orlamünde. His duties included preaching in the Wittenberg church and teaching at the university.

[53] According to WA 18, 90, footnote 6, and 94, footnote 7, Luther's account is not altogether factual, for Karlstadt seems to have received the parish by arrangement with his superiors. Cf., however, MA' 4, 360-370.

to devour a whole harness, when opportunity came. He who is so venturesome that he dares in full view of a reigning prince greedily and wantonly to arrogate his property, jurisdiction, and statutes, what would he do behind the back of a prince, if he found occasion? This is the way to honor and fear the authorities and to teach the masses both with word and example`that the priest is like the people, as Isaiah says [Isa. 24:2].

Even if the devil bursts, he will be unable to deny that the princes of Saxony sit as governing authorities ordained by God. The land and the people are subject to them. What kind of a spirit then is this that despises such a divine order, proceeds with headstrong violence, treats princely possessions and rights as though they were his own, and doesn't even once recognize the prince or confer with him about it, as though he were a blockhead, and he himself were prince in the land? Should not a good spirit fear God's order a little more, and since the estate, the pastorate, and the land belong to the prince, first humbly beg permission to leave and resign one position, and beg the favor of being installed in another?

Now, however, Dr. Karlstadt forsakes his duties at Wittenberg behind the prince's back, robs the university of his preaching and lectures and what he is obligated to do by reason of the prince's endowment, and retains nevertheless the salary or revenue for himself, and puts no one else in his place. At Orlamünde he also takes the pastorate belonging to the university, drives out him whom he had not appointed, nor had the power to appoint, much less to dismiss. Dear friends, why all this? Some suppose in order that he might draw that much more income, and because he believed the elector would be lenient and not quick to punish. But I believe that a secondary reason was that the prophets sought a hide-out on the Saale, where they could spread their spirit and poison, creeping around in the darkness like mice—something they would not be able to do for long in Wittenberg.

He cannot pretend that he could not remain in Wittenberg on account of heresy, for, thank God, the gospel itself is there, pure and fine. And if it were not, he would not for that reason be driven to godless behavior. Even if the devil and his members are around us in the world, we dare not on that account be devils or members of the devil. Dr. Karlstadt was unusually free to devote himself alone to God's Word, letting the other priests do what they would.[54] And even if there had been nothing but devils in Wittenberg, he should nevertheless not therefore, behind the prince's back, move without leave or permission, meanwhile retaining his income, and shamelessly appropriating the prince's possessions at another place.

Nor can he say that he moved out of pity for Orlamünde, to teach the erring sheep. For this pastorate was served through the university by a Christian pastor, namely Master Konrad [Glitzsch][55] who correctly understood and taught the gospel. And even if it had been so, he should nevertheless have petitioned the authorities about it. For one is not to do evil for the sake of the good (Rom. 3 [:8]).[56] It has been done only to give room and place for the evil spirit to circulate its poison, as I have said, so that we might be pictured as remarkable masters, with no one equal to us.

If he did not seek to gain money or to concentrate his poison, but sought only the glory of God, why did he not request to preach God's Word at other cities, where he would not have found such income? Yet the preaching might well have been needed and the cities could have been closer. Indeed it was because it wasn't convenient for the spirit and the belly. However if such mischief is to occur "out of the inner call of God," then it is necessary that it be proved with miraculous signs. For God does not change his old order for a new one unless the change is accompanied with great signs. Therefore one can believe no one who relies on his own spirit and inner feelings for authority and who outwardly storms against God's accustomed order, unless he therewith performs miraculous signs, as Moses indicates in Deut. 18 [:22].

When, however, he alleges, together with the Orlamünders, that he has been elected by them as their minister, and thus externally called, I answer: To me it doesn't matter that they afterward have elected him. I speak about his first coming. Let

---

[54] Karlstadt was troubled by scruples of conscience because his office as arch-deacon of the cathedral church required his presence at the celebration of the mass according to Roman rite. Cf. MA³ 4, 376.

[55] Konrad Glitzsch, vicar in Orlamünde, whom Karlstadt ousted in the spring of 1523.

[56] The editor has followed the suggested reading of Otto Scheel: um Guts willen, in Luther's Werke, Ergänzungsband 1 (Berlin, 1905), p. 188, rather than the reading of the text umb Gotts willen in WA 18, 96.

him produce letters to show that they at Orlamünde have summoned him from Wittenberg and that he did not himself run over there.[57] Dear friends, if being called means that I, out of a sense of duty and obedience, run to another city, and thereafter place myself in so favorable a light and persuade the people to choose me and oust another, then I say that no principality is so great, but that I would be prince therein and drive out the incumbent. How easy is it not to persuade a people? That is not the way to extend a call. It is to promote faction and rebellion and to despise authority.

Nor did the Orlamünders have a right to elect a pastor on another's salary, for it belonged to the prince and his jurisdiction. Nor is the prince or the university un-Christian, burdening them with wicked pastors. And even if he had appointed a godless one to Orlamünde, which he had not done, they should nevertheless not deprive their sovereign of his right, possession, and authority, and behind his back elect a pastor and give away revenues (which were not their own) to whomever they would. Much less should he [Karlstadt] have accepted it without petitioning the prince. Rather, as is becoming of subjects, they should humbly have made complaint with the prince and the university, and requested that a Christian pastor be given them. If then he had not been willing, they could thereafter have planned as best they could.

Now however they plot without the knowledge of the prince, elect pastors and appoint them as they themselves please. They appear to regard their natural liege lord and reigning prince as so much dirt, whose possessions and prerogatives they wantonly wrest from him and take into their own hands. Indeed both Karlstadt and the Orlamünders have deserved a good strong jolt, as an example to other such bands, so that they would know that they have a sovereign and are not themselves lords in the land. However I would pardon and excuse the good people of Orlamünde on the ground that they were too feeble in the face of Dr. Karlstadt's overbearing spirit. Overcome by his humble bearing and high-sounding words (as is his custom), they were unable to see how they acted against their own lord. Possessed of a factious spirit, Dr. Karlstadt has my answer on the basis of what is apparent from

---

[57] Luther seems unaware of a letter from the Orlamünde parish asking Duke John that Karlstadt might be sent to this place.

the manner in which he has carried on in this situation, for he will not rest until he has tied the pitiable people to his person and set at naught temporal authority.

Beyond this, all would have been forgiven in honor of the gospel, if only he had not so stubbornly undertaken to defend himself. For when the university, by order of the prince, wrote and summoned him back to his duties and office in Wittenberg[58]—yes indeed, my Karlstadt, will you come?—he aroused the poor people to reply to the university in such proud and arrogant tones that it was too much.[59] The university's summons was considered papistic and I don't know what. Nothing was evangelical, only what Dr. Karlstadt said and did with the Orlamünders. Now may a pious reader tell me, have not the princes of Saxony had enough patience with this mad spirit? Yes, unfortunately all too much. Had they been more diligent in wielding the sword, the rabble on the Saale would today be more peaceable and disciplined, and the spirit would not be domiciled there.

When no end to this game was in sight, but only rash action with total disregard of both the prince and the university, I nevertheless came to the Saale by order of the prince, and preached against such fanaticism as well as I could. Then the devil also welcomed me, in a way which I have no doubt long deserved. How he panted, rushed and writhed, just as if Christ had come to drive him out. Dr. Karlstadt even caught me off guard at the table with such a mild manner and gentle words that I instantly felt the "spirit" speak from him. Thereupon I pointed out to my gracious young lord, Duke John Frederick,[60] that his grace should not put up with this, for what was being done [rather than said] was apparent. He would be factious and make naught of the authorities. This is how much I know about the matter, and no more.

And what should I say? There is no earnestness nor truth in what this spirit proposes. They do not even themselves believe what they say, nor keep what they promise, except this that the devil

---

[58] The summons was issued by letter, March, 1524.
[59] The reply was given in a letter, dated May 12, 1524.
[60] Cf. p. 103, n. 29. Following his discussion with Karlstadt at Jena Luther reported to the duke who subsequently banished Karlstadt from his territories.

seeks only to cause trouble in the world. For when Dr. Karlstadt was last in Wittenberg he willingly agreed to leave the pastorate,[61] since he saw that nothing else would do, and promised then that he would return to Wittenberg. Had he then been certain that he had been called to be pastor, he should not have given it up, but rather have given up his life, as until then he had struggled and defended himself. For one ought not to renounce a divine call when they [with whom one is associated] boast of having pure fellowship with God.

He seems to have been of the opinion that his poison was already sufficiently spread abroad, and the trouble now was rooted deeply and strongly enough, and that the populace would now stay with him as unfortunately is all too true, so that he could probably remain as pastor there, even though the prince and the university wouldn't like it. Also an apparent surrender of the pastorate would do no harm, since the populace was so prepared that no one who succeeded him would prosper. Hence eventually the princes would have to leave him there, as indeed has been publicly suggested. Such devious and clever designs the spirit did not think that God could see or prevent. Thus he planned treacherously to secure his advantage before anyone was aware of it. Now we men easily lose in a gamble. The spirit surely lost, and God is found to be wiser than he is.

I have had to make this extended explanation, although very unwillingly, because the spiteful spirit is so prone to embellish himself to the shame of the princes of Saxony, by whose favor he receives honor and goods. I think also if he had not fled in such misery and despondency, but had had the moral courage at that time to request reasons [for his banishment] from the princes of Saxony, these and others, of which I am perhaps unaware, might have been indicated to him. Though more could be said about that, I am of the opinion that the land belongs to the princes of Saxony and not to Dr. Karlstadt, who is a guest therein and has nothing. When they take from no one what belongs to him and at the same time, for reasons of their own, no longer want someone in their

---

[61] April, 1524.

land, I do not believe they are obligated to say to each one what has actuated them, nor to take the matter to court. For princes must conceal many things and keep them secret. If a landlord did not have the right and the power to ask a guest or a servant to move out, without first giving a reason and settling the matter in court, he would be but a poor landlord imprisoned in his own estate, and the guest would himself be landlord.

This spirit does not consider this, but presses on and attacks the princes with public abuse, as though he were their equal lord in the land of Saxony and defies them with the law in their own possessions. How shall one answer such an arrogant and venture-some head other than as the householder in the gospel says: "Friend, I am doing you no wrong. . . . Take what belongs to you and go. . . . Shall I not do what I choose with what belongs to me?" [Matt. 20:13-14]. This evil-eyed rogue also wanted to know the reason and justification for the householder's dealing with his possessions as he chose. Oh you fine spirit, to what extent are you able to conceal what you have in mind? You would be lord, and that which you affirm and do is to be considered right. That is the sum of it.

What think you now? Is it not a fine new spiritual humility? Wearing a felt hat and a gray garb,[62] not wanting to be called doctor, but Brother Andrew and dear neighbor, as another peasant, subject to the magistrate of Orlamünde and obedient as an ordinary citizen. Thus with self-chosen humility and servility, which God does not command, he wants to be seen and praised as a remarkable Christian, as though Christian behavior consisted in such external hocus-pocus. At the same time he strives and runs counter to duty, honor, obedience, and the power and right of the reigning prince and the governing authority, which God has instituted. This is God's new sublime art, taught by the heavenly voice, which we at Wittenberg, who teach faith and love, do not understand and cannot know. This is the nice "turning from the material," the "concentration," the "adoration," the "self-abstraction," and similar devil's nonsense.[63]

---

[62] Cf. p. 81, n. 5. When Luther preached in Jena prior to his interview with Karlstadt, the latter attended wearing a felt hat.
[63] Cf. p. 88, n. 13.

Concerning the Mass

Herewith an answer has been given to several of Dr. Karlstadt's books.[64] We shall now give our attention to the book which has to do with the mass,[65] so that we may deal specifically with the sacrament. For I do not know why he makes so many books, all of which deal with the same subject. He could well put on one page what he wastes on ten. Perhaps he likes to hear himself talk, as the stork its own clattering. For his writing is neither clear nor intelligible, and one would just as soon make one's way through brambles and bushes as to read through his books. This is a sign of the spirit. The Holy Spirit speaks well, clearly, in an orderly and distinct fashion. Satan mumbles and chews the words in his mouth and makes a hundred into a thousand. It is an effort to ascertain what he means.

Dr. Karlstadt has observed that we at Wittenberg opposed the mass as a sacrifice and a good work with great earnestness, both with writings[66] and in action. Moreover, we were the first ones to do so. He was probably concerned that we receive honor therefrom and thus through vainglory be led to sin. He reasoned with himself how he might help us in the following way: What shall I do to bring the Wittenbergers into such disrepute that all their writings and deeds concerning the mass will mean nothing, and that they be defamed in their holding the mass as a sacrifice and a good work, and I alone be the hero that has brought into the world the awareness that the mass is not a sacrifice? I will do this. I will not pay attention to what they write, confess, or do. Then I could be no knight, for all this is too evident. I will inveigh against them because they call it a mass, which means a sacrifice, and because they elevate the sacrament as though they offered it. Then I can

---

[64] Luther has the following books of Karlstadt in mind: *Ob man gemach fahren soll; Ursachen, der halben Andres Carolstadt vertrieben;* and *Von dem Sabbat und geboten Feiertagen.*

[65] In the following remarks Luther directs his attack against Karlstadt's *Wider die alten und neuen papistischen Messen* (*ca.* September, 1524) in St.L. 20, 2306ff.

[66] Cf. *A Treatise on the New Testament That Is the Holy Mass* (1520), WA 6, 353ff.; PE 1, p. 28ff. *The Babylonian Captivity of the Church* (1520), WA 6, 484ff.; PE 2, p. 167ff.

say: The Wittenbergers all grievously err, and with them the "poor bishop at Zwickau." [67]

Well then, we must in turn be thankful for the good deed and see to it that the high honor also does not deceive the rich vagabond and "uncalled" preacher Karlstadt. In matters relating to the name of the mass and the elevation of the sacrament, we shall make reply in such manner that more shame than honor will come to him. Not that it is necessary to refute such childish tomfoolery other than to show that no good spark of true understanding is left in Dr. Karlstadt. Therefore, let everyone be on guard against this mad spirit, and not trust his splendid words. Lurking behind them are false, murderous snares, confusing the conscience with utterly unnecessary trickery.

First of all he takes us to task for calling the sacrament a mass, and accuses us of being Christ's hangmen and murderers, using other horrible words even worse than those used by the papists, because mass is supposed to mean sacrifice in Hebrew. [68] Having taken the risk of contending with such earnestness that the mass is not a sacrifice is of no help to us. Even in the eyes of the world it is disgraceful, childish, and effeminate to be in agreement in substance and yet to quarrel about words. In forbidding this Paul calls such people, *logomaxous*, "word warriors," and wranglers, etc. [I Tim. 6:4; II Tim. 2:14]. However it is the devil, as I have said, who would like to use Karlstadt's head, to burden conscience grievously with sin and horrible danger in things which are in themselves free and without sin. Therefore he has no peace unless he destroys good consciences and kills souls, which should live, as Ezekiel [13:19] says.

In the second place, if it really were true that mass means sacrifice, and there were a fragment of good in Dr. Karlstadt, he should have first informed and admonished us before publicly attributing to us such great vices before the whole world. Since we in fact deny and struggle against the mass as a sacrifice, it might

---

[67] "Poor bishop at Zwickau" refers to Luther's friend, Nikolaus Hausmann, pastor at Zwickau.
[68] The derivation of the word "mass" from the Hebrew *missah* (Cf. Deut. 16:10) is incorrect. Luther does not make the mistaken meaning central in his argument. Cf. below. The word "mass" is derived from the Latin *missa* as contained in the liturgical form, *Ite, missa est.* . . .

have been expected that we would very gladly also drop the name, were we instructed that by using the name we make the mass a sacrifice. What has happened to brotherly love in the high spirit? Is it no sin for these saints so grievously and shamefully to calumniate the neighbor without any cause? Plagued with blindness, Dr. Karlstadt pays no attention to nor does he recognize such truly great sins, as is apparent from his desire to burden the whole world with erroneous, imagined, and great sins. Acting in this manner is, in my opinion, to have the log in one's own eye and to want to take the speck out of another's eye [Matt. 7:5; Luke 6:42].

I have never known, also do not know now, that mass means sacrifice. Dr. Karlstadt must excuse me. Although I do not know much Hebrew, yet I am more competent to speak and to judge than he. I have now also almost translated the whole Bible into German, and I have not yet found that mass means a sacrifice. I think he must have found it written in the vent of a chimney, or recently invented his own Hebrew language, as he can invent sins and laws and a bad conscience, or probably the heavenly voice speaks in this way. It would be in order, when one does not understand a language, not to make claims for oneself in the field, and to give honor to those who are competent in it, so that no one might say: See, what a presumptuous ass he is! And especially when one would establish an article of faith, as Karlstadt here does, and hence raves: "I have dreamt that mass in Hebrew means sacrifice. Therefore the Wittenbergers seize, hang, murder, scourge Christ and are worse than Caiaphas, Judas, Herod, because they call it mass." Take it easy, factious spirit. If it were a carnival play, buffoonery would be in place.

In my Hebrew language I find that *mas* means tribute or tax, which one annually gives to the government, as in Gen. 49 [:15]: "Issachar was tributary." [69] And the Books of Kings often tells how land and people became tributary to the children of Israel. Hence on one occasion Moses calls the mass (Deut. 16 [:10]) not the sacrifice, as Dr. Karlstadt dreams, but the first fruits, which they were willingly to bring to the priests on Pentecost, as an annual tribute, and there before the Lord through offering confess and

---

[69] In the RSV the whole passage is: "Issacher . . . became a slave at forced labor." "Forced labor" is the term Luther translates "tributary."

give thanks, that they had received such fruits and the iand from the Lord, as Moses very beautifully teaches (Deut. 26 [:10, 13]). Even as also each tenant confesses through his tribute that he has received such money or goods from his liege lord. Sacrifice, however, is no tribute. It was also not commanded in the same way as the tribute. Thus one had to kill the sacrifice and burn it, so that mass and sacrifice agree together like the fist and the eye, although I have been compelled to translate Deut. 16 [:10], "freewill offering." Of course, these spirits, who alone have the heavenly voice, do not pay any attention to my interpretation.

When the Hebrew language was still common among them, the apostles and the first Christians called the bread and wine, which they had gathered for observance of the sacrament, "mass," in Hebrew in accordance with Jewish custom. A part of it was consecrated for use in connection with the sacrament, the other was distributed among the servants of the congregation and the poor. For a long time afterwards this practice was also referred to as "collections," as the *Historia tripartita* testifies.[70] Though the practice was discontinued the word "collect" still remains in the papist mass to indicate that collect and mass belong together, until the abomination [Mark 13:14; Dan. 11:31–12:11] came and made a sacrifice out of it. Therefore the word mass does not refer to the consecrated sacrament, which is an action involving God and man, but only to the gathering of bread and wine, involving men. It was not something given or offered to God, but distributed among men.

Where are you now, dear factious spirits and sin drovers, with your Hebrew language? Tell me why I should not call the Christian office a collect or mass, as the apostles and first Christians did? Yes, tell me, where have you gotten the lie from to blame us with calling the consecrated bread and wine a mass, even if mass means sacrifice? One calls the whole office a mass and says, "during the mass," or "in the mass," one consecrates the bread and wine. Also, in the mass one receives the sacrament. Who has ever heard it said, "I will receive the mass," or "I have received the mass," when

---

[70] The *Historia ecclesiastica tripartita*, a compilation of extracts from Socrates, Sozomenus, and Theodoret, was the principal handbook of church history used in the Middle Ages. Its author and compiler, Cassiodorus (d. *ca.* 570), wished to augment the reworking of Eusebius' church history by Rufinus.

one has received the sacrament? I do not know if I have even once written or said it. Be that as it may, I know for sure that we do not teach or speak so at Wittenberg, although there would be no danger if the sacrament were or were not called a mass. The lying spirit has certainly invented this about us, just as he as the result of his own dream calls mass a sacrifice, to demontsrate his wantonness.

What, however, if the apostles had also called the sacrament itself a mass? I think they would defend themselves quite well before the factious spirit and say: The Jews had to bring their mass, that is, their first fruits, to the priests, by which they gave nothing to God, but rather thereby confessed and thanked God, that they received these and the whole land from his grace. We observe the sacrament or our mass in a similar way. We do not celebrate it in order to give or offer something to God, but only that we may thereby confess and thank God, who has given us the same, together with all the riches of the kingdom of heaven, as also the words of Christ state: We should do this in his remembrance [I Cor. 11:24, 25]. With this I think they would have quite well stopped the mouth of the spirit and instructed him, so that he might better learn the Hebrew language and Moses, before he slanders and condemns that which he neither knows nor understands.

This I say as though it were proven that mass is a Hebrew word, which I would not depend on. Whether it is Hebrew or not makes no difference, although it is much like the Hebrew. However what one would make into an article of faith by which to rule conscience must be something that is known much more definitely than one knows that mass is from the Hebrew. There is nothing of this in the Scripture. Besides, whatever occurs to or strikes the fancy of the scatterbrained, factious spirit must be a definite article of faith. After that speedily force it with fury and raging upon poor consciences, create sin where none exists, as is the nature of all his teaching and spirit. If a good spirit were moving him, he would first be sure of the matter, and prove that "mass" is Hebrew, before he interprets it in a Hebrew manner. Then he should also prove that it means sacrifice. Finally he should also demontsrate that one must not call it mass. He does none of this. He only slavers his drivel about, and this we are all to accept as an article of faith.

However, to portray the devil better, and show that he has no reason for lying in this way, but his whole undertaking is a pretense, I'll even suppose that mass means a sacrifice, and that in addition we expressly call not the office but the sacrament a sacrifice (neither of which occurs, but the factious spirit lies about both). What would that mean to him? Would we therefore be Christ's hangmen and murderers, as the factious spirit spurts? Or does it follow therefrom, that we consider the sacrament a sacrifice? Since he himself confesses that we do not consider it a sacrifice, how is he able to lie so brazenly and say we do at the same time consider it a sacrifice? But we cannot simultaneously believe and confess two contradictory things in one heart.

Yes, I will say further, that if we publicly confess with hearts, tongues, pens, and actions that it is no sacrifice, and besides that imprudently were to call it the mass, as do those who do not know that a mass is a sacrifice, would God not judge us more according to the heart and all other outward evidence rather than so on account of giving the appearance and using the name [mass] condemn us as the devil does through Dr. Karlstadt? For God himself says that he sees and judges according to the heart, not according to appearance (Isa. 11 [:3]). Dr. Karlstadt, however, because of the external appearance of a name of whose meaning we are not sure slanders us so shamefully, and will neither judge according to the heart, nor take into account all of its fruits, which we show forth with deeds.

How often does not a mother call her daughter a little whore, both in anger and in love? How often does not a father call a son, "you fool," "you rogue"? Or they may call the daughter *putana*,[71] and not know that *putana* means a whore, but think of a virgin. If Dr. Karlstadt's spirit would hear of this, he would curl his lip and rail: "Oh, the mother and the father are of the devil. They bring infamy upon God's creatures. They murder, hang, strangle, and mangle the precious virtue of virginity in their own child. They are indeed more evil than any keeper of prostitutes or murderer. With the heart and other outward evidence they show that the daughter is a pious virgin, but in calling her a little whore or *putana*, they do as much as a keeper of prostitutes who would take her to a

---

[71] *Putana*, derived from the mediaeval Latin *putena* and used in French as *putain*.

brothel." Dear friend, what would the mother say to such a judge? She would beg for God's sake that one bind him with chains as a mad, raving man. By the same token, as Karlstadt well knows, we are not in earnest, even should we call the sacrament a sacrifice, although we do not do it. Yet in his judgment we consider it a sacrifice and for that reason he continues to slander us so outrageously. As is apparent, he only seeks occasion to slander us out of pure wantonness.

So senseless and possessed have envy and vain ambition made this man, that he no longer sees how the heart gives the name to the deed, and not the deed the name to the heart. If the heart is right and good, no matter what the name, it can do no harm. How can there be good and proper understanding of dealing with the Scripture or divine things in the head of one whose mind is so perverted that he has lost even the common understanding of the function of human reason? Does he not know that one must judge everything according to the belief and the fruits of the heart, not according to the name or appearance, as also all natural law teaches? Let those who will believe that such a teacher who, seeing all things through a colored glass and judging according to his embittered and false heart, writes correctly and in a Christian way about the sacrament. If he knows this and writes wantonly nevertheless, it's all the worse, as thereby one clearly perceives that he must be possessed. For a man who is in his right mind does not act so wantonly.

Now, what if in these days we went on and called the sacrament not mass, but in plain German a sacrifice, just to spite the factious spirit? Do you think we would be equal to the task? According to our way of thinking, all we have done at Wittenberg, and yet intend to do, will be so fashioned by God's grace that the devil with all gates of hell and factious spirits may assault, but will gain nothing, as is borne out by the past. Come now, I shall call the sacrament a sacrifice anew, not because I consider it a sacrifice but because the god of this factious spirit, the devil, would prevent me from calling it thus. I shall therefore do what he does not want me to do, and not do what he wants me to do. Moreover, I shall set forth the reason and basis for the action I propose.

I will call St. Peter a sinful fisherman, as he calls himself in the gospel [Luke 5:8], and say: "St. Peter, the poor sinner, has converted the world with his gospel" [Acts 2:41-42]. St. Paul, the persecutor of Christendom, is teacher of the gentiles [Acts 9:4; I Cor. 15:9]. St. Mary Magdalene,[72] the sinner, has been saved [Luke 7:48], and the like. This I write in order to give Karlstadt's spirit occasion to write still more books (although nothing is commanded him) and thunder at me, saying: "The Wittenberg 'highminded preacher' [73] defames the grace of God, the blood of Christ and the Holy Spirit, since he calls the saints sinners. With the heart he regards them as holy, but 'shrieks' [74] (according to his German manner of speech) otherwise with the pen. Since he calls them sinners, he also regards them as such and turns them into sinners, murders and hangs Christ, and sheds his blood, etc." In this manner the "depth-minded" vagabond preacher is accustomed to carrying on.

Yes, I will even make it worse. I will call Jesus Christ, the Son of God, the crucified and one who died. Let the factious spirit demonstrate his skill and say: "Christ now sits in heaven and is no longer crucified. Since you however still call him thus, well then, to that extent you crucify him, and are worse than the Jews by whom he was crucified, even though you say otherwise with the heart and pen." How does that strike you? This spirit would eventually prevent us from using any names from previous history. For if I may not say of the mass, that it has been a sacrifice, and this is an abominable thing, in case I say: "Here is a sacrifice of the papists, or we receive the sacrifice" (note, that formerly was a sacrifice), then also we can no longer in the gospel call Simon the leper, Peter a sinner, nor Paul a persecutor, nor Christ the crucified. For all this is past and due to the devil and now is no more.

How often does it not happen that the evil name of a thing remains when the evil is gone? Should he who calls it by the evil name thereby make the same evil by so doing? Nothing could be worse than that someone now should crucify and kill God's Son.

---

[72] Luke does not use this name. Luther is following an ancient Christian legend in identifying Mary Magdalene with "a woman of the city, who was a sinner" (Luke 7:37).

[73] Karlstadt had applied this epithet to Luther in one of his writings. Cf. WA 18, 108.

[74] "Shrieks" is a rendering of *kirren*, a word belonging to the peculiar German dialect of Karlstadt as spoken in Würzburg. Cf. *ibid.*

Yet since it occurred once the evil name remains forever; but no harm is done, since our heart, disposition, and all our deeds are turned in another direction than the name suggests. Should not allowance be made for a charitable interpretation when from habit, or the evil influence which the papists have exerted upon the sacrament, it is called a sacrifice, although we do not do it? Might I not call it a martyred, crucified, murdered sacrament, as Dr. Karlstadt himself does? For all this is included in the word "sacrifice." Can it be said that I martyr, crucify, and murder, and am like him who does it in deed, when I only use the name?

Therefore I ask the factious spirit and stuff his own words down his throat: "Say on, why do you call the bread and wine a 'martyred, crucified, murdered sacrament'? Are you not also executioners and murderers of Christ, even if you no doubt shriek otherwise with the pen?" If you say, however, that you don't thereby intend this, but only point out what others are doing—ah, dear squire, why can I not then also call it a sacrifice, with the meaning others have developed, rendered, and given? Do you not see, what all the world and even children see, that one is not to judge according to names and appearance, but according to the heart and the deed? I have said all this at greater length than necessary (as though there were some among us who call it a sacrifice), in order to show how unable the spirit is to accomplish anything. For even if his dreams were true, he would still achieve nothing. It stands to reason that a spirit who has lost the fundamental truth and deals only with externals, should have a theology of semblance and shadows.

To be sure, it is a sin and a shame, as has been said, to waste so many words and so much time and paper over these trifles. However it has been fruitful in that the mask has been pulled from this spirit and he has been brought into the light. Being aware of where Dr. Karlstadt has taken up his position, and what he has in mind, everyone will beware of him as of the devil. For that could be granted him as a person, if he taught something about names and semblance, but left alone and did not touch the fundamental truth in the heart and the deed. No one but the devil would stage such a useless show and with high-sounding words pretend as though everything depended on his contention. In addition, he outrageously condemns and slanders the true internal basis [of our position] which he himself admits we have and would eagerly have destroyed. For no upright, pious man behaves this way. Were he able to bring it about, he would do everything in his power to destroy utterly the good light of truth and the grace of God which has been given us at Wittenberg, and to persuade the people that through him the true sun had arisen at Orlamünde.

How does it look to you now? He who depended on Dr. Karlstadt's argument—how well would he manage with his mass? For he has not proved that the word "mass" is derived from the Hebrew, that it is a sacrifice and that one should not so call it. And even if he had proved all this, he would thereby have accomplished nothing except making himself and us the object of ridicule. If the papists would only cease offering the mass, dear God, how gladly would I not let them call it what they pleased. While the name makes no difference to me, Dr. Karlstadt makes everything depend on it, paying too little attention to the main argument, the foundation.

The other matter about the elevation[75] of the sacrament is of the same kind. This must also be anti-Christian and papistic. Oh if someone could advise this man to leave both preaching and writing alone and do some other work! He is unfortunately not suited for it. He wants to make new laws and sins and set up new articles of faith. Whether it pleases God or not, he can do nothing else.

Already, at an early date,[76] we have taught Christian liberty from [the writings] of St. Paul. There is to be freedom of choice in everything that God has not clearly taught in the New Testament, for example, in matters pertaining to various foods, beverages, attire, places, persons and various forms of conduct [Rom. 14:2-6; I Cor. 8:8-10]. We are obligated to do nothing at all for God, except believe and love. Now tell me, where has Christ forbidden us to

---

[75] Cf. Karlstadt's *Wider die alten und neuen papistischen Messen*, St.L. 20, 2309: "They elevate the host and similarly the cup. Through this act they indicate that He, whom they elevate, is still a sacrifice and that their bread and wine also is a sacrifice." Cf. also *WA* 18, 110.

[76] Cf. Luther's *Eight Wittenberg Sermons* (1522), PE 2, 395f.; also *Von beider Gestalt des Sakraments zu nehmen (On Receiving Both Kinds in the Sacrament)*, WA 10², 11ff.

elevate the sacrament or commanded us to elevate it? Show me one little word, and I will yield. Yet Dr. Karlstadt ventures to burst out and say that it is forbidden by Christ, and considers it a sin as great as the denial of God. He is unable to prove this. Nor is it true. Is it not a woeful, pitiable blindness, so to burden souls with sin and murder them, and make laws where none exist?

Tell me, my brother, what do you think of the spirit who dares command and direct the Christian to do what Christ does not do, yes to do that of which Christ does the opposite? For Christ does not forbid elevation, but leaves it to free choice. This spirit forbids it, and ensnares the conscience due to his own wanton ambition. Is not this to slander Christ? Is not this to deny Christ? Is not this to set oneself in Christ's place and in Christ's name to murder souls, bind consciences, burden with sins, make laws, and, in short, so to deal with souls as if one were their God? All this, and what more there is to be added, he does who makes law and sin where Christ would have freedom and no sin. For this same reason we have shown the pope to be the Antichrist, in that he infringes on such freedom with laws, where Christ would have freedom. And my factious spirit blunders upon the same way. He would make captive what Christ would have free.

However in this respect the profile of the factious spirit differs from that of the pope. They both destroy Christian freedom, and they are both anti-Christian. But the pope does it through commandments, Dr. Karlstadt through prohibitions. The pope commands what is to be done, Dr. Karlstadt what is not to be done. Thus through them Christian freedom is destroyed in two ways: on the one hand, when one commands, constrains, and compels what is to be done, which is nevertheless not commanded or required by God; on the other hand, when one forbids, prevents, and hinders one from doing that which is neither prohibited nor forbidden by God. For my conscience is ensnared and misled just as much when it must refrain from doing something, which it is not necessary to refrain from doing, as when it must do something, which it is not necessary to do. When men must refrain from doing that from which they need not refrain and are compelled to do what they need not do, Christian freedom perishes in either case.

The pope destroys freedom in commanding outright that the

sacrament is to be elevated, and would have it a statute and a law. He who refrains from keeping his law sins. The factious spirit destroys freedom in forbidding outright that the sacrament be elevated, and would have it a prohibition, a statute, and a law. He who does not act in accordance with this law sins. Here Christ is driven away by both parties. One pushes him out of the front [door], the other drives him out the rear [door]. One errs on the left side, the other on the right, and neither remains on the path of true freedom. I am very much surprised, however, and had I not read it myself in Dr. Karlstadt's books, the whole world could not have convinced me that he should not know this, for I have, you know, instructed him in this and considered him sensible. Oh, Lord God, what are we when thou lettest us fall? What can we do when thine hand is removed? What can we achieve when thou no longer enlightenest us? Is this free will and its power, that so quickly makes out of the learned man a child, out of the intelligent a fool, out of the wise man a madman? How terrible art thou in all Thy works and judgments [Ps. 66:3].

Well, dear Sirs, let us walk in the light, while we have it, lest the darkness overtake us [John 12:35]. And let him who can, perceive. I will discuss the matter in broad terms.

Teaching and doing are two things. I say, furthermore, that one should separate teaching and doing as far from each other as heaven from earth. Teaching belongs only to God. He has the right and the power to command, forbid, and be master over the conscience. However, to do and refrain from doing belong to us so that we may keep God's commandment and teaching. Where doing or to refrain from doing is in question, and concerning which God has taught, commanded, and forbidden nothing, there we should permit free choice as God himself has done. Whoever though goes beyond this by way of commandments or prohibition invades God's own sphere of action, burdens the conscience, creates sin and misery, and destroys all that God has left free and certain. In addition he expels the Holy Spirit with all his kingdom, work, and word, so that nothing but devils remain.

Now the elevation of the sacrament, wearing the tonsure, putting on the chasuble and alb, etc., are matters concerning which God has given neither commandments nor prohibitions. Therefore everyone is to have freedom of choice to do these things or refrain from doing them. God wants us to have such freedom, etc. Since the pope does not allow for such freedom of action, but curbs it with his teaching and commandment, he usurps the office of God and sets himself arrogantly in God's place, as St. Paul has forewarned concerning him [II Thess. 2:4]. He makes sin where God would have no sin, and thereby kills souls and binds consciences. Since Dr. Karlstadt does not allow for freedom to refrain from doing what need not be done, but compels with prohibitions and teaching, saying one must not elevate the host, etc., he also usurps the office of God and sets himself in his place. He makes sin where there neither can nor should be any sin. Thus he kills souls on this side, as does the pope on the other side, and both of them, like murderers of souls, destroy Christian liberty.

We however take the middle course and say: There is to be neither commanding nor forbidding, neither to the right nor to the left. We are neither papistic nor Karlstadtian, but free and Christian, in that we elevate or do not elevate the sacrament, how, where, when, as long as it pleases us, as God has given us the liberty to do. Just as we are free to remain outside of marriage or to enter into marriage, to eat meat or not, to wear the chasuble or not, to have the cowl and tonsure or not. In this respect we are lords and will put up with no commandment, teaching, or prohibition. We have also done both here in Wittenberg. For in the cloister we observed mass without chasuble, without elevation, in the most plain and simple way which Karlstadt extols [as following] Christ's example. On the other hand, in the parish church we still have the chasuble, alb, altar, and elevate [the host] as long as it pleases us.

Therefore my factious spirit ought not fight against us Wittenbergers in this manner: "They elevate the sacrament. Therefore they sin against God." But this might be said, "They teach and command that one must elevate the sacrament lest there be mortal sin. Therefore they sin against God." For so the papists do and teach. We however do not so teach, and yet permit freedom to do this as long as it pleases us. The doing does no harm; the teaching, however, is the very devil. On the other hand, in the cloister we refrain from it, but we do not so teach as Dr. Karlstadt does.

The refraining does no harm; the teaching, however, is the very devil. From this you may gather, who are "the cousins of the Antichrist," [77] we or Dr. Karlstadt. We do as the papists, but we do not tolerate their teaching, commandment, and constraint. We refrain from doing like the Karlstadtians, but we do not tolerate the prohibition. Thus the pope and Dr. Karlstadt are true cousins in teaching, for they both teach, one the doing, the other the refraining. We, however, teach neither, and do both.

Now, dear sirs, we are speaking of minor matters, insofar as the doing is concerned. For what does it mean to elevate the sacrament? But when the teaching is taken into account we are dealing with the most important matters. The factious spirit is too frivolous and meddles all too impudently in this matter. He has such a low regard for teaching and such a high regard for the doing that he does not see the beam in his own eye, and is too much concerned with the splinter in our eye [Matt. 7:5]. For with teaching he manhandles conscience, which Christ has won with his own blood, and kills souls, which God has dearly purchased, with commandments and sins. For thereby the kingdom of Christ will be destroyed and everything that the gospel has brought us exterminated. For Christ cannot remain in the conscience that goes whoring after alien teaching and the commandments of men. There faith must perish. Therefore let everyone know that Dr. Karlstadt has a spirit which is hostile to faith and to the whole kingdom of God, which he in turn would destroy with his conceit and human nonsense, as you may well understand from this part of the discussion and concerning which you will hear more later.

However, we thank him kindly for teaching us that Christ did not elevate the sacrament in the Last Supper, although we also already knew this, and almost as well as he. We are talking here about teaching, not doing, and beg him to show us where Christ teaches or forbids elevation. We already know where he refrains from doing it or does not do it. But we are of the opinion that it is not necessary to do or refrain from doing all that Christ has done or refrained from doing. Otherwise we would also have to

---

[77] Karlstadt employed this phrase in describing Luther and his associates in his tract *Auhslegung dieser Wort Christi Das ist mein Leib etc.* (1524). Cf. *WA* 18, 89.

walk on the sea, and do all the miracles that he has done. Further-more, we would have to refrain from marriage, abandon temporal authority, forsake field and plow, and all that he has refrained from doing. For that which he would have us do or not do, he has not only done or not done himself, but in addition he has explained in words that command and forbid what we are to do and refrain from doing. For when he says, John 16 [John 13:15]: "I have given you an example, that you also should do as I have done to you," he applies this, not to Lazarus, whom he had raised from the dead, but to the act of footwashing.

Therefore we will admit no example, not even from Christ himself, much less from other saints, for it must also be accom-panied by God's Word, which explains to us in what sense we are to follow or not to follow it. We do not consider works and ex-amples adequate, indeed we do not want to follow any example: we want the Word, for the sake of which all works, examples and miracles occur. For certainly he is sufficiently wise and articulate, and able to anticipate the future so as to indicate in words every-thing which is commanded or forbidden.[78] Well now, heigh, you factious spirits, rave on as best you can and show us, where has Christ with one tittle forbidden the elevation of the sacrament? Since you still boast and bluster that Christ prohibits it, where is the prohibition? I imagine it is to be found in the nightgown of the bride in Orlamünde, or in the trousers of the bridegroom in Naschhausen.[79]

If the rule is to be that one is so strictly to follow the example of Christ and not the Word alone, then it will follow that we should observe the Last Supper nowhere but in Jerusalem, in the upper room.[80] For if incidental circumstances are to be strictly binding, the external places and persons must also strictly be adhered to. And it will come to this, that this Last Supper was only to be ob-served by the disciples, who were the only ones who were ad-dressed at that time and commanded to observe it.[81] And what St. Paul says (I Cor. 11 [:17ff.]) will become utter foolishness.

---

[78] Cf. p. 173.
[79] Cf. p. 101.
[80] Luke 22:12.
[81] Cf. Karlstadt's *Wider die alten und neuen papistischen Messen.* St.L. 20, 2310.

Also since we do not know and the text does not state whether red or white wine was used, whether wheat rolls or barley bread were used, we must by reason of doubt at this point refrain from observing the Last Supper, until we become certain about it, so that we do not make any external detail differ a hairsbreadth from what Christ's example sets forth. Yes, we must also previously in a Jewish manner have eaten the paschal lamb. Also, since the text does not state whether Christ took it in his hands and himself distributed it to each one, we must also wait until it is ascertained, so that we do not elevate and administer it differently than Christ did. For where we overlook this, the factious spirit appears and cries: We hang, murder, and crucify Christ. This matter is so very important, and salvation is buried here much more than in Christ's wounds, blood, word, and spirit.

Oh the blindness and the mad fanaticism of such great heavenly prophets, who boast of daily speaking with God! Children would be ashamed to jest in so coarse a manner. At this point I recall a prediction which was made concerning Dr. Karlstadt when he first embraced our teaching. It was said: "Yes, Dr. Karlstadt will not stay with it long. He is an unstable person, and has never stuck to one thing." [82] At that time I would not believe it. Now I see it before my very eyes. For he has completely fallen again from faith into works, and unfortunately into human or rational works, which he himself has invented. In summing up we assert that we observe everything in the sacrament that Christ by his words has commanded, when he says: "Do this in remembrance of me" [I Cor. 11:24]. However, in matters which he has not forbidden we act as freely as it pleases us, saying: No one is to command or prohibit anything which he has neither commanded nor forbidden.

And although I had intended also to abolish the elevation, now I will not do it, to defy for a while the fanatic spirit, since he would forbid it and consider it a sin and make us depart from our

---

[82] Scheel believes that Karlstadt's interpretation of the Christian faith reveals his connection with a mystical conception of Christianity via Thomism and Augustinianism. Cf. Otto Scheel, *Luthers Werke* (Ergänzungsband I: Berlin, 1905), p. 67.

liberty.[83] For before I would yield a hairsbreadth or for a moment to this soul-murdering spirit and abandon our freedom (as Paul teaches) [Gal. 5:1], I would much rather tomorrow become a strict monk and observe all the monastic rules as stringently as I ever did. This matter of Christian liberty is nothing to joke about.[84] We want to keep it as pure and inviolate as our faith, even if an angel from heaven were to say otherwise [Gal. 1:8]. It has cost our dear, faithful Savior and Lord Jesus Christ too much. It is also altogether too necessary for us. We may not dispense with it without the loss of our salvation.

At this point you should carefully examine Dr. Karlstadt's spirit, noting the way he proceeds, how he would tear us from the Word and lead us toward works. To achieve this all the better, and to make a good impression, he holds before you the works of Christ himself, so that you might thereby be alarmed and think: Oh, really, who should not follow Christ? And yet all the while he conceals the Word. For he has none to which he can point.[85] For after he has seen how we will pay no attention to human words and works, be they ever so holy or ancient, etc., and would have Christ alone as our master, the rogue divides Christ into two parts. Namely, how Christ, on the one hand, without words does and refrains from doing certain works, and, on the other hand, how with words he does and refrains from doing works. Dr. Karlstadt is so knavish that he presents Christ alone as he does and refrains from doing without words, wherein he is not to be followed by us, and is silent where Christ does and refrains from doing with words, wherein we are to follow him.

Do you see here the devil, who before has misled us through saints? He would now mislead us through Christ himself. Beware where you do not hear God's word commanding or forbidding you

---

[83] The elevation of the host was not abolished in Wittenberg until 1542, after the death of Karlstadt.

[84] Luther refers to Karlstadt's taunt: ". . . *sie sprechen, sie meinen's nicht also, und rühmen sich, dass sie vom Gesetz so hoch gefreit sind, dahs sie Gottes Wort auch verkehren dürfen und anders deuten, dewn Gott sein Wort und Weise gedeutet hat. . . ."* St. L. 20, 2310.

[85] Karlstadt is unable to cite a prohibition of Christ with respect to elevation of the sacrament. He must content himself to point out that Christ has not commanded it. *Welchem hat Christus befoh'en, dahs er sein Abendmahl in die Höhe auf heben und dem Volk zeigen möge? ibid.,* p. 2311.

so that you may not be led astray and pay no attention to it, even if Christ himself did it. Has not enough been said? We read: "Thy word is a lamp to my feet" (Ps. 119 [:105]). The Word, the Word is to be followed, don't you hear? When one now holds before you how Christ has done it, speak up briskly: Very well, he has done it. Has he also taught and commanded it to be done? Also if one holds before you, this Christ has not done, then speak up briskly: Has he also forbidden it? And if they cannot point to his Word, then say: Put it aside, let it be. That doesn't apply to me. Nor is it an example, it is his work, done for his own part. If they say: All of Christ's doing is for our instruction, let them say it. But note carefully what is meant with instruction. A man has said it. He has as much authority as you yourself.

So it is in the world, as the saying goes: He who cannot sing always wants to sing, whoever cannot preach or write, he wants to preach and write. But whoever can, he hesitates and does so reluctantly. Dr. Karlstadt, who hereby proves that he doesn't understand Christ at all, just as above he doesn't understand Moses, must preach and write when no one has commanded or requested him to do so, and when he is requested to do so, he does not do it. He interprets Moses in such a way that the disorderly populace is incited to punish public misdeed. However, Dr. Karlstadt does not and cannot teach Moses spiritually, as he reveals sin and physically drives rough and rude people to works. He constructs his own Moses. Thus here he also constructs his own Christ, that we are to follow his works without the Word. But he does not understand how Christ is first of all our salvation, and thereafter his works with the Word are our example. He knows no more about the New Testament than he does about the Old, and yet he would write about the sacrament and such matters, as though there were great need for his absurd and blind art, and, indeed, his folly.

For how is a true understanding of Moses or the law possible, so that the knowledge of sin is taught (Rom. 3 [:20], and rough people are driven to works (Lev. 18 [:4-5]), when one so interprets it that the disorderly populace is to revolt and usurp the office of the temporal authority, and thereby overturn the whole order and meaning of the law? Furthermore, how is it possible for anyone to understand Christ correctly, as he is given to us in faith unto life, and his words and works are given in love as an example, who goes off in another direction and only emphasizes how we, bidden and unforbidden, are to regard Christ's works as a necessary example and are to follow them? There faith and love together with the whole gospel must perish. And that is why they speak so scornfully of the doctrine of faith and love, as even Dr. Karlstadt himself threw it in my face in Jena, just as if they knew something much higher and better. Yet they do not speak out plainly, nor do they want to bring it out into the open. Even when taken by itself this behavior shows that the devil speaks through them, since they ridicule the doctrine of faith and love, that is, Christ himself with his gospel.

Thereafter the man comes again in his Hebrew language and contends thus against us: "The Wittenbergers elevate the sacrament. Therefore they regard it as an offering. For they do precisely what the law of Moses prescribes, in which there were two offerings, the heave offering and the wave offering. [Exod. 35:5; 22; Num. 18:8; 11]. He who elevates makes a heave offering, etc." This goes beyond all bounds! If this is not blindness, what then is blindness? This spirit calls everything that one elevates an offering, and argues from the particular to the universal. Thus, there is one elevation in the law which is an offering; therefore all elevation is offering. This would be as if I were to say: One finds an elevation which is an offering; therefore elevation of all kinds is an offering.[86] Or thus, a cow in Orlamünde is black; therefore all cows in the world are black. I must speak in a lay and rustic manner with the new layman[87] and peasant. Here we see what the plowman from Naschhausen is able to do, of whom Dr. Karlstadt boasted at Jena, that he would put all the doctors in the world to shame.[88] When the maid lifts the mirror to look at herself, she offers it. When the farmer lifts the ax or the flail, to chop or to thresh, he offers it. When the mother raises the child and dandles it, she offers it. Therefore she trespasses against Christ's prohibition, hangs, mur-

---

[86] Karlstadt did not draw the conclusion attributed to him by Luther.
[87] Karlstadt speaks of himself as "a new layman" in the titles of two treatises in the spring of 1523. Cf. WA 18, 118.
[88] According to the Acta Jenensia Karlstadt said: "I intend to make my living by means of the plow; you will indeed become aware of what the plow can produce." WA 15, 340.

ders, slays, crucifies Christ and does all the evil that those do who offer Christ. How the fanatic spirit raves! For the plowman at Naschhausen has said it: he who elevates, offers.

Tell me, has not this peasant amply deserved that one should set his plow right? In this manner God ought to cast down those who rise and set themselves against the knowledge of God and resolve to act on a knowledge of their own. The Egyptians were not to be stricken with a common darkness, but with one that could be felt [Exod. 10:21]. In my opinion an attitude of this kind implies the loss of reason, sense, and understanding. The papists themselves have never been so foolhardy nor of the opinion that they offered the sacrament by elevating it, although they otherwise regard it as a sacrifice. But they elevate it in order to show it to the people, to remind them of the passion of Christ, etc.[89] For this reason the priest doesn't say a word, either about sacrifice or anything else, when he elevates it. How should we then offer it through the elevation, we who insist so strongly that it is no sacrifice?

But it is the same fiddle upon which he always fiddles, namely, that the external appearance is the main thing, according to which everything that the heart, mouth, pen, and hand confesses is to be regarded and judged. Therefore it does not help that we believe with the heart, confess with the mouth, testify with the pen, and demonstrate with deeds that we do not regard the sacrament as a sacrifice, though we still elevate it. The elevation is so important and by itself counts for so much, that it outweighs and condemns everything else. Is this not a vexatious spirit, who so juggles with external appearance against the truth in the spirit? If only the elevation were permitted to remain an external matter, the brides would be truly undressed[90] and naked regardless of how one felt about it in his heart.

However enough has been said above about this harping on external appearance. I point it out now only in order that I might also undress the spirit and expose how he is occupied with sheer foolishness. He is unable to deal properly with the main articles of Christian doctrine, and yet he presses such foolishness so severely on the conscience, with such bombastic words, as though these

---

[89] The elevation was also a summons to adore the host.
[90] Cf. p. 101.

were the main articles, on which everything depended. I do it so that everyone will know how to guard against this spirit, who is always seeking to set up new articles of faith, though God knows nothing of them, and to enforce a new teaching, which has not been entrusted to him.

This however I have said as though it were true and conceded that possibly an elevation could take place which would be an offering, as this spirit pretends. But no man on earth calls elevation an offering, except this spirit, who has invented this and sought to burden us with it, since he did not know anything else to write about. Nor will he ever be able to show where elevation means a sacrifice. He himself has forgotten his own words, where he says: Sacrifice is equivalent to slaying, killing, hanging, murdering, burning, etc. Who, however, would be so mad as to say that elevating was the same as slaying, killing, murdering, burning? Only this spirit, who perhaps also learns a new German from his heavenly voice. Thereupon he raves and fights against himself, in that whoever elevates, sacrifices.

To demonstrate his excellent command of the Hebrew language, he produces from the Hebrew the two words *thnupa* and *thruma*,[91] which I have translated wave offering and heave offering, or heave and wave. The world is to marvel at the plowman of Naschhausen's understanding of the Hebrew language. Yet it is not the common Hebrew, which every one speaks, but that which the spirit teaches anew and daily, with the aid of the heavenly voice. For my Hebrew language teaches me that before one offers something according to the law, one must heave and wave it. And it must be heaved and waved so as to acknowledge God and give thanks to him as for a gift, which is not offered or given to God, but received from him. Just as I have said above about the term "mass."[92] Only after it had been heaved and waved was it offered and kindled, so that even in the law heave and wave cannot by any means be sacrifice.

Behold, what expert knowledge this spirit has of the law of

---

[91] For a description and interpretation of *tenûphāh* (wave offering) and *terûmāh* (heave offering). Cf. S. R. Driver in *A Dictionary of the Bible*, ed. James Hastings, III, 588.

[92] Cf. p. 122.

Moses and the Hebrew, and yet he is so arrogant and wanton that he builds articles of faith on such dreams of his, and would have the consciences so completely ensnared thereby, that they become Christ's murderers, hangmen, and executioners, if they elevate the sacrament. Thus the devil must always have his mouth full of slander in order to destroy Christ.

Dr. Karlstadt has fallen from the kingdom of Christ and has suffered shipwreck with respect to faith. Therefore he wants to get us out of the kingdom right into works and simply make Galatians of us also. For take note, dear reader, what gross blindness it is to fight as he does. "If anyone circumcise himself, should he not in all fairness be called a Jew? Thus, whoever elevates is rightly called one who brings a sacrifice, etc." [93] You poor, miserable spirit, where on earth have you read that he is rightly called a Jew who circumcises himself? Did not Paul circumcise Timothy, when he was already baptized and a Christian? (Acts 16 [:3]). Does not Paul declare circumcision a matter of free choice (I Cor. 7 [:19]), "Neither circumcision counts for anything nor uncircumcision," that is, one may circumcise himself or not, have a foreskin or not. And this spirit pits his judgment blithely and boldly against that of Paul, saying it is not a matter of free choice, but makes one a Jew. He ought rather say that whoever circumcises himself as though he were compelled to do so by law and for conscience's sake, he is rightly a Jew. For circumcision does not make a Jew, since one does find those who due to illness or on account of an infection must be circumcised. Should they therefore be called Jews?

He, however, is a Jew who, compelled in his conscience by law, feels he must be circumcised. This Jewish disposition and conscience makes one a Jew, even if he never externally circumcised himself or could circumcise himself. The foreskin thus makes no one a Jew. But if he thinks in his conscience, he must have a foreskin, this one is a gentile, even if he permitted himself to be circumcised a thousand times externally. Similarly, since he thinks it necessary to have the foreskin and to condemn circumcision without leaving it free choice as Christ would have it, Dr. Karlstadt actually is a

---

[93] A quotation from Karlstadt's *Wider die alten und neuen papistischen Messen,* St.L. 20, p. 2310.

gentile and has lost Christ. Here one sees clearly how this man is completely swallowed up in works and drowned in external appearance, so that he is not able to give one single right judgment in spiritual matters of conscience. For it is impossible that a spark of Christian understanding should still be found in him, since he holds that an external work makes a Jew or Christian, gentile or Turk, and does not judge according to the conscience, but according to semblance and appearance, which even reasonable people do not do.

In this instance, too, he should have said, "Whoever elevates the sacrament out of necessity of conscience, as if he had to elevate it, would also be a Jew." But we do not do so, as he well knew. Therefore he feared that he would be put to shame, as one who publicly lies against us. But he did not see that he hereby acquires much greater shame, in that he lies against God and forbids an action, as condemned by God's prohibition, that God, however, has not forbidden. On the other hand, whoever insists that the sacrament may not be elevated, as a matter of necessity is a gentile. In doing this Dr. Karlstadt sets up a law compelling the conscience, which only God has a right to do. But whoever elevates the sacrament with such a conscience and the intention of making it an offering, is one who sacrifices, and a papist. For where such a conscience exists, there one sacrifices, even if one never elevated the sacrament or even sank it into a deep well. Where, however, such a conscience does not exist, there one does not sacrifice, even if one raised it above the heavens and the whole world shouted: Sacrifice, sacrifice! For everything depends on the conscience. Of this the fanatic spirit knows nothing, or does not want to know anything.

I imagine the reading of this treatise will annoy many, since it deals with such charlatanry. But how can I avoid it? This mad spirit drives me to it. Yet, as I said above, we have some fruit from it in that we defend and understand more clearly our Christian freedom.[94] We also recognize this false spirit for what he is and see how he is blind and stupid in all things. Everyone may therefore govern himself accordingly. For since he does not understand such trifling [external] things, but so magnifies them as to usurp the office of God, making laws, sin, and matters of conscience, where

---

[94] Cf. p. 88, par. 4.

none exist, destroying Christian liberty, and enticing consciences away from an understanding of grace to external works and appearance, so that Christ is denied, his kingdom destroyed, and the gospel reviled—who then can hope that he will ever be able to write or teach anything that is good? For certainly one can prove from this matter that the spirit of Christ is lacking. It must be the devil that is there, and so he is. Let each one govern himself accordingly.

I am happy the mass now is held among the Germans in German. But to make a necessity of this, as if it had to be so, is again too much.[95] This spirit cannot do anything else than continually create laws, necessity, problems of conscience and sin. To be sure, I have read in I Cor. 14 [:27-28] that he who speaks with tongues is to be silent in the congregation when no one understands anything of what he says. One tends however to skip over the other words: "Unless there is someone to interpret." That is, St. Paul permits speaking with tongues, "if at the same time it is interpreted," so that one understands it. Therefore he also commands that they are not to prevent those who speak with tongues, etc. Now we administer the sacrament to no one unless he understands the words in the sacrament, as one well knows. So in this matter we do not act contrary to St. Paul, since we satisfy his intention. If we do not satisfy this spirit, who only looks at external works and has no regard for either conscience or intentions, it is of no importance. We attach no importance to his new articles of faith.

I would gladly have a German mass today. I am also occupied with it. But I would very much like it to have a true German character.[96] For to translate the Latin text and retain the Latin tone or notes has my sanction, though it doesn't sound polished or well done. Both the text and notes, accent, melody, and manner of rendering ought to grow out of the true mother tongue and its inflection, otherwise all of it becomes an imitation, in the manner of the apes. Now since the enthusiast spirit presses that it must be, and will again burden the conscience with law, works, and sins, I will take my time and hurry less in this direction than before, only to spite the sin-master and soul-murderer, who presses upon us

---

[95] On the basis of I Cor. 14, Karlstadt insisted on the use of the German. Cf. *Wider die alten und neuen*, etc., *op. cit.*, p. 2308.
[96] Luther's German mass appeared in 1526.

works, as if they were commanded by God, though they are not.

For whoever goes to the sacrament understanding these words in German or having them clearly in his heart: "Take, eat; this is my body," etc. [Matt. 26:26], which he has learned and borne in mind from a foregoing sermon, and thereupon and therewith receives the sacrament, he receives it rightly and does not merely hear speaking with tongues, but something which has real meaning. On the other hand he who does not comprehend or understand these words in his heart, nor thereupon receives the sacrament, such a one would not be helped if a thousand preachers stood around his ears and shouted themselves into a frenzy with such words. However for the mad spirit everything depends on external works and appearance, which out of his own head he would continually set up as necessary and as an article of faith, without God's commandment.

Also the fool doesn't understand St. Paul's words correctly when he writes of speaking with tongues (I Cor. 14 [:2-29]). For St. Paul writes of the office of preaching in the congregation, to which it is to listen and to learn from it, when he says: Whoever comes forward, and wants to read, teach, or preach, and yet speaks with tongues, that is, speaks Latin instead of German, or some unknown language, he is to be silent and preach to himself alone.[97] For no one can hear it or understand it, and no one can get any benefit from it. Or if he should speak with tongues, he ought, in addition, put what he says into German, or interpret it in one way or another, so that the congregation may understand him. Thus St. Paul is not as stubborn in forbidding speaking with tongues as this sin-spirit is, but says it is not to be forbidden when along with it interpretation takes place.

Hence has come the custom in all lands, to read the gospel immediately before the sermon in Latin, which St. Paul calls speaking in tongues in the congregation. However, since the sermon comes soon thereafter and translates and interprets the tongue, St. Paul does not reject or forbid it. Why should I then, or anyone condemn it? Yes, would to God, that only this order of St. Paul were everywhere in effect so that after the Latin gospel nothing else

---

[97] Luther interprets I Cor. 14 to refer to speaking in foreign languages in the sense of Acts 2. Actually, I Cor. 14 refers to a form of ecstatic speech (glôssalalta).

was preached than its exposition. Now this enthusiast spirit would condemn everything that St. Paul permits and forbids one not to condemn. In addition he will allow no singing or Latin word, and applies the teaching of St. Paul about speaking with tongues not to the office of preaching alone, but to all external forms. This is always his method, though these forms are not essential.

Not that I would oppose using nothing but German in the mass, but I will not endure that some one without God's Word and out of his own arrogance and wantonness forbids the reading of the Latin gospel and makes sin where none exists, lest we get the factious spirit with his fanaticism as master in the place of God. For we cannot establish or strengthen our cause against the papists with such charlatanry. Otherwise we would stand before them in disgrace. Our whole basis must be certain and the words of God pure upon which we build and do combat against the papists, so that they are unable honestly to oppose our arguments. For even if we now get the mass in German, it will still not be enough to speak the words of the sacrament in German. For they must be spoken earlier and beforehand, before we receive the sacrament, so that they who go to receive it might have the words in the heart and not in the ears. What difference does it make if they do not hear in the sacrament, if, immediately preceding the reception they have heard the words in the sermon and have comprehended them, and then make their confession, unless one would yell the same words in the ears of everyone who goes to receive the sacrament, and consecrate the sacrament as many times as there are individuals to receive it.

I had intended to answer everything in one book, but I am too pressed and it will become too large. Therefore I must abruptly break off here and begin another about the sacrament. Nor do I have all of his poisonous books of which they boast. You will not have to wait long, for I have written this in a short time. The other one will follow in the footsteps of this one, if God wills. To him be praise and glory eternally. Amen.

PART II

Our controversy has no doubt given great joy to the papists and inspired among them the hope that our cause would thereby suffer defeat. So be it, let them boast and exalt over us. Often and repeatedly I have said that if our cause is of God no one will be able to suppress it. If it is not of God, I will not be able to support it whatever some one else does. I can lose nothing by it for I have won nothing. But this I know that no one but God himself can take it from me. However much I regret this vexation, I am glad that the devil now reveals himself and his shamefulness through these heavenly prophets. They have long grumbled to themselves and would not even have come out into the open unless I had lured them out through a gulden.[98] This I believe, by God's grace, to be a good investment which I do not regret.

I am not worried as long as God is with me. I know and am sure who is Master of the situation. He has not hitherto failed me in the face of many a hard blow. He will not now fail me. He who has the gospel can be confident and calm. We have a joyful trust and are of good courage. We have as adversaries dejected, stupid, despairing, and anxious spirits who tremble at the rustling of a leaf [Lev. 26:36], but, as always with the godless (Ps. 36 [:2]), know no fear of God but do violence to his Word and work. God is concealed and cannot be seen or felt. Were he a present, visible person, he could drive them out of the land with a stem of straw.

For this spirit has wrought thus: At first he sneaked around in the land upsetting things and seeking followers. Then when he thought he had a following he emerged boldly, thinking all was won. But his trust is not in God, though his followers claim that God speaks to them. Rather, he depends on the favor of the populace and builds on flesh and blood. For when God compels anyone to speak, such a one makes public proclamation, even if he is alone and no one follows him, as in the case of Jeremiah

---

[98] Luther invited Karlstadt to express his opposition openly and gave him a coin as a challenge to do so. Cf. WA 15, 339f.

144

[Jer. 2:2ff.]. I too can claim that this was my way. It is the way of the devil to glide around in secrecy and in conspiracy, afterward making the excuse that at first his spirit was not strong enough. No, Sir Devil, the spirit that is of God makes no such excuse. I know you well.

The true nature of the devil is not yet apparent. For he has still other ideas which I have smelled for a long time. They too will be revealed, if God wills. It has come to the point, God be praised, when this is not particularly my affair. There are plenty of others who can answer such a spirit, without my having to be involved with him during my life. I am well aware that Dr. Karlstadt has been cooking this brew for a long time without being able to get anything under way. I have also known that he could not do it any better than he has done no matter how long he chewed on his clever notions. For no art or wit or imagination is of avail before God. With one word he can bring all to shame. He knows that human thoughts are vain [Prov. 21:30].

If anyone is so weak that he has fallen before this onslaught and now has doubts about the sacrament, let him follow that advice[99] and get along for a while without the sacrament. Let him busy himself with the Word of God, in faith and love, and let those who are secure in their conscience concern themselves with the sacrament. You are not condemned if you are without the sacrament. But let the papists who rejoice over this controversy beware lest they harden their hearts. For it is not the first time God has ordered things so that he appears foolish and weak and his Word and purpose seem on the point of extinction, in order that the godless should thereby be hardened and blinded. At such times God's purpose has emerged the more strongly, and they who were hardened and blinded by his seeming foolishness and weakness have been the more terribly destroyed. Such was the case of the Jews when Christ was crucified and such the case when the martyrs were made to suffer [I Cor. 1:18ff.].

---

[99] Karlstadt had stated that it was possible to be saved without the reception of the sacrament. Cf. his *Dialogus oder ein Gesprächbüchlein von dem greulichen und abgöttischen Missbrauch des hochwürdigen Sakraments Jesu Christi.* WA 18, 135. Throughout the following discussion, almost without exception, Luther refers to this treatise of Karlstadt.

Just as the devil is disorderly and jumbles things together, so Dr. Karlstadt's treatise and head are equally disordered and mixed up, so that it is exceedingly annoying to read and difficult to remember what he writes. Yet I will try to create some order in view of his passion and poison and to consider his argument part by part. I would first present in broad outline the fundamental idea from which all his raving emanates, so that the reader may be more clear in observing and judging this spirit. This is the argument.

Out of his great mercy God has again given us the pure gospel, the noble and precious treasure of our salvation. This gift evokes faith and a good conscience in the inner man, as is promised in Isa. 55 [:1], that his Word will not go forth in vain, and Rom. 10 [:17], that "faith comes through preaching." The devil hates this gospel and will not tolerate it. Since he has not succeeded hitherto in opposing it with power of sword, he now, as indeed always, seeks victory by deceit and false prophets. I ask you, Christian reader, to observe carefully. If God wills I will help you to discern the devil in these prophets so that you can yourself deal with him. It is for your good, not mine, that I write. Follow me thus:

Now when God sends forth his holy gospel he deals with us in a twofold manner, first outwardly, then inwardly. Outwardly he deals with us through the oral word of the gospel and through material signs, that is, baptism and the sacrament of the altar. Inwardly he deals with us through the Holy Spirit, faith, and other gifts. But whatever their measure or order the outward factors should and must precede. The inward experience follows and is effected by the outward. God has determined to give the inward to no one except through the outward. For he wants to give no one the Spirit or faith outside of the outward Word and sign instituted by him, as he says in Luke 16 [:29], "Let them hear Moses and the prophets." Accordingly Paul can call baptism a "washing of regeneration" wherein God "richly pours out the Holy Spirit" [Titus 3:5]. And the oral gospel "is the power of God for salvation to every one who has faith" (Rom. 1 [:16]).

Observe carefully, my brother, this order, for everything depends on it. However cleverly this factious spirit makes believe that he regards highly the Word and Spirit of God and declaims passionately about love and zeal for the truth and righteousness of

God, he nevertheless has as his purpose to reverse this order. His insolence leads him to set up a contrary order and, as we have said, seeks to subordinate God's outward order to an inner spiritual one. Casting this order to the wind with ridicule and scorn, he wants to get to the Spirit first. Will a handful of water, he says, make me clean from sin? The Spirit, the Spirit, the Spirit,[100] must do this inwardly. Can bread and wine profit me? Will breathing over the bread bring Christ in the sacrament? No, no, one must eat the flesh of Christ spiritually. The Wittenbergers are ignorant of this. They make faith depend on the letter. Who ever does not know the devil might be misled by these many splendid words to think that five holy spirits were in the possession of Karlstadt and his followers.

But should you ask how one gains access to this same lofty spirit they do not refer you to the outward gospel but to some imaginary realm, saying: Remain in "self abstraction"[101] where I now am and you will have the same experience. A heavenly voice will come, and God himself will speak to you. If you inquire further as to the nature of this "self abstraction," you will find that they know as much about it as Dr. Karlstadt knows of Greek and Hebrew. Do you not see here the devil, the enemy of God's order? With all his mouthing of the words, "Spirit, Spirit, Spirit," he tears down the bridge, the path, the way, the ladder, and all the means by which the Spirit might come to you. Instead of the outward order of God in the material sign of baptism and the oral proclamation of the Word of God he wants to teach you, not how the Spirit comes to you but how you come to the Spirit. They would have you learn how to journey on the clouds and ride on the wind. They do not tell you how or when, whither or what, but you are to experience what they do.

Again, in external matters which they believe God has not directly ordered, they act like incendiaries as if they were out of their minds. Just as they have fashioned their own inner spirit, so they have created also their own external order, though God has given neither commands nor prohibitions to the effect that we may not have images, churches, or altars, that we may not use the word

---

[100] A reference to Karlstadt's repeated use of the term.
[101] One of the seven stages in the mystic apprehension of God. Cf. p. 88, and MA' 4, 373.

"mass," speak of a sacrament and its elevation, or wear chasuble instead of gray coats,[102] and we ought to address one another as neighbor "dear." They advocate the murder of godless rulers,[103] will endure no injustice, and assume, in many cases, a pretense of humility and piety of much importance to themselves but of no meaning before God. Whoever differs from them is a papist twice over who crucifies or murders Christ; indeed, those who differ from them are Scribes. Whoever agrees with them, however, is up to his boots in the spirit and is a learned light. O wonderful saints! If you ask who directs them to teach and act in this way, they point upward and reply, "Ah, God tells me so, and the Spirit says so." Indeed all idle dreams are nothing but God's Word. What do you think of these fellows? Do you fully grasp what kind of a spirit this is?

They pay no attention to God's design of inward things, such as faith. They approach and force all external words and Scriptures belonging to the inward life of faith into new forms of putting to death the old Adam. They invent such things as "turning from the material," "concentration," "adoration," "self-abstraction," [104] and other such foolishness which has not an inkling of foundation in Scripture. My Karlstadt plunges in like a sow to devour pearls, and like a dog tearing holy things to pieces [Matt. 7:6]. What Christ has said and referred to the inner life of faith, this man applies to outward, self-contrived works, even to the point of making the Lord's Supper and the recognition and remembrance of Christ a human work, whereby we in like manner, in "passionate ardor" and (as they stupidly put it) with "outstretched desire," put ourselves to death. By throwing up a smoke screen, he obscures the clear words of Christ, "My blood poured out for you for the forgiveness of sins," etc. [Matt. 26:28; Mark 14:24; Luke 22:20]. Their meaning undoubtedly is grasped, received, and retained only by faith, and by no kind of work. This will become clearer as we proceed.

Enough has been said so that you may know that it is of the nature of this spirit to press for a way the reverse of that ordered by God. That which God has made a matter of inward faith and

---

[102] Cf. p. 81.
[103] Münzer, not Karlstadt, was an advocate of such action.
[104] Cf. pp. 88, 117.

spirit they convert into a human work. But what God has ordained as an outward word and sign and work they convert into an inner spirit. They place the mortification of the flesh prior to faith,[105] even prior to the Word. In devil's fashion they go out where God would enter and enter where he goes out. It ought surprise no one that I call him a devil. For I am not thinking of Dr. Karlstadt or concerned about him. I am thinking of him by whom he is possessed and for whom he speaks, as St. Paul says, "For we are not contending against flesh and blood—but against the spiritual hosts of wickedness in the heavenly places" [Eph. 6:12].

So, my brother, cling firmly to the order of God. According to it the putting to death of the old man, wherein we follow the example of Christ, as Peter says [I Pet. 2:21], does not come first, as this devil urges, but comes last. No one can mortify the flesh, bear the cross, and follow the example of Christ before he is a Christian and has Christ through faith in his heart as an eternal treasure. You don't put the old nature to death, as these prophets do, through works, but through the hearing of the gospel. Before all other works and acts you hear the Word of God, through which the Spirit convinces the world of its sin (John 16 [:8]). When we acknowledge our sin, we hear of the grace of Christ. In this Word the Spirit comes and gives faith where and to whom he wills.[106] Then you proceed to the mortification and the cross and the works of love. Whoever wants to propose to you another order, you can be sure, is of the devil. Such is the spirit of this Karlstadt, as you will more clearly see presently.

So to our task, by the power of God.

First, what a fuss this spirit makes over the word and name, "sacrament." He makes a mountain out of a molehill. I regret to have to answer him. But it is necessary in view of his overbearing attitude. Christ and the apostles, he says, never used the word. He wants a biblical word. God has given names to what he has created. We men should not give names to divine things. At last

---

[105] Karlstadt claimed this was a misreading of his statements. *Anzeig etlicher Hauptartikel christlicher Lehre Bl. A 4⁶*, WA 18, 139.
[106] Cf. Augsburg Confession (1530), Art. 5: ". . . the Holy Spirit who effects faith where and when it pleases God in those who hear the Gospel. . . ."

he becomes a Jew and calls it a *"sekerment,"* [107] as the Jews ridicule us Christians, deriving the word from *seker theminith,* that is, a false image. So Hebrew is taught at Naschhausen,[108] *seker* meaning false, and *ment,* an image. Why this parading of words? In order to impress the mad mob who with open mouth and nostrils exclaim, "Believe me, that is something. Here is a learned man. Here is a spirit."

This illustrates what I have said above.[109] Outward names and signs which God has neither commanded nor forbidden, become the main subject on which all stress is laid, just as in the matter of the names of mass and elevation. If you don't speak of sacrament, you are supposed to be spiritual and holy. But whoever uses the word sacrament, he makes black white, and deceives the people about God and perpetrates similar horrible vices. In short, he denies Christ. But is it not a terrible thing for this frivolous spirit to make so much of nothing? Listen, murderer of souls and sinful spirit! We admit that God has not called it a sacrament, nor commanded us to call it a sacrament. But tell me, on your part, where has he forbidden it? Suppose it is only a name. What then? Who has given you the power to forbid what God has not forbidden? What reason is there for your sacrilege in framing up great sins where God has not considered them such? Are you not indeed a murderer of souls who sets himself above us in God's place and takes away our Christian liberty and subordinates consciences to himself?

Indeed you do not use the name employed by Christ and the apostles. Why do you lie so grossly? We also call it the Lord's Supper, or the bread and cup of the Lord, as we read it in the words of the Apostle in I Cor. 11 [:25]. Yet, stupid spirit, you ought to accuse us, saying, "They forbid us to call it a sacrament and forbid us to speak of it as the Lord's Supper." If you were to pin something like that on us, your bitter poisonous hatred would have something on us. Since we neither command nor forbid anything in

---

[107] *"Sekerment"* is derived from a contraction of the two Hebrew words *seker,* meaning false, and *theminith,* meaning image, the latter word having been abbreviated to "ment." Karlstadt referred to this derivation, but did not himself accept it. Cf. *WA* 18, 140 and *MA'* 4, 410.

[108] A suburb of Orlamünde. Cf. also p. 110.

[109] Cf. p. 148.

this respect, but, in free conscience call it a sacrament, you are the one who denies and blasphemes Christ when entirely on your own, without God's command, you forbid, condemn, and slander a freedom which we have from God, as a gift, and when you make so great and necessary and spiritual a thing out of your external names and signs.

May I not call my Lord Jesus Christ by a name not in Scripture? How about such names as crown of my heart, joy of my heart, my ruby—if I do not make it a matter of conscience, claiming that thus and in no other way is he to be designated? But where do you find these names in Scripture? If we want to speak of baptism and the Lord's Supper collectively, what are we to do? We find no word in Scripture which comprehends all the sacraments or signs. So we must be silent or not speak of them collectively, else these prophets judge us as deniers of Christ. Similarly in regard to the several articles of faith, the various points of Christian doctrine, the various chapters in the Bible. How are we to treat them? These names, articles, points, chapters are not in the Bible. So we are no longer to say anything about articles of the faith, points of doctrine, chapters of the Bible. What will even these heavenly prophets do, since they refer by name to chapters of the Scriptures? Are not also they murderers of Christ, by their own judgment, since they give names which are not in the Bible to divine things?

We might let it pass if we were dealing with clowns in carnival time. But surely we are not dealing with a good spirit when we find these lofty minds, these heavenly prophets, clowning so childishly in such serious matters and on top of it wanting us to look on these trifles as chief articles of the Christian faith. What light can there be in heads that hold such tangible darkness? I say this in order to expose for you this devil and prove what I have said above.[110] Observe therefore how this rogue institutes ordinances which God has not commanded, and calls spiritual what he has himself contrived. Also, he slanders and deprives us of the Christian freedom which is ours in spirit and conscience. Dear friend, do not lightly regard this prohibition of what God has not forbidden, or the violation of Christian freedom which Christ purchased for us

---

[110] Cf. p. 147, par. 1.

with his blood, or the burdening of conscience with sins that do not exist. Whoever does and dares do this, dares also do any evil. Indeed he denies thereby all that God is, teaches and does, as well as his Christ. So it is no wonder that in the sacrament he wants nothing else than bread and wine, and is the cause of still other disaster. What good can the devil do?

Therefore, my brother, listen to me. You know that for the sake of every article of the Christian faith including that of Christian freedom we ought to be willing to risk body and soul. Therefore do what is prohibited and allow what is commanded by those opposing freedom. Even so St. Paul taught the Galatians [Gal. 5: 1ff.]. Since this same Christian freedom is in danger in regard to this word and name, sacrament, you are henceforth obligated to call the Lord's Supper a sacrament, in defiance of these prophets of the devil. And if you are among them or come upon them, you must call it a sacrament, not on account of your own conscience, but in order to confess and maintain Christian freedom. Do not allow the devil to make a commandment, prohibition, sin, or matter of conscience, where God wants none. If you allow them to make this a sin, Christ is no more, they take him away. For with that kind of a conscience we deny the true Christ, who takes away all sin. So you see that though it may seem a small thing there is no small peril when you make these issues a matter of conscience.

It is the same as in regard to the prohibition of meat on a fish day. Eat meat on that day. Don't eat it on a day you are commanded to do so. If you are forbidden to marry, get married, or declare your willingness to do so. So also in other matters. When men want to make commandments, prohibitions, designations of sin, good works, scruples, and perils where God gives freedom and neither commands nor forbids, you must hold firmly to such freedom and always do the contrary until you gain this freedom. Paul would not consent to the circumcision of Titus (Gal. 2 [:3]) when others sought to compel him and said it was necessary. Yet he had Timothy circumcised (Acts 16 [:3]), when he was under no compulsion. So in this instance you may or may not call it a sacrament. But when these prophets try to force you and forbid you, then you should and must call it a sacrament.

Furthermore, when he goes on to prove that the body and

152

blood of Christ are not in the sacrament, he himself confesses to having been influenced by the traditional statement that the natural body of Christ is as large, broad, thick, and long in the sacrament as it was on the cross.[111] This he says, he cannot believe. This he (as Caiaphas) was compelled by God to say of himself, so that everyone can see that he did not derive his interpretation from but outside of Scripture, and that he wants to bring this kind of notion to Scripture, bending, forcing, and torturing it according to his own conceit instead of letting his stupid mind be changed and directed by the word and Scripture of God.

But it happens that the populace and reason easily fall for such talk and conceit, and there is really no cause to boast of heavenly voices and lofty minds. Even the most mediocre intellect is inclined thus and would rather believe that only bread and wine were present than that the body and blood of Christ are here concealed. One needs no unusual spirit for that which any one easily believes. All that the stupid populace needs is that some one with a bit of reputation is smart enough to preach this and he has pupils enough. It would not be hard for me to believe and preach such a doctrine,[112] so Dr. Karlstadt need not in this respect boast of much knowledge or skill.

But if we are so to treat our faith that we bring our pet ideas into Scripture and deal with Scripture according to our understanding, attending only to what is common to the crowd and generally accepted notions, then no article of the faith will remain. For there is none in Scripture that God has not placed beyond the reach of reason. On this account, Dr. Karlstadt's error reveals itself in his attitude toward faith and the Word of God, namely that reason readily and willingly accepts it, while in reality reason balks at the Word of God and the articles of faith. And he dares to make this the chief foundation of an article of his own. I too could say that I cannot believe that the Son of God has become man and

---

[111] Luther exaggerates Karlstadt's words here to mean more than Karlstadt himself stated, namely, that he doubted the presence of Christ in the sacrament.
[112] In his treatise, *Vom Anbeten des Sakraments des heiligen Leichnams Christi* (1523) (*WA* 11, 417ff.), Luther made his stand clear regarding the symbolic interpretation of the Words of Institution espoused by the Waldensians. Five years prior to writing this treatise his mind was not altogether closed to a symbolic interpretation. Cf. *WA* 18, 143 and *MA'* 4, 410.

comprehended a majesty which heaven and earth could not contain in the narrow womb of a woman and then allowed himself to be crucified. And I could then twist and interpret all Scripture and the word of God according to my opinion, as Mani[113] did. So at the very beginning it is sufficiently known that he has brought his pet ideas into Scripture and not drawn them thence, as indeed he cannot derive them thence. He could have kept this method to himself, but God has so ordered it that the cuckoo should call out his own name.

Then he proceeds to Scripture, before which he fears for his life, and seeks to bewitch it so that it will not fell him, saying, "This verse," etc.[114] But while he is mumbling in the dark out of fear, let me set forth his meaning a bit more clearly. He interprets the words in which the Evangelists describe the Lord's Supper in this manner, "Jesus took the bread, gave thanks and broke it and gave to his disciples, saying, take, eat, this is my body which is given for you, do this in remembrance of me."

He says that the words, "this is my body given for you," form an independent sentence and do not belong to the preceding ones, "Take, eat." Their meaning and message is isolated from the rest so that, although they have been added, the passage would be complete without the preceding words.

In short Dr. Karlstadt's contention is that Christ might as well have omitted the words, "This is my body given for you" in the Lord's Supper, and that it would be sufficient to say, "Jesus took the bread, gave thanks and broke it, and gave it to his disciples saying, Take, eat, do this in remembrance of me" [I Cor. 11:24; Matt. 26:26].

That he has given his body [life] for us, he holds, is mentioned in many other places in Scripture. Here it is introduced super-

---

[113] Mani (ca. 215-276), Persian founder of Manicheism, whose method of thinking is characterized by a fusion of mysticism and rationalism.
[114] The complete sentence from Karlstadt's *Dialogus* (*op. cit.*, p. 145) reads: "This verse, 'This is my body which is given for you,' is complete in itself. At other points in the gospels it appears independently, though in different words, where Christ says nothing of the sacrament, for example in Matt. 16 [:5ff.]; John 3 [:1ff.]; 6 [:25ff.]. . . ." Karlstadt makes the point that this verse is not related to the preceding action. "This" refers to "my body" not the bread in the preceding verse. The thirteenth-century Waldensians sought to interpret this verse in a similar manner. Cf. WA 18, 144 and MA³ 4, 411.

fluously, but to remind them why they should hold him in remembrance. You might almost think that Christ was a drunkard who had indulged so much that night that he became loquacious with his disciples.

How think you? Is not his an irresponsible spirit who so shamelessly deals with God in his word and twists it as he pleases? While these spirits boast that they dare not use a word unless it is enforced by clear passages of Scripture, and that this must be the procedure, as he constantly urges Gemser[115] in his treatises, saying, show the basis for your argument, cite Scripture, compel, force, pin down, and insist on your interpretation so no one may escape you. But we are willing to accept his own rule and say, dear spirit, you claim two things, first, that the passage "This is my body given for you," is an independent assertion and does not depend on its context. We ask you, don't heed what we see but show us the basis for your argument, cite Scripture, forcing and compelling us to acknowledge your position. How about it? Can you do it? For God's sake, show us at least one syllable which clearly declares or compels us to believe that this passage is an isolated one, and we will believe it. Won't you? Where is your spirit? Where is your God? Is he asleep? [I Kings 18:27]. Or is he vanquished? Alas, dear children, how silent and speechless the spirit is now who has written so many books and yet cannot adduce one word to prove that this passage stands by itself.

Well then, since the high spirit is silent and can give no evidence, we beg for grace to believe our eyes and ears. We plainly see and hear that this passage is not a kind of unnecessary addition, as this wanton spirit insists, but is a part of the context and is as intimately associated with it as any phrase could be. For it follows immediately on the words, "Take and eat, this is my body," so that no one hearing them in succession would get the idea that they are a new sentence. So there will have to be stronger evidence and more convincing proof from Scripture to persuade us that they are a new independent sentence and do not depend on the preceding words. We may confidently suppose and be sure that his spirit will produce such evidence and proof when the devil becomes God.

---

[115] Gemser is one of the fictitious characters in Karlstadt's *Dialogus* (*op. cit.*, p. 145) whose name may refer to Karlstadt's opponent, Jerome Emser.

For if it were an additional statement it ought not be in the midst of other words nor involved with such as refer to eating. Instead, if the other sentence is complete, the words should follow, and according to Karlstadt the text would read thus: "Take and eat. Do this in remembrance of me. For I say to you that here sits the body which will be given for you."

So Christ would have spoken, if it were an additional sentence and Christ had followed Dr. Karlstadt's opinion. But he is not so loquacious or confused in the head as Dr. Karlstadt, though Dr. Karlstadt thinks that because he himself mixes everything and brews without any order, Christ does the same. But this he should first prove. That he himself has such a mind and method needs no further proof.

In the second place this spirit is under obligation to prove his statement that, "This is my body," is added here in order to teach and remind the disciples why they are to remember Christ. Well, it's out in the open, because the spirit has said so. But where is the basis and proof that Christ for this reason added these words? O Peter of Naschhausen,[116] show your poor companion one little syllable so as to press, force, and compel him so to confess. For he hears well enough what you say, but it is a great shame that you have forgotten that you must prove it. Where is it written? What passage in Scripture says that these words were added to give instructions about remembrance? I know that we are to remember the death of Christ. But that these words were added for this purpose I don't know, namely, that the Supper is complete without this sentence, and plenty of other passages indicate why we should remember Christ. Had I been with you, Peter, I would have introduced you to another kind of Gemser who would have set the ruffian straight.

This then is the situation. Is Dr. Karlstadt one who has power to define articles of faith, so that we must believe him, even when he speaks without scriptural foundation about what he dreams? Then what he writes is correct, and this passage must be forced out of its context. It has only a special meaning which has been added

---

[116] Peter Rültz of Naschhausen is another fictitious character in Karlstadt's *Dialogus, ibid.*

and patched on the whole text in the manner of a sea shell fastened to a pilgrim's cape,[117] and has nothing to do with the Supper. But if he is not the one, then you see how the devil rides him, so that he tears, establishes, alters, interprets, and tortures the Word of God according to his whim and fancy, in view of which I almost believe proof that the man is not in earnest. It seems he is an opportunist who cares for neither God nor man. For how could a man without guidance of a particular devil undertake to close eyes and ears to a crystal-clear word, and to speak without authority of Scripture, and set up whatever opinion he desires. He exalts such idiosyncrasy as if nothing more firm were to be found on earth, and he slanders and insults those who oppose him, as if he were possessed by devils. This is clearly seen in his books.

His tearing and torturing of God's Word reminds me of an author whose book I read as a young Master of Arts. He twisted and tortured the Lord's Prayer thus: Our Father, hallowed be Thou in heaven, Thy name come, Thy kingdom be done, etc. The subdivisions were strange and rare, and reasons for doing so were not lacking. It also reminds me of the way some Jews have treated Gen. 2 [1:27]: "God created man in his own image; male and female he created them." This they interpret to mean that God created Adam in such a way as to include both a male and female image.[118] If such cutting and dividing were valid, especially in passages of importance, and such as are the basis of articles of faith, what a fine Bible we would have. In other passages it may not be so important.

This then is our basis. Where Holy Scripture is the ground of faith we are not to deviate from the words as they stand nor from the order in which they stand, unless an express article of faith compels a different interpretation or order. For else what would happen to the Bible? For instance, when the Psalmist says, "God is my rock" [Ps. 18:3], he uses a word which otherwise refers to a natural stone. But inasmuch as my faith teaches me that God is not a natural stone, I am compelled to give the word "stone," in

---

[117] Pilgrims who made a pilgrimage to St. Jacob de Compostella followed the custom of fastening a seashell to their cape.

[118] Already Philo was familiar with the view that the first man was bisexual in nature. Cf. Otto Scheel, op. cit., p. 194.

this place, another meaning than the natural one. So also in Matt. 16 [:18], "On this rock I will build my church." In the passage we now are treating no article of faith compels us to sever it and remove it from its place, or to hold that the bread is not the body of Christ. Therefore we must take the words just as they stand, making no change and letting the bread be the body of Christ.

But, says my Peter Rültz,[119] it is a special sentence, because the phrase, "This is my body," begins with a capital letter, and it is preceded by a period which usually indicates the beginning of a new passage.[120] What do I hear? I demanded a reason and basis in Scripture, and you give me a period and capital letter. Is a period and a capital letter Holy Scripture in the mind of the Naschhausen plowman? [121] Indeed I hear you give me your peculiar notion in place of divine Scripture and return dirt for gold. Because you have the opinion that a period and capital letter indicate something different and new, you want to talk me into thinking the same without scriptural authority. Peculiar notions and crying Scripture, Scripture, Scripture, compel, urge, force me by a word of God, will not prove that a period and capital letter introduce something new. Where in Scripture do you find a clear assertion that a period and a capital letter mark the beginning of an independent statement? Don't you hear, Peter? Peter, do you hear?

Is it not a sin and shame that this spirit seeks to base so important a matter on such idle prattle yet makes so terrible a racket if we do not give a scriptural basis? Suppose my book had no periods or capitals and yours had both. Our faith might come to depend on ink and pen, and even on the disposition of writer and printer. That would be a fine foundation! To put it briefly, we must have sober, lucid words and texts which by reason of their clarity are convincing, regardless of whether they are written with capital or small letters, with or without punctuation. For even if it were true (which it is not) that a period and capital indicated something new, should it follow in regard to Holy Scripture that my

---

[119] Cf. p. 156, n. 116.
[120] In his *Dialogus*, Karlstadt actually employed this form of argument. "The pronoun *hoc* begins with a capital 'H.' A capital letter indicates the beginning of a new statement and verse." . . . "*Hoc est corpus*, etc., is separated by periods and capital letters. . . ." Cf. *WA* 18, 148; *St.L.* 20, 2321.
[121] Cf. p. 136.

faith should rest not on expressions and words alone but on frail periods and capitals which really say or sing nothing. That would indeed be a false foundation.

How about the use in some books (not all are alike) of capital letters and punctuation marks to indicate the importance of what is said, so that the reader will the better observe and remember it, rather than that something new is signified? On what doubts my faith would then be founded if it were claimed that period and capital introduced something new? How often do we consistently spell the name Christ with a capital letter? How often do we underline or draw a hand or some figure alongside the text, though it is not a question of something new. Punctuation marks and letters are a human invention and means and man has full freedom to put them wherever he wills. My Dr. Karlstadt wants to establish a divine faith and word on such changing human conventions.

Alas, what can one say? The spirit can hardly mean it. It is clear that he is concerned only about self-contrived matters and not much about faith and God's Word. Woe to a faith which, compelled to seek support and aid from such scraps, is not grounded on any word from the great and wide Scriptures, where all articles otherwise have a substantial and solid base. Even if Dr. Karlstadt's opinion were correct and true, I ought and could not believe it, because of his tomfoolery with points and capitals. He produces no part of the Word and does nothing more than deny our clear, forthright, ordered text. I cannot but think, "O my, this is foolishness and gives me no foundation."

Herewith I address myself to all who accept the opinion of Dr. Karlstadt. I say that Dr. Karlstadt's sole and best argument rests on the passage, "This is my body," as a separate text, as a beginning of a new and additional sentence, as we have heard. If he cannot prove or explain this, his whole case falls. He has nothing more than his *touto*,[122] and such like, and everything depends on its being a new and separate sentence. If this falls and our contention stands, that this part is connected with the other, Karlstadt is helped neither by *touto* nor *tatta*,[123] and we have won. The context forcibly

---

[122] The Greek word for "this."

[123] *Tatta* is either sarcastic mimicry or a corruption of the Greek *tauta*, plural of *touto*.

urges and compels us to accept the meaning that the bread is the body of Christ. Since the words read, "Take, eat, this is my body," and are dependent on each other, they compel us forcibly to hold that what he asks them to eat is his body. Dr. Karlstadt himself recognized this and therefore was so anxious to tear and divide the words from each other. But he found only a period and a capital, and even they are not in all books. Even if they were, it would be uncertain whether they were there as an introduction of a new thought or for the sake of the reader's devotion, and the latter is the more likely.

But faith should and must rest on certainty, not on punctuation marks and capitals. It must have clear, distinct passages and altogether plain words out of Scripture as its foundation. There now, you Karlstadtians and as many as there may be of you, you all lie in one heap. Your faith rests on frail, uncertain points and letters. That Belial may wager his conscience and salvation on such, not I. My dear Karlstadtian sirs, you write many books, but for God's sake give attention to the point where you are in trouble and consider how you may prove the passage "This is my body," to be the beginning of a new thought. Everything depends on this, this is the focal point, dear brother, whether you sever, divide, or separate. Even if you write as many books as there is sand on the seashore, if you cannot prove this point, you have lost. As I have said and repeat once more, the text combines, "Take, eat, this is my body." If you let the word "eat" remain with "body of Christ," you must meet the argument that the bread is the body, and it is the body that is to be eaten. This you cannot escape. I dare you and I dare you twice over.

Tell me how you can depend on a spirit who dares gamble on so priceless a truth without the authority of Word and Scripture, solely on the basis of a single period and a capital letter. Is he not sufficiently foolhardy and foolish? Do you think he has a conscience? What more would he not venture if he had opportunity? What devout heart would entrust him with anything that is good or upright? All right, I have done my duty. Whoever wants to fall into error, let it be his lot. And though this is sufficient answer to all of Karlstadt's books, since it is established that the bread is the body of Christ, he ought to learn to tone down his shameful insults by calling us dogcatchers and heaping abuse on us. He has fought against us with his period and capital as his one wretched weapon, as one would attack a cliff with a broken straw. It serves him right. Why did he not stay away from his prophets?

Yet I am willing to give further answer, in order to reinforce my position. To begin with, if he should demand that I should also prove my faith that this sentence, "This is my body," belongs to the preceding words, whereas he denies it and cannot prove that the one passage is separable from the other, I would reply thus: I let the one stand with the other as I find them in the text because in speaking, hearing, and reading the one naturally follows the other and I know no reason why I may or should separate the natural order and sequence of the words. Since I find them connected, the burden of proof lies on him who would separate them. This is sufficient confirmation for me. Just as I take the words of "The Lord's Prayer" as they stand, "Our Father who art in heaven." I need no further confirmation than that this is the order of the words. I know no reason why I should divide thus "Our Father who art, in heaven hallowed be," etc. If you so divide I want to know the reason and offer objection. So here the natural manner of speaking is, "Take, eat, this is my body." One word follows the other, and I know no reason for separating them. For Karlstadt's period and capital mean nothing, and neither he nor any one else has another reason. For good measure, we shall go on to show from the clear message and meaning of Scripture, not from punctuation or capitals, that the one word should and must follow the other. For the present, let this be answer enough to the objection of the devil.

In the third place he comes with his Greek and chokes at the *touto*. For in Greek the sentence reads, *"Touto esti to soma mou."* Originally and still today these Greek words mean in translation, "this is my body." In Latin the words, *"Hoc est corpus meum,"* are a complete and correct rendering of the Greek, without missing the point by one whit, as all those would have to affirm, who know Greek. Peter Rültz of Orlamünde[124] alone has discovered something new. Pretending that one cannot adequately translate the whole phrase, he thinks it would be well to let *touto* remain untranslated, and we read *"touto* is my body." What can I say? I would laugh

---

[124] Cf. p. 156, n. 116.

at the monkey business if it did not concern matters of such great importance. The ass's head wants to master Greek, and knows neither German nor Latin, let alone Greek and Hebrew. He presents himself unashamedly before the whole world as if there were only Peter Rültz of Naschhausen here who does know Greek.

Now this rebel spirit only intends to rouse the evil mob and draw it to himself, for always it desires the unusual and what is new. They will smack their lips and exclaim, "What a wonderful man this Dr. Karlstadt is. He discovers what is concealed from all the world, yet, in his humility wears the gray coat and felt hat of a peasant, and does not want to be called Doctor but neighbor Andrew." [125] Here God dwells and the Holy Spirit with all his feathers and eggs.[126] Karlstadt certainly does not appeal to the crowd because they understand his reasoning. This they cannot do, for he mumbles, strains himself to the breaking point, and chokes on his words and can hardly express what he wants to say. Perchance God resists him, or he simply lacks the ability to speak German. I know that no one of them can tell what his reasoning is, even though one had consumed all his books. On the other hand, they fall for him because of his great cleverness and big words and because he calmly blasphemes in suggesting how contrary to reason it is to believe that the body of Christ is in the sacrament. In this way he can arouse and make a fool of the crowd. That he knows nothing about the foundation of faith doesn't much matter. But this thing doesn't last.

I have two tasks in hand. First, I must more clearly expose Dr. Karlstadt's basis and reasoning; secondly, I must give my answer. Now with regard to Dr. Karlstadt's dream about his *touto*, this needs be said. The German, Latin and Greek languages employ three genders in their pronouns: masculine, where we in German use *der, dieser, jener;* feminine, where we use *die, diese, jene;* and neuter where we use *das, dies, jenes.* So we say *der Himmel* (the heaven), *der Mond* (the moon), *der Stern* (the star), *der Mann* (the man), *der Knabe* (the boy), *der Hund* (the dog). So also *die Sonne* (the sun), *die Erde* (the earth), *die Luft* (the air), *die Stadt* (the city), *die Frau* (the woman), *die Magd*

---

[125] Cf. pp. 81, 117.
[126] An allusion to the dove, symbol of the Holy Spirit.

(the maid), *die Kuh* (the cow). Also, *das Wasser* (the water), *das Holz* (the wood), *das Feuer* (the fire), *das Licht* (the light), *das Pferd* (the horse), *das Schwein* (the pig). But the Hebrew language does not have these genders, only the masculine and feminine *der* and *die.*

Now Karlstadt contends thus. In the Greek and Latin languages bread is preceded by *der,* not *das.* For they say *der artos, der panis.* We Germans, however, say *das Brot.* Body, however, is *das* in Greek and Latin. For they say, *das soma, das corpus.* We Germans say, *der Leib.* Since Christ here says, "*Touto esti to soma mou,*" "*Das ist mein Leib,*" and does not say, "*Der ist mein Leib,*" he cannot be referring to bread, which would be *der* in Greek, but to his body, which is *das* in Greek. Do you now understand what Dr. Karlstadt is after? It is his Greek *touto,* which in German is *das.* As a modern Greek he wants to contend from the Greek language that the body of Christ is not in the sacrament, for Christ does not say, "*Der ist mein Leib,*" but, "*Das ist mein Leib.*" To speak of bread as "*Das ist mein Leib,*" is not in keeping with Greek grammar.

Such skill no Greek ever witnessed, from Christ's time to ours, even if he were a native in the language. But now they have discovered this skill at Orlamünde, perhaps in an ancient image when they destroyed the images, or they have it from some heavenly voice. And the man who has hardly seen "a-b-c" in Greek, gives no credit to those born and bred in the language, or to those who now in Germany and other lands have competent knowledge of Greek. Since nothing is easier than to sense and observe a discrepancy of this kind, surely they would have done so in all this time. For there is no child reared in the German language, who would not laugh if someone said to him about a woman, "*Der Frau ist schön*" (the woman—masculine—is beautiful), "*Das Mann ist fromm*" (the man—neuter—is devout), and would say that you are a Tartar or a gypsy. Would not all Greece and the whole world have sensed the same, if Christ had said, "*Touto* is my body," though all the world knows that *touto* has been and still is understood as referring to "bread"! If a Greek child heard some one say, *das artos* (the—neuter—bread) he too would soon laugh. Yet no one has laughed when all the world has said of the bread, "*Das ist mein Leib*" (this is my body).

163

Yet this stupid spirit presumes now to instruct the Greeks. But as I have said, the man has lost head, eyes, brain, and heart, since he knows neither shame nor fear, and dares wager all according to his whims. He knows well enough that he is ignorant of Greek, and proves it fully by translating the Greek, *"Touto esti to soma mou,"* into Latin *"Istud panis est hoc corpus meum,"* and into German, *"Touto ist der Leib mein,"* making of the article *to* a pronoun and inserting *panis,* etc. What German speaks thus: "This is the body, mine?" Yet on such ignorance he consciously ventures to build a faith for himself and all the world. If some one dares build articles of faith on conscious and admitted ignorance and so to teach the world, how much more he would dare do it on a vague illusion or doubt? Indeed, what would such an impudent spirit not dare? I am terror-stricken at the boldness and outrage of men in divine things, while in their attitudes to men on earth they are weak, unstable, and despairing.

Let me now explain why Christ said *touto* or *das* of the bread instead of *der.* In German we have a way of speaking which allows us when we point to something before us to designate and call it *das,* whether in itself it be *der* or *die.* So I say, *"Das ist der Mann* (that is the man) of whom I speak," *"Das ist die Jungfrau* (that is the young lady) whom I mean," *"Das ist die Magd* (that is the maiden) who sang there," *"Das ist der Geselle* (that is the fellow) who told me," *"Das ist die Stadt* (that is the city) that did it," *"Das ist der Thurm* (that is the tower) that lies there," *"Das ist der Fisch* (that is the fish) which I brought." Here I call to witness all Germans, if I am speaking German. After all, this is our mother tongue, and we commonly speak so in German lands.

The Greeks do the same in their language in regard to *touto* and the bread, when they point to it and say, "That is my body, given for you." I call to witness all those who know Greek. But the Latin language is different—it has no [definite and indefinite] articles as do the Greek and German. Especially is it so among my Saxons who *"tutten"* and *"tatten"* [127] just like the Greeks, with whom they

---

[127] The phrase is a play on the Greek words *touto* (neuter, singular) and *tauta* (neuter, plural) which in their onomatopoeic effect bear a resemblance to *taten,* the past tense of the German verb *tun.*

are in complete agreement in saying, *"Touto esti to soma mou,"* this is your body, this is the woman, this is my body. Were Dr. Karlstadt's dream to prevail, one would have to claim that it would not be German to say, *"Das ist mein Leib"* (this is my body) given for you, since *Leib* (body) requires *der* in German. Though we say, *"der Leib* (the body) is large," yet we say, *"Das ist der Leib"* (this is the body) that pleases me. So also, *"Das ist der Leib"* (this is the body) given for you. But Dr. Karlstadt thus reveals that he knows no more German than Greek.

In the sacrament, thus, when I speak German and have a wafer or host before me in my hand, though both would require *"die,"* I say, *"Das ist die Speise"* (this is the food), and not, *"Die ist die Speise."* So also Christ said of the same wafer or host, "This is my body," etc. You ask, why I cannot say *das Man* and yet say *Das ist der Mann.* I cannot say: *das Frau, das Magd, das Stadt, das Geselle* and yet I have to say; *"Das ist die Frau," "Das ist die Magd," "Das ist die Stadt," "Das ist der Geselle."* I know no other reason than that this is the genius of languages as God has created them. Thus no Greek will say *"das artos"* and yet he will say *"Das ist der artos."* So also he says, "This is my body, given for you."

Again, dear Peter Rültz, Gemser[128] wants to try to open your ears. You say *touto* refers to the body of Christ and not to the bread, when Christ says *touto*, or, this is my body. Tell me, dear Peter, to what then does the other *touto* which follows refer? Luke 22 [:20] and Paul in I Cor. 11 [:22] speak thus of the second part of the sacrament: "In the same way he took the cup, after supper, and said, *touto*, or this cup is the new testament in my blood," etc. Here the word *touto* is clearly expressed in the text and refers to the cup, which he offered, and not to the blood of Christ contained therein. For in Greek it reads, *"Touto to poterion he kaine diatheke estin en to haimati mou"* (this cup is the new testament in my blood). Tell me, if the *touto* must refer to Christ and yet here in the text it expressly refers to the cup, do you believe and call the blood of Christ or Christ himself, the cup? Would it not be better if you made all your ideas completely new and did not call his blood a cup, but a dinner basket or a spoonbowl?

---

[128] Cf. p. 155, n. 115.

Do you hear, Peter? Why do you sweat so? It is winter and freezing weather. Do you want a handkerchief? Won't a capital letter or period help here? [129] Or will not the *touto* become a *das* and the cup a *der*, so that grammar might come to your aid when the spirit fails! For "cup" in Greek is also a *das* and not a *der, touto poterion.* Are you not the man who loves the straight truth? And who boasts that he is bold in the face of lies but yielding before the truth? Well, yield now and listen. Acknowledge the truth and confess that you have been mistaken about the *touto*, and that the one who came and told you was not your heavenly Father, as you lied and blasphemed, but the harassing devil or his mother, who pointed you to the *touto* referring to the bread but said nothing about the one referring to the cup.

What can you mumble against this, the whole bunch of you Karlstadtians? You have nothing to say, but to condemn your blasphemous treatise and lying tongue. As those who have been publicly and irrefutably vanquished,[130] confess that just as the *touto* in connection with the cup does not refer to the seated Christ but to the cup and his blood, which Christ offered to the disciples, bidding them drink and saying that this was a new testament in his blood, so also you must confess that the *touto* in connection with the bread referred not to the body of Christ but to the bread that he gave them and told them to eat. Do you object to this? Let us hear. Behold how God can catch the wise in their craftiness [Cf. I Cor. 3:19; Job 5:13]. For these prophets thought they could overturn the world with their *touto* in connection with the bread, but overlooked that the *touto* with the cup immediately plunged them into the mire so that they could not as much as give forth a peep.

Is this man not plagued by misfortune? The Evangelists have placed *touto* at this point to make certain it would be understood to refer to the bread and have spoken most simply to avoid the error that Dr. Karlstadt pursues. But he grasps for it and arrogates it to

---

[129] Karlstadt applied the same method of argument to the words, "This cup is the new testament in my blood." Cf. *WA* 18, 156.

[130] In the preface (March 16, 1525) to his treatise *Von dem neuen und Alten Testament*, Karlstadt maintained he had been exiled by Luther, "unheard and unvanquished." Cf. *ibid.*, p. 85.

himself to fortify his error. Tell me, now, Peter Rültz, who has the sword by its edge and who by its hilt? I think you have been struck and your companion has thrust you with your own *touto*, with which you thought you were doing valiantly. You ought clearly to see which of us two has the spirit and the right skill. If I were to repay you in slanderous words for the way you have blasphemed so maliciously and terribly the exalted sacrament of the body and blood of Christ, where would I find enough words? For your sins and blasphemy are immeasurable.

Even if, in spite of everything, Dr. Karlstadt remained unshaken with his *touto*, and it were as he fancies, yet I have already proved that it would not help him, since he has not achieved and cannot achieve that the phrase, "This is my body," is something new and separated from the rest of the passage. When my poor factious spirit finds himself in straits, he wants to get out. For if it is not an independent passage, but dependent on the other part, everything is swept away which Dr. Karlstadt "*toutos* or *tautas*, clucks or cackles." Firmly and defiantly, the truth remains that the body of Christ is in the sacrament. If that stands, the Holy Spirit also has the power to say, *der Magd* and *das Mann;* it is of no consequence, neither does it help or hurt if he says, *der Brot* or *das Brot.* Not that He does so here, but even if He had done so, Dr. Karlstadt would have gained nothing. Something higher than rules of grammar must always be present when the grounding of faith is concerned. For even John in Chapter 1 [:10] of his Gospel speaks of light and calls it *das*, but shortly afterwards uses *der* and says, "The world knew him not," rather than, "The world knew it not." So Dr. Karlstadt fares ridiculously not only in his knowledge of Greek but in that he tries to ground articles of faith on grammar. If my faith had to rest on Donatus[131] or A-B-C books, I would be in a bad way.

How many new articles we would have to establish, if we were to master the Bible in all passages according to grammatical rules? How often it speaks contrary to custom in regard to number, gender, person, etc. Indeed, what language does not do so? We Germans use *die* before *Nacht* (night) and say *die Nacht.* Yet at times we change the *die* to *das* and speak of *des Nachts.* "*Es ist des Nachts*

---

[131] Aelius Donatus (*ca.* 350 A.D.) is the author of an elementary Latin grammar which was used as a textbook for a long time.

still und gut schlafen" ("It is still at night and good to sleep"). So Dr. Karlstadt had better have stayed at home with his grammar. He could have produced words and text more fittingly from Scripture so as to win us over to his *touto* as a reference to the person of Christ instead of the bread. He asks us to produce passages from Scripture. So we require him to do the same. All right, tackle the task briskly, Peter. Show us one syllable from Scripture that *touto* applies to the person of Christ and not to the bread. Why not? We don't believe your grammar, for its foundation is sandy and uncertain.

So you see, my dear reader, how this *touto* matter stands. Dr. Karlstadt obstinately denies that it refers to the bread, saying it is not clearly and certainly proved. So he holds to his position, which shows a purely malicious objection to the natural meaning and order of the language. He has to be convinced that it refers to the bread. Though the nature of speech supports us, yet we have for good measure and overwhelmingly proved from the text that it must refer to bread since in the following part it refers to the cup. Consequently his mouth has been stopped.

So we, on our side, hold to our "no" and demand that he prove how the *touto* refers to the body of Christ, as he says and affirms. For whoever affirms must prove his assertion against him who denies. Despite objection let him produce a text for his affirmation, as we have done for ours. That he says "no" to what we affirm, despite the nature of language, and affirms what we deny, means nothing. He must refute our "no" with a clear biblical text and prove his assertions, just as we have refuted with a clear text what he denies and have established our assertion. If he overcomes our objection, he will have won. We pray, however, for his mercy and ask that he doesn't burn the marsh.[132]

But it is as I said. The spirit does not take important matters seriously. The devil merely finds an opportunity to pursue his game and hold the whole business up to ridicule. All right, I will turn over Dr. Karlstadt with his grovelling Greek to those competent in it who can knock the nonsense out of his head and whip him soundly, so that another time he does not presume to use Greek

---

[132] That is, do the impossible.

before he knows it. I will deal with him, using Scripture, and demand that he use Scripture. If he will do that he will become a knight with his *touto*. I hope, however, that we will at least be spared from him this Shrovetide, by God's help. Let this be said of the dear *touto* about which the heavenly prophets have made such an ado.

Let us now take the text and see how fine it would turn out if this passage, "This is my body," were a separate phrase and referred to the person of Christ, and not to the bread. For as Christ took the bread in his hand, gave thanks, and broke it, giving to his disciples and saying, "Take and eat," and immediately went on without transition, "This is my body," the meaning and natural order of the words compel us to conclude that he speaks of the bread which he took in his hand and gave and told them to eat of it. Otherwise the disciples could not have understood him nor could any one else who heard him say it. For their eyes must have turned to his hand as he took the bread, broke it, gave and distributed it, and their ears must have heard the words which he spoke while he offered and gave it to them. For in the administration he only spoke the words, "This is my body."

Were it not his body which he offered and told them to eat, as he said, "Eat, this is my body," he would have deceived them and mocked them with words. How would it sound if I gave someone a gray coat, saying, "Here, put this on, this is my white cape trimmed with martin," etc., and applied the words to the garment I have on? Would that not be deceit and mockery if after I had said, "Here, put this on," I immediately went on without a break to say, "This is my white cape trimmed with martin"? Of course, there must be words of transition which would turn his attention from the gray coat I offer him and tell him to put on my cape. Otherwise he would not be able to understand. And how would it sound if I gave someone a piece of bread and said, "Take and eat," and as I offered and asked him to eat it, I immediately went on to say, "This is a pound of gold in my pocket"?

Truly it must not be a *touto* or *tauta* or period or capital that comes between, to indicate the beginning of a different and new meaning, for the words follow each other too closely. Clearly expressed words must be interposed to separate the parts, as,

"Take, eat, for I have, or there is still, a pound of gold in my pocket." Or, "Here, put this on, I still have, or there is still, another white cape with martin trim." So here Christ would have had to say, "Take, eat, for I tell you here my body is seated, which will be given for you." Otherwise it would be mocking and ridiculous. As if one were to hand a drink to another and would say, "Take, drink, here I sit, Hans in the red pants," or "Here, drink, the Turks have slain the Sultan," or otherwise bring in an alien notion that has nothing to do with drinking. So it would be if Christ said "Take, eat, this is my body, given for you," and were introducing a new thought.

If he had not said these words just in the same moment as he offered the bread, but a little before or after, there might have seemed to be some argument. But now that he said, "This is my body," just as he gave and offered to them the bread and bade them eat, no one can draw any other conclusion from the meaning of words than that it was his body which he offered and asked them to eat. Or else it must be admitted that no one can be sure about what one says to another. If any one so tears apart these clear and distinct words, let no one hereafter speak with me without knowing I may interpret his words differently, or I must be concerned that he will misinterpret my words. Why should Christ have to say such a word in the moment that he offered them bread and bade them eat, when he had plenty of other occasions to say it and well knew that they would not apply it except to the bread which he gave them and asked them to eat.

It is not true, therefore, as Dr. Karlstadt claims, that he spoke so as to teach them wherein the remembrance should consist. This he said boldly from his own imagination and cannot prove it by Scripture or otherwise. One does not teach by abruptly, suddenly, and deceivingly breaking off a thought and, without warning and notice going on to another matter, while offering something of which he is not speaking. In so doing one obscures, deceives, and deludes. In teaching one must proceed with simplicity, plainness, and clarity, even showing what one teaches, and not giving or showing one thing while teaching or referring to something else. It is not good teaching to show you white while teaching you about black, or to show you the devil while teaching you about God.

Clowns and deceivers or scoffers and jesters do so either to mislead or to ridicule. A devout man who is in earnest does not do so.

Or why was it necessary for Christ to point twice to himself— once toward his body, once toward his blood? Had it not been enough if he had said, "I am he," or, "This is my body, of which the prophets have said that it will be given for you," as Dr. Karlstadt wants it? Now, however, everything points toward eating and drinking and both are expressed. He takes something hard, similar to the bread, namely his body, and something liquid, similar to what they drink, namely his blood. Why did he have to do that? He could just as well have taken something else, not as similar to bread and wine. As we said, he could simply have asserted, "I am the man who is given for you," and there would have been no reference to anything that could be eaten or drunk.

Now that he gives both, the one in the bread in the form that is eaten, and the one in wine in a form that is drunk, and only does it at the time they are at the table eating, and even in the moment that he offers it and asks them to eat and drink, no conscience denying this can ever be certain. And I am sure that even Dr. Karlstadt's conscience is uneasy and uncertain so as to render it unable to digest such blows, however hardened and blinded he may be. For Christ could have taught this at some other time and not saved it up until they ate and drank, and until he offered it to them and told them to eat and drink.

What does it mean? When he had given the bread and said, "This is my body," etc., he begins anew with the cup and this time gives the wine and says, "This is my blood." If he begins something new when he says, "This is my body," wanting thereby to teach on what the remembrance was based, he would not have separated and divided the one part from the other, but would have combined body and blood closely with one another and said, "This is my body and blood, which is given for you and shed for you," and then the teaching could be considered clear and complete. But now that he separates, and says one word about eating and another about drinking, and inserts other words between the two, namely, "Likewise he took the cup, gave thanks, and gave it to them, saying drink ye all of this," one certainly can conclude that the eating and drinking is of concern to the Lord, as he says, "This is my body, this is my blood."

See, indeed, how neatly this spirit soils himself with his cleverness. He pretends that the passage, "This is my body given for you," does not belong to what immediately precedes, namely, "Take, eat," but is to be considered a new, independent, sentence. Yet he admits, and must admit, that this last passage, "This do in remembrance of me," belongs to the first words, "Take, eat." Is it not obstinate mischief, when in a passage three parts follow each other and are related to each other, some one dares claim that the first and last belong together, but that the second and middle part is independent and belongs to neither, and does this on his own initiative without any basis in Scripture? How can a mind tolerate that the third or last should belong to the first, and the second or middle part between the two belong to neither of them?

It would be the same as saying that in this passage, "Jesus said to his disciples, beware of false prophets, who come to you in sheep's clothing" [Matt. 7:15], the middle part, "Beware of false prophets," did not belong to the first or last part, but was a new, independent, sentence. The text then would read, "Jesus said to his disciples, who come to you in sheep's clothing, for you should beware of false prophets." A shameless obstinacy might say so, but no one is so mad as to believe him. Just so is it with this shameless spirit who raves in this place, when he sees that the passage, "This is my body," follows immediately upon the first, without so much as an "and" between them, and that the sense requires that the two belong together.

But Dr. Karlstadt patches things over with an interpolation, saying, "It is as if Christ were to say, 'Dear disciples, you have heard that the prophets speak of a body, which should be given for sins. I say to you, I am that body,'" etc. My answer is, Who has said so? Who has authorized him to make an interpolation here? How do we know that this interpolation and addition are correct? Where is the Scripture and basis for it? How does the text require it? Indeed where is there a single syllable in support of it? Karlstadt says so. If this is enough, then it is much more sufficient that I say otherwise, for I have the clear text and natural meaning of the words on my side. Was Christ inferior to Dr. Karlstadt in wisdom, in that he did not add this himself, when it was so highly necessary to have this meaning here? Where are now the lofty prophets, who do not call the Lord's Supper a sacrament, but wanted a name from the Bible? They will not even tolerate the word *enim*.[133] Tell me, now, what sense does it make to decry the addition of a little word or name (which imperils nothing), as the greatest of all vices, while the addition of a lot of loose talk and an interpolation which ruins everything is permissible? Don't you see the devil in this again who makes that which is nothing and optional a matter of necessity and makes nothing of the Word of God which is of supreme importance? But that is his nature throughout.

Good God! though we have such clear and certain passages of Scripture, it is still trouble and toil to remain ahead of the devil. And this lying spirit would have us depend on his own word, so that we would need have no other support than to say, Dr. Karlstadt said so. What fine shape we would then be in? Is this to bring the people to Christ? Indeed to the devil in the depths of hell. I think I know what he had in mind. He imagined, forsooth, the rascal spirit, "They will come at me with these clear Scripture passages, and what shall I do? By anticipating their plans, I shall render their verses weak and blunt their edges by my own interpolations." But the mad fool did not realize that by weakening and making blunt the edges of our clear passages of Scripture with his own interpolations without Scripture would accomplish nothing, other than to make the edges sharper. For when people see that he has no scriptural basis and only comes with his own self-contrived interpolation, they sense that he himself must have felt the text was too clear and overpowering for him. So his lying is on a par with his doubtful confession, and his patchwork as poor as a double tear. But, my lying spirit, you can't patch things that way. You must lead with Scripture and text.

Secondly, I would very much like to hear a text from the prophets which speaks of a body and blood which are to be given for sins, as this lying spirit pretends. They say, of course, of the whole person that he must suffer, but nothing of body and blood. Since Christ here clearly names body and blood and refers to the

---

[133] In Latin the words, "This is my body," read, "*Hoc est enim corpus meum.*"

prophets, as this spirit says, the words "body and blood" should be found somewhere in the prophets and should be identical with Christ, who would be reminding the disciples of them and they would understand him. Now, you lying spirit, who suffers not that a word be added to God's Word, show us where the prophets speak of a body or blood? Where in the prophets had the disciples heard it? Again you see that with this spirit everything is forced and feigned? The whole Christ must suffer, but at the table he makes a division so as to give his body to be eaten, and his blood to be drunk. Such a separation was not necessary nor could it take place in his suffering. Consequently the prophets have spoken of suffering and not of this division or of the Supper.

Thirdly, if we are to make so extensive an addition, how will this fit in with what follows thereupon, "This do in remembrance of me"? For it should connect with "eat" in his saying, "Take, eat." Shall it jump back over so many words and so long a statement to that with which it belongs? Where is the language whose nature and character permits interposing so many other words and so long a statement between two words that belong together. Quite obviously we are dealing with mischievous wantonness. Still, as we have said, Karlstadt must produce the proof for his contentions which we shall await.

Let this be our answer to the arguments and reasons that Dr. Karlstadt presents for his dream from Scripture. They were threefold. First, a capital letter is found in some books, not all. Second, there was a punctuation mark. Third, the dear *touto*. What wonderful arguments, which no one would use except such heavenly prophets, who hear the voice of God. A fourth now is, that he cannot present a single verse of Scripture in his favor. This is the most damaging argument and will forever remain so. I shall not overthrow it but will rather strengthen it. Furthermore he teaches us what Frau Hulda,[134] natural reason, has to say in the matter, just

---

[134] In Germanic mythology, Frau Hulda is the name of the leader of a group of elfin creatures who were looked upon as the instigators of good and evil among men. Like them Frau Hulda is of a capricious nature, now friendly, now hostile especially in times when disorder arises among men. She may therefore be regarded as a personification of order and clever reasoning. However, in matters of faith Luther looked upon reason as seductive, hence as "the devil's prostitute." Cf. *MA⁴*, p. 413.

as if we did not know that reason is the devil's prostitute and can do nothing else but slander and dishonor what God does and says. But before we answer this arch-prostitute and devil's bride, we first want to prove our faith, not by setting forth capitals or periods or *touto tauta* but by clear, sober passages from Scripture which the devil will not overthrow.

In the first place no one can deny that the three Evangelists, Matthew [26:26], Mark [14:22], and Luke [22:19], and Paul in I Cor. [11:24] agree in their descriptions of the first part of the sacrament and use almost identical words. Christ took the bread, gave thanks, broke it, and gave to his disciples, saying, "Take and eat, this is my body, given for you." Since they all speak of the same thing, our understanding of the Evangelist Matthew's report must agree with that of the Evangelists Mark and Luke, and that of Paul. Is it not surely this, in spite of what else could be said? It is certain that the meaning of all four is that Christ did not here bid the disciples to dance or pipe a tune, but to eat, according to the words, "Take, eat, this is my body," etc.

So then it must be admitted, without danger of contradiction, that the same four, in describing the second part of the sacrament, also are in agreement and in their narrative all have sought to speak of the same event. This despite of what else could be said here also. So what Matthew [26:28] says, "This is the blood of the new testament, which is poured out for many, for the forgiveness of sins," must be the same and mean the same as when Mark [14:24] says, "This is the blood of the new testament, which is poured out for many." So also, when Luke [22:20] and Paul [I Cor. 11:25] say, "This is the cup of the new testament in my blood, which is poured out for you," it is and means the same as Matthew and Mark seek to say in these words, "This is my blood, poured out for many." Who can still here say or think otherwise? With the words, "This is the cup," Luke and Paul do not refer to the visible body or the visible blood of Christ, but to the visible cup, as the word forcefully requires since it clearly stands there and says, "This is the cup." Therefore the body or blood of Christ is neither cup nor jug, neither dish nor plate. We must likewise conclude that Matthew and Mark speak of the same visible cup and not of the visible blood of Christ when they say, "This is my blood." Thus the word *das* in all the gospels never does or can refer or point to anything else than what Christ offered, namely, the cup or the drink, when he asked them to drink. Or else we must say that the Evangelists were not in agreement and were not writing of the same thing in the second part of the sacrament.

So now enough for this time. As stated above, Karlstadt's *touto* and *tauta* are lost. It is established that the Evangelists and Paul do not speak of the visible blood of Christ but of the cup or the wine, and it must be conceded that they say, "This is my blood of the new testament." Also, "This is the cup of the new testament in my blood." If we have maintained that in the sacrament the blood of Christ is truly present as these words require, then it is likewise confirmed that also the body of Christ is truly present in the other part of the sacrament. Thus all of Dr. Karlstadt's objections have fallen to the ground, and it is clear that they were nothing but his own dream, which with utter carelessness he hoped to inject into Scripture, but which now is excluded.

He reviles us with many scornful and jeering words, asking how we get Christ into the bread and wine, whether He must strike up the tune we demand and many similar words of shameful blasphemy. We can plainly see that they are the words of a thoughtless spirit or devil, which serve to excite the profligate mob and charm those who are not much worried about faith and conscience. But sincere hearts who are concerned about conscience and faith are surely not satisfied with such jesting and words of abuse and sacrilege. They want the Word of God and say, "Why should I care for Karlstadt's dreams, sneers, and slanders? I see the clear, distinct, and powerful words of God which compel me to confess, that the body and blood of Christ are in the sacrament." Such should be our answer, and ridicule we can meanwhile disregard. How Christ is brought into the bread or strikes up the tune we demand, I do not know. But I do know full well that the Word of God cannot lie, and it says that the body and blood of Christ are in the sacrament.

Here I will not yet answer the sophistic and miserable interpolation with which Dr. Karlstadt mends and patches the words about the cup. He must bite sharper who would make any dent in this text. Karlstadt's words will not do it, they are only

Karlstadtian. Later I will show up his sophistry. For the present, it is sufficient to have proven in powerful fashion that the Evangelists and Paul refer the words, "This is my body," "This is my blood," "This is the cup," not to the visible body or blood of Christ, as Karlstadt dreams, but to that which he offers the disciples, bidding them eat and drink. This passage we have won and secured beyond the power of Karlstadt and all devils with their sophistry, of that I am sure. But, as I have said, it is the nature of this spirit to pay no attention to the external Word and sign of God. This he attacks boldly and does with it as he pleases. Then he devises something sheerly out of his own imagination, without any basis in Scripture, and this is supposed to be the true spirit.

Furthermore beside these four strong passages we have yet another. I Cor. 10 [:16] reads thus: "The cup of blessing which we bless, is it not a participation in the body of Christ?" That is a verse which is a thunderbolt on the head of Dr. Karlstadt and his whole party. This verse has been also the life-giving medicine of my heart in my trials concerning this sacrament. Even if we had no other passage than this we could sufficiently strengthen all consciences and sufficiently overcome all adversaries. O, how Dr. Karlstadt feared this verse and set out to build a great strong dome above himself against this thunderbolt. But when he sought for stone and lime, he found only cobweb and chaff, as we will see when we come to the fragile interpolation of his spiritual and scriptureless brain.

But observe first that Paul says nothing about *touto* or *tauta*, nor does he busy himself with small or capital letters. Clearly he declares, "The bread that we break." Especially, he notes, "that we break." Not only Christ broke it at the Supper. Thereby Dr. Karlstadt's lie is demolished, for he holds that even if Christ had given his body and blood in the Supper as a food it would not necessarily follow that Christians also or we should afterwards do so. Our answer is this, "The bread that we break," "we, we, we." Who is "we"? I hope that Dr. Karlstadt will find yet another *touto* in Greek, which will tell us that "we" means "Christ alone." His Peter Rültz will then boast that the Greek language does not permit otherwise.

Observe, secondly, that Paul is speaking of bread in the

sacrament, which Christ broke, and afterwards also the apostles broke it. "Breaking" is nothing but breaking into pieces and distributing, in Hebrew fashion—Isa. 58 [:7]: "Break[135] your bread with the hungry"; Lam. 4 [:4]: "The children beg for bread, but no one breaks it unto them." So the factious spirits have no reason to charge us again as betraying Christ, because we do not break the bread into crumbs with our fingers, but take the host in larger pieces. For they insist on such breaking and are not satisfied if it is otherwise broken into pieces, as by hand, knife, or other means as it was broken among the Jews. Remember also that Paul does not call it the form of bread as the papists do,[136] but calls it frankly and simply bread. Thus we may know that we do not sin in this respect either when we call it bread and use it in St. Paul's fashion, though the papists call it heresy.

Observe, in the third place, that he clearly and distinctly asserts, "The bread which we break is a participation in the body of Christ." Do you hear, my dear brother? The bread which is broken or distributed piece by piece is the participation in the body of Christ. It is, it is, it is, he says, the participation in the body of Christ. Wherein does the participation in the body of Christ consist? It cannot be anything else than that as each takes a part of the broken bread he takes therewith the body of Christ. This fellowship is really a participation, so that in communion with each other they receive the common body of Christ, as he himself said, "We who are many are one body, for we all partake of the same loaf." On this account it has from ancient times been called *communio*, that is a fellowship [participation; *koinōnia*].

At this point Dr. Karlstadt distorts meaning in masterful fashion, and would gladly take the edge off this verse and make it dull in advance, so that no one would see how badly he was hit. Because of the perverted nature of his spirit, he makes everything spiritual and inward which God has determined should be outward and bodily; on the other hand he makes that outward and bodily

---

[135] In his German Bible Luther rendered the past tense of *paras* with "break." The RSV has translated the word as "share."

[136] The Roman church distinguishes between the essence (*substantia*) and the form (*accidentia*) of bread in the Lord's Supper, the former being changed into the body of Christ while the latter remains bread.

which God wills should be inward and spiritual, as I have already said. So here he turns his attention to the word "participation" and wants to become spiritual and make of it a spiritual participation. He holds that they have participation in the body of Christ who with "desire" recall the suffering of Christ and suffer also with him, etc., which is a new terminology they have invented to describe their new understanding.[137]

But if we ask for the reason and Scripture to prove this interpretation or where is the text that requires this meaning, he points us to the vent of a chimney,[138] or to the man who came and told him this. How could he do otherwise? He could not tolerate the verse, yet could not defend himself. So, rather than thus read it, he thought, I will twist it to suit myself. If Scripture will not help, my big head will, for it is full of spirit. It is enough, it tells me even more about it, namely that the participation in the suffering of Christ is identical with participation in the body and blood of Christ. Isn't that fine? Indeed, very fine. Only one letter is involved here so that we change the "d" to "b" and the "b" to "d." So we get the word for body [Leib] from the word for suffering [Leid], and vice versa. There you have it, as an eel by the tail. For this you need produce no Scripture.

Let the mad spirit go his way. We shall refute his interpretation in the following manner. First, participation in the suffering of Christ cannot be participation in the body and blood of Christ. For whoever suffers with Christ or partakes in his sufferings, must be devout, spiritual, and believing. A sinful, carnal person does not do thus. But even the unworthy partake of the body of Christ, according to Paul in I Cor. 11 [:29]: "Whoever eats the bread in an unworthy manner eats judgment upon himself." This happened at the Supper to Judas the traitor who participated with the other disciples in the body and blood of Christ and partook with them. For he received it, ate, and drank just as the other disciples did.[139]

Dr. Karlstadt makes a spiritual participation out of the par-

---

[137] Cf. p. 88.
[138] Cf. p. 120.
[139] In opposition to Thomas Aquinas and Luther, Karlstadt denied that the unworthy receive the body and blood of Christ in the Lord's Supper. Cf. WA 18, 170.

taking of the body and blood of Christ and does not want to accept the idea that it is a receiving of the body and blood in bread and cup. I shall let St. Paul take care of this view, when he says, "The bread that we break is the participation in the body of Christ" [I Cor. 10:16]. Now no one can deny that the breaking of bread is a bodily, outward, act. They themselves say that an outward breaking or eating is nothing, but we must eat the body of Christ in a spiritual manner, etc. How then can the outward breaking of bread and eating be a spiritual participation, as Dr. Karlstadt claims? Moreover, the unworthy and godless also break bread and eat, as Judas Iscariot and certain Corinthians did (I Cor. 11 [:29]). They, thus, participate in the body of Christ and partake of it, as an interpretation of this verse requires, since the breaking of bread is a participation in the body of Christ. We must let this verse stand as it is, so that, when one breaks this bread, there is a participation in the body of Christ.

We are driven to the conclusion that Paul does not here speak of the spiritual participation, which only the saints have, of which Dr. Karlstadt dreams. But he speaks of a bodily participation, both by the holy and unholy, just as both break bread. So we see that the dream of Dr. Karlstadt is a lie. Probably he thought, "I will seize on the word 'participation' alone and torture it and will not notice the following words, 'the bread which we break,' etc. Otherwise they will not put up with my participation. But if I do not notice this, no one will observe it or have anything against the word 'participation,' and I will have won. I need do no more than I think: people are altogether blind."

Why then did St. Paul not simply say, "The bread, which we break, is the body of Christ," instead of adding, "The participation in the body of the Lord"? I reply, why did he not also simply say, "The bread is the body of the Lord," as the Evangelists did and he himself said in I Cor. 11 [:24; 10:16], instead of adding, "which we break"? He added this phrase undoubtedly because he wanted to speak as clearly and distinctly as ever he could and that he might forcefully guard against the error of Dr. Karlstadt. He wanted to speak of the bread of the sacrament and this he could not do better than by speaking of the broken bread. Also he wanted to teach that each one in his piece received the body of Christ. Therefore he did not want to call only the whole loaf the body of Christ, but also that which was distributed in the congregation and through the breaking of bread given to all in common. Thus this breaking of bread was not the body of Christ alone but participation in the body of Christ, that is, a body distributed to and received by all in the congregation. He could not have spoken more clearly and strongly. For with these words during the breaking, distributing, and receiving of the bread, he can see what happens when we break and offer and receive the bread. He says that such broken bread is participation in the body of Christ, so that they all in common and as one receive the one body of Christ and become partakers of it bodily.

So observe and mark well once again how this evasive devil has no other recourse than, as is his custom, to spiritualize that which God has made to be bodily, yet gives or cites no argument or reason for doing so. He does it rather as one who had power to establish articles of faith as he wishes. So here he says the bodily participation in the body of Christ must be spiritual, just as afterwards he does with the unworthy eating and drinking. As we shall see, he proceeds in a similar manner in regard to the discerning of the body of Christ [I Cor. 11:29]. I will give you a good description of him only so that you may learn to know and recognize the devil.

It is a very fine little discovery that I too could well employ if a verse which spoke of a bodily act were too much for me and hit me on the head so that my brain was dazed. I would go to it and say, "I wasn't hit. The verse speaks of spiritual things," and so I would be free from providing any proof for such an interpretation. Under such circumstances it would be easy to be a heavenly prophet. If I were compelled to produce proof, I would withstand all argument as butter does the sun. I would need a towel for my sweat, and say, "My proof seemed to me to be so perfect and correct."

So this verse of Paul stands like a rock and forcefully requires the interpretation that all who break this bread, receive, and eat it, receive the body of Christ and partake of it. As we have said, it cannot be spiritual, so it must be a bodily participation. For one cannot partake of the body of Christ except in two ways, spiritually or bodily. Again, this bodily participation cannot be visible or perceived by the senses, else the bread would not remain. Nor can it be merely natural bread, otherwise it would be ɛ bodily partaking not of the body of Christ, but of bread. Consequently, where the broken bread is present, there the body of Christ is truly and bodily present, though not of course visibly. Whoever boasts that he can dent this verse, will, I promise, find hard chewing.

In the third place we have the verse in I Cor. 11 [:27], "Whoever eats the bread or drinks the cup of the Lord in an unworthy manner will be guilty of profaning the body and blood of the Lord." Here again the sectarian spirit goes off and makes into spiritual that which St. Paul affirms is body, and attributes unworthy eating to those who do not have a right understanding of Christ and remembrance of his body. If again you ask, where is this written? What is the basis for it? Where is the text? He will show his anger and give no other evidence than that he has been burned by such verses, and would rather forestall them as impertinent, just as if I would seek to persuade some one who waved a naked sword over me to believe that it was a straw, so that he would not strike me. But it doesn't help to tremble before death. O helpless spirit, how long do you think you can evade the producing of Scripture or text? Are you not ashamed to have been active so long in injecting your anger, your lies, your dreams into Scripture?

All right, when Paul here says, "Whoever eats and drinks unworthily," etc., he made a mistake. He should have said thus, "Whoever remembers the Lord unworthily or does not know him," etc. "The unworthy eating and drinking is the unworthy understanding and remembrance of the Lord,' unless perchance Dr. Karlstadt's spirit fails him here. But who would believe that? You must imagine that St. Paul was drunk that evening, and when he spoke of unworthy eating and drinking, he forgot and talked too much, for he should have spoken about unworthy remembrance. But Dr. Karlstadt has caught the right meaning on a sober morning and has now put St. Paul's word straight in its right order. So he is thanked by Peter Rültz and the bride of Orlamünde.[140]

---

[140] Cf. pp. 101, 110, 132.

Now let us have our say. St. Paul connects here the bread and the body of Christ with each other, even as he did above, when he said, "The bread that we break is the participation in the body of Christ." He does not say, "The bread that we break is the participation in the bread of the Lord," though this would have sounded fine to Dr. Karlstadt. So here he does not say, "Whoever is unworthy of this bread, he sins or is guilty of profaning the bread of the Lord," as again Dr. Karlstadt would like to have it, but, "is guilty of profaning the body of the Lord," so that in both places he maintains that the bread of the Lord is the body of the Lord. For if this is not what he meant, he would have had to say, as above, "Whoever is unworthy of this bread, he is guilty of profaning the bread of the Lord." How can you sin in eating the body of the Lord, if he is not present in the eating or the bread? Or you would have to say thus, "Whoever is unworthy of this bread, he is guilty of profaning the Lord's Supper, or God, or the commandment, or the ordinance of the Lord."

Now the nature and character of the sentence requires us to interpret it to mean that whoever eats unworthily is guilty in regard to what he eats. Therefore, it is not enough for Dr. Karlstadt to say "no" and insert an interpolation. Since the text here is clear, and the nature and meaning of the language used affirm that whoever eats this bread unworthily is guilty of profaning the body of the Lord because the body of the Lord is eaten in the bread, and sin is committed in the eating and drinking, therefore he would have to bring forward convincing verses and text, if we were to believe him. For the text forcefully compels the interpretation that sin is committed in the eating and drinking, as it says, "Whoever eats and drinks unworthily," and yet claims that the same sin has to do with the body and blood of the Lord. This strongly indicates that it is in the eating of the body and drinking of the blood of Christ that the unworthy one has offended and therein committed evil.

For the unworthy remembrance of the Lord is a separate sin other than the unworthy eating, and St. Paul says nothing of it in this place. All the words in the entire chapter where he condemns the unworthy eating indicate that the sin consists wholly in eating and drinking. St. Paul terrifies them lest they think it is merely

183

bread or wine which they eat and drink, thereby becoming unworthy, when it is the body and blood of Christ, which makes them guilty of such unworthy eating. Such, I said, is the natural meaning, and one can see that Dr. Karlstadt's mocking objections are altogether artificial, forced and obstinate, on which no conscience or faith can rely.

It is not sound reasoning arbitrarily to associate the sin which St. Paul attributes to eating with remembrance of Christ, of which Paul does not speak. For he does not say, "Who unworthily holds the Lord in remembrance," but, "Who unworthily eats and drinks." Now there would be no rhyme or reason in saying one becomes guilty of profaning the body of Christ through unworthy eating or the blood of Christ by unworthy drinking, if the body was not in that which was eaten and the blood in that which was drunk. Why too should it be necessary for him even to distinguish between the two offenses, unworthy eating in regard to the body of the Lord and unworthy drinking in regard to the blood of the Lord?

Why does he not put it thus: Whoever unworthily eats this bread is guilty of profaning the blood of the Lord. Who unworthily drinks of this cup is guilty of profaning the body of the Lord? If Dr. Karlstadt's meaning were correct, one of the two would be enough. Indeed it would be sufficient if he had said, "Who eats and drinks unworthily is guilty of profaning Christ or the death of Christ," since Dr. Karlstadt interprets the sin of unworthy eating to be that one does not rightly honor and observe the suffering and death of Christ. But inasmuch as Paul makes the unworthy drinking of the cup to mean the same as profaning the blood, and the unworthy eating of the bread to mean the same as profaning the body, the clear, natural sense of the words is that the body is in the eating, and the blood is in the drinking. And no one can produce an argument to the contrary which has any show of validity.

In brief, this is the spirit of whom I have already said that he makes inward whatever God makes outward. So he has to do here. The guilt which Paul places in the bodily eating and drinking he makes an inner one, in a spiritual eating and drinking. From the fact that he fumes that those unworthily eat and drink who do not inwardly acknowledge the body of Christ nor rightly hold him in remembrance, we can understand that he transfers the eating and drinking into the spirit, though Paul considers it an outward act. For spiritual eating is the right recognition and remembrance of the body of Christ. Do you not again become aware of this devil with all his spirituality, though he has no basis, Scripture, argument, or other evidence than what he spins from his own brain?

Fourthly, St. Paul writes in the same chapter, "Let a man examine himself, and so eat of the bread and drink of the cup. For any one who eats and drinks without discerning the body eats and drinks judgment upon himself" [I Cor. 11:28-29]. But here comes Peter Rültz again, blowing his own horn, posing as a Greek, and says that the word *diakrinōn* means "discerning." It also refers to remembrance, meaning that we must in spirit sharply discern the body of Christ and imitate the suffering of Christ with "calm desire" [141] and fervor, etc. Everything that this spirit teaches must be related to the spiritual remembrance of Christ. Rültz knows no other tune. Would that he knew it well and were not using it as a cloak to spread his poison.

Dear Peter, I beg you put your glasses on your nose, or blow your nose a bit, to make your head lighter and the brain clearer. Look a little closer with us on the text. You say that the discerning belongs to the remembrance. But Paul says it applies to the eating and drinking. For he does not say, "Who unworthily holds the Lord in remembrance merits judgment, since he does not discern the body of the Lord." But he speaks thus, "Who eats and drinks unworthily, he eats and drinks judgment to himself, for he does not discern the body of the Lord." Do you hear that, Peter? In an unworthy eating and drinking this discerning is lacking, therefore judgment is the penalty. Is that not clear enough? Does not the text demand this?

I should like to give Dr. Karlstadt two gulden again[142] if only once in all this discussion he would help, not me, but his own cause by doing one of two things: either by producing passages from Scripture, or by showing that a selected text demands an interpretation proving his cause to be right. Now, however, he does nothing more than latch on to a small word and smears over with

---

[141] Cf. p. 88.
[142] Cf. p. 144, n. 98.

his spittle as he pleases, but meanwhile he does not take into account other texts which overthrow him who smears and spits, so that he is up-ended with all four limbs in the air. So here, after he has raved and smeared for a long time that the discerning belongs to the remembrance of the Lord, he does not see that the text clearly states that it belongs to the unworthy eating and drinking. So also, as above,[143] when he wanted to make the participation of the body of Christ spiritual, he did not notice that the bodily breaking of bread broke his neck.

He is like the ostrich, the foolish bird which thinks it is wholly concealed when it gets its neck under a branch. Or like small children, who hold their hands in front of their eyes and seeing nobody imagine that no one sees them either. This spirit acts in the same way. He grabs at a small word, with which he covers himself, but lets the whole text be, which leaves him uncovered and shames him. I don't know if he imagines that there are no Bibles or people left in the world. Against me he will accomplish nothing, though I verily warned him at Jena he had better make sure of hitting his mark, for I would not miss mine. But he interpreted my words as he interprets the Bible, and calls it a hit when he calls me "mad sophist," "bloody sow," "papist twice over," and epithets of similar nature. But I want him to take the matter seriously and hit the mark. I was about to say, the mass for the soul is invalid, for the coin is a "copper" [instead of silver]. But it was the work of God which hardened and blinded the heart of Pharaoh [Exod. 4:21ff.] to the honor of his truth and word, bringing comfort to all believers and terror to the arrogant.

So we conclude that this discerning is to take place in the eating and drinking, as above; guilt and sin occurs in relation to the body of the Lord. Who, thus, eats and drinks unworthily eats unto his judgment. Why? Because, Paul says, he does not discern the body of Christ. Now tell me, how does one discern the body of the Lord in eating and drinking? The Greek word, *diakrinein,* in Latin, *discernere,* means to make a distinction, and not to think of one thing like the other, but to consider the one thing nobler, better, more precious than the other. St. Paul means that whoever eats and drinks unworthily, fittingly deserves judgment or severe

---

[143] Cf. pp. 179-181.

punishment, because with his unworthy eating and drinking he does not distinguish, does not discern, the body of Christ, but thinks of and treats the bread and wine of the Lord as if it were merely bread and wine, though it is the body and blood of the Lord. For if he seriously thought of it as the body of the Lord, he would not act so carelessly, as if it were ordinary bread, but would eat with fear, humility, and reverence. He ought of course have a sense of awe before the body of the Lord.

If this is not the correct view, you give another and tell what it means to discern the body of Christ. For the word has only this meaning, that we should look on the body of Christ as something better and more precious than any thing else having a significance all its own. This is sufficiently required by these words. Since St. Paul bears witness to and wants such discerning in the eating and drinking of the Lord's bread and cup, it is sufficiently borne out by the text that we should consider the body of Christ as better and more important than the bread and the cup. So it must follow that the body and blood of Christ are there in the bread and cup. They eat to judgment who eat unworthily by not discerning the body of Christ, and those who eat worthily do rightly discern it.

But one ought not blame Dr. Karlstadt. As I have said, since his spirit is bent on making spiritual what God wants to be bodily, he has to treat the discernment in this way, making recognition and remembrance a spiritual discernment, inward in the spirit, when God intends a bodily discernment, between bread and the body of Christ. Should one require him to show the basis and reason for his position, or to present a compelling argument on the basis of the text? Brother, do not bewilder him with such a request. Don't you see that he has other things to do? It is enough that such a man says it. If you don't believe him, believe his gray peasant coat and felt hat,[144] in which, as you ought to know, the Holy Spirit must be.

This high art of Dr. Karlstadt reminds me of that practiced by those who are fond of allegories, whom St. Jerome[145] in his

---

[144] Cf. pp. 81, 117, 162.
[145] Luther seems to have in mind the letter of St. Jerome (331-420) to Paulinus in which he objects to seeing prophecies of Christ's coming in some of the verses of Homer and Virgil. WA 18, 178.

Prologue compares to jugglers. I might make out of Dietrich of Bern,[146] Christ; out of the giant with whom he fought, the devil; out of the dwarf, humility; out of his prison, the death of Christ. Or I might take any other tale or legend of knights to exercise my imagination or toy with, as he did who applied Ovid's *Metamorphoses* entirely to Christ.

Or to anticipate the objection of my spirits that I compare their ways to secular fables, let me take the legend of St. George and say that St. George was Christ, the maiden he saved was Christendom, the dragon of the sea was the devil, the horse was the human nature of Christ, the spear was the gospel, etc. Likewise, when St. Peter sank in the sea [Matt. 14:27ff.] and Christ helped him, I might say that the sea is the persecution and tribulation in the world, Peter any Christian in doubt, and Christ the grace of God, etc.

Such is the trifling art with which these prophets busy themselves. They have discovered many similar interpretations in the Old Testament and daily find more. They teach much about the sevenfold sprinkling,[147] and fill their books with this kind of skill, as if it were such a priceless thing which nobody but themselves knew about. In general, their interpretation is so stupid that it makes one feel like vomiting, especially their sevenfold sprinkling. They do not consider that such has to be proved from Scripture and that it means nothing unless it is clearly expressed elsewhere, as I have explained in the sermon on the ten lepers.[148] For them, however, it is enough just to have contrived it, thereby it is proved.

So Dr. Karlstadt does here. Since he had learned these things from his prophets, and by nature has a strange head which always looks for that which is unusual and no one hitherto has known, he launches out and tries to play dice with the words of St. Paul, as was his custom in treating the Old Testament, interpreting them allegorically. Consequently he must make St. Paul speak of spiritual, not bodily participation, of spiritual, not bodily discerning, of spiritual, not bodily unworthiness in eating, of spiritual, not

---

[146] Dietrich von Bern is that name of Theoderic the Great (454-526) which became the center of a growing number of Germanic legends in medieval times.
[147] Cf. p. 88, n. 13.
[148] *WA* 8, 336ff.

bodily guilt in regard to the body of the Lord. And the silly, feeble devil thinks no one sees him. No, my fellow, we see you well enough. You haven't used enough make-up; you need more and other colors.

You may say that it is nonetheless true that the sea signifies persecution, and Christ, the grace of God, and sinking, weakness or despair. And it is true, that the grace of God helps in despair. And it is not wrong or false that there is a spiritual participation, a spiritual discerning of the body of Christ, a spiritual unworthy eating, a spiritual guilt of the body of Christ. Generally, all such allegories or interpretations are in fact true and very attractive and fine. My answer to this is that I am not contending as to their falsehood or truth. But I know well, that they often are amiss and pure fancy, because they are brought forward without any scriptural foundation, just as these prophetical sprinklings, with which they toy, are pure nonsense.

What I do contend against is not only Dr. Karlstadt's attempt to establish his views without basis in Scripture, but also his attempt through such lofty spiritual semblance forcefully to suppress, deny, and falsify the true, scriptural meaning, which naturally derives from the text but which his mockery will not endure. If he lets the natural meaning remain inviolate, I will let him interpret allegorically and spiritually, juggle and play, until he tires. If someone will permit me to retain the meaning that Peter, according to the scriptural sense, did walk on the sea and sank, etc., it is no longer my concern how he interprets it afterwards, provided no harm is done to faith.

So if Dr. Karlstadt leaves untouched the bodily participation of the body of Christ, the bodily discerning, the bodily unworthiness in eating, the bodily guilt in unworthy eating, etc., I for my part will let him do what he wants. For St. Paul also in Rom. 12 [:6] says, "Let prophecy be in proportion to our faith," so that each one does not interpret what and how he pleases and thereby lead the conscience astray. For it is real jugglery to make a thing seem to have happened and to exist, when there is nothing to it. Just as Dr. Karlstadt's spiritual interpretation seems to him and his followers to be a remarkably precious one. But when one examines it under the light and according to the text, it is revealed as pure jugglery. Devoid of foundation or truth, it is the product of his own fancy, and forced upon the text.

If such spiritual juggling were to prevail, I would like to put Dr. Karlstadt and all his prophets to school for another three years. I was thoroughly drilled in this method when I first began to study the Bible ten years ago, before I discovered the true method. I too would carelessly say: "In the beginning God created heaven and earth," Gen. 1 [:1]: Heaven refers to the angels and the spiritual creatures; earth refers to the bodily creatures. Don't you think this was splendidly and truly said? Yes, but meanwhile what happened to the text? How could I prove, that in this verse heaven and earth are not the natural heaven and earth, as the words say? Brother, the natural meaning of the words is queen, transcending all subtle, acute sophistical fancy. From it we may not deviate, unless we are compelled by a clear article of the faith. Otherwise the spiritual jugglers would not leave a single letter in Scripture.

In this manner even the great teacher Origen[149] played the fool, and led St. Jerome and many others astray with him. In former times his books were justly forbidden and condemned on account of such spiritual tomfoolery. For it is dangerous so to play with the Word of God by which conscience and faith are to be guided. Therefore, interpretations of God's Word must be lucid and definite having a firm, sure, and true foundation on which one may confidently rely.

These are the main points in this matter, by which, through the grace of God, we satisfy every good conscience in order to confirm their faith. If we do not thereby convert the hardened Karlstadtians, we have nonetheless successfully contended against them in these two matters. First, that they can neither prove their assertions with Scripture nor wrest them from the text, but produce only their own notions and ideas, presuming thereby to obscure clear passages but in vain. To our interpretation he said,

---

[149] Origen (ca. 182-251) is considered the author of the allegorical interpretation of the Scriptures in Christendom. Corresponding to the trichotomy of man the Scriptures must be interpreted in accordance with a threefold sense: the literal (sômatikôs), the moral (pschychôs), and spiritual (pneumatikôs). The spiritual sense of Scripture, by means of which its hidden or concealed meaning is brought to light, came particularly to be identified in the narrower sense with an allegorical method of interpreting the Scriptures.

"No," for which we demanded no proof without giving our own, which we then did. But he proposed another interpretation without offering any foundation—a scandalous thing of so lofty a spirit! Secondly, everything they brought against us was unconvincing and did not stand the test. Finally, we defied them to do their best. We are determined to stand up to them and their cleverness, whether past, present, or future, with no other passages from Scripture [than those adduced by us]. They shall not thus deprive us of them. For the only source of Dr. Karlstadt's strength lies in applying arbitrarily and without proof everything attributed by the evangelists and apostles in clear words to the eating and drinking [in the sacrament] to the remembrance of the Lord. Let another come, who can do better.

Suppose now, despite all, Dr. Karlstadt's bluster prevailed and overcame our faith (though this is impossible). What would he then have accomplished? Not on that account would his faith thereby be right or certain. For he proves nothing, but only recites his claims, as one might recite a fairy tale, giving no basis, or Scripture, or reason. No conscience can rest or depend on such a foundation, which would be nothing more than the word of Dr. Karlstadt. Thus, whoever follows Dr. Karlstadt's opinion must fall between two chairs and be suspended between heaven and earth. Of the sacrament he would retain nothing at all. For he who has neither a basis nor a single passage of Scripture on his side, forsakes our faith, and cannot comprehend it. I have often asserted that the ultimate goal of the devil is to do away with the entire sacrament and all outward ordinances of God. Then as these prophets teach, all that would count would be for the heart to stare inwardly at the spirit.

Everyone now clearly sees, I think, that Dr. Karlstadt's spirit is one that seeks to fool the people with the word "spiritual," and undertakes to make everything spiritual which God has made bodily. With this talent he manages to put on a good show and attract attention. If only he would establish a basis for his view, not only claiming, thus, thus it is, but prove that it is and must be so because of what is in the text, then he would be a fine spirit. But since he speaks only on his own, we can say: You lie, dear spirit. All men are liars [Ps. 116:11]. The pope has lied in the same manner. But his spirit has rather busied itself in making spiritual things bodily, as he transforms a spiritual Christendom into an outward, bodily community. This sectarian spirit, on the other hand, is mostly concerned about making spiritual what God makes bodily and outward. We therefore proceed between the two, making nothing spiritual or bodily, but keeping spiritual what God makes spiritual, and bodily what he makes bodily.

If now some still persist and remain in this error and view of the Karlstadtian sacrament, or later fall into it, what would be their lot? What indeed would be our attitude even if the whole world rejected our interpretation? How are we to consider the gospel, on which certainly more depends? Does not the whole world reject and resist it? How few are they who rightly hold to it? Don't let yourself be misled if only a few rightly treat and believe the sacrament. Let him who will be gone, but make sure where you stand. It is not surprising that many go astray. The wonder is that there are some who do not go astray, few though they are. Christ himself said, "Do you think when the Son of man comes, he will find faith on earth?" [Luke 18:8]. I am not to blame for any one who now errs. I have surely warned and taught faithfully.

Concerning Frau Hulda,[150] Dr. Karlstadt's Shrewd Reason, in this Sacrament

Now that we have shown our scriptural foundation and proven our faith, while refuting Dr. Karlstadt's argument, let us see how splendidly he speaks in this matter when he seeks counsel of his reason, which first of all gives him his proper foundation. For Dr. Karlstadt is now much madder than ever the papists were. The papists at least have always been anxious to adduce evidence from Scripture, though they have used it falsely. But Dr. Karlstadt has only *touto* and *tauta*, periods and capitals, and interpolations out of his own head, with never a verse from Scripture. Thus, the papists confess that in the matter of the sacrament we are to follow Scripture, not reason. But Dr. Karlstadt scrapes and collects whatever reason can show, teach, or judge. Are they not merry prophets and heavenly spirits?

---

[150] Cf. p. 174, n. 134.

The first sample of this highly praised reason is its conclusion that if the body and blood of Christ were in the sacrament, it would have to follow that the bread was crucified and given for us and not Christ himself, since the text reads, "This is my body given for you." This Frau Hulda interprets to mean the same as saying, "The bread is given for you." This again means, "My body is not given for you before it has become bread," etc. How does this cleverness appeal to you? Defy them and say that they are no heavenly prophets. If you ask where they learned such grammar, or by what reasoning they thus interpret the word of Christ, you may probably hear the heavenly voice.

Let us proceed. This is pure knavery with which the devil here deals. Tell me, Frau Hulda, you who are so pure and will not tolerate our adding or taking away a syllable from the word of God, why are you here so filthy? You add so many words and say, "My body is not given for you before it has become bread"? Also, why do you break up the sentence and say, "The bread which is given for you"? Show me where it is written that we should understand or explain the words, "This is my body, which is given for you," to mean, "This bread is given for you," or "My body is not given for you before it becomes bread." In any language this sentence cannot be understood except in this sense, "This is my body, given for you," etc. There is no other body, given for you, than the one which in death I give you to eat. From this it does not follow that it would at the same moment be eaten and crucified, but that which was eaten in this moment, the same would afterwards, when it is not eaten, be given for you.

Let me take John the Baptist as an example, when he pointed to Christ and said, "Behold, the Lamb of God who takes away the sin of the world" [John 1:29]. Listen to this, sectarian spirit: John said there that Christ bears or takes away the sin of the world, yet he is not on the cross. My dear friend, continue and say from this it follows that Christ is not crucified for us. For the words read that Christ did not bear the sins of the world before John pointed him out and called him the Lamb of God. For there is no other Christ crucified for us, and he is not crucified at any other time or place than when John pointed him out by the Jordan river. There he bore our sins, before he was crucified, just as here he is given for us in the bread.

In John 10 [:11] Christ says, "I am the good shepherd and lay down my life for my sheep." Ha, dear sectarian spirit, let us learn from you that since Christ says of himself that he gives his life for us, it must follow that this happens in the moment when in the synagogue of the Jews he says this of and about himself, and not on the cross, so that he is not afterwards crucified for us. For the words say nothing else than, "I give my life" [John 10:15]. They do not say, "I will give my life," just as here he says, "which is given for you," and not, "which shall be given for you." So also one has to understand him when he says, "I give them eternal life" [John 10:28], and not, "I will give them." So also in John 19 [17:19], he says, "And for their sake I consecrate myself"; he does not say, "I will consecrate myself." You ought to feel shame in your hearts, you great gruff asses' heads, who pretend to such great skill in interpreting the Scriptures that you let such stuff go out into the world, from which it is clear that either on account of your great wickedness you do not want to, or on account of your great ignorance you cannot, either rightly speak or understand what is spoken.

If this devil insists so strongly on the words, "Which is given for you," as present in tense, and not to be understood as "Which in the future shall be given for you," we throw his word back at him and say that if the words, "This is my body," refers to the body of the seated Christ, then it must follow that Christ is not crucified for us. For the word is attributed to Christ as he sits there, and not to him on the cross. For he could not hang on the cross and at the same time be at the supper table. So he could not be given for us at any other time than when he sat there and said this of himself. Is not this a case where cleverness becomes ridiculous?

If now you heavenly prophets can allow that Christ sits at the table and his word, "Which is given for you," is to be so interpreted that the "is given" means "Shall be given," or "It is so determined and ordained that he shall be given," thus agreeing that his sitting at the table and referring to his body takes place at one time and his being crucified and giving himself at another, then we ask that you do not object to the statement that his body is in the bread and afterwards on the cross when it is not in the bread.[151] Then we may say concerning the bread, "This is my body given for you," in the sense that it shall be given for us, or it is already determined and ordained to be given, as if it were already given.

Where are you now, Frau Hulda, with your cleverness? Indeed, where is your inner witness, since you do not need the outer witness? This I tell you, my dear reader, so that you may get to know the annoying devil who takes advantage of Dr. Karlstadt. For in this matter of reason Peter Rültz boasts very loftily, and here speaks aptly in the manner of the heavenly prophets, namely, as we said, they do not come through the external Word to the spirit but from the spirit they come to the external Word. They hold to the word of Christ in John 12 [John 15:26-27]: "The Spirit of truth will bear witness and you also will be witnesses," just as if the apostles had received the Spirit without the external Word of Christ. Satiated with the inner witness, Peter Rültz boasts that he receives the external in order to teach and correct others.

There you have their theology: Others are to learn outwardly by their word, which they call an external witness. But they themselves are better and superior to the apostles, and pretend to learn inwardly in their spirit without an external Word and without means, though this possibility was not given to the apostles, but alone to the only Son, Jesus Christ. Thus you see how this devil, as I said already, disregards the external Word and does not wish to have it as a forerunner to the Spirit. Learn to shy away from such and be assured that these prophets are full of the devil. This is clear from this first aspect of the way they employ reason, and will become clearer. Such an exalted spirit which is above the apostles ought also forsooth demonstrate his superiority by great signs. But in the same manner as they prove their doctrine and external witness with Scripture, so they prove their spirit and inward witness with signs. The one devil is like the other.

If only Dr. Karlstadt and his gang could forego their sophistry and rationalism, since the word of Christ spoken over the bread, "This is my body," is a source of difficulty and anxiety for them. They

---

[151] In his *Dialogus* Karlstadt maintained: "If Christ had entered the sacrament he would have left the place where he was seated, for Christ always left his previous abode before he came to or entered another city or place." WA 18, 184.

neither can nor want to understand how bread might still be the body, and ought to do one of two things: Either give God honor and let his Word remain right and true, even though they don't understand how it can be that it is right and true, and be satisfied with it and believe it when they hear that God so speaks and wants it this way. Or, if they want to be really clever, let them follow the customary meaning of Scripture and simple sense of its language, setting aside their subtleties and craftiness.

For if we heed the simple sense of the language we can say of a glowing piece of iron, "It is fire," or, "The iron lying there is pure fire." If now a contentious sophist wanted to show off his smartness and set himself up against the whole world, declaring iron and fire were two different things and it could never be that iron was fire, tell me, would he not be a senseless fool? He would be trying to teach the people to exchange their simple way of speaking for his keen and sharp sophistry, though the simple sense of the words, "The iron is pure fire," is nothing more than saying that the iron and fire are in each other,[152] so that where the iron is there the fire is also. And no one is so stupid that he here needs some great and clever sophistry to tell him that wood is not stone, fire is not iron, water is not earth.

Since now iron is fire and fire is iron, according to the simple sense of language, and the two are in each other and as one, though each retains its own nature, they might well have exercised humility, foregoing their cleverness and smartness, and following Christ and all the world in the simple meaning of the word and say of the bread, "This is my body." This would mean the same as saying, bread and body are as one or in each other, as fire and iron. No one is so stupid as to deny that body and bread are two different things. We use similar expressions about the human nature of Christ, when we say, "He is God," and, "God is man." Yet no one stupidly avers that the divine and the human are not two different natures, or that one can be transformed into the other. The simple statement means that in Christ divinity and humanity are as one

---

[152] The homely illustration of "iron and fire," employed by Luther in this connection to demonstrate the need for giving priority to "the simple sense of language," has led some to describe—quite erroneously—Luther's understanding of the Lord's Supper with the word "consubstantiation."

so that God is bodily present [Col. 2:9] where the human person is, as Paul asserts.

So the simple meaning of the words could easily have given them what they sought for in their cleverness and contrived sharpness of reason at the expense of so much unnecessary toil and work for themselves and others. And you will see, as they progress, that they do not want to honor the Word of God in faith nor receive it according to the simple use of language. Instead, with their sophisticated reason and refined subtlety they want to measure and master it until they finally come to the point where they will deny that Christ is God. For to reason it sounds just as foolish to say, "Man is God," as, "The bread is the body." And as they deny the one they will soon also boldly deny the other. Such is also the aim of the devil, who has led them away from Scripture into their own reason, thereby bringing back again all the ancient heresies.[153] You will be surprised how clever reason can be, especially in the mad mob, when it shakes its head and says, yes, godhead and humanity are two different things, separated infinitely from each other as the eternal from the temporal. How then can the one be the other, or any one say, "Man is God"? You must therefore reply: the temporal is eternal, mortal is immortal and the like, as reason foolishly imagines in Dr. Karlstadt's head against the sacrament, and it will thus have come upon the truth in splendid fashion!

Or if this sort of speaking does not please them, they form their judgment in accordance with the manner of speech employed in Scripture which contains a common figure of speech called synecdoche. This occurs when the name of a whole is given to a part, as Scripture does when it calls the people of Israel a "possession" and a peculiar people of God [Exod. 19:5], though a majority always belonged to the devil and only a minority was God's people. So also Paul, in his letters to the Galatians [Gal. 1:2] and Corinthians [I Cor. 1:21] and elsewhere, called the congregation God's though only the smaller part consisted of true children of God. Indeed in I Cor. 10 [:1] he calls them all one bread and one body who drink of the one cup, though many of them drink unworthily of the cup, as he himself says.

---

[153] Arianism (fourth century) denied Jesus' complete divinity, while Sabellianism (fourth century) denied his complete humanity.

These sophists and keen smart alecks in this place could have applied the whole passage about bread and body, of which Jesus spoke when he said, "This is my body," solely to the body, regardless of the bread. Not that the bread did not belong here, but in his words he placed as much importance on the body as if only the body were present and everything else, be it bread or color, was nothing more than the body. Just as if a mother should point to a cradle in which her child lay and should say, "That is my child," and a sophist should ridicule her, saying, "What? Is the cradle your child?" Don't you think she would think him a fool or a crank? In his obstinacy he did not want to understand her words, as she pointed to both the cradle and the child, and yet meant especially the child, as if the cradle were not there.

Thus St. Paul, in Rom. 1 [:16] calls the preached gospel a power of God. Now let a clever sophist interrupt who knows that the power of God (which is eternal) is to be distinguished from utterance by word of mouth which immediately dies away. He wants to prove his skill and bring forward a *touto* or *tauta* and concludes, the bodily voice cannot be the power of God. So St. Paul is lying when he speaks of a bodily vocal sound as the power of God. St. Peter, too, is subject to the same criticism, as he says (I Pet. 1 [:25], "The Word of God remains forever." Isaiah [40:8] also speaks thus meaning the Word that is preached among us. How can this be true, that an eternal thing can be transient?

A sophist cannot believe this, but whoever knows the common use of Scripture is not misled by it, but rather easily understands. It is well explained by the use of synecdoche which is much employed not only in Scripture, but in all languages. So here you see that this evil spirit cannot speak or understand even his mother tongue. Dr. Karlstadt, who pretends to a great knowledge in Greek and Hebrew would benefit if he and his prophets were led back to their mothers or to a German school, so that they might first learn how to speak and understand German.

A second aspect of such high-sounding reason is Dr. Karlstadt's claim to have proved that nothing other than bread and wine are in the sacrament, and that when Christ commanded us to receive his body, he meant, take the bread and eat. Therefore the decrepit preachers[154] (*Hutzelprediger,* what beautiful German) should have proclaimed how one eats worthily of the Lord's bread, as Paul said. If now again I ask these lofty spirits, where is it written that Christ said, "Take the bread and eat," they most likely will point to the inward witness; let the Wizard of Oz[155] believe that, not I. I know of no place where Christ told us to take the bread and eat. He did say, "Take, eat, this is my body." Here he tells me to take his body and eat, not bread. But this spirit has supreme power to fix and to change, to add and to take away, as he pleases. How can he err?

To confirm this kind of reason he blames the pope for many more grievous errors. First, the pope steals the honor due God, in that he tells us to respond to the form of the bread, My God, be merciful to me. Second, he contradicts the truth by teaching us to honor the bread and letting us forget the body of Christ. Third, he destroys the teachings of Paul, exalting the form of the bread to the point that we forget the remembrance of the Lord. Fourth, that he makes us foolish by teaching us to eat the bread with solemnity though we may never give a thought to Christ. Fifth, that he renders the suffering of Christ unnecessary in his teaching that Christ in the form of the bread forgives our sins and has redeemed us, and thus his death on the cross was in vain. There you have it, pope, you are done for. I hold that you have been vanquished. These five points he has spewed out in such disorder that I find it painful to bring any order into them.

What shall I do? If I answer him, then I am a priest. But Dr. Karlstadt has reasoned with himself. "The pope's errors have been brought to light by others before me. Now I, too, would be glad to win a medal of honor in combat with the dead body of Hector. But if I write what others have written and adduce nothing new, it would bring disgrace on me as a great heavenly prophet. All right, I will attack him and write pure lies about him." Now the pope and his followers have done me much more injury than Dr. Karlstadt, and still do so daily. In fact they have hitherto

---

[154] A phrase used by Karlstadt about his opponents, meaning literally "dried and shrunken."

[155] The original speaks of *Kolkryb,* a kind of demonic, chameleon-like mythical character.

greatly despised Dr. Karlstadt. Yet I would not be so mad as to attack the pope with what is generally known as a stinking lie. The pope and his crowd do not care when I hit the mark with obvious truth and clear Scripture. Why then should they pay any attention when Dr. Karlstadt strikes at them with what he knows are palpable falsehoods?

I am not concerned with the life of the pope and his people. We speak now of his teaching—not of his morals, but of his dogmas. Here I do not say that Dr. Karlstadt errs, but his conscience tells him that he obviously lies in what he says of the pope. For he too has been a sophist[156] who has studied and taught the theology of the universities and of the pope. The pope nowhere teaches that one shall say to the sacramental bread, "My, God, be merciful to me," as all the world knows. Nor does he teach that we should hold in remembrance the bread but forget the body of Christ. Nor does he ever teach so high a regard for the bread that we forget remembrance of the Lord. He does not teach that we can eat the bread worthily even if in so doing we never give a thought to Christ. And he does not render unnecessary the suffering of Christ when he teaches that Christ in the form of the bread forgives our sins and redeems us, which in fact he does not teach. In these five points Dr. Karlstadt himself, as well as all the world, knows that he lies in his own conscience against the pope.

He should use other examples and reasons if he wants to show that the pope is guilty of stealing the honor due God, contradicting the truth, destroying the teaching of St. Paul, making people foolish, and the suffering of Christ unnecessary. For these examples rather prove that Dr. Karlstadt has a deceitful and evil spirit, who openly robs the people of their honor, contradicts his own conscience, and as a foolish rascal reveals his sin and shame before all the world. What a fine spirit we have here, who would drive out the devil by a devil. Indeed he would disgrace public truth with public lies.

What could be the purpose of Dr. Karlstadt in this shameless lying? I can imagine two reasons. First, that he might get the mob to think that what Luther and the others have done to the pope

---

[156] Before joining forces with the Reformation Karlstadt was a Thomist and published two tracts interpreting the scholastic theology of Thomas Aquinas.

amounts to nothing. They all play the hypocrite with him. **Here is our man.** Dr. Karlstadt knows how to do it. He knows how to show up the pope. How about it, neighbor Andreas [Karlstadt] and dear cousin Peter? Second, in lumping Luther and the pope together, he might impress upon his bungling associate, Rültz, that Luther's teaching is identical with that of the pope—indeed that Luther is a papist twice over,[157] for that is what he calls me, too. This Dr. Karlstadt's devil does, not because he is hostile to the pope's devil, who sent him to Dr. Karlstadt so as craftily to help the pope up again, but in order that he might destroy everything that God had accomplished hitherto by the gospel through us and the many souls who had been saved, which was bitter medicine to the devil.

So my readers now understand how bold and wicked this spirit of Dr. Karlstadt is, as he shamelessly and openly lies before the people against his own conscience in such great and important matters, where we should avoid as poison all error and doubt (to say nothing about obvious lies). They know that such a spirit cannot be anything else than an evil, wrathful devil. For it is not necessary to treat these questions, but through Dr. Karlstadt's envious hatred this spirit would take revenge on us and destroy our gospel. For we do not teach that the form of the bread should be adored, feared, or honored to the disregard of the Lord's death. Rather we do honor the body and blood of Christ in the bread, as he himself well knows, and he has furthermore attacked us throughout his book because we do not regard it as only bread or the form of bread. Yet he charges that we honor only bread, and in his folly contradicts himself.

So with more fairness on our side we could say that Dr. Karlstadt robs God of his honor, contradicts the truth, destroys the teaching of St. Paul, and makes the passion of Christ unnecessary, since he denies, in the face of clear and strong texts, that the body and blood of Christ are in the sacrament. He devises interpolations out of his head, which are supported neither by a semblance of truth nor by argument, Scripture and context. Finally he cannot help

---

[157] To the title of his treatise *Auhslegung dieser Worte Christi, Das ist mein Leib,* etc., Karlstadt added the subtitle *Wider die einfältigen und zwiefältigen Papisten.* . . . WA 18, 73. Cf. also p. 186.

himself but spews out good, fat, strong lies, and like a mad person speaks against himself. And thus you have a second good example of the manner in which dear Reason pretends to authority in divine things. We had better wait until later to consider how it can be true that Christ forgives sin in the sacrament since he makes himself quite useless in this regard.

Frau Hulda's third example is her proof that the body of Christ is not in the sacrament because of the words of Christ, "The flesh is of no avail" (John 6 [:63]) and, "It is to your advantage that I go away, for if I do not go away, the Counsellor will not come to you" [John 16:7]. Where, he says, has Christ commanded us to receive his body? This is a question he keeps bringing up in connection with his *touto* as though it were certain that he has won. We again reply as to one who has gone down to defeat in disgrace. Christ commands us to receive his body when he says, "Take, eat, this is my body." Let this be said once and for all as though it were said a thousand times in reply to this question. For the *touto* and capital letter and period have lost the day, as we have already proved.

Is this not a demonstration of consummate skill and a forceful conclusion: The flesh is of no avail, therefore one does not receive the body of Christ in the sacrament? What a perfect fit! Why not try this? Dr. Karlstadt is no longer at Orlamünde, therefore the body of Christ is not in the sacrament. It follows as well in one case as in the other. What difference does it make to the sacrament, either for or against, that the flesh of Christ is of no avail? Of what avail is it, when he sits at the supper table and, according to their dream, refers to himself in *touto*? You spirits, rather let me use your skill! The flesh of Christ is of no avail, therefore he does not sit at the table, and the *touto* cannot refer to him. Is this not as valid a conclusion as yours? Tell me, where is the flesh of Christ of avail? On the cross? In heaven? In the mother's womb? Where then? I suppose I'll soon hear that he cannot be anywhere, since his flesh is of no avail. For if it follows that Christ is not in the sacrament since the flesh of Christ is of no avail, it follows equally well that he is nowhere. For that the spirit must be present if the flesh is to be of avail is as true on the cross or in heaven as in the sacrament. What do you think? These are indeed heavenly prophets, and thus you should attack the sacrament if you wish to overthrow it!

Further, tell me, what is the benefit of your sacrament, your bread and wine? If it is not of any benefit, then there is no sacrament in the Supper and no one receives anything. For where that is which does not avail, there is nothing, as you yourselves say that the body of Christ cannot be there since his flesh is of no avail. What then of the Supper? For surely none will be or become as holy which will be of avail, since the flesh of Christ is of no avail, though it is the most holy of all. If that is not fanaticism and frenzy, brother, what is fanaticism and frenzy? I will not here show how the blind and bold spirit employs and perverts the word of Christ. For Christ does not say, "My flesh is of no avail," but thus, "Flesh is of no avail" [John 6:63]. But of his own flesh he says, "My flesh is food indeed" [John 6:55].

"Flesh" and "the flesh of Christ" are two very different things. So also, "The flesh of Christ is of no avail," is quite different from, "The flesh of Christ is of no avail to you or me." This I must further expound to prove that these spirits, who so despise the outward Word, do not have a right understanding of Scripture. God is good [Luke 18:19], and all that he has created is good also (Gen. 1 [:3]). What is good, is also "of avail." To the godless, however, nothing is good or "of avail," nothing pure and salutary, but everything is harmful, evil, unclean, and damnable, even God himself, not because of God or of what he has created but because of the lack of faith of those who misuse everything. So we should not say that the flesh of Christ is of no avail, but flesh is of no avail, as Paul says, "Flesh and blood cannot inherit the kingdom" [I Cor. 15:50]. Here "flesh" means a carnal mind, will, understanding or self-contrived opinion, as Paul in Rom. 8 [:6] says, "To set the mind on the flesh is death." When Christ (John 6 [:55]) speaks of his flesh and says it is "food indeed," he corrects the Jews who understand him in a carnal manner, by adding that his words are "spirit and life" [John 6:63]. Flesh is of no avail, that is, to understand his spiritual words in a carnal manner brings only death.

Yes, you say, the bread of the Lord and the cup are of benefit, if we worthily eat and drink, which means that we acknowledge and taste Christ, heartily and ardently. Brother, what can we say?

Your bread and wine are of avail, if one eats and tastes of them with ardent knowledge. Why is not our sacrament also of avail when we eat and receive it in true faith? Or is the body and blood of Christ, when it is received with true faith in the sacrament, not as powerful as your frail bread and wine? Or is a true faith inferior to an ardent acknowledgment of Christ? But tell me, you lying spirit, when or where have we ever taught that the sacrament (though in itself always "of avail," salutary, and good) is "of avail" to everyone, unless he receives it in faith through the words of God which are in with it?

In dealing with these matters, Dr. Karlstadt employs nothing but real devilish tricks. First, he uses wonderfully beautiful words (heartily, ardently, taste, knowledge), so that one might think him in earnest. But he saw clearly that bread and wine are too ordinary in themselves, so he had to blow them up with such additions, but without showing either way or means of arriving at them. Secondly, he does not use the word, faith, to make it seem as if he were teaching of other and much higher things than we, and as if true faith was nothing compared to "ardent knowledge," though he knows as much of the acknowledgment of Christ as of faith and a good conscience. Thirdly, he strikes a treacherous blow in seeking to picture us as teaching merely a reception of the sacrament, without Word and faith, though he well knows otherwise, and lies continuously, poisonously, and wantonly. As I have said above, to employ obvious lies in these great matters is not the work of a good spirit, but of a vengeful devil, by which indeed Dr. Karlstadt is possessed.

He comes next upon the word *sacramentaliter* and says, the sacramental flesh of Christ is of no more avail than his natural flesh, for it presents neither death nor resurrection, etc. Here he boasts that with this piece he has boxed the ears of the pope so that his whole face was blackened, together with all papists, old and new. For a nobody you boast pretty loftily. I do not know whether the spirit purposely puts on such irrational and mad demeanor, or whether God plagues him so horribly. Out of his own fancy, without any basis, he makes a bare, naked, impotent, statement that the sacramental body of Christ is of "no avail," etc. By such a word the pope and all of us are supposed to be vanquished. Were it the heathen Priapus[158] he would probably pass wind in the face of such well-aimed terror.

I have already said that it is not right, but blasphemous before God, if one says the body of Christ is of no avail, as this mad spirit raves. He is ever beneficial, wherever he is, however he may seem of no avail because of my unbelief. The sun is always shining, though unseen by the blind man. The Word of God is ever salutary, though a poison and "a fragrance of death to death" [II Cor. 2:16]. The body of Christ is always in the sacrament, even if not to these mad and blind spirits, who have not yet learned so much from their high, heavenly spirit as to know that flesh and the flesh of Christ are not one and the same flesh, but one is a flesh of life, the other a flesh of death. But what difference do life and death mean to such prophets? If only they had the honor of being holy spirits, that would be quite enough.

But he says that one cannot see in the sacrament the death and resurrection of Christ, therefore Christ is of no avail there. Brother, is this true? What high prophets! But tell me, how do you see the death and resurrection in the body of Christ seated at the supper table, to which the *touto* refers? Is it marked on his brow? No? Then even there he does not benefit us. How this spirit makes a fool of himself in all his words. He can say nothing but that it boomerangs on his own head and hits him so that he not only is blackened but is made to stagger as a drunkard. If now the words of Christ lead and teach us to see the death and resurrection in the seated Christ, why should they not do so also in the body and blood of the sacrament? For it is not the body of Christ, either seated at the table or present in the bread, but the word that he speaks, "This is given for you," which teaches us about the death and resurrection of Christ.

But suppose your knowledge and remembrance of Christ were this pure passion, pure heart, pure ardor, pure fire, before which also the sectarian spirits were to melt away and were to blow up their spirituality with words which are a thousand times more high-sounding, what then? What would be gained? Nothing except new monks and hypocrites who would with greater devotion and

---

[158] The reaction ascribed to Priapus by Luther, is described by Horace, *Satires* i., 8, 46, only for a different reason. Cf. WA 18, 194.

earnestness stand before the bread and wine (if everything went well), as hitherto the sensitive consciences have stood before the sacrament. Indeed as great a concern and anxiety would manifest itself about this knowledge and remembrance as hitherto has been felt for the worthy reception of the body of Christ. For the acknowledgment which they advocate accomplishes nothing. Even the devil knows full well and recognizes that the body of Christ is given for us, yet this does not help him.

The knowledge, however, does help if I do not doubt, but in true faith hold firmly that the body and blood of Christ is given for me, for me, for me (I repeat), in order to take away my sins, as the word in the sacrament affirms, "This is the body, given for you." This knowledge produces joyful, free, and assured consciences. This is the meaning in Isa. 53 [:11], "By his knowledge he will make many to be accounted righteous." This teaching is as hostile as death to Dr. Karlstadt's spirit, and in his desire to eradicate it he makes a great ado about "passionate, heartfelt, earnest knowledge of the body of Christ," as if he were much in earnest, yet he really stifles it. He thinks one does not see that out of the word of Christ he makes a pure commandment and law which accomplishes nothing more than to tell and bid us to remember and acknowledge him. Furthermore, he makes this acknowledgment nothing else than a work that we do, while we receive nothing else than bread and wine. But more of this later.

I will, however, show up this spirit. With such high-sounding words he hopes to anticipate the accusation and outcry that he despoils the sacrament by making it merely bread and wine. Therefore he vaunts himself and spruces up these great words, so that one might suppose he wanted to exalt the sacrament. But basically it is the devil's intention to dash it to the ground and institute instead a festive meal, where finally it ends up in excessive eating and drinking and throwing of jugs and cans against the walls, brawling, and fighting. For if hitherto it has not been possible to maintain reverence when it has been believed that the true body of Christ was present, what kind of reverence will remain if it is thought that only bread and wine are present? What jolly companions we then would be, revelling and carousing until the heath begins to wave.

So you can clearly see how the devil makes a commandment out of a promise of Christ and in place of faith institutes a human work, as I have said of him above. For all that Dr. Karlstadt spews out in this matter about the knowledge of the body of Christ derives from referring his *touto* to the seated body of Christ, all from his own fancy, as we have heard. For with this *touto* he means that we are asked only to practice the knowledge of Christ in this sacrament, though Christ in this place says not a word about such knowledge, commandment, or work. Nor can he show any basis, Scripture, or reason except his hopeless *touto* and his own notions, which let him believe who believes the devil. He makes also this knowledge a pure work, destroying thereby both faith and the promise of Christ.

From this you can grasp that Dr. Karlstadt's theology has not gotten beyond teaching how we are to imitate Christ, making of Christ only an example and lawgiver. From this only works can be learned. He does not know and teach Christ as our treasure and the gift of God, from which faith follows, and which is the highest of doctrines. All this he wants to dress up and obscure with these words: passionate knowledge, ardent remembrance, and the like. He descends from faith to works in a manner that I long ago observed would lead his teaching and skill to a point where he would affirm that the free will plays a part in the things of God and in good works.

Further, the mad spirit is so ignorant of Scripture that he interprets the word, "remembrance," where Christ says, "This do in remembrance of me," only in the manner of the sophists [scholastic teachers] to mean, the inner thoughts of the heart, as one would think of any one. For this spirit must be inward, and make inward and spiritual what God wants to be outward, so that nothing will be external. But it is still more mischievous and malicious, that he gives such remembrance the power to justify, as faith does. The proof he gives is, he says, that it is written, "That they have done this in remembrance of me." What think you? It is written, "They have done it in remembrance of me." Therefore such remembrance justifies. There you comprehend how well Dr. Karlstadt understands the Lord's Supper, his remembrance, and justification, namely, that the devil shows only ridicule and scorn in these matters.

207

You should, however, know and hold that this remembrance of Christ is an outward remembrance, as one can speak of remembering any one. This is the way the Scriptures speak of it, for example, in Psalm 15 [Ps. 16:4]: "I will not take their names upon my lips"; Psalm 10 [Ps. 9:6]: "The very memory of them is perished"; Psalm 72 [Ps. 83:4] "Let the name of Israel be remembered no more"; Psalm 111 [Ps. 112:1]: "The righteous will be remembered for ever." By the words, "This do in remembrance of me," Christ meant what Paul meant by his words, "Proclaim the death of the Lord," etc. [I Cor. 11:26]. Christ wants us to make him known when we receive the sacrament and proclaim the gospel, so as to confirm faith. He does not want us to sit and indulge in such fancies and make out of such a remembrance a good work, as Dr. Karlstadt dreams. Would that these prophets had put in more time in study before they published books.

From this you know well that such remembrance does not justify, but that they must first be justified who would preach, proclaim, and practice the outward remembrance of Christ, as it is written in Rom. 10 [:10], "For man believes with his heart and so is justified, and he confesses with his lips and so is saved." The righteousness which Dr. Karlstadt produces out of remembrance, however, avails nothing and you should beware of it. He lies to you and deceives you. For he does not make such knowledge spiritual as it ought to be. For Isaiah [Isa. 53:11] speaks of a spirit and of a spiritual knowledge which the Holy Spirit works in us, not we ourselves. I know and am convinced beyond doubt that this is the same as, Christ is given for me. But Dr. Karlstadt makes of it a human, carnal devotion and a passionate, ardent work in the heart, though not higher than the knowledge and recognition that Christ is given for us, which the devil and the hypocrites also know. He can teach knowledge, but not the use of knowledge. He spews out much about knowledge, but does not develop or rightly apply it, but permits it to remain a mere human work. That is to make it a carnal instead of a spiritual knowledge. For his spirit will not tolerate anything less than making carnal what is spiritual.

Frau Hulda gives us a fourth example when she takes St. Paul's words in I Cor. 11 [:24], "Take, eat, this is the body which is broken for you," and seeks to master these. God help, how the spirit pales and trembles before this thunder! Still he summons courage and says, "O you poor, ignorant man, do you mean that the body of Christ was broken as bread is broken," etc.? But hear, brother, how he here chokes and writhes in pain. Tell me (he says), has Christ broken himself in the bread? If he was not in the bread that he broke you will not be able to convince any apostle that Christ broke his body in the bread. He will finally make the claim that no bone of Christ was to be broken, therefore this breaking must be understood as his suffering, thus, "This is the body which is broken for you," equals, "Which is crucified for you." See, brother, how the spirit here walks on eggs, how he twists and turns, how he talks as if he had mush in his mouth and mumbles like a half-dead, despairing person.

No, dear little spirit, you do not thus escape me. I should have treated of this phrase above with the others, but could not because of the sloppy and confused arrangement of this book. In the first place it does not help that he understands "broken" as referring to suffering and crucifixion, for Scripture does not so speak and he cannot prove otherwise. So his interpolation and peculiar fancy mean nothing. We do find that Scripture calls the troubled soul "a broken heart and spirit" [Ps. 51:17], but not with reference to bodily suffering. Even if it did so, we can thereby not be sure that such is the meaning here, unless better evidence can be produced. Nor is it germane to the argument here that no bone of Christ is to be broken. For none of us is mad enough to say that Christ was broken in the sacrament visibly as a thief might be broken on a rack. Our proof is that Christ and the apostles have broken the body of Christ, according to the word, "This is my body, which is broken for you," and that in the breaking he was in it, unless Paul lies.

Let us take the rogue by the throat. We have already thoroughly and convincingly proved that Dr. Karlstadt's *touto* must refer to the bread, when Christ says, "Take, eat, *touto* or this is my body, which is given for you." When St. Paul also uses *touto* and says, "This is the body which is broken for you," it too must refer to the bread. So the text requires that this bread be the body which is broken. Consequently this breaking must necessarily remain in the supper and in the eating at the table, and cannot mean anything else, as I have said above, than that the body is distributed in the congregation, as one breaks bread and distributes it in the congregation. It is not necessary here to indulge in fantasy as to just how the body of Christ is broken in the bread. It is enough that it is broken, that is, distributed in all its parts and pieces completely.

So it is established that the body of Christ and the bread are one, and that where the bread is broken it means that the body of Christ is broken or distributed, so that it is divided between and received by many. For had St. Paul not wanted to say that the body of Christ was in the bread—he would not have attributed to the body of Christ the breaking (which in the usage and meaning of Scripture applied especially to the bread). Now, however, no one can disregard the fact that he joins the two together, and thus refers to the bread and calls it the broken body of Christ, so that in one breaking both bread and the body are broken, and we must confess that the body of Christ is there in the bread. Just as the bread does not lose its character or name because it is broken, but remains bread and is called so, though in pieces, so also the body of Christ remains such though divided in many places among many people.

Still another point remains. St. Paul says of the bread, "This is the body which is given for you." Brother, how can it be for us? "Broken among us" would have been better. What nimble feet this spirit has, to jump so easily over this word "for us." Brother, why? This is the reason: He has undertaken to deny that the forgiveness of sins is in the sacrament. Such an undertaking is filthy, where the word "broken for us" still stands. It cannot mean otherwise than that such breaking of bread and body takes place and is instituted that it might avail us and redeem us from sins. For Christ has placed the strength and power of his suffering in the sacrament, so that we may there lay hold on it and find it according to the word, "This is my body, which is given for you for the forgiveness of sins," as we shall hear now, right soon. Therefore, this word was to remain untouched by this spirit.

Frau Hulda's fifth attempt is directed especially toward the Luther[159] who has taught that when a person has a conscience

---

[159] Actually, the attack was directed against the Roman rite. Because Luther held that the forgiveness of sins is imparted in the sacrament, he could conclude that the attack was also directed against him.

troubled by sin he should go to the sacrament and there obtain comfort and the forgiveness of sins. Here Peter Rültz is first of all a fine fellow and speaks boldly: "O you false prophets, you promise the kingdom of God to the people for a piece of bread. I know that you do not improve the bread by your secret breathing and whispering, why then do you say that sins can be forgiven when you have blown upon it? Why do you not just as well take a handful of barley, etc., and eat it in God's name, so that you may be free from your sins?" Here I must speak with Dr. Karlstadt himself.

My dear Dr. Karlstadt, if you could not or would not attack this point in any other way, why did you not stay at home? You have your hands full, even if there were a thousand of you, if you would win me over by Scripture and argument. Then you sally forth and attack me only with insulting words and with obvious and shameless lies. Do you mean that I am afraid of lies when you yourself know that you lie? In worldly affairs when someone dishonors another with lies, and both know that these are lies, will not, brother, the one say to him who lies, you lie as an arch rascal and disgraceful scoundrel? What shall we then say of one who shamelessly lies against his conscience in divine things? All right, who still does not believe these prophets to be full of the devil, let him listen. I will show them up with their shameless lies.

Tell me, first, spirit of lies, when have we ever taught that a piece of bread forgives sins? Ah, Peter Rültz and Victus Knebel,[160] prove it by one single syllable or punctuation mark, since it is your custom to prove your points in this way. Since you know that we do not teach so, what kind of a spirit is it that makes you lie so scandalously? If it were because you forgot or did not know, I could regard you as human. But since you lie so maliciously, knowingly, and poisonously, no one can see in you anything else than the evil spirit. But it is the nature of these prophets to speak thus scornfully and insultingly in divine matters in order to excite the mad mob which gets the idea through such words that here is the real victory and triumph, though they hear no real sense.

Secondly, tell me when we whisper or breathe upon the bread?

---

[160] The name of another fictitious character in Karlstadt's *Dialogus*. Cf. also p. 155.

Ah, now, show me! And where have we ever taught that our whispering and breathing have improved the bread? Ah, now, why don't you answer? All right, I will take an oath. If Dr. Karlstadt believes there is any God in heaven or on earth, may Christ my Lord never more be merciful and gracious to me. I know that is a serious oath. My reason for it is that Dr. Karlstadt knows that we do not breathe or whisper over the bread, but do speak the divine, almighty, heavenly, and holy words which Christ himself spoke at the supper with his holy lips and commanded us to speak. I shall remain silent concerning the evil and sinful papists. I affirm this, that if an ass, as Balaam's ass [Num. 22:28], spoke these words, or if even a devil spoke them, still they are the words of God and are to be held in all honor, as is fitting.

Tell me, if some one certainly knows that it is a Word of God and yet dares consciously to noise abroad with disdain and ridicule that it is a human whispering and breathing, thus perverting the poor mob by such lies and poison, and does this without any fear or trembling and shows no contrition for it, but rather feels joy and glee in such wickedness, as if God would give him a crown for such blasphemy and perversion of souls and dub him a knight of grace, how can such a one believe or think that there can be any God? He cannot be possessed by one devil. Let it be. Dr. Karlstadt will discover this, if he has not already done so. If God rewards him I too will say that there is no God. But in friendliness I warn Dr. Karlstadt to do penance. God has been tempted enough. It has lasted long enough. It will and must soon become otherwise. Would to God that in this respect I may be a liar and false prophet. Alas, dear Lord, what can we do if Thou dost forsake us?

Miserable spirit, why don't you lay hold of the right thing? Why don't you correct our teaching? You impute a strange teaching to us, which you impose on us deceitfully since it is not ours. What is easier than to imagine a lie and attribute it to someone, and then to fight about it and become a knight? Our teaching is that bread and wine do not avail. I will go still farther. Christ on the cross and all his suffering and his death do not avail, even if, as you teach, they are "acknowledged and meditated upon" with the utmost "passion, ardor, heartfeltness." Something else must always be there. What is it? The Word, the Word, the Word.

Listen, lying spirit, the Word avails. Even if Christ were given for us and crucified a thousand times, it would all be in vain if the Word of God were absent and were not distributed and given to me with the bidding, this is for you, take what is yours.

Even if I followed the Karlstadtian teaching and preached the remembrance and knowledge of Christ with such passion and seriousness that I sweated blood and became feverish, it would be of no avail and all in vain. For it would be pure work and commandment, but no gift or Word of God offered and given to me in the body and blood of Christ. It would be as if I had a chest full of gold and great treasure buried or preserved in a certain place. I might think myself to death and experience all desire, great passion, and ardor in such knowledge and remembrance of the treasure until I became ill. But what benefit would all this be to me if this treasure were not opened, given, and brought to me and placed in my keeping? It would mean truly to love, but not to enjoy. It would mean to be satisfied with the scent and to become drunk from the sight of the glass, as Isaiah [Isa. 29:8] says: One dreams that he eats and drinks, but when he awakes, his soul is faint, etc.

The entire teaching of Dr. Karlstadt is a fantasy of this kind. For by his high-sounding words, "passionate remembrance, ardent knowledge, experiential taste of the suffering of Christ," he mocks us and does not bring us any farther than showing the health-giving treasure in a glass or vessel. We may look and smell until we are satisfied, but as in a dream. He gives nothing, opens nothing, lets us have nothing. Indeed by such high-sounding words he seeks to obscure the word that gives us such a treasure, namely, "Take, eat, this is the body given for you." To him the words, "for you," are poison and bitter death. But they are our comfort and life. For they open the treasure to us and allow us to appropriate it.

So that our readers may the better perceive our teaching I shall clearly and broadly describe it. We treat of the forgiveness of sins in two ways. First, how it is achieved and won. Second, how it is distributed and given to us. Christ has achieved it on the cross, it is true. But he has not distributed or given it on the cross. He has not won it in the supper or sacrament. There he has distributed and given it through the Word, as also in the gospel, where it is preached. He has won it once for all on the cross. But the distribution takes place continuously, before and after, from the beginning to the end of the world. For inasmuch as he had determined once to achieve it, it made no difference to him whether he distributed it before or after, through his Word, as can easily be proved from Scripture. But now there is neither need nor time to do so.

If now I seek the forgiveness of sins, I do not run to the cross, for I will not find it given there. Nor must I hold to the suffering of Christ, as Dr. Karlstadt trifles, in knowledge or remembrance, for I will not find it there either. But I will find in the sacrament or gospel the word which distributes, presents, offers, and gives to me that forgiveness which was won on the cross. Therefore, Luther has rightly taught that whoever has a bad conscience from his sins should go to the sacrament and obtain comfort, not because of the bread and wine, not because of the body and blood of Christ, but because of the word which in the sacrament offers, presents, and gives the body and blood of Christ, given and shed for me. Is that not clear enough?

Yet this mad spirit has attacked us and said, O you false prophets, you have no word in the sacrament which presents or gives you the forgiveness of sins. I repeat, he should have attacked the word in the sacrament on which we stand, defiantly and persistently, and should have proved that we do not have it there. Then he would have been a valiant knight. Even if only bread and wine were there present, as they claim, as long as the word, "Take, eat, this is my body given for you," etc., is there, the forgiveness of sins, on account of this word, would be in the sacrament. Just as in the case of baptism we confess that only water is present, but since the Word of God, which forgives sin, is connected with it, we readily say with St. Paul, that baptism is a bath of regeneration and renewal. Everything depends on the Word.

There you have, my reader, Dr. Karlstadt's devil and can see how he has proposed to destroy the external Word of God, which also he does not regard or consider or designate as anything more than a whisper, breath, or blowing. Also, you can see how he has wanted to abolish the sacrament altogether, both bodily and spiritually, denying the bodily presence of the body and blood of

Christ and the spiritual presence of the forgiveness of sins, so that neither the sacrament nor its fruits remain. And in place of a divine ordinance and word he has wanted to institute his own fancied remembrance and knowledge. But he lacked the necessary skill. Now you know how to judge him.

I must add that at the very end of his book he spews out great wisdom and cleverness. He says, the mortal body of Christ was at the supper, but now he is immortal and cannot be given for us, according to the words, "This is the body which is given for you." So now he neither is nor can be given for us, and the words are now in the past and must be false, since we now speak of the immortal body. So it must also be false to say that the mortal body is in the bread and wine, as we hold such suppers even after the death of Christ. Now he is immortal and is not given in the sense Christ held when he was mortal. How say you? How Frau Hulda seeks for loopholes and escape!

To this we answer. First, the blood of Christ does not become the blood of Gabriel or Michael when it becomes immortal, but remains the blood of the same Christ. For we believe and hold that the blood of Christ now at the right hand of God in heaven was shed for us once only. If we consider the act by which the forgiveness of sins was achieved, we know that it did not take place at the supper. But now it has taken place and is accomplished. When we consider the application of the forgiveness, we are not dealing with a particular time, but find that it has taken place from the beginning of the world. So St. John in the Book of Revelation [13:8] says that the Lamb of God was slain before the foundation of the world.

Since now all they who are forgiven still have sins, the body and blood of Christ are necessary for them. Thus it is still true that he is given for them. For while the act has taken place, as long as I have not appropriated it, it is as if it had not taken place for me. Frau Hulda gets nowhere with her sharp sophistry, for she does not see that the question concerns completely the application of what Christ has won for the sake of the distribution and has placed in the distribution. As we have mentioned above, St. Paul therefore says, "The body of Christ was broken for us" [I Cor. 11:24]. It neither hinders nor helps the forgiveness to speak of mortal or immortal, or of what has happened or will happen. It is sufficient that the blood be one and the same. When it is given for and to me, it is shed for me. That which is shed for me, does and must take place daily.

This is the best and finest illustration of Frau Hulda's ability in these matters, showing us how she acts and speaks as a bride of the devil, expressing what he inspires. Dr. Karlstadt further juggles and says that Christ does not descend from heaven, since Paul says, "We are to proclaim his death until he comes" I Cor 11 [:26]. Again he ridicules the Word of God asking if Christ must leap up on account of the stinking breath of a drunken priest, and if we can call or conjure him down from heaven? Also he objects that Christ would have to leave the place where he sat in order to creep into the bread, and would have to leave heaven, were he to come into the bread, etc. All blasphemous words of this kind are nothing but childish, mad, sacrilegious ideas, and lies which are not worthy of answer.

For we do not say that he comes from heaven or leaves his place vacant. Otherwise this spirit would have to say that the Son of God, when he became man in the womb of his mother, also had to leave heaven. All the ridicule that Karlstadt heaps on the sacrament, he has to direct also to the deity of Christ in the flesh, as he also surely will do in time. When St. Stephen saw Jesus, Acts 8 [7:55], he did not say that he came down from heaven, but he saw him standing at the right hand of God. When Paul, in Acts 9 [:4], heard him speak, Christ did not come down from heaven. In short, the mad spirit thinks in childish terms, as if Christ went up and down. He does not understand the realm of Christ which is in every place, and as Paul says, fills all in all (Eph. 1 [:23]). We are not bidden to search out how it can be that our bread becomes and is the body of Christ. It is the Word of God that says so. We hold to that and believe it. Chew on it, you poor devil, and search for as long a time as you need to discover how it occurs.

He also ridicules us, claiming that we say and teach that the cup is in the blood, and jests that we see no blood there. Always he turns his ears away from the Word of God and sees with single vision the bread and wine. For this spirit will not believe what the Word of God says, but only what he sees and feels. What a fine faith. Our answer to this wicked devil is this: This word in Luke 22 [:20], "This cup is the new testament in my blood," does not and cannot mean that the word, "in my blood," should belong to the word "this cup," as this spirit in his great and pure malice pretends, but to the word "a new testament," as also these words naturally follow each other in text and meaning. This is to say, "This cup is a new testament, not in itself, for it is perhaps glass or silver, but because my blood is therein, it is a new testament because of this blood." For whoever so receives the cup as to receive the blood of Christ which is shed for us, he receives the new testament, that is, the forgiveness of sins and eternal life.

But I will tell you why Dr. Karlstadt must blaspheme, juggle, and ridicule at this point. The text is too clear and too powerful and he is at a loss to know what to say. For this word more forcibly and powerfully than any before requires that the blood is in the sacrament. So he hopes to fill the ears of the mob with other pranks, so as to divert attention from these words of Luke. I think I find evidence here that it is against his own conscience that Dr. Karlstadt denies that the blood and body of Christ is in the sacrament, and that in his heart he is hostile to God and wants to blaspheme and dishonor him, to the injury and vexation of his Word and sacrament. I believe, I say once more, that Dr. Karlstadt has surrendered himself and dared to become an avowed enemy of God, wanting to race rather than trot to hell. God grant that I be mistaken and lie.

For this word of Luke and Paul is clearer than sunlight and more overpowering than thunder. First, no one can deny that he speaks of the cup, since he says, "This is the cup." Secondly, he calls it the cup of the new testament. This is overwhelming, for it could not be a new testament by means and on account of wine alone. For what else is the new testament than forgiveness of sins and eternal life won for us by Christ and allotted to us in the sacrament? If now the cup is to be a new testament, there must be something in and connected with it as effectual as the new testament. Is it not the blood of Christ, as he says, "in my blood"? If not, tell us what it is. So we can well say to these spirits, O you false prophets who give and promise the new testament to the people for and in a drink of wine. Then the text should read, this is the cup of the new testament in wine. But now the words read: This is the cup of the New Testament in my blood. Thereby Dr. Karlstadt's skill, writings, books, both those he has written and can yet still write, are thrust to the ground and so overwhelmed that he can in no way resist. Were he able he would be still more malicious.

There our text stands. However you bite, chew, ridicule, confidently blaspheme, or wickedly act, dear heavenly prophets, the cup you must let remain as the new testament, even though there be no *touto* here referring to it. And even if all *toutos* were on your side, you still would have to admit that it is the new testament not because of or in its nature but through and in the blood of Christ. The blood, the blood of Christ makes this cup to be a new testament. It cannot be understood as the blood of the Christ who sits there, for the cup cannot be the new testament on account of a blood that is not in it, or does not touch or concern it. Cup and blood must here be one, as we have said above, so that whoever has or takes the cup also has and takes the blood. Whither now, dear factious spirits? I will let you write and shriek for a thousand years and need not oppose you with more than one word, "This is the cup of the new testament." O how the words, "new testament," smash the prophets and spirits into one lump in the gutter.

I have also heard said (for I have not seen or read all these poisonous books) how they seek help from what Christ, in Matt. 16 [:18] says to Peter, "You are Peter and on this rock I will build my church." Here they say is a parallel. Christ begins to speak of Peter, whom he calls a rock, and then immediately turns the thoughts to another rock and says, "On this rock I will build my church." So also here, when he says, "Take, eat, this is my body," and then turns from speaking about bread to speaking about his seated body. See, what a perfect match. Clutch at any straw. One lie must be accompanied by seven other lies in order to make it look like and seem to be the truth.

To this we reply. Even if it seemed that Christ spoke in the manner of Matthew 16, that it must be so here would still not be enough for us to base an article of faith and establish conscience on it. It would have to be proved by clear text that it is and must be so read in this place. It means nothing if these spirits say that Christ in Matt. 16 [:18] turns the meaning from one rock to another, therefore here also the thought turns from bread to the body. Who will guarantee and assure us that it must be so here? You of course say so, but how can one believe you when you have no proof? You have to prove the parallel with Scripture and not simply assert it of yourself. For faith (as I have often said), does not want some one simply to say or sing thus, but wants a word of God that plainly says: So it is and not otherwise. For faith wants to be no reed that the wind shakes [Matt. 11:7].

Furthermore, it is not true that Matthew 16 reads similarly. For the word "and" stands between the two and the word "rock" is repeated, thus, "You are Peter, and on this rock," etc. So the phrase, "You are Peter," is one complete sentence, and then a new thought begins, namely, "On this rock," etc. Such an "and" and a repetition of the word, "body," do not occur in the Supper, but the words follow immediately. "Take, eat, this is my body." If Matthew 16 had read thus, "You are Peter or rock, on it or on which I will build my church," then it would be similar in structure. Or if in the account of the Supper, we were to read, "Take, eat the body and this is my body," it would be like Matthew 16.

Now, however, there is an "and" in Matthew 16 and in our passage no "and" is inserted, and Christ repeats the word, "rock," in Matthew 16 and says, "On this rock," but in the supper does not repeat the word, "body." This shows that he used the word, "rock," about himself or the word which Peter spoke, and the word, "body," about the bread. So these two sentences are as alike as water and fire. Also the Evangelist in Matthew 16 carefully distinguished and pointed out the second part as a new phrase concerning the rock. For he refers to Peter as der [masculine] but to the second rock as die [feminine] to make clear that Peter, der, was not the other rock, which he makes die, on which Christ would build his church. He puts der and die in two distinct parts, while in the account of the supper he uses the pronoun das for both the bread and the body in one sentence when he says, "This [das] is my body."

Finally in order not to speak entirely without scriptural basis, he does (God be praised) produce one verse, probably in parting. It is from Matt. 24 [:23]: "If any one says to you, 'Lo, here is the Christ,' or 'There he is!' do not believe it." When we say Christ is in the bread it is supposed to be the same as saying, here and there Christ is, therefore it is not truly so. Here, here, they think they've hit upon something. All right, I will sing "Eli" to the prophets [161] and proclaim a recess. So blind does hate make these spirits, that they do not look around to see what comes before or after these words, but fall for what seems to be the meaning on first sight. So again we have to make it clear to them.

There is quite a difference between speaking of Christ and of the body and blood of Christ. For when the Evangelist says, "Here or there Christ is," and the like, he speaks of the whole Christ, that is, of the kingdom of Christ. This is the meaning which the text in Luke 17 [:20] strongly requires, when it says, "The kingdom of God is not coming with signs to be observed; nor will they say, 'Lo here it is!' or 'There!'" This the other Evangelists express thus: Christ is here or there. All of this means that the kingdom of God does not consist in external things, places, times, persons, works, but as he himself says, "The kingdom of God is within you." From this it follows not that Christ is nowhere, but that he is everywhere and fills all things (Ephes. 1 [:23]). He is bound to no particular place, so that he must be there and nowhere else, as they make out who do not let our consciences be free but bind them to a particular place, work, or person.

Now, as Christ himself and his kingdom are not bound to any one place or external thing, so all that belongs to his kingdom is free and bound to nothing—the gospel, baptism, the sacrament, and Christians. For the gospel is and must be free in regard to all places and is bound to no particular spot. For it is not at Rome alone or here or there to the exclusion of some other place. So also baptism and the sacrament. For it is not necessary that in the churches alone and nowhere else there be preaching, baptism, and the sacrament. They can be in any place where there is need. It does not follow now that Christ in the sacrament is as if bound to one place, here or there. He and his sacrament are or may be free to be in any place. Consequently, these prophets wrongly apply words about the kingdom of Christ to the sacrament.

Were what they say true, then one would also have to deny that gospel, baptism, and sacrament are nowhere. For Christ is

---

[161] A reference to an expression of Karlstadt wherein he compares Luther's despair to Christ's word on the Cross.

present in the gospel and yet must be, orally and bodily, in places and localities. And Christ could not be in heaven at the right hand of the Father, since here too we might say, "See, there Christ is." And of St. Stephen, when he saw Christ stand (Acts 8 [7:56]), we might say, "Thou liest, for Christ is neither here nor there," if the carnal thoughts of these prophets were worth anything. Indeed their own teaching about the knowledge and remembrance of Christ could not stand, for these imply that he is at one place.

This phrase, "here nor there" must be understood, first of all as referring to bodily, external places and things, and second, as referring to such bodily places as are particularly prescribed by false prophets for others as necessary for salvation, instead of permitting freedom in regard to such things, as we have discussed in regard to the papacy. We teach not that the body and blood of Christ are visibly present in external things, but that they are hidden in the sacrament. Nor do we say that he is and must be in particular places and is not free to be in all. Rather we claim that he and the bread and wine are and must be free in regard to all localities, places, times, and persons.

The reason for saying, "This is my body," and not, "This is Christ," is that we might not regard the whole Christ, that is, his kingdom, as in the sacrament, but see in it clearly and particularly the true and real body, as a part of his kingdom and of the whole Christ. In the same manner we do not call the gospel Christ or the kingdom of Christ, but speak of it as an oral, bodily preaching, regarding it as a part of the whole Christ or his kingdom. It has the character of the whole Christ in that it is not necessarily bound to any particular locality but is free as to all places. Therefore when we speak of Christ, it is of the whole, but when we speak of the body, it is as of a part of the whole.

Herewith I will be content for this time. To Dr. Karlstadt's contention as to our authority to bring the body and blood of Christ into the sacrament we have given sufficient proof, and he will have to let us keep our belief that the bread that "we" break is the body of Christ. This "we" has truly its authority from the words of Christ himself at his supper. What he imagines concerning the righteousness of mortification, and its coming before the inner righteousness of the spirit, is his own fancy and is without any foundation. For above you have heard of the right order: At the beginning and first of all is the faith in the heart, the righteousness of the spirit, then follows the mortification and death of the old nature (Rom. 8 [:13]), "For if by the Spirit you put to death the deeds of the body you will live." By the Spirit, he says, which thus must be there.

This is my answer to all the books of Dr. Karlstadt on the sacrament which he has written and contrived over the past three years. I have answered him in three weeks, and will give him another three years, and three more, or six in all, to make a decent reply to me. I warn them once more to see to it that they meet the issue, for they need it. For my part I courteously give them thanks from my whole heart and ask for none in return, because they have so greatly confirmed me in regard to this article of faith. For now I see that it is not possible to produce anything in opposition to this article. I have gone to such lengths and written so much in order to show clearly how obscurely and disorderly Dr. Karlstadt writes. I hope that from this book Dr. Karlstadt first of all may better understand himself. For I do not doubt that up to now he has not himself understood what he has been doing or whither his teaching may lead. He cannot rightly grasp or understand anything, much less develop his ideas or write.

In closing, I want to warn everyone truly and fraternally to beware of Dr. Karlstadt and his prophets, for two reasons. First, because they run about and teach, without a call. This God condemns through Jeremiah [23:21], who says, "I did not send them, yet they ran. I did not speak to them, yet they prophesied." For this reason they are judged by Christ (John 10 [:1]), as thieves and murderers who do not enter by the door, but climb in by another way. They boast of possessing the Spirit, more than the apostles, and yet for more than three years now have secretly prowled about and flung around their dung. Were he a true spirit he would at once have come forward and given proof of his call by signs and words. But he is a treacherous, secret devil who sneaks around in corners until he has done his damage and spread his poison.

The second reason is that these prophets avoid, run away from, and are silent about the main points of Christian doctrine. For in no place do they teach how we are to become free from our sins, obtain a good conscience, and win a peaceful and joyful heart before God. This is what really counts. This is a true sign that their spirit is of the devil, who can use unusual new words to excite, terrify, and mislead consciences. But their spirit cannot give quietness or peace, but goes on and teaches special works in which they are to exercise and discipline themselves. They have no idea how a good conscience can be gained or ought to be constituted. For they have not felt or ever recognized it. How can they know or feel it, when they come and teach of themselves, without a call. No good can come in this way.

The grace of God be with us all. Amen.

CONCERNING REBAPTISM

1528

Translated by Conrad Bergendoff

INTRODUCTION

Early in the Reformation period the teachings of the Anabaptists came into conflict both with the Reformers and the defenders of the old order. Switzerland was the center, but the ardent advocates of the rebaptism of believers spread over many lands. Luther had some contact with them in the appearance of the "Zwickau prophets" early in his career, but it was after the Peasants' War that both the activity of the Anabaptists and attempted suppression of them increased. The secular authorities were aroused on the charge that the Anabaptists really were insurrectionists who threatened all government. Burning and drowning were the usual forms by which the heretics were executed. In March 1528 one of their noblest leaders, Dr. Balthasar Hubmaier, was burned in Vienna, and his wife drowned.

Luther was averse to this kind of punishment, but could not change the attitude of those who feared the heretical teachings. He observed that the movement was spreading, and in December 1527 and January 1528 wrote a treatise on the subject in reply to an inquiry of two pastors. They were apparently in a Roman Catholic diocese but had turned to Luther for counsel on how to deal with the heresy.

Luther gives the impression that he does not know sufficiently what the teachings of the Anabaptists were. Yet he had been receiving information from his followers in many places, and Melanchthon had let him see a tract he had prepared against them. The above mentioned Hubmaier had written a book in defense of the Anabaptist doctrine in 1525. There is no evidence that Luther had read it though he knew that Hubmaier had claimed him as a friend. Luther disavows this, and goes on to give the two pastors advice as to counteracting the heresy. He challenges the Anabaptists to produce a reasoned account of their system, lacking this, he can only write more generally, hoping in the future to treat of it in more detail.

There is no later or more elaborate treatise on the subject by

Luther. But the controversy seems to have stimulated him to deeper study of the significance of baptism, and the result is a number of thorough interpretations in sermons and other writings of the scriptural meaning of child baptism.

The translation follows the text of *WA* 26, 144-174.

CONCERNING REBAPTISM

A Letter of Martin Luther to Two Pastors

Martin Luther, to the worthy and beloved pastors N. and N., my dear friends in Christ.

Grace and peace in Christ our Lord. Unfortunately, I know full well, dear sirs, that Balthasar Hubmaier[1] has included my name among others in his blasphemous booklet on rebaptism, as if I shared his perverted views. But I have comforted myself with the thought that no one, either friend or foe, would believe such a transparent lie as his. Not only is my conscience at rest in this, but my reputation is sufficiently safeguarded by the number of my sermons and especially by the latest Postil [containing sermons for the Sundays] from Epiphany to Easter, wherein I have made known abundantly my faith concerning infant baptism.[2] Therefore I have deemed it unnecessary to answer his kind of book. For who can stop the mouths of all people, even of all devils? I have long ago found that if I stop one mouth of the devil, he opens ten others, and the lie grows constantly greater. So, whether I wish it or not, I commit my cause to God, and if I have told the truth I depend on him as a true judge, who knows how to bring things to a right end. This he does daily as we may well discern.

---

[1] Balthasar Hubmaier studied theology at the University at Freiburg and became a professor in the theological faculty at Ingolstadt in 1512. In 1519, while serving as cathedral preacher at Regensburg, he declared himself in favor of the Reformation. Subsequently, he associated with rebellious peasants at Waldshut and embraced the cause of the Anabaptists. In thus denying the validity of infant baptism, Hubmaier became a heretic in Catholic and Protestant territories. After fleeing from Waldshut in Austria to Zurich in Switzerland and thence to Moravia, he was burned at the stake in Vienna in 1528.

[2] Cf. *EA*' 11, 52ff. The name, Postil, is derived from the Latin words, *Post illa verba textus* (after those words of the text), which were spoken after the reading of the text and prior to its interpretation in the sermon. In medieval times a collection of sermons was called a Postil (*postilla*). In his preface to the *Large Catechism*, Luther cites the titles of some of these volumes of sermons. Cf. WA 30^I, 125.

So far we have escaped such rabble preachers in the territory of our prince, God be thanked and praised in eternity. We also have none of the foes of the sacrament, but are at peace and in harmony in doctrine, faith, and life. May it be God's will graciously to keep us thus. Amen. Since there has not been much occasion here for it, I have not, for my part, given much thought to these baptizers. But it serves you right as papists (I must call you such, as long as you are under your tyrants). You will not suffer the gospel, so you will have to endure these devil's rebels, as Christ says in John 5 [:43]: "I have come in my Father's name, and you do not receive me; if another comes in his own name, him you (i.e., the ones who are among you) will receive." Still, it is not right, and I truly grieve, that these miserable folk should be so lamentably murdered, burned, and tormented to death. We should allow everyone to believe what he wills. If his faith be false, he will be sufficiently punished in eternal hell-fire. Why then should we martyr these people also in this world, if their error be in faith alone and they are not guilty of rebellion or opposition to the government? Dear God, how quickly a person can become confused and fall into the trap of the devil! By the Scriptures and the Word of God, we ought to guard against and withstand him. By fire we accomplish little.

I am not sure as to the ground and reason of their faith, since you do not tell me, and yet ask advice as to what to do in such cases. My answer cannot be very definite. In a sense you are yourselves Anabaptists. For many among you rebaptize in Latin when someone has been baptized in German, though your pope neither does nor teaches thus. For we know well enough that the pope recognizes it as a baptism when midwives administer emergency baptism, even though it be in German. Still you rebaptize persons whom we have baptized in German, as if our German baptism by pastors were not as valid as German baptism by midwives. So the bonehead of Leipzig[3] recently did at Mühlhausen.

---

[3] A professor at Leipzig, Hieronymous Dungersheim, denied this accusation of Luther and wrote both a letter and a booklet to defend himself. The letter is in Enders, *Briefwechsel* 6:251ff., the treatise in *EA* (2d ed.; 28 vols.; 1862-1885), 26:322ff. Luther had carried on correspondence with Dungersheim in 1519 regarding the power of the papacy. St. *L* 18, 426ff.

But the pope has never commanded that baptism should be only in Latin and not in another language. So you have your reward. You favor rebaptism, so you get plenty of Anabaptists, though you will not tolerate them, and yet you want to be rebaptizers in opposition to your own teacher and master, the pope.

But I pass by now what wrong your people do in their rebaptizing. Your shame is the greater since by your rebaptizing you at the same time contradict your idol, the pope. Teacher and pupil do not agree with each other. I will not speak further of this, but rather help you by appearing to be a papist again and flattering the pope. For my dear enthusiasts will put no other interpretation on it (as they already have done) than that I hereby flatter the pope and seek his favor. Who does not follow their folly must bear the name of a new papist.

In the first place I hear and see that such rebaptism is undertaken by some in order to spite the pope and to be free of any taint of the Antichrist. In the same way the foes of the sacrament want to believe only in bread and wine, in opposition to the pope, thinking thereby really to overthrow the papacy. It is indeed a shaky foundation on which they can build nothing good. On that basis we would have to disown the whole of Scripture and the office of the ministry, which of course we have received from the papacy. We would also have to make a new Bible. Then, also, we would have to disavow the Old Testament, so that we would be under no obligation to the unbelieving Jews. And why the daily use of gold and goods which have been used by bad people, papists, Turks, and heretics? This, too, should be surrendered, if they are not to have anything good from evil persons.

The whole thing is nonsense. Christ himself came upon the errors of scribes and Pharisees among the Jewish people, but he did not on that account reject everything they had and thought (Matt. 23 [:3]). We on our part confess that there is much that is Christian and good under the papacy; indeed everything that is Christian and good is to be found there and has come to us from this source. For instance we confess that in the papal church there are the true holy Scriptures, true baptism, the true sacrament of the altar, the true keys to the forgiveness of sins, the true office of the ministry, the true catechism in the form of the Lord's Prayer, the Ten Commandments, and the articles of the creed. Similarly, the pope admits that we too, though condemned by him as heretics, and likewise all heretics, have the holy Scriptures, baptism, the keys, the catechism, etc. O how do you dissemble? How then do I dissemble? I speak of what the pope and we have in common. He on his part dissembles toward us and heretics and plainly admits what we and he have in common. I will continue to so dissemble, though it does me no good. I contend that in the papacy there is true Christianity, even the right kind of Christianity and many great and devoted saints. Shall I cease to make this pretense?

Listen to what St. Paul says to the Thessalonians [II Thess. 2:4]: "The Antichrist takes his seat in the temple of God." If now the pope is (and I cannot believe otherwise) the veritable Antichrist, he will not sit or reign in the devil's stall, but in the temple of God. No, he will not sit where there are only devils and unbelievers, or where no Christ or Christendom exist. For he is an Antichrist and must thus be among Christians. And since he is to sit and reign there it is necessary that there be Christians under him. God's temple is not the description for a pile of stones, but for the holy Christendom (I Cor. 3 [:17]), in which he is to reign. The Christendom that now is under the papacy is truly the body of Christ and a member of it. If it is his body, then it has the true spirit, gospel, faith, baptism, sacrament, keys, the office of the ministry, prayer, holy Scripture, and everything that pertains to Christendom. So we are all still under the papacy and therefrom have received our Christian treasures.

As a veritable Antichrist must conduct himself against Christendom, so the pope acts toward us: he persecutes us, curses us, bans us, pursues us, burns us, puts us to death. Christians need indeed to be truly baptized and right members of Christ if they are to win the victory in death over against the Antichrist. We do not rave as do the rebellious spirits, so as to reject everything that is found in the papal church. For then we would cast out even Christendom from the temple of God, and all that it contained of Christ. But when we oppose and reject the pope it is because he does not keep to these treasures of Christendom which he has inherited from the apostles. Instead he makes additions of the devil and does not use these treasures for the improvement of the temple. Rather he works

232

toward its destruction, in setting his commandments and ordinances above the ordinance of Christ. But Christ preserves his Christendom even in the midst of such destruction, just as he rescued Lot at Sodom, as St. Peter recounts (I Pet. 2 [II Pet. 2:6]). In fact both remain, the Antichrist sits in the temple of God through the action of the devil, while the temple still is and remains the temple of God through the power of Christ. If the pope will suffer and accept this dissembling of mine, then I am and will be, to be sure, an obedient son and devoted papist, with a truly joyful heart, and take back everything that I have done to harm him.

So it is of no consequence when these Anabaptists and enthusiasts say, "Whatever is of the pope is wrong," or, "Whatever is in the papacy we must have and do differently," thinking thereby to prove themselves the foremost enemy of Antichrist. Not realizing that they thus give him most help, they hurt Christendom most and deceive themselves. For they should help us to reject abuse and accretion, but they would not get much credit for this because they realize they were not first to do this. So they attack what no one yet has attacked in the hope that here perchance they might have the honor of being first. But the honor turns to disgrace, for they attack the temple of God and miss the Antichrist who sits therein, just as the blind, who grope after water, take hold of fire.

In fact they remind us of what one brother in the forest of Thuringia did to the other. They were going through the woods with each other when they were set upon by a bear who threw one of them beneath him. The other brother sought to help and struck at the bear, but missed him and grievously wounded the brother under the bear. So these enthusiasts. They ought to come to the aid of Christendom which Antichrist has in his grip and tortures. They take a severe stand against the pope, but they miss their mark and murder the more terribly the Christendom under the pope. For if they would permit baptism and the sacrament of the altar to stand as they are, Christians under the pope might yet escape with their souls and be saved, as has been the case hitherto. But now when the sacraments are taken from them, they will most likely be lost, since even Christ himself is thereby taken away. Dear friend, this is not the way to blast the papacy while Christian saints are in his keeping. One needs a more cautious, discreet spirit, which attacks the accretion which threatens the temple without destroying the temple of God itself.

Again, those who depend on such arguments say that they know nothing of their baptism, and exclaim, "How do you know you have been baptized? You believe people who say you have been baptized. But you should believe God himself and not people, and you must be sure of your baptism." Surely this seems to me to be pretty shaky argument. For were I to reject everything which I have not seen or heard, I would indeed not have much left, either of faith or of love, either of spiritual or of temporal things. I might reply, "My friend, how do you know that this man is your father, this woman is your mother? You cannot trust people, you must be sure of your own birth." In this manner all children would forthwith be free from obedience to the commandment of God, "Thou shalt honor thy father and thy mother." For I could retort, "How do I know who is my father and mother? I can't believe people. So I will have to be born again by them in order to see for myself, else I will not obey them." By acting in this way God's command would indeed be made altogether null and void.

Likewise I might refuse to recognize anyone as brother, sister, cousin, or relative, constantly repeating, "I did not know we were related, because I am uncertain who my parents were," etc. But (if I were ruler of the land) I would repay such a spirit by forbidding him to retain, expect, or receive any inheritance, either house, land, or a single penny from his parents, and so play with him at his own game until his spirit takes on flesh for him again. For since he neither recognizes nor trusts his parents, he cannot know or hope for their possessions. O, how well society would be ordered when no one would want to be related to another as child, brother, sister, cousin, relative, heir, or neighbor! To be among such Christians would be no better than being among wild wolves.

Then too I might refuse to be subject to any lord or master, explaining that I am not sure he was born a prince, because I did not see it, but had to accept popular opinion. So I will be a free man, pay no attention to the command of God, have no authority above me, but run away from people to wolves, among whom there is no such commandment of God to honor parents and government. That the devil really desires this in these baptizers is apparent from the fact that these disciples of his are prepared (as it is said) to forsake wife and children, house and land, and go to heaven altogether alone. More of this later.

Indeed I might then claim that holy Scripture meant nothing, Christ meant nothing. The apostles, too, never preached. For I have not seen nor felt these things. I've only heard them from people. So I won't believe them unless they are re-enacted anew and happen and are done again before my eyes. So I am above all a wholly free fellow, free also from the commands of God. That's the way I would have it, if I could, the devil declares. That would be a foundation for the Anabaptists on which nothing in heaven and earth could stand.

You reply: Have you not yourself taught that we should obey God and not man? You think thereby to slay me with mine own sword, don't you? But since you are in such a fighting mood, I would ask you if we are to obey God when he commands us to honor parents and superiors? If you say, "Yes," I would ask, How then do you know who they are, since you don't want to believe men? Where are you then? I see full well that your mistake is in not knowing what it means to believe men, and so stumble into error as hopelessly as the Anabaptists do. Therefore listen to me.

When we teach that we are not to obey men, we mean of course that they are speaking entirely for themselves and God is not in their minds, that is, they speak only as men in what they think up, without reference to the Word and work of God, and cannot therefore prove anything either by the words or works of God. For who would call that a human teaching which is presented by God through man? And who would say that faith in such teaching meant faith in man and not in God? In Col. 2 [:23], Paul chides the human teaching which has never proven what it proclaims, that is, it is imagined only and cannot be proved by a single word or work of God. So when you hear that men are not tᵣ be believed you are to understand that this applies only to what is purely human speculation and not to statements wherein a word or work of God is declared or affirmed. You are to distinguish simply (as the words indicate) between faith in God and faith in what is only of man.

When you were born, for example, it was no secret event, nor was it a human invention. Your birth was a work of God which became publicly known and could not be denied. And if anyone wants to contradict it as the Jews presumed to contradict the miracles and signs of Christ, it is of no avail. For those who see and witness to the divine public deed will nonetheless prevail and stop the mouths of the others in deed and truth. For the law of God holds here rigorously, that by the mouths of two or three witnesses all things are to be confirmed [Deut. 19:15]. You must truly believe people like that. For they bear witness to the work of God, namely, your birth. They prove that these were your parents. Besides, no one but they took care of you, and no one but they alone strove and labored for you. God's work progresses in public so that neither devil nor man can controvert it, but every man can so know and declare it as he declares that you are living.

When anyone bears witness to the work of God it does not mean believing men, but God. In sum, when any one declares and bears witness to the work of God and which is not the figment of man's imagination, and this can be controverted neither by the devil nor man, then you believe God and not man, for it is the work of God which He so publicly discloses that even the devil cannot deny it.

This truth is in no way affected by the occasions when children are put or sent away and never know their true parents throughout their lifetime, for we are speaking here of ordinary divine public order. Such children are dishonestly and secretly dealt with, against the will of God, so it is not surprising that theirs is a different lot. They are reared in secret, so that who their parents are remains a secret to them. Whatever the devil does is darkness: let it remain in darkness. But God's order functions in the light.

If now you ask why I believe this man and this woman to be my parents I reply: First, I am sure that I am a work of God and am a human being, wherefore I have to have a mother and father and am not sprung from a rock.[4] God says in Gen. 1 [:28] to the man and woman, "Be fruitful and multiply," from which it is clear that all persons are born of man and woman, and have a father and mother. This is confirmed by the commandment to all men,

---

[4] The metaphor is derived from Homer's *Iliad* 22, 126.

"Thou shalt honor father and mother." (In both instances Christ as the Son of God is of course an exception.) Since I am sure that I came from parents and am not grown on a tree, I am compelled, secondly, to believe, that it is from this man and this woman, who are represented to me by other people as being my parents, according to the word, "On the evidence of two or three witnesses all things shall be established." So I am compelled by God to rely on such people. Thirdly, it is a work of God that no one other than these two in all the world in his own name has taken me as a natural child, or in case of their death, those relatives or pious people who took me in their name. Such an indisputable fact is like any other of God's evident works before devil and man. For neither world nor devil can doubt the evident works of God. They may try, but it will be to no avail. The devil can of course skilfully attack the Word of God, while the work is still hidden.

The reason that God speaks in Rom. 13 [:1], "Let every person be subject to the governing authorities," is that I might believe in him who is my prince or lord. I conclude from this word that I must have a superior and I must be a subject. Secondly, since all the world testifies and says this is he and everyone recognizes him as such and no one denies that this is an evident work of God, I must believe such testimony. If any one contradicts, he does so in vain, for finally every one admits that he lies. Thirdly, it is an evident work of God, that no one else considers me as his subject. I live under his protection, justice, law, and peace, as I should under government, and all other authorities leave me alone; nor do they call my status into question or oppose it, provided I keep my place in the light of law and God's order. Robbers and murderers may well find their place under foreign rulers in secrecy and darkness, but these are rightly judged as not being their subjects.

Wait, you say, I will test you. Why do you not now believe in the pope as your lord? Instead, you make him the Antichrist, though all the world testifies that he is the head of Christendom, and they will prove it indeed that he has the rule. I answer, there you almost caught me! But let me tell you, that if you can convince me that the papacy meets the three requirements I have shown to hold in regard to parents and government, then I will consider the papacy as a work of God, submitting to it, and deeming it a work of God. But, dear fellow, if you cannot do this, allow me to judge it as a human fancy, without the word and work of God, which is under no circumstances to be believed. I can forcefully prove that the papacy is a human fancy.

In the first place, the Word of God clearly tells me that parents and government exist, and that I should and must have parents and government as I have said. But there is no Word of God that says there is a pope, and that I must have a pope and be subject to him. Since the Scriptures command nothing concerning the pope and his rule, there is no papacy which can be considered the work of God. For the Scriptures give testimony concerning what are the works of God. Therefore I said above, that we should believe in men when they show and prove, not their own fancies or works, but the Word or work of God. For, before considering the question as to what a thing is, make sure that it exists.[5] Before you tell me what the pope is, you must convince me that there is a divinely appointed pope. If he cannot exist one does not ask who he is. Secondly, though many bear witness to him, their testimony is not only in vain, since it cannot make a work of God out of the papacy, or prove it to be such, but is not unanimous and complete. For not only has the Eastern church borne testimony against the papacy and opposed it, but also many subjects of the pope himself, who have been burned at the stake for their opposition and still are strangled daily. His rule thus has never been accepted or unopposed, or been peacefully established as has the rule of parents or government, as we have related already.

Thirdly, it is not a work of God. For he exercises no office to the welfare of his subjects. Indeed, he persecutes the gospel and Christians, let alone that he ought to be a teacher and guardian. He only teaches his filth and poison as human notions, discards the gospel, even persecutes it, though without avail. He makes a sacrifice out of the sacrament, faith out of works, work out of faith. He forbids marriage, [and issues prohibitions concerning] food, seasons, clothes, and places. He perverts and abuses all Christian treasures to the injury of souls, as we have sufficiently proved elsewhere. Since on all three counts the papacy is deficient, we

---

[5] Luther quotes a rule in medieval logic.

must judge it as a pure human invention, which is not worthy of belief and is in no way comparable to the institutions of parenthood and government.

Baptism, too, is a work of God, not invented by man but commanded by God and witnessed to by the gospel. Secondly, there are people who can witness to the fact that you have been baptized, and no one can contradict or prove the opposite. In the third place, there is the work, i.e., you are reckoned among Christians, admitted to the sacrament, and to the use of all Christian privileges. This would not be the case if you had not been baptized and all were not sure of it. So all of this is clear proof of your baptism. For all the world knows and sees that everyone is baptized as a child. Whoever refuses to believe all this refuses to believe God himself, since God says, Two witnesses are to be believed [Deut. 19:15; Matt. 18:16]. Such witnesses he does not punish, though he never leaves false witness unpunished or inviolate.

Herewith I have sufficiently proved that no one ought to have doubts as to his baptism, as if he did not know that he is baptized. He sins against God who will not believe it. For he is much more certain of his baptism through the witness of Christians, than if he himself had witnessed it. For the devil could easily have made him uncertain so that he imagined he had been dreaming or had an hallucination instead of being properly baptized. So he would have to fall back finally on the testimony of Christians to be at peace. This kind of testimony the devil cannot confuse or make dubious.

In the third place, it is said, as I also have read, that they base their faith on this verse, "He who believes and is baptized will be saved" [Mark 16:16]. This they interpret to mean that no man should be baptized before he believes. I must say that they are guilty of a great presumption. For if they follow this principle they cannot venture to baptize before they are certain that the one to be baptized believes. How and when can they ever know that for certain? Have they now become gods so that they can discern the hearts of men and know whether or not they believe? If they are not certain if they believe, why then do they baptize, since they contend so strenuously that faith must precede baptism? Are they not contradicting themselves when they baptize without being certain if faith is there or not? For whoever bases baptism on faith and baptizes on chance and not on certainty that faith is present does nothing better than he who baptizes him who has no faith. For unbelief and uncertain belief are one and the same thing, and both are contrary to the verse, "Whoever believes," which speaks of a sure faith which they who are to be baptized should have.

You say, I know, that he confesses that he believes, etc. Dear sir, confession is neither here nor there. The text does not say, "He who confesses," but "He who believes." To have his confession is not to know his faith. With all your reasoning you cannot do justice to this verse unless you also know he has faith, since all men are liars and God alone knows the heart. So whoever bases baptism on the faith of the one to be baptized can never baptize anyone. Even if you baptized a person a hundred times a day you would not at all know if he believes. Why then do you carry on with your rebaptizing, since you contradict yourself and baptize when you are not sure that faith is present, and yet you teach that faith must most certainly be present. This verse, "Whoever believes," altogether opposes their rebaptizing, since the verse speaks of a certain faith. They base their rebaptizing on an uncertain faith, and in not a syllable do they follow the meaning of the verse.

I say the same thing about the baptized one who receives or grounds his baptism on his faith. For he is not sure of his own faith. I would compare the man who lets himself be rebaptized with the man who broods and has scruples because perhaps he did not believe as a child. So when next day the devil comes, his heart is filled with scruples and he says, Ah, now for the first time I feel I have the right faith, yesterday I don't think I truly believed. So I need to be baptized a third time, the second baptism not being of any avail. You think the devil can't do such things? You had better get to know him better. He can do worse than that, dear friend. He can go on and cast doubt on the third, and the fourth and so on incessantly (as he indeed has in mind to do), just as he has done with me and many in the matter of confession. We never seemed able to confess sufficiently certain sins, and incessantly and restlessly sought one absolution after the other, one father confessor after the other. Just because we sought to rely on our confession, as those to be baptized now want to rely on their faith. What is the end result? Baptizing without end would result. All this is nonsense. Neither the baptizer nor the baptized can base baptism on a certain faith. This verse of Scripture is far more a judgment on them than on us. And these are the people who don't want to trust the men who are witnesses of their baptism, but now as men are ready to trust themselves that they are baptized as if they were not men, or as if they were more certain of their faith than the witness of Christendom allows.

So I contend that if they want to do justice to this passage, "Whoever believes," according to their understanding, they must condemn rebaptism much more earnestly than the first baptism. Neither the baptizer nor the baptized can maintain his position, for both are uncertain of their faith, or at least are in constant peril and anxiety. For it happens, indeed it is so in this matter of faith, that often he who claims to believe does not at all believe; and on the other hand, he who doesn't think he believes, but is in despair, has the greatest faith. So this verse, "Whoever believes," does not compel us to determine who has faith or not. Rather, it makes it a matter of every man's conscience to realize that if he is to be saved he must believe and not pretend that it is sufficient for a Christian to be baptized. For the verse does not say, "Whoever knows that he believes, or, if you know that anyone believes," but it says, "Whoever believes." Who has it, has it. One must believe, but we neither should nor can know it for certain.

Since our baptizing has been thus from the beginning of Christianity and the custom has been to baptize children, and since no one can prove with good reasons that they do not have faith, we should not make changes and build on such weak arguments. For if we are going to change or do away with customs that are traditional, it is necessary to prove convincingly that these are contrary to the Word of God. Otherwise (as Christ says), "For he that is not against us is for us" [Mark 9:40]. We have indeed overthrown monasteries, mass-priests, and clerical celibacy, but only by showing the clear and certain scriptural arguments against them. Had we not done this, we should truly have let them stand as they previously existed.

When they say, "Children cannot believe," how can they be sure of that? Where is the Scripture by which they would prove it and on which they would build? They imagine this, I suppose, because children do not speak or have understanding. But such a fancy is deceptive, yea, altogether false, and we cannot build on what we imagine.

There are Scripture passages that tell us that children may and can believe, though they do not speak or understand. So, Ps. 72 [106:37f.], describes how the Jews offered their sons and daughters to idols, shedding innocent blood. If, as the text says, it was innocent blood, then the children have to be considered pure and holy—this they could not be without spirit and faith. Likewise the innocent children whom Herod had murdered were not over two years of age [Matt. 2:16]. Admittedly they could not speak or understand. Yet they were holy and blessed. Christ himself says in Matt. 18 [19:14], "The kingdom of heaven belongs to children." And St. John was a child in his mother's womb [Luke 1:41] but, as I believe, could have faith.

Yes, you say, but John was an exception. This is not proof that all baptized children have faith. I answer, wait a minute. I am not yet at the point of proving that children believe. I am giving proof that your foundation for rebaptism is uncertain and false inasmuch as you cannot prove that there may not be faith in children. Inasmuch as John had faith, though he could not speak or understand, your argument fails, that children are not able to believe. To hold that a child believes, as St. John is an example, is not contrary to Scripture. If it is not contrary to the Scripture to hold that children believe, but rather in accord with Scripture, then your argument, that children cannot believe, must be unscriptural. That is my first point.

Who has made you so sure that baptized children do not believe in the face of what I here prove that they can believe? But if you are not sure, why then are you so bold as to discard the first baptism, since you do not and cannot know that it is meaningless? What if all children in baptism not only were able to believe but believed as well as John in his mother's womb? We can hardly deny that the same Christ is present at baptism and in baptism, in fact is himself the baptizer, who in those days came in his mother's womb to John. In baptism he can speak as well through the mouth of the priest, as when he spoke through his mother. Since then he is present, speaks, and baptizes, why should not his Word and baptism call forth spirit and faith in the child as then it produced faith in John? He is the same one who speaks and acts then and now. Even before, he had said through Isaiah [Isa. 55:11], "His word shall not return empty." Now it is up to you to bring forth a single Scripture verse which proves that children cannot believe in baptism. I have cited these many verses showing that they can believe, and that it is reasonable to hold that they do believe. I grant that we do not understand how they do believe, or how faith is created. But that is not the point here.

Furthermore, he commands us to bring the children to him. In Matt. 19 [:14] he embraces them, kisses them, and says that theirs is the kingdom of heaven. The misled spirits like to fend this off by saying, Christ is not speaking of children, but of the humble. But this is a false note, for the text clearly says that they brought to him children, not the humble. And Christ does not say to let the humble come to him, but the children, and reprimanded the disciples, not because they kept the humble, but the children away. He embraced and blessed the children, not the humble, when he said, "Of such is the kingdom of heaven." So also Matt. 18 [:10], "Their angels behold the face of my Father," is to be understood as referring to such children, for he teaches us that we should also be like these children. Were not these children holy, he would indeed have given us a poor ideal with which to compare ourselves. He would not have said, you must be like children, but rather, you must be otherwise than children. In sum, the misled spiritualist cannot make children here to mean the humble, except through his own imagining, for the words are too clear and forceful.

Some want to take the force out of this text by saying that the Jewish children were circumcised. Therefore they were holy and could be brought to Christ, whereas our children are heathen, etc. I answer: But suppose there were also girls among these children who were brought to Jesus, and who were not circumcised? For surely all kinds of children were among those brought to him, and since it does not expressly say that they were boys only we cannot exclude girls, but must let it mean children of both sexes. They are not brought to him because of their circumcision, but that they might be blessed, coming to Christ out of the Old into the New

Testament, according to his word, "Let the children come to me for of such is the kingdom of God." He says that those who come to him are of the kingdom of God. By their coming and being brought to Christ they are so holy that he embraces, blesses, and gives them the kingdom. Let him who wills follow his fancy. I maintain as I have written in the Postil[6] that the most certain form of baptism is child baptism. For an adult might deceive and come to Christ as a Judas and have himself baptized. But a child cannot deceive. He comes to Christ in baptism, as John came to him, and as the children were brought to him, that his word and work might be effective in them, move them, and make them holy, because his Word and work cannot be without fruit. Yet it has this effect alone in the child. Were it to fail here it would fail everywhere and be in vain, which is impossible.

It cannot be denied that Ps. 77 [106:37] speaks of girls and uncircumcised when it says that they were offered to the idols of Canaan. Yet they were described as innocent blood. And surely Moses in Lev. 12 [:5] included girls in the regulation of offerings for purification and atonement. Everybody knows that boys alone were subjected to circumcision, but that girls participated in its benefits also by virtue of the saying spoken by God to Abraham (Gen. 17 [:7]): "I will be the God of thy descendants, and circumcision shall be a covenant between me and you and your descendants after you." Surely girls are the descendants of Abraham, and through this promise God is indeed their God, though they are not circumcised as are the boys.

If they now believe that through the covenant of circumcision God accepts both boys and girls and is their God, why should he not also accept our children through the covenant of baptism? He has in fact promised us that he wants to be God not alone of the Jews but also of the Gentiles (Rom. 3 [:29]), and especially of the Christians and those who believe. If the circumcision of boys avails both boys and girls, so that they become the people of God because of the faith of Abraham from whom they are descended, how much more then should not baptism help each one to become a member of the people of God because of the merit of Christ to whom he is

---

[6] Cf. p. 229.

244

brought and by whom he is blessed. Let everyone know how uncertain is the foundation of the Anabaptists and how vainly they build thereon.

But, you say, he has not commanded the baptism of children, there is no reference to it in the writings or epistles of the apostles. I answer, neither has he specifically commanded the baptism of adults, nor of men or of women, so we had better not baptize anybody. But he has commanded us to baptize all Gentiles, none excepted, when he said, "Go and baptize all heathen in my name," etc. (Matt. 28 [:19]). Now children constitute a great part of the heathen. We read in Acts and the Epistles of St. Paul how whole households were baptized, and children are surely a good part of the household. So it seems that just as Christ commanded us to teach and baptize all heathen, without exception, so the apostles did, and baptized all who were in the household. Had they not overlooked that the troubling spirits would seek to differentiate between young and old, they would have considered this more expressly, since otherwise in all the Epistles they write so much about there being no respect or difference of persons among Christians. For St. John in I John 2 [:14] writes to the little children, that they know the Father. And, as St. Augustine writes, child baptism has come from the apostles.[7] So the Anabaptists proceed dangerously in everything. Not only are they not sure of themselves but also they act contrary to accepted tradition and out of their own imaginings create differences between persons which God has not made. For even if they contended that they had not been sufficiently subdued, they ought, however quarrelsome they are, to be concerned and frightened at their wrongdoing in rebaptizing on such uncertain grounds. For they are already convicted of doing wrong in their being so uncertain. For in divine matters one should act on certain, not on dubious, grounds.

For if an Anabaptist hears (that is, if he does not want to be obstinate but teachable) that just as John believed and was made holy when Christ came and spoke through the mouth of his mother, so a child becomes a believer if Christ in baptism speaks to him through the mouth of the one who baptizes, since it is his Word,

---

[7] *De Genesi ad literam* X. Cap 23. *Migne* 34, 426.

his commandment, and his word cannot be without fruit, then the Anabaptist must admit that it may be so, that he cannot altogether and firmly deny it, nor cite any Scripture to the contrary. But if he cannot clearly and convincingly deny it, then he cannot firmly defend his rebaptism. For he must first firmly prove that children are without faith when they are baptized, if he is to justify rebaptism. I hold that it has been sufficiently proved that his reasoning is uncertain and supercilious throughout.

Yet even if they could establish that children are without faith when they are baptized, it would make no difference to me. I would want to know their reason for rebaptizing when later on faith or the confession of faith is supposed to be present. For it is not enough to claim they were baptized without faith, therefore they should be rebaptized. Some reason is needed. You say it is not proper baptism. What does it matter, if it is still a baptism? It was a correct baptism in itself, regardless of whether it was received rightly. For the words were spoken and everything that pertains to baptism was done as fully as when faith is present. If a thing is in itself correct you do not have to repeat it even though it was not correctly received. You correct what was wrong and do not have to do the entire thing over. Abuse does not change the nature of a substance, indeed it proves the substance.[8] There can be no abuse unless the substance exists.

When ten years after baptism faith appears, what then is the need of a second baptism, if baptism was correctly administered in all respects? For now he believes, as baptism requires. For faith doesn't exist for the sake of baptism, but baptism for the sake of faith. When faith comes, baptism is complete. A second baptism is not necessary.

It is as if a girl married a man reluctantly and altogether without a wife's affection for the man. She is before God hardly to be considered his true wife. But after two years she gains affection for him. Would then a second engagement be required, a second wedding be celebrated, as if she had not previously been a wife, so that the earlier betrothal and wedding were in vain? Of course you would be considered a fool, if you believed that,

---

[8] A proverb in jurisprudence. Cf. WA 26, 159.

especially since everything is in order now because she has come into her right and properly keeps to the man she had not properly accepted. So also if an adult falsely allows himself to be baptized but after a year comes to faith, do you mean, dear sir, that he should be rebaptized? He received the correct baptism incorrectly, I hear you say. His impropriety makes baptism improper. Should then human error and wickedness be stronger than God's good and invincible order? God made a covenant with the people of Israel on Mt. Sinai. Some did not receive that covenant rightly and in faith. If now these later came to faith, should the covenant, dear sir, therefore be considered invalid, and must God come again to each one on Mt. Sinai in order to renew the covenant?

Likewise God provides for the preaching of the Ten Commandments. But since some people only grasp them with their ears, albeit improperly, they are not Ten Commandments, are no good, and God ought hence to issue ten new commandments in place of the former. It can't be enough that people let themselves be rightly converted and give heed to the original Ten Commandments. It would be a curious situation when the Word of God, which abides forever [Isa. 40:6-9; I Pet. 1:24], has to be changed and be renewed as often as men change and want something new. Yet it does remain firm and unique, so that they who do not now cleave to it or have fallen from it, may still have an immovable rock to which to return and to hold. If subjects paid homage to their liege with the intention of putting him to death, but after three days repented and gave sincere allegiance to him, dear fellow, would it be necessary here to set up anew the conditions of allegiance? Of course not, inasmuch as now their allegiance is sincere which formerly was treacherous.

Were we to follow their reasoning we would have to be baptizing all of the time. For I would take the verse, "Whoever believes," with me and whenever I find a Christian who has fallen or is without faith, I would say that this man is without faith, so his baptism is fruitless; he must be baptized again. If he falls a second time, I would again say, see, he has not faith, there must be something wrong about his first baptism. He will have to be baptized a third time, and so on and on. As often as he falls or there is doubt about his faith, I will say, he doesn't believe, his baptism is defective. In short, he will have to be baptized over again so often that he never again falls or is without faith, if he is to do justice to the verse, "Whoever believes." Tell me, what Christian will then ever be sufficiently baptized or consider that his baptism is completed? But verily baptism can be correct and sufficient even if the Christian falls from faith or sins a thousand times a year. It is enough that he rights himself and becomes faithful, without having to be rebaptized each time. Then why should not the first baptism be sufficient and proper if a person truly becomes a believing Christian? Since there is no difference in baptism whether lack of faith precedes or follows, baptism doesn't depend on faith. But if faith is lacking, the Anabaptists would have us believe we must alter the nature of baptism to accord with the verse, "Whoever believes."

I claim therefore that even if the Anabaptists could prove their thesis, that children are without faith (which they cannot do), they would not have proved more than that the correct baptism, instituted by God, has been wrongly and not properly received. But whoever proves only an abuse, only proves that the abuse should be corrected and not that the thing should be changed. For abuse does not alter the nature of a thing.[9] Gold does not become straw because a thief steals and misuses it. Silver doesn't turn into paper if it is dishonestly obtained by a usurer. Since then the Anabaptists demonstrate only the abuse of baptism, they fly in the face of God, nature, and reason, when they want to alter and make anew baptism itself in treating the abuse. All heretics do the same with regard to the gopsel. They perceive it wrongly and so hear it wrongly in connection with an abuse, and then hasten to change and make a new gopsel out of it. So no matter which way you look at it the Anabaptists are in error. They blaspheme and dishonor the order of God, calling baptism wrong on account of the wrongs and abuses of man, though even their claim of man's wrongs and abuses is unconvincing.

There is, however, a devil who promotes confidence in works [*Werkteufel*] among them. He feigns faith, whereas he really has a work in mind. He uses the name and guise of faith to lead the poor people to rely on a work. Just as it happened under the papacy,

---

[9] Cf. p. 246, n. 8.

when we were driven to the sacrament as a work of obedience. For no one went in order to nourish his faith, but everything was finished and the work accomplished when we had received the sacrament. So here again the Anabaptists are urging on to a work, so that when the people are baptized they may have confidence that everything is right and complete. In reality they pay little attention to faith, but only seem to praise it. For, as we have already said, were they to be sure beforehand of faith, they would never again baptize anyone. If they did not rely on works but earnestly sought for faith, they would not dare to rebaptize. The unchanging Word of God, once spoken in the first baptism, ever remains standing, so that afterwards they can come to faith in it, if they will, and the water with which they were baptized they can afterwards receive in faith, if they will. Even if they contradict the Word a hundred times, it still remains the Word spoken in the first baptism. Its power does not derive from the fact that it is repeated many times or is spoken anew, but from the fact that it was commanded once to be spoken.

It is the devil's masterpiece when he can get someone to compel the Christian to leave the righteousness of faith for a righteousness of works, as he forced the Galatians and Corinthians on to works though, as St. Paul writes, they were doing well in their faith and running rightly in Christ [Gal. 5:7]. So now, as he sees the Germans through the gospel acknowledging Christ in a fine way and believing as they should, so that they thereby were righteous before God, he interferes and tears them away from this righteousness, as if it were vain, and leads them into rebaptizing as if this were a better righteousness. He causes them thus to reject their former righteousness as ineffectual and to fall prey to a false righteousness. What shall I say? We Germans are and remain true Galatians.[10] For whoever permits himself be rebaptized rejects his former faith and righteousness, and is guilty of sin and condemnation. Of all things such behavior is most horrible. As St. Paul, says, the Galatians have severed themselves from Christ [Gal. 5:4], even making Christ a servant of sin, when they circumcise themselves.

Satan does these things against us, in order to make our teach-

---

[10] Cf. WA 18, 121. Cf. also *Against the Heavenly Prophets*, p. 139.

ing seem contemptible, as if we could not have the right spirit or teaching because we had not been rightly baptized. But we know the tree by its fruits [Matt. 7:16f.]. For neither among the papists nor among these rebellious spirits do we find men who can handle and interpret Scripture as skilfully as do those on our side by the grace of God. This is not the least of the Spirit's gifts (I Cor. 12 [:10]). We see among them the natural fruit of the devil, namely, that some of them on account of rebaptism desert wife and child, house and land, and will recognize no authority. Yet St. Paul teaches that whoever does not provide for his own has disowned his faith and is worse than an unbeliever (I Tim. 6 [5:8]). And in I Cor. 7 [:13] he expresses as his desire that a wife who believes should not divorce an unbelieving husband. Nor does Christ want a marriage broken, except where adultery becomes a reason for it. Our spirit not only allows but commands that every estate should remain and be held in honor, and that faith should exercise itself peacefully in love [Cf. Gal. 5:6] so that no uprising or complaint could fairly be charged to our teaching. The papists of course by their lies blame us for all manner of ills, but even their own consciences are here in many instances their own judges.

This refutes too their position that baptism does not avail in case the priest or he who baptizes did not have faith. For even if St. Peter baptized, no one would know for certain if in that moment he stood in faith or in doubt. For no one can discern his heart. In brief, such arguments once led the Donatists[11] to separate themselves and to rebaptize, when they saw how unholy some were who preached and baptized. They began to base baptism on the holiness of men, though Christ had based it on his Word and commandment. That is also the attempt of our rebellious spirits, the foes of the sacrament. They maintain, of course, that the truth and Scripture compel them, but they lie nevertheless. They are offended (as they sometimes experience) that any rogue may bring Christ into the bread of the sacrament,[12] as if all the world were sure that they themselves have faith and are completely holy. They act as

---

[11] The Donatists were the group against whom Augustine defended the validity of the church's sacraments even if wicked priests administered them or wicked people received them. Cf. LW 13, 89.

[12] Cf. WA 18, 165ff. Cf. also Against the Heavenly Prophets, p. 147.

though they were not great rogues in the eyes of God, just as much as they who sharply condemn wickedness and call others rascals, forgetting the beam in their own eye.

We recall that St. John was not averse to hearing the Word of God from Caiaphas and pays attention to his prophecy [John 11:49f.]. Moses and the people of Israel received the prophecy of the godless Balaam as a word from God [Num. 24:17]. So also St. Paul recognized the heathen poets Aratus and Epimenides and honored their saying (as a word of God).[13] And Christ bids us hear the godless Pharisees in the seat of Moses, though they are godless teachers. We need to be much less self-complacent. Let God judge their evil lies. We can still listen to their godly words. For if they are evil, it is to their own harm. If they teach correctly, we can be correctly instructed. Consider the pious Magi in Matt. 2 [:4ff.]. They heard the Word of God from the book of Micah through the mouth of Herod, the cruel king, who in turn had heard it from the godless high priests and scribes. Still on that Word they set out for Bethlehem and found Christ. It was no great hindrance that they heard the Word of God only through Herod the murderer of Christ.

Still we must admit that the enthusiasts have the Scriptures and the Word of God in other doctrines. Whoever hears it from them and believes will be saved, even though they are unholy heretics and blasphemers of Christ. It is not a minor grace that God gives his Word even through evil rogues and the godless. In fact it is in some respects more perilous when he proclaims it through holy than through unholy folk. For the thoughtless are tempted to attach themselves to the holiness of the people rather than to the Word of God. Greater honor is then given to man than to God and his Word. This danger does not exist when Judas, Caiaphas, and Herod preach, though no one can make this an excuse for an evil life if God can make some use of such. Now if a godless man can have and teach the Word of God correctly, much more can he baptize and give the sacrament properly. For it is a greater thing to teach the Word of God than to baptize, as St. Paul boasts

---

[13] "For we are indeed his offspring" [Acts 17:28], is a quotation from *Phainomena* 5, by Aratus of Sicily. "Cretans are always liars," etc. [Titus 1:12] is a quotation from the work of Epimenides of Gnossus (600 B.C.). WA 26, 163.

in I Cor. 1 [:17]. As we have said, whoever makes baptism dependent on the faith of him who baptizes will never receive baptism from anyone. For if I ask you if you have been rebaptized, and you say, yes, I again ask, how do you know that you now are rightly baptized? Were you to reply, because he who baptized me has faith, I would ask, how do you know that? Have you looked into his heart? So there you are, like butter in sunshine.

Our baptism, thus, is a strong and sure foundation, affirming that God has made a covenant with all the world to be a God of the heathen in all the world, as the gospel says. Also, that Christ has commanded the gospel to be preached in all the world, as also the prophets have declared in many ways. As a sign of this covenant he has instituted baptism, commanded and enjoined upon all heathen, as Matt. [28:19] declares: "Go therefoıe and make disciples of all nations, baptizing them in the name of the Father," etc. In the same manner he had made a covenant with Abraham and his descendants to be their God, and made circumcision a sign of this covenant. Here, namely, that we are baptized; not because we are certain of our faith but because it is the command and will of God. For even if I were never certain any more of faith, I still am certain of the command of God, that God has bidden to baptize, for this he has made known throughout the world. In this I cannot err, for God's command cannot deceive. But of my faith he has never said anything to anyone, nor issued an order or command concerning it.

True, one should add faith to baptism. But we are not to base baptism on faith. There is quite a difference between having faith, on the one hand, and depending on one's faith and making baptism depend on faith, on the other. Whoever allows himself to be baptized on the strength of his faith, is not only uncertain, but also an idolator who denies Christ. For he trusts in and builds on something of his own, namely, on a gift which he has from God, and not on God's Word alone. So another may build on and trust in his strength, wealth, power, wisdom, holiness, which also are gifts given him by God. But a baptism on the Word and command of God even when faith is not present is still a correct and certain baptism if it takes place as God commanded. Granted, it is not of benefit to the baptized one who is without faith, because of his lack of faith, but the baptism is not thereby incorrect, uncertain, or of no meaning. If we were to consider everything wrong or ineffectual which is of no value to the unbeliever, then nothing would be right or remain good. It has been commanded that the gospel should be preached to all the world. The unbeliever hears it but it has no meaning for him. Are we therefore to look on the gospel as not being a gospel or as being a false gospel? The godless see no value in God himself. Does that mean he is not God?

If an adult wants to be baptized and says, "Sir, I want to be baptized," you ask, "Do you believe?" Just as Philip asked the chamberlain in Acts 4 [8:37] and as we daily ask those to be baptized. Then he will not blurt out and say, "Yes, I intend to move mountains by my faith." Instead he will say, "Yes, Sir, I do believe, but I do not build on this my faith. It might be too weak or uncertain. I want to be baptized because it is God's command that I should be, and on the strength of this command I dare to be baptized. In time my faith may become what it may. If I am baptized on his bidding I know for certain that I am baptized. Were I to be baptized on my own faith, I might tomorrow find myself unbaptized, if faith failed me, or I became worried that I might not yesterday have had the faith rightly. But now that doesn't affect me. God and his command may be attacked, but I am certain enough that I have been baptized on his Word. My faith and I make this venture. If I believe, this baptism is of value to me. If I do not believe, it is not of value. But baptism in itself is not therefore wrong or uncertain, is not a matter of venture, but is as sure as are the Word and command of God."

Of his baptism as a child he would say, I thank God and am happy that I was baptized as a child, for thus I have done what God commanded. Whether I have believed or not, I have followed the command of God and been baptized and my baptism was correct and certain. God grant that whether my faith today be certain or uncertain, or I think that I believe and am certain, nothing is lacking in baptism. Always something is lacking in faith. However long our life, always there is enough to learn in regard to faith. It can happen that faith fails, so that it is said, "See, he had faith but has it no more." But one cannot say about baptism, "See, baptism was there but is no longer present." No, it remains, for the command of God remains, and what is done according to his command stands and will ever remain.

Up to this point we have clearly and sufficiently proved, in my opinion, that the Anabaptists do wrong in denying the first baptism, as if they were sure that children were baptized without faith, though of this they cannot be certain. On the other hand we cannot prove that children do believe with any Scripture verse that clearly and expressly declares in so many words, or the like, "You are to baptize children because they also believe." Whoever compels us to produce such a statement has the upper hand and wins, for we cannot find such words. But sincere and sensible Christians do not require such proof. The quarrelsome, obstinate rebellious spirits do in order to seem to be clever. But on their side they can produce no statement which says, "You are to baptize adults but no children." We are however persuaded by many good reasons to hold that child baptism is right and that children do believe.

First, because child baptism derives from the apostles and has been practiced since the days of the apostles. We cannot oppose it, but must let it continue, since no one has yet been able to prove that in baptism children do not believe or that such baptism is wrong. For even if I were not sure that they believed, yet for my conscience's sake I would have to let them be baptized. I would much rather allow them baptism than to keep them from it. For if, as we believe, baptism is right and useful and brings the children to salvation, and I then did away with it, then I would be responsible for all the children who were lost because they were unbaptized—a cruel and terrible thing. If baptism is not right, that is, without value or help to the children, then I would be guilty of no greater sin than the Word of God had been spoken and his sign given in vain. I would not be responsible for the loss of any soul, but only of an ineffectual use of the Word and sign of God.

But this God would easily forgive me, since it was done in ignorance and more than that out of fear. I did not invent it. It came to me by tradition and I was persuaded by no word of Scripture that it was wrong. I would have been unwilling to do it, had I been convinced otherwise. It would be very much as when I preach the Word, also according to his command, among the unbelieving and without fruit, or as it is said, cast pearls before swine, or holy things to the dogs [Matt. 7:6]. What could I do? Here, too, I would rather sin in preaching fruitlessly than in refusing to preach at all. For in fruitless preaching I would not be guilty of a soul [being lost] while in refusing to preach I might be held accountable for many souls. That would be too much for any individual. This I say even if there were uncertainty about the faith of children in baptism, for we cannot set aside baptism which is certain, on account of faith which is uncertain. Baptism did not originate with us, but with the apostles and we should not discard or alter what cannot be discarded or altered on clear scriptural authority. God is wonderful in his works. What he does not will, he clearly witnesses to in Scripture. What is not so witnessed to there, we can accept as his work. We are guiltless and he will not mislead us. If we knew or believed that child baptism was useless, it would be a wicked thing to still baptize. So the Waldenses do, but that is to despise God and his Word.

In the second place, this is an important consideration: No heresy endures to the end, but always, as St. Peter says, soon comes to light and is revealed as disgraceful. So St. Paul mentions Jannes and Jambres and their like [II Tim. 3:8f.], whose folly is finally plain to all. Were child baptism now wrong God would certainly not have permitted it to continue so long, nor let it become so universally and thoroughly established in all Christendom, but it would sometime have gone down in disgrace. The fact that the Anabaptists now dishonor it does not mean anything final or injurious to it. Just as God has established that Christians in all the world have accepted the Bible as Bible, the Lord's Prayer as Lord's Prayer, and faith of a child as faith, so also he has established child baptism and kept it from being rejected while all kinds of heresies have disappeared which are much more recent and later than child baptism. This miracle of God is an indication that child baptism must be right. He has not so upheld the papacy, which also is an innovation and has never been accepted by all Christians of the world as has child baptism, the Bible, faith, or the Lord's Prayer, etc.

You say, this does not prove that child baptism is certain. For there is no passage in Scripture for it. My answer: that is true. From Scripture we cannot clearly conclude that you could establish

255

child baptism as a practice among the first Christians after the apostles. But you can well conclude that in our day no one may reject or neglect the practice of child baptism which has so long a tradition, since God actually not only has permitted it, but from the beginning so ordered, that it has not yet disappeared.

For where we see the work of God we should yield and believe in the same way as when we hear his Word, unless the plain Scripture tells us otherwise. I indeed am ready to let the papacy be considered as a work of God. But since Scripture is against it, I consider it as a work of God but not as a work of grace. It is a work of wrath from which to flee, as other plagues also are works of God, but works of wrath and displeasure.

In the third place, it is likewise the work of God that during all the time children were being baptized, he has given great and holy gifts to many of them, enlightened and strengthened them with the Holy Spirit and understanding of the Scripture, and accomplished great things in Christendom through them. John Huss[14] and his colleagues are examples from that time, and many other holy men before him. He does the same to very many of his people in our day. He has not hitherto driven them to the Anabaptists, which undoubtedly he would have done if he had judged his commandment concerning baptism improperly observed. He does not contradict himself, nor would he favor with his gifts those who disobey his commands. Since he thus gives such gifts as we must admit to be holy gifts of God, he confirms, of course, thereby the first baptism and considers us rightly baptized. By these works we thus prove the first baptism to be proper and rebaptism to be wrong, just as St. Peter and St. Paul (Acts 15 [:8f]) from the miracle of the gift of the Holy Spirit to the heathen proved that it was the will of God that heathen need not heed the law of Moses.

In the fourth place, if the first, or child, baptism were not right, it would follow that for more than a thousand years there was no baptism or any Christendom, which is impossible. For in that case the article of the creed, I believe in one holy Christian church, would be false. For over a thousand years there were hardly any

---

[14] John Huss, reformer of Bohemia, was burned at the stake at Constance on June 6, 1415, as a heretic. Luther found himself in agreement with many views held by Huss, notably concerning the papacy. Cf. LW 31, 321.

other but child baptisms. If this baptism is wrong then for that long period Christendom would have been without baptism, and if it were without baptism it would not be Christendom. For the Christian church is the bride of Christ, subject and obedient to him. It has his Spirit, his Word, his baptism, his sacrament, and all that Christ has. If, indeed, child baptism were not common throughout the world, but (like the papacy) were accepted only by some, then the Anabaptists might seem to have a case and might attack those who receive it, just as we oppose the clergy who have made a sacrifice out of the sacrament though among the laity it still remains a sacrament. But the fact that child baptism has spread throughout all the Christian world to this day gives rise to no probability that it is wrong, but rather to a strong indication that it is right.

In the fifth place, the words of St. Paul in II Thess. 2 [:4] concerning the Antichrist, that he shall sit in the temple of God, of which we have already spoken, accord with our position. If it is the temple of God it is not a haunt of heretics, but true Christendom, which must truly have a baptism which is right beyond any doubt. We see and hear of no other than child baptism, whether under the pope, among the Turks, or in all the world. Christ commands the children to come and to be brought to him, and, in Matt. 19 [:14] says that theirs is the kingdom of God. The apostles baptized entire households [Acts 16:15]. John writes to little children [I John 2:12]. St. John had faith even in his mother's womb, as we have heard [Luke 1:41]. If all of these passages do not suffice for the enthusiasts, I shall not be concerned. They are enough for me, to stop the mouth of anyone from saying that child baptism does not mean anything. If they are still uncertain, I am satisfied if they do not henceforth do away with it but let it be in doubt among themselves. We, however, are certain enough, because it is nowhere contrary to Scripture, but is rather in accord with Scripture.

In the sixth place, since God has made a covenant with all heathen through the gospel and ordained baptism as a sign thereof, who can exclude the children? If the old covenant and the sign of circumcision made the children of Abraham believe that they were, and were called the people of God, according to the promise, I will be the God of thy descendants [Gen. 17:7], then this new covenant and sign must be much more effectual and make those

257

a people of God who receive it. Now he commands that all the world shall receive it. On the strength of that command (since none is excluded) we confidently and freely baptize everyone, excluding no one except those who oppose it and refuse to receive this covenant. If we follow his command and baptize everyone, we leave it to him to be concerned about the faith of those baptized. We have done our best when we have preached and baptized. If now we have no particular passage of Scripture on the baptism of children, they on their side have just as little of Scripture which bids us baptize adults. But we have the command to offer the common gospel and the common baptism to everyone, and herein the children must be included. We plant and water and leave the growth to God [Cf. I Cor. 3:6].

In sum, the Anabaptists are too frivolous and insolent. For they consider baptism, not as a God-given ordinance or command, but as a human trifle, like many other customs under the papacy relating to the consecration of salt, water, or herbs. For if they looked on it as a God-given ordinance and command they would not speak so disgracefully and shamefully about it even if it were not rightly used. But now they have the insane idea that baptism is something like the consecration of water and salt or the wearing of cowl and tonsure. So they carry on and call it a dog's bath, or a handful of water, and other such vile things. Those who hold the gospel to be the right Word of God do not speak lightly of it even though there are many who do not believe or accept it, or who falsely use it. He who does not hold it as the Word of God is the one who treats it lightly, blasphemes and says it is fable, fairy story, or a counsel of fools, and the like. It ought to be easy for such a one to acquire disciples who believe such blasphemy.

Observe this well, that if the Anabaptists at first had presented their idea with good arguments, they would not have misled or won many persons. For they have no substantial or certain arguments. But they attract a great many people by using great, high-sounding words of slander against baptism. For the devil well knows that if the mad mob hears high-sounding words of slander, it falls for and readily believes them, asking for neither reason nor proof. So they hear it said, baptism is a dog's bath and those who baptize are false and foolish servants of bathkeepers. So they conclude, aha, so the devil baptizes, and God shame the false servants of bathkeepers. That is the position they take and have nothing else with which to attack baptism. For all those to whom I have ever listened when discussing these things with me delivered themselves of these high-sounding words of slander (dog's bath, servant of a bathkeeper, handful of water, etc.) and then stood there as shorn monks, having nothing more with which to defend their errors.

Very much in the same manner the devil also deceives those who blaspheme the sacrament. When he realizes that his lies do not produce much effect, he fares forth and fills the ears of the mad mob with high-sounding sacrilege, such as, our sacrament is an eating of flesh and guzzling of blood and the like. When they have exhausted those same high-sounding words their art is soon exhausted, and they begin to talk about the ascension of Christ.[15] The Jews do the same to this day. In order to keep their children in their faith they blaspheme Christ shamelessly, refer to him as "the hanged one" and confidently lie about him. This frightens an innocent, simple heart and misleads it, as St. Paul observes in Rom. 16 [:18]. For this reason they always have an easy time of it, for their high-sounding sacrilege has enabled them to lead the people whither they wanted, nor have they dared to establish firm ground for their error. Had they first formulated a good and solid foundation for their case then it would be sufficient to give the lie a good blow and set it forth in its true light.

We who know that baptism is a God-given thing, instituted and commanded by God himself, look not at its abuse by godless persons, but simply at God's ordinance. We find baptism in itself to be a holy, blessed, glorious, and heavenly thing, to be held in honor with fear and trembling, just as it is reasonable and right to hold any other ordinance and command of God. It is not the fault of baptism that many people abuse it. It would be as wrong to call the gospel a vain babbling because there are many who abuse it. Since then, as far as I have been able to see and hear, the Anabaptists have no argument but high-sounding words of sacrilege, everyone ought properly to shun and avoid them as messengers of none

---

[15] An allusion to Zwingli's doctrine of the bodily presence of Christ at the right hand of God.

other than the devil, sent out into the world to blaspheme the Word and ordinance of God so that people might not believe therein and be saved. For they are the birds who eat the seed sown by the wayside (Matt. 13 [:4]).

Finally I claim that if some one had not been baptized, but did not know it and firmly believed that he had been rightly baptized, that faith would be sufficient for him. For before God he has what he believes. All things (Christ says) are possible to him who believes [Mark 9:23]. To rebaptize such a one would be to imperil his faith. How much less, then, should we rebaptize those who are sure they have been baptized! God grant they then believed, but it makes no difference if they did not. The Anabaptists cannot be sure their baptism is a right one, since they base their rebaptizing on a faith of which they cannot be sure. Hence they play a gambling game with those they rebaptize. To be uncertain and dubious in godly things is to sin and tempt God. Whoever teaches deceit for uncertainty in place of sure truth lies in the same way as he who speaks openly against the truth. For he speaks that of which he is himself not sure and yet wants it to be taken as truth. But whoever would base baptism on the commandment and ordinance of God would soon realize that rebaptism is neither necessary nor useful. The first baptism sufficiently meets the requirement of God.

They are guilty also of blaspheming and denying the commandment and work of God. For while the first baptism is in accord with the commandment of God and justice is done to it by its very performance, they still insist it is wrong and only a dog's bath. What else are they saying but that God's command and work are wrong and amount to a dog's bath? This they say for no other reason than that they demand a certainty of faith in baptism though it is impossible to have this certainty. This is to deny and blaspheme a sure command and work of God for an uncertain delusion.

Assume that the first baptism is without faith. Tell me which is the greater and the more important in the second baptism, the Word of God or faith? Is it not true that the Word of God is greater and more important than faith, since faith builds and is founded on the Word of God rather than God's Word on faith? Furthermore faith may waver and change, but God's Word remains forever [Isa. 40:6-9; I Pet. 1:24]. Then too, tell me, if one of these two should be otherwise, which should it rather be: the immutable Word or the changeable faith? Would it not more reasonably be the faith that should be subject to change rather than the Word of God? It is fairer to assume that the Word of God would change faith, if a right one were lacking, than that faith would change the Word of God. So they must confess that in the first baptism it was not the Word of God that was defective, but faith, and that what is needed is another faith and not another Word. Why then do they not concern themselves rather with a change of faith and let the Word remain unaltered? Shall we call God's Word and ordinance false because we do not truly believe it? In that case a true word would be rare and far between. If they were to act rightly according to their own peculiar logic they should be urging a rebelieving, not a rebaptizing. For baptism is by the Word and ordinance of God and dare not be opposed to it or other than it is, while faith may be otherwise than it is (if it is not present). So really they should be "Anabelievers" and not Anabaptists, if they were right, which, of course, they are not.

Since then these baptizers are altogether unsure of themselves, and reveal that they are lying, and thereby deny and blaspheme the ordinance of God through their deceitful uncertainty, making the last first, basing the Word and ordinance of God on human work and faith, urging baptism when they should be urging faith, every devout Christian, convinced that they are misleading, uncertain, and perverted spirits, should avoid them at the peril of his soul's salvation. May Christ, our Lord, grant this and help us. Amen.

This is as much as I can undertake now, briefly and hastily. For at this time I am not able to go into this matter more thoroughly. As mentioned I am not sure what they do believe. For the devil is mad and talks so wildly and stirs up so much confusion that absolutely no one knows what he believes. The Anabaptists agree with the foes of the sacrament that only bread and wine are in the Lord's Supper. Yet the sacramentarians disagree with the Anabaptists on baptism. Also, the sacramentarians are not agreed among themselves nor the Anabaptists among themselves. They are at one only in regard to and in opposition to us. Likewise the papacy is divided into innumerable factions of priests and monks who once devoured each other among themselves, until now, in their opposition to us, they are united. It is the same among temporal princes and lords. Pilate and Herod become one over against Christ, though previously they were mortal enemies. But in this particular case, the error of the Anabaptists is more tolerable than that of the sacramentarians. For the sacramentarians altogether destroy baptism, while the Anabaptists give it another character. Still there is reason to hope that they will right themselves. It is enough to have demonstrated that the Anabaptists' faith is uncertain and deceptive and that they cannot prove their case.

For Satan needs do no more through the enthusiasts than always to produce doubt. He thinks it is enough where he can speak haughtily and contemptuously about us, as the rebel sacramentarians do. None of them take pains to make clear and to prove their arrogance, but their concern is to make our interpretation contemptible and uncertain. They teach doubt, not faith, calling this Scripture and the Word of God. The devil knows he can accomplish nothing in the bright light of truth, so he stirs up the dust, hoping to raise a cloud before our eyes so that we cannot see the light. In the cloud he dazzles us with will o' the wisps to mislead us. Having made up their minds concerning their peculiar notions, they attempt to make the Scriptures agree with them by dragging passages in by the hair. But Christ has faithfully stood by our side up to this point and will continue to trod Satan under our foot. He will protect you all against the seductions of your tyrant and Antichrist and mercifully help us to gain his freedom. Amen.

INSTRUCTIONS
FOR THE VISITORS OF
PARISH PASTORS
IN ELECTORAL SAXONY

1528

Translated by Conrad Bergendoff

INTRODUCTION

In the confusion that resulted from the overthrow of the power of the Roman bishops by the Reformation a need arose to reform the parish life of the congregations according to the doctrines now recognized as evangelical. Luther was not primarily interested in matters of organization, but he recognized increasingly that new forms would have to take the place of those rejected. Among the first of his proposals were those in the field of worship, the *Formula Missae* in 1523 and the *Deutsche Messe* in 1526.

Everywhere it was difficult to find clergymen who understood the import of the Reformation doctrine for the pastoral work in the congregation. Nor were the laity ready to support the pastors and care for the churches on a voluntary basis. In some places the people even interpreted the new movement as a liberation from all obligation to the servants or institutions of the church. The princes realized that strong leadership was needed. In January, 1524, Duke John Frederick of Saxony turned to Luther for guidance, but whatever might have been contemplated was made impossible by the events of the Peasants' Uprising.

In October, 1525, Luther urged Elector John of Saxony to give attention to the plight of the clergy and the churches. The prince felt that the cities should help economically, but he encouraged Luther to propose a specific plan, which Luther did in November. He recommended a visitation to discover the actual situation. The territory was to be divided into regions which were to be visited by representatives of the nobility and the court, and where need existed the government should make provision for clergy, churches, or schools, out of public funds.

Not much was done until November of the following year when Luther pointedly told the Elector that the confiscation of monasteries and church property was not meant to enrich the aristocracy, but that the taking over of former church property obligated the government to support the schools and the churches which formerly had been supported by this property. He wanted a team of four visitors: two to examine the economic; two, the religious affairs of the parishes. Communities were to be made to pay, according to their ability, for the support of the church on the same principle as they were taxed for bridges, roads, and defense. In the present emergency the government was bound by its duty to its citizens to assume this responsibility in the church.

Luther's importunity caused the Elector to act, and in February, 1527, the visitation began. Lack of sufficiently explicit directions hampered the visitors, who made suggestions as they proceeded. As they reported, Luther made further observations, and more complete instructions were gradually formulated and studied by various officials in September. Melanchthon drew up a short guide as a doctrinal foundation for the visitation, entitled *Articles of Visitation*. This was not acceptable to John Agricola, who felt Melanchthon was giving the papists reason to think the reformers were yielding to Rome on some points. Luther found it necessary in November to bring him and Melanchthon together to reconcile their views on the relationship of faith and repentance. This became one of the first internal controversies between the Lutherans.

In January of 1528 the Elector asked Luther to provide a preface which would explain the origin of the *Instructions*. The Elector also recommended that no new regulations be published regarding forbidden degrees in marriage, and to this Luther assented, since the pastors could be counselled orally on this point. But he refused to follow the Elector's suggestion and omit the passages which gave pastors permission to administer the sacrament in one kind in cases where weak consciences seemed to justify this as a temporary measure. But in 1538 when a second edition was printed Luther did withdraw this concession. Luther refused, too, to be concerned about the Romanist claim that the treatment on repentance represented a retraction of his earlier stand.

Melanchthon was the author of the *Instructions*, but Luther's ideas underlie the whole and some passages reflect his pen. Because of the endorsement of it by Luther, and the fact that he not only wrote the preface but made revisions in later editions, the work is generally included in the works of Luther. Duke Henry made the revised form of 1538 the basis of a Saxon visitation in 1539, bringing out an edition for his duchy. Again in 1545 Luther wrote a preface for an edition which served as a guide for the visitation of the Diocese of Naumburg. Bugenhagen provided a Latin translation of the second edition (1538) and used it in reorganizing the church in Denmark.

The translation follows the Wittenberg text of 1528, as given in the WA 26, 195-240.

INSTRUCTIONS
FOR THE VISITORS OF
PARISH PASTORS
IN ELECTORAL SAXONY

Preface

Both the Old and the New Testaments give sufficient evidence
of what a divinely wholesome thing it would be if pastors and
Christian congregations might be visited by understanding and
competent persons. For we read in Acts 9 [:32] that St. Peter
travelled about in the land of the Jews. And in Acts 15 [:2] we are
told that St. Paul together with Barnabas revisited all those places
where they had preached. All his epistles reveal his concern for all
the congregations and pastors. He writes letters, he sends his
disciples, he goes himself. So the apostles, according to Acts 8 [:14],
when they heard how the Word had been received in Samaria, sent
Peter and John there. Also we read in the Old Testament how
Samuel travelled around, now to Ramah [I Sam. 7:17], now to Nob
[I Sam. 21:1], now to Gilgal [I Sam. 10:8; 11:14; 13:8; 15:12] and
other places, not out of delight for taking a walk but out of love
and a sense of duty in his ministry and because of the want and
need of the people. Elijah [I Kings 17–21] and Elisha [II Kings
2–13] did the same, as we read in the books of Kings. More than
any, Christ has done this kind of work on behalf of all, and on this
account possessed no place on earth where he could lay his head
or which he could call his own. This began even while he was in
the womb, for he went with his mother over the hills to visit
St. John [Luke 1:39].

Formerly, in the days of the ancient Fathers, the holy bishops
diligently followed these examples and even yet much of this is

found in the papal laws. For it was in this kind of activity that the bishops and archbishops had their origin—each one was obligated to a greater or lesser extent to visit and examine. For, actually, bishop means supervisor or visitor, and archbishop a supervisor or visitor of bishops, to see to it that each parish pastor visits and watches over and supervises his people in regard to teaching and life. And the archbishop was to visit, watch over, and supervise the bishops as to their teaching. But in time this office became such a show of secular pomp when the bishops made themselves princes and lords, that the duty of supervision was turned over to a provost or vicar or dean. Then the provosts and deans and chapter heads became servile courtiers and left supervision to deputies who with their notices of summons plagued the people with their extortions and visited no one.

Finally, when things reached their lowest, the deputies themselves remained at home in a warm house and sent perchance some rascal or ne'er-do-well who wandered around the countryside and in towns, and what he heard from mean mouths or gossip among men and women in the taverns he reported to his superior who then exercised his fleecing office, scraping and skinning innocent people of their goods and leaving murder and misery where there had been honor and good name. The holy synods were forgotten. In brief this is what befell so worthy an office and nothing remained of it except the burdening and banning of people because of money, debts, and temporal goods and the making of a divine order out of the bellowing of antiphons and versicles in churches. No attention is paid to how one teaches, believes, loves, how one lives a Christian life, how to care for the poor, how one comforts the weak, or punishes the unruly, and whatever else belongs to such an office. They are altogether officious and gluttonous fellows who destroy what belongs to the people and do worse than nothing for them. This office has fared like all holy and ancient Christian doctrine and order—it has become the farce and contempt of the devil and Antichrist with awful and terrible destruction of souls.

Who can describe how useful and necessary this office is in the Christian church? One can sense it in the abuses which have come through a period of deterioration and perversion. But no doctrine or vocation has remained sound or pure. On the contrary, a host of frightful sects and mobs, like the chapters and monasteries, have cropped up, whereby the Christian church has been altogether suppressed, faith has died out, love turned into wrangling and war, the gospel put in the shadow, and purely human inventions, teachings, and dreams have ruled in place of the gospel. Surely the devil enjoyed success when he tore down this office and brought it under his own power, setting up instead these spiritual scarecrows and monk calves,[1] so that no one resisted him. Even when the office is rightly and diligently administered it takes a lot of effort to exercise it properly, as Paul complained to the Thessalonians, Corinthians, and Galatians, for the apostles themselves had their hands full to keep things in order. What good purpose then can these lazy, sluggish bullies accomplish?

Now that the gospel through the unspeakable grace and mercy of God has again come to us or in fact has appeared for the first time, and we have come to see how grievously the Christian church has been confused, scattered, and torn, we would like to have seen the true episcopal office and practice of visitation re-established because of the pressing need. However, since none of us felt a call or definite command to do this, and St. Peter has not countenanced the creation of anything in the church unless we have the conviction that it is willed of God, no one has dared to undertake it. Preferring to follow what is certain and to be guided by love's office (which is a common obligation of Christians), we have respectfully appealed to the illustrious and noble prince and lord, John, Duke of Saxony, First Marshall and Elector of the Roman Empire, Landgrave of Thuringia, Margrave of Meissen, our most gracious lord and prince,[2] constituted of God as our certain temporal sovereign, that out of Christian love (since he is not obligated to do so as a temporal sovereign) and by God's will for the benefit of the gospel and the welfare of the wretched Christians in his territory, His Electoral grace might call and ordain to this office several competent persons. To this His Electoral grace through the goodness of God has

---

[1] Cf. *Deutung der zwo greulichen Figuren, Babstesels zu Rom und Mönchkalbs zu Freiberg in Meissen funden* (1523), WA 11, 357ff., in which Luther interpreted the appearance of a freak calf as a sign betckening judgment on monasticism.

[2] John the Steadfast (1468-1532), who succeeded his brother, Frederick the Wise, as elector.

graciously consented, and he has commissioned and commanded for this purpose these four persons, namely, the gracious and honorable Herr Hans of Planitz, Knight,[3] etc., the worthy and learned Jerome Schurff, Doctor of Laws,[4] etc., the honorable and constant Asmus of Haubitz,[5] etc., and the worthy Philip Melanchthon, Master,[6] etc. May God grant that it may be and become a happy example which all other German princes may fruitfully imitate, and which Christ on the last day will richly reward. Amen.

But the devil through his poisonous, worthless gossips can leave no godly work unstained and uncaricatured. Already he has used our enemies to criticize and condemn us so that some boast that we have regretted our teaching and are retreating and recanting.[7] (Would to God that their boast were true, and that our recanting were accepted by them! Surely they would more approach us than we them and would have to confirm our teaching and recant their stand.) Therefore I have been led to publish everything which the visitors have prepared and shown to our gracious lord after I have carefully reviewed it in collected form, making it known in published form, so that everyone may see that we are not trying to cover up or hide anything, but would gladly and sincerely seek light and permit it. While we cannot issue any strict commands as if we were publishing a new form of papal decrees, but are rather giving an account or report which may serve as a witness and confession of our faith, we yet hope that all devout and peaceable pastors who find their sincere joy in the gospel and delight to be of one mind with us will act as St. Paul teaches in Phil. 2 [:2], and will heed our prince and gracious lord. We hope they will not ungratefully and proudly despise our love and good intention, but will willingly, without any compulsion, subject themselves in a spirit of love to

---

[3] Hans von der Planitz (d. 1535), lawyer and diplomatic representative, who was in the service of the electors of Saxony, present at the Leipzig Debate (1519) and at the Diet of Augsburg (1530).
[4] Jerome Schurff (1481-1554), professor of jurisprudence at Wittenberg, who was present on the occasion of Luther's trial at the Diet of Worms (1521) and remained faithful to the Reformation cause throughout his life.
[5] It has not been possible to further identify Asmus of Haubitz.
[6] Philip Melanchthon (1497-1560), who served as professor at Wittenberg and became one of Luther's closest co-workers.
[7] Because of the advice, not only to confess to God but also to the pastor (Cf. p. 296) some, notably Erasmus, held that evangelical Christians were edging back toward Rome. Cf. WA 26, 183.

such visitation and with us peacefully accept these visitors until God the Holy Spirit brings to pass something that is better, through them or through us.

If some obstinately want to set themselves against us and without good reason demand something else, as there always are undisciplined heads who out of utter perversity are able to do nothing in common or in agreement, but are different and self-centered in heart and life, we must separate these from ourselves as chaff on the threshing floor and refuse to accommodate ourselves to them. In this matter, too, we shall not neglect to solicit the help and counsel of our gracious lord. While His Electoral grace is not obligated to teach and to rule in spiritual affairs, he is obligated as temporal sovereign to so order things that strife, rioting, and rebellion do not arise among his subjects; even as the Emperor Constantine summoned the bishops to Nicaea since he did not want to tolerate the dissension which Arius had stirred up among the Christians in the empire, and constrained them to preserve unity in teaching and faith.[8] May God, the Father of all mercy, grant us through Jesus Christ, his dear Son, the spirit of unity and the power to do his will. Even though the finest spirit of unity prevails among us we still have our hands full to do good and to be established by the power of God. What would happen if there were to be disunity and disagreement among us? The devil has become neither pious nor devout this year, nor will he ever be so. So let us be on guard and anxious to keep (as Paul teaches) the spiritual unity in the bond of love and of peace [Eph. 4:3]. Amen.

Contents of the Instructions

The Doctrine
The Ten Commandments

---

[8] Constantine the Great, Roman Emperor (306-337), summoned the bishops of the eastern and western branches of the church to Nicaea in A.D. 325 to establish unity and peace between two opposing parties, one of which rallied about the point of view held by Arius (d. 336), presbyter in Alexandria, the other about the one espoused by Athanasius (d. 373), deacon and later bishop of Alexandria. Arius held that there was a time when Christ was not, while Athanasius stoutly defended the eternal divinity of Christ. Temporary peace and unity were established by the emperor through the banishment of Arius and adherents of his point of view while declaring the signatories to the position maintained by Athanasius as correct.

True Christian Prayer
Tribulation
The Sacrament of Baptism
The Sacrament of the Body and Blood of the Lord
True Christian Penance
True Christian Confession
True Christian Satisfaction for Sin
The Human Order of the Church
Marriage
Free Will
Christian Freedom
The Turks
Daily Worship in the Church
The True Christian Ban
The Office of Superintendents
Schools—the First, Second, and Third Divisions[9]

The Doctrine

In regard to doctrine we observe especially this defect that, while some preach about the faith by which we are to be justified, it is still not clearly enough explained how one shall attain to this faith, and almost all omit one aspect of the Christian faith without which no one can understand what faith is or means. For Christ says in the last chapter of Luke [24:47] that we are to preach in his name repentance and forgiveness of sins.

Many now talk only about the forgiveness of sins and say little or nothing about repentance. There neither is forgiveness of sins without repentance nor can forgiveness of sins be understood without repentance. It follows that if we preach the forgiveness of sins without repentance that the people imagine that they have already obtained the forgiveness of sins, becoming thereby secure and without compunction of conscience. This would be a greater error and sin than all the errors hitherto prevailing. Surely we need to be concerned lest, as Christ says in Matt. 12 [:45] the last state becomes worse than the first.

---

[9] Omitted in the first edition of the *Instructions* (1528), this classification was included in the Table of Contents of the second edition (1538-1539).

Therefore we have instructed and admonished pastors that it is their duty to preach the whole gospel and not one portion without the other. For God says in Deut. 4 [:2]: "You shall not add to the word . . . nor take from it." There are preachers who now attack the pope because of what he has added to the Scriptures, which unfortunately is all too true. But when these do not preach repentance, they tear out a great part of Scripture. They have very little good to say about the eating of meat and the like, though they should not keep silent when they have an opportunity to defend Christian liberty against tyranny. What else is this than what Christ says in Matt. 23 [:24]: "Straining out a gnat and swallowing a camel."

So we have admonished them to exhort the people diligently and frequently to repent and grieve over their sins and to fear the judgment of God. Nor are they to neglect the greatest and most important element of repentance, for both John and Christ condemned the Pharisees more severely for their hypocritical holiness than for ordinary sins. The preachers are to condemn the gross sins of the common man, but more rigorously demand repentance where there is false holiness.

But some[10] hold that nothing should be taught to precede faith and that repentance follows from and after faith, in order that our opponents might not be able to say that we have recanted our former teaching. One ought to remember that repentance and law belong to the common faith. For one must of course first believe that God is the one who threatens, commands, and frightens, etc. So it is best for the unschooled, common people that such phases of the faith retain the name of repentance, commandment, law, fear, etc., so that they may the better distinguish and understand the faith in Christ which the apostles call justifying faith, i.e., which makes righteous and takes away sin. This the faith which stems from commandment and repentance does not do, yet it causes the common man to have doubts concerning the meaning of faith and to raise pointless questions in his mind.

[10] John Agricola of Eisleben maintained that repentance follows faith; Melanchthon that it precedes faith. Their opposing points of view were reconciled temporarily in the formula above after a meeting with Luther and Bugenhagen at Torgau, August 26-29, 1527. Cf. Melanchthon's letter to Justus Jonas. C.R. 1, 914ff.

The Ten Commandments

The preachers are to proclaim and explain the Ten Commandments often and earnestly, yet not only the commandments but also how God will punish those who do not keep them and how he often has inflicted temporal punishment. For such examples are written in order to forewarn people, for instance, how the angels spoke to Abraham in Gen. 19 [:12f.], and told how God would punish Sodom and destroy it with the fire of hell. For they knew that he would tell it to his descendants so that they would learn to fear God.

So too they are to point out and condemn various specific vices, as adultery, drunkenness, envy, and hate, and how God has punished these, indicating that without doubt after this life he will punish still more severely if there is not improvement here.

The people are thus to be urged and exhorted to fear God, to repent and show contrition, lest their ease and life of false security be punished. Therefore Paul says in Rom. 3 [:20]: "Through the law comes (only) knowledge of sin." True repentance is nothing but an acknowledgment of sin.

Then it is important that faith be preached. Whoever experiences grief and contrition over his sins should believe that his sins are forgiven, not on account of his merits, but on account of Christ. When the contrite and fearful conscience experiences peace, comfort, and joy on hearing that his sins are forgiven because of Christ, then faith is present—the faith that makes him righteous before God. We are to teach the people diligently that this faith cannot exist without earnest and true contrition and fear of God, as it is written in Psalm 110 [Ps. 111:10] and Prov. 1 [:7], "The fear of the Lord is the beginning of knowledge." And Isaiah says in the last chapter: "On whom does God look except on the trembling and contrite heart?" [11]

This shall be proclaimed repeatedly, so that the people do not entertain false notions and think they have faith when they are far from having it. It shall be made clear that only if they have faith can they truly repent and grieve over their sins. Without repentance theirs is an imagined faith. True faith brings comfort and joy in

---

[11] Isa. 66:2: "But this is the man to whom I will look, he that is humble and contrite in spirit, and trembles at my word." Cf. also Ecclus. (Sirach) 1:16.

God, and we do not feel such comfort and joy where there is no repentance or fearfulness, as Christ says in Matt. 11 [:5]: "The poor have good news preached to them."

These two are the first elements of Christian life: Repentance or contrition and grief, and faith through which we receive the forgiveness of sins and are righteous before God. Both should grow and increase in us. The third element of Christian life is the doing of good works: To be chaste, to love and help the neighbor, to refrain from lying, from deceit, from stealing, from murder, from vengefulness, and avenging oneself, etc.

Therefore again and again the Ten Commandments are to be assiduously taught, for all good works are therein comprehended.

They are called good works not only because they are done for the welfare of our neighbors, but because God has commanded them, and so they also are well pleasing to God. God has no delight in those who do not obey the commandments, as is stated in Mic. 6 [:8]: "O man, I will show you what is good and what God requires of you, namely, to do justice. Yea, do justice, delight to do good to your neighbor, and walk humbly before God."

The first commandment teaches us to fear God. For God threatens those who do not reverence him. It teaches us also to believe in and trust God, for God promises to do good to those who love him, that is, look to him for blessings, as we read in Isa. 64 [:4] and I Cor. 2 [:9]: "What no eye has seen, nor ear heard, nor the heart of man conceived, what God has prepared for those who love him."

The second commandment teaches us not to misuse the name of God. We rightly use his name when we call on him in every need, bodily or spiritual, as he has commanded in Ps. 49 [Ps. 50:15]: "Call upon me in the day of trouble; I will deliver you, and you shall glorify me." And in the same psalm, God tells what is the right kind of service by which we may serve him: to call upon him and pray, that he may help, and to give him thanks because of his goodness. For God says in this place: "And you shall glorify me." Also, "He who offers thanks, praises me, and in this way, I shall show him the salvation of God" [Ps. 50:23].

The pastors and preachers are to exhort the people to pray. For we fulfil this commandment by praying, that is, asking God for his help in all our trials and troubles. They are to instruct the people what prayer is, and how one is to pray.

True Christian Prayer

First, they should teach that God has commanded us to pray. Just as it is a great sin to commit murder so also it is sinful not to pray or to ask God for something. Indeed this commandment is meant to urge us on to pray. So great is the goodness of God that not only does he help those who ask for help but also bids us pray, as we read in Luke 18 [:1] and many other passages, which pastors should teach their people. If we knew of a prince who not only gave what was asked of him, but commanded everyone to ask for what he needed, we would look on such a one as a gracious master and ask much of him. Our Lord gives the more freely as we pray the more of him, as he said of Mary Magdalene in Luke 7 [:47]: "Therefore is much given her, because she has looked for so much from me."

Secondly, they should make clear that God also has promised to hear us (Matt. 7 [:7]; Luke 11 [:9]): "Ask and it will be given you." We should depend on such a promise and not doubt that God will hear our prayer. So Christ speaks in Mark 11 [:24]: "Therefore I tell you, whatever you ask in prayer, believe that you receive it, and you will."

The fact that we are sinners should not frighten us away. For He does not hear us because of our merits, but on account of his promise. Thus, in the last verse of Micah [7:20]: "Thou wilt show faithfulness to Jacob and steadfast love to Abraham, as thou hast sworn to our fathers from the days of old."

But no answer is promised the prayer of the sinner and the hypocrite who knows no repentance for his sin and hypocrisy. For of him Ps. 18 [:42] says: "They cried for help, but there was none to save, they cried to the Lord, but he did not answer them."

But those who are penitent, and believe that on Christ's account God has forgiven them, should not hold back because of the sins they have committed and their hypocrisy. For God does not want any doubting, but wants us to believe that he hears and will help us. Therefore the pastors should also instruct their people that

278

prayer includes faith that God will hear us, as James writes in Jas. 1 [:6f.]: "But let him ask in faith, with no doubting, for he who doubts is like a wave of the sea that is driven and tossed by the wind. For that person must not suppose that he will receive anything from the Lord."

But it cannot be called prayer when one repeats heedlessly a great number of *Pater Nosters* or psalms, pays little regard to or places no reliance on God's promise to hear, or does not wait for God's help. Indeed such a one has no God, and it happens to him what Ps. 114 [115:6] says, "Their idols have ears but do not hear," that is, such a one imagines a god who does not hear.

Thirdly, the people are to be instructed to pray God both for temporal and spiritual things. Indeed each one is to be encouraged to bring his wants to God. One suffers from poverty, another from sickness, a third from sin, a fourth from lack of faith and another from shortcomings. Many therefore seek help of St. Anthony,[12] or St. Sebastian,[13] etc. But whatever it may be, help should be sought from God.

And if God delays in helping us we should not therefore cease to pray, as we are taught in Luke 18 [:1]. For in this manner God gives us practice in faith. Even if God does not give what we pray for, still we should not doubt that he has heard our prayer. We should realize that instead of what we have asked he will give something better. Committing such requests to him, we ought not set time or measure for his answer. How long did not Abraham and the other patriarchs have to wait before the promised land was given them? Such examples are plentiful in the Scriptures.

The third commandment teaches us to keep the Sabbath holy. Even though God now has not given us a command to observe the Sabbath in an external way as in the case of the Jews so that no manual labor could then be done, yet certain external aspects of the Sabbath are to be observed, such as the hearing and learning of the Word of God and for the people to have stated times on which to assemble, etc.

---

[12] St. Anthony of Padua (1195-1231) who was canonized within a year after his death by Gregory IX.
[13] St. Sebastian who died a martyr's death probably toward the close of the third century is considered a protector against the plague.

The fourth commandment teaches us to honor our parents and to obey them. Here the young people shall frequently be confronted with the promise of God in Exodus 20 [:12]: "Whoever honors his parents shall long live." That is, he shall prosper all his life. Whoever dishonors parents and disobeys them will have adversity. Thus Ham was cursed by his father Noah (Gen. 9 [:25]). For his father said, "Cursed be Canaan; a slave of slaves shall he be to his brothers." Thus Absalom came to an evil end because he had pursued his father, and was finally caught in a tree and hanged as we read in II Sam. 18 [:9]. Thus Jacob cursed Reuben because he violated his wife, for his father said (Gen. 49 [:4]): "You shall not have pre-eminence because you went up to your father's bed; then you defiled it—you went up to my couch." For it is needful to instruct the people that all success and adversity come from God, success to those who fear God and keep his commandments, adversity to those who despise him. And even if God lets ill befall the righteous, yet he will afford help and comfort not only through spiritual but also temporal gifts, as Psalm 33 (Ps. 34 [:19]) says: "Many are the afflictions of the righteous; but the Lord delivers him out of them all." And the entire Thirty-seventh Psalm proclaims, "Fret not yourself because of the wicked." It is a great mistake not to urge the people to hope and ask for temporal goods from God, for in the use of these faith is practiced.

Nor is it necessary to engage in subtle debate as to whether or not God gives these things on account of our works. It is enough to teach that God demands such works and rewards them because he has promised to do so without our merit.

It is necessary to teach that God forgives our sins without reference to any of our works, on account of Christ. So hostile is God to sin that the work of no creature can make satisfaction for it— only the sacrifice of God's own Son could do this.

But then many clamor: good works are not meritorious. It would be much better to teach people to do good works and drop the sharp disputes. For the truth is that God gives blessings because of his promise, not because of our works, yet the good works which God has commanded must be done.

Therefore undisciplined people need forcefully to be reminded how severely God punishes those who are disobedient toward parents with all kinds of misfortune. For God permits them to suffer shame, poverty, sickness, and other evils.

Also we need to teach parents their responsibility to instil in their children the fear of God, to teach and let them learn the Word of God. Thus we read in the Proverbs of Solomon 12 [Prov. 22:15]: "Folly is bound up in the heart of a child, but the rod of discipline drives it far from him." So Paul in Eph. 6 [:4] says: "Fathers, do not provoke your children to anger, but bring them up in the discipline and instruction of the Lord." Such is the example of Eli who according to I Sam. 2 [:30] was punished by God and deprived of his priestly office because he had not taken seriously the rearing of his children. Never has youth been more insolent than today—we see how little they obey, how little they respect their parents. On this account, undoubtedly, the world is full of plagues, war, rebellion, and other evils.

To this commandment, too, belongs the reverence for old age.

Also that we honor the office of the priesthood, which ministers to us with the Word of God. For the ministry is a servant of God's Word and through it we have the Word of God, as St. Paul writes in I Tim. 5 [:17]: "Let the elders who rule well be considered worthy of double honor, especially those who labor in preaching and teaching."

Also that we obey the government. In Romans 13 Paul enumerates three points concerning government.

First, the payment of taxes, namely that each shall give the authorities such money and labor as is required of him [Rom. 13:6f].

Second, respect, that is, that we have sincere respect for government. Even if government cannot in every instance punish our violations, still we should know that God will punish, for he has established and maintains government. Also we can be assured that all the rebellious will be punished, as Paul says in Rom. 13 [:27]: "Therefore he who resists the authorities resists what God has appointed, and those who resist will incur judgment." So also Solomon declares in Prov. 24 [21-22]: "My son, fear the Lord and the king, and do not disobey either of them; for disaster from them will rise suddenly, and who knows the ruin that will come from them both?"

It is well to remind the people of examples of God's punishment of the rebellious, as we read of Datham and Abiram who set themselves against Moses, in Num. 16 [:31ff.]: "The ground under them split asunder; and the earth opened its mouth and swallowed them up, with their households and all the men that belonged to Korah and all their goods. So they and all that belong to them went down alive into Sheol; and the earth closed over them. . . . And fire came forth . . . and consumed the two hundred and fifty men offering the incense."

Abimelech, who set himself against the sixty-nine sons of Gideon, met his end, according to Judg. 9 [:53] and II Sam. 11 [:21] when a woman on a tower in Thebez threw a part of a millstone on his head and crushed his skull.

Sheba, who drew Israel away from David, as we read in II Sam. 20 [:22], was for this reason beheaded.

Absalom, who rose up against his father David, was hanged at last in an oak tree, as also related in II Sam. 18 [:9].

Zambri or Zimri, who conspired against his lord Elah, king of Israel, and killed him, was king only seven days. For Omri, king of Israel besieged him at Tirzah, and when Zimri saw that the city would be won, he went into the palace and burned the king's house over him. So we read in I Kings 16 [8ff.].

Clearly, God lets no wickedness go unpunished. Murder never goes unavenged, as Christ says in Matt. 26 [:52]: "For all who take the sword will perish by the sword." That is, whoever takes the sword on his own initiative without the authority of government will be punished. Scripture abounds in such passages, which the people should be taught diligently. For instance Solomon says in Prov. 16 [:14]: "A king's wrath is a messenger of death, and a wise man will appease it." Or, in Prov. 20 [:2]: "The dread wrath of a king is like the growling of a young lion; he who provokes him to anger, sins against his soul."

The third duty we owe government is honor. For how can we imagine that we have paid the government something when we have given it tax or tithe or served it with physical labor? God requires of us a much higher service toward the government, namely, honor. This means, first, that we recognize that government is from God and that through it he gives us much greater benefits. For if God did not maintain government and justice in the world, the devil, who is a murderer, would everywhere bring about murder, so that none of us could be sure of life, wife, or children.

But God sustains government and through it gives peace and punishes and guards against the wicked, so that we may support wife and children, bring up children in the discipline and knowledge of God, have security in our homes and on the streets, that each may help the other, and communicate and live with another. Such gifts are altogether of heaven, and God desires that we consider and recognize them as gifts of God. He desires us to honor government as a servant of his and to show gratitude to it because through it God gives us such great benefits.

Whoever, thus, might see God in government, would have sincere love towards government. Whoever could estimate the blessings which we receive through government, would be heartily thankful toward government. If you knew that someone had saved your child from death, you would thank him warmly. Why then are you not grateful to the government which saves you, your children, your wife, daily from murder? If the government did not restrain the wicked, when could we be secure? Therefore when you look on wife and children, bear in mind that these are gifts of God which you may possess through the government. And as you love your children, you should also love the government. Because the common man does not acknowledge such blessings as peace, justice, and punishment of the wicked, we need often to remind him of them and diligently to explain them to him.

Secondly, we give greatest honor to the government when we pray for it, that God may give those in authority grace and understanding to rule peacefully and wisely, as St. Paul has taught in I Tim. 2 [:1ff.]: "First of all, then, I urge that supplications, prayers, intercessions, and thanksgiving be made for all men, for kings and all who are in high positions, that we may lead a quiet and peaceable life, godly and respectful in every way. This is good, and it is acceptable in the sight of God our Savior." And Bar. 1 [:11f.]: "Pray for the life of Nabuchodonosor king of Babylon, and for the life of Balthasar his son, that their days may be upon earth as the days of heaven." For since peace is a divine gift we need to ask and pray for it from God.

Some ask, how can government be from God, since so many

have come to power by evil use of force? Julian[14] is an example. And Scriptures call Nimrod a hunter, because he had grasped for so much (Gen. 10 [:9]).

This is the answer. When in Rom. 13 [:1] Paul says that the government is of God, this is not to be understood in the sense that government is an affliction in the way that murder or any other crime is inflicted by God, but in the sense that government is a special ordinance and function of God, just as the sun is a creature of God or marriage is established by God. An evil man who takes a wife with evil intent can abuse the ordinance of marriage. So also a tyrant can abuse the ordinance of God, as Julian or Nero[15] did. The ordinance, by which peace and justice is maintained, remains a divine creation even if the person who abuses the ordinance does wrong.

The preachers, accordingly, should faithfully remind the authorities to maintain peace, justice, and security for their subjects, to defend the poor, the widow, and the orphan, and not to look on them as chattel, as God commanded Jeremiah, in Jer. 7 [:2ff.], to preach to all the people of Judah and proclaim his promise to dwell with them. So also Paul writes in Col. [4:1]: "Masters, treat your slaves justly and fairly, knowing that you also have a Master in heaven." The same Lord will in his own time take care of evil authorities. Rehoboam, the son of King Solomon, was a mighty king who grievously oppressed his people by following the counsel of his young companions. So when the people asked that their burden be lightened, King Rehoboam gave this answer: "My little finger is thicker than my father's loins. My father made your yoke heavy, but I will add to your yoke; my father chastised you with whips, but I will chastise you with scorpions" [I Kings 12:10-11]. Then all Israel deserted King Rehoboam, so that he ruled only over the children of Israel who dwelt in the cities of Judah, as we read in I Kings 12 [:17], and retained only one tribe. King Jeroboam had ten tribes, as is recorded in I Kings 11 [:31].

---

[14] Julian, Roman emperor from 361-363 A.D., also known as "the Apostate," defected from the Christian religion and sought to re-introduce hellenistic paganism as the religion in his empire.
[15] Nero, Roman emperor from 54-68 A.D., whose name is associated with the first great persecution of Christians known to history.

Yet citizens are to be diligently instructed not to be less obedient and subject toward harsh government. So St. Peter teaches in I Pet 2 [:18]: "Servants, be submissive to your masters with all respect, not only to the kind and gentle but also to the overbearing." For God yet lives whose word is in Deut. 32 [:35]: "Vengeance is mine, and recompense." He will not let the untoward authority escape.

Some are in doubt if in matters of taking possession of property or punishment of the wicked we should follow laws made by the emperors or heathen. Should we, for instance, hang thieves when the law of Moses taught otherwise? (Exod. 22 [:1ff.]).

We can be assured that we should follow these laws and that it is right to observe the law of emperors.

For as St. Peter writes in I Pet. 2 [:13]: "Be subject for the Lord's sake to every human institution, whether it be to the emperor as supreme, or to governors as sent by him to punish those who do wrong and to praise those who do right."

As circumcision is not enjoined on us, so we are not commanded to follow the administration of the laws of Moses. Thus we read in Acts 15 [:10] that the yoke of the law is not to be laid on the heathen. The gentiles do not need to become Jews, but may remain gentiles. That is, in matters of temporal government they may follow gentile ordinances. Property may be apportioned and punishment administered, not according to the law of Moses but according to their own laws.

According to Exodus, Leviticus, Numbers, and Deuteronomy, Moses ordered tithes to be given only to the priests. But we should give tithes to whomever the government orders.

Moses declares that the eldest or first-born son should inherit a double portion [Deut. 21:17]. We should follow our own laws of inheritance.

Moses teaches in Exod. 22 [:1ff.] that thieves shall be punished by being made to repay [that which has been stolen] partly twofold, partly fourfold.

In such cases our own nation's laws shall govern. It were well, however, that we punished thievery with discrimination and not too severely. For it is a common and frequent experience that very minor thefts are just as severely punished as grave offenses.

But ancient laws are not to be discarded for the sake of peace just because they are severe.

The ancients who instituted these laws were convinced that hard punishments were necessary for those among our people who are disorderly.

Thus each shall follow his own national law. This is a form of Christian liberty, as St. Paul says in Col. 3 [:11]: A Christian is not "Greek, Jew, circumcision, uncircumcision, barbarian, Scythian, slave, free, but Christ is all and in all." So also Paul confirms Gentile justice in Rom. 13 [:1], where he teaches that all authority is of God, whether Jewish or Gentile.

So, we are to be subject to all authority, not only Christian but Gentile.

Yet all law is to be judged by this standard, that it teaches what Paul says in Rom. 13 [:3], the praise of good conduct and the punishment of evil. If a law punishes more severely than the Mosaic law, it is not on that account unjust.

We mention these things because of those who clamor against the law of the land in regard to tithes, hanging, and the like. Partly on this account the rebellion of two years ago was instigated. Those who raise this clamor should be punished as rebellious. For we are to fear all temporal laws and ordinances as the will and law of God. For Solomon says in Prov. 16 [:10]: "Inspired decisions are on the lips of a king," that is, the order or commandment of the authorities is to be respected as an ordinance of God. Much is said about this in Rom. 13 [:1ff.]. The other commandments Christ himself explains in Matthew 5.

The people are also to be exhorted to pay honestly and willingly the tax imposed on each. Even if some obligations are heavy each one is bound to pay on account of his duty and his obedience to government so that peace may rule throughout the land. For what else is unwillingness to pay tax or render service than giving rise to thievery and murder?

So they especially who bear the name of Christian should do this in love which willingly bears all burdens, and gives beyond what is due, which pays, even when burdened unjustly, and seeks no revenge through its own powers, as Christ teaches in Matt. 5 [:39]. We ought to bring honor to the holy gospel by paying honestly, as a matter of course, so that the holy gospel is not slandered and disgraced as happens in the case of those who claim in the name of the holy gospel to be free from tithes and other temporal burdens.

Tribulation

To the third part of Christian life, that is, the doing of good works, belongs also the knowledge of how one shall meet tribulation.

First, we are to teach the people that all tribulation, not only of the spirit, but also of the body, is sent from God, whether it is poverty or illness, danger to children, peril of possessions, or hunger. God would thereby admonish us and awaken us to penitence. As we read in I Cor. 11 [:32]: "But when we are judged by the Lord, we are chastened so that we may not be condemned along with the world."

Now it is not enough to know that God sends such experiences. We must also teach that in the midst of these tribulations we are to call upon him and confidently believe that he will help, as we have explained above in regard to prayer. So God says in Psalm 49 [Ps. 50:15]: "Call upon me in the day of trouble; I will deliver you, and you shall glorify me."

Besides all this we should teach the people how weak man is, and how the devil always knows in what way he can entice us into evil, bringing temporal and eternal shame and misery on us. For Christ says in John 8 [:44] that the devil is a murderer. And Peter in I Pet. 5 [:8] says: "The devil prowls around like a roaring lion, seeking some one to devour." We need therefore to stand constantly in the fear of the Lord, watching and praying that God will direct and protect us. We rightly practice our faith when we fight such peril with prayer. So Christ says in Luke 21 [:36]: "Watch at all times and pray."

We have given these instructions to the pastors and explained to them that they should clearly and correctly present to the people these most important matters of the Christian life which we have here described, namely, repentance, faith, and good works, while passing by many other things of which the poor masses understand little.

The Sacrament of Baptism

Baptism shall be retained as hitherto, and children are to be baptized. For baptism has the same import as circumcision, and as children were circumcised so also children shall be baptized. And as God said, he wills to take into his care and protection the children who were circumcised. For such is the Word of God in Gen. 17 [:7]: "I will be God to you and to your descendants after you." Also, "And I will be their God." So also the children who are baptized are in God's care. Therefore we should earnestly pray to God because of this his promise.

The common people are to be taught what great benefits baptism brings, namely that God will care for and protect the child and receive it as his own.

It is well that we use the German language in baptism so that they who witness the act may understand the prayer and the word in baptism.

Occasionally also it should be explained to the people in preaching on the sacrament that baptism does not only mean that God wills to receive children when they are small, but throughout life. Therefore, baptism is not a sign only to children, but also to the older people it is an incitement and exhortation to repentance. For the water in baptism signifies penitence, contrition, and sorrow. So baptism should awaken the faith that those who repent of their sins are cleansed and forgiven. This kind of faith is a complete baptism.

One need not quarrel over the use of chrism.[16] The true chrism with which all Christians are anointed by God himself is the Holy Spirit. So we read in Isa. 61 [:1] and in Eph. 1 [:17].

The Sacrament of the Body and Blood of the Lord

These three articles concerning the sacrament of the true body and blood of our dear Lord Jesus Christ shall be explained to the people.

---

[16] Chrism is a specially consecrated oil employed in the administration of baptism, confirmation, and holy orders in Roman and Eastern Orthodox churches. The 1538-39 edition of the *Instructions* inserted the additional qualification that "chrism is an unnecessary, free matter." WA 26, 213.

First, they are to believe that the true body of Christ is in the bread and the true blood of Christ is in the wine. For thus reads the word of Christ in the Evangelists Matthew, Mark, and Luke: "This is my body" [Matt. 26:26]; "Drink of it all of you" [Mark 14:22]; "This is my blood of the new testament, which is poured out for many for the forgiveness of sins" [Luke 22:19]. So also Paul declares in I Cor. 11 [10:16]: "The bread which we break, is it not a participation in the body of Christ?" Were this now taken to mean not the true body, but only the Word of God, as some interpret it, then it would be a participation not in the body of Christ but only in the Word and Spirit. In this same epistle Paul also declares that this meal is not to be regarded as ordinary food, but as the body of Christ, and he judges those guilty who carelessly receive it as ordinary food [I Cor. 11:27].

Pastors also are to read what the Fathers have written, so that they may the better instruct themselves and others. So Hilary in Book 8[17] on the Holy Trinity says that we should not doubt that this is the true body and blood of Christ, since Christ has so declared.

It is to be remembered that so great a miracle happens through no merit of the priest but because Christ has ordained that when we commune his body is present, just as the sun rises daily without any merit of ours but solely since God has so ordained.

Secondly, the people are to be taught that it is right to receive both bread and wine. For now the holy gospel (God be praised) has been restored and we have clear witness that both elements are to be offered and received. For Christ has so ordained, as the three evangelists point out, and St. Paul has so done in the early church, as we see in I Cor. 11 [:24f.]. No human being may alter such a divine ordinance. We dare not annul a man's last will, as St. Paul writes in Galatians [Gal. 3:15]. Much less is God's own last testament to be changed.

Accordingly we have instructed pastors and preachers to proclaim this teaching of the gospel concerning both kinds to everyone, be he strong, weak, or obstinate. They are in no way

---

[17] Cf. *Nicene and Post-Nicene Fathers of the Christian Church* (New York: 1902), IX, 141.

to favor celebration in one kind, but condemn this as wrong and contrary to the institution and last testament of our Savior and Lord, Jesus Christ. Thus the doctrine itself will be spread in a free, pure, public manner.[18] Inasmuch, however, as no one is to be forced to believe, or driven by command or force from his unbelief, since God likes no forced service and wants only those who are his servants by their own free will, and in view of the fact that the people are confused and uncertain, it has been and still is impossible to establish a rule concerning persons to whom both kinds are to be offered or from whom they are to be withheld according to the teaching of Christ.

So while we can easily say that the doctrine is to be preached purely and freely as Christ himself has given it, we have not been able to bring it about that in all cases, and in every way and by every person, the use and practice conform to this teaching. We must remember that the people are strongly accustomed to receive only one kind, and that there are not a few who on account of this custom are in serious doubt. So one has to let the day have its twelve hours and leave the matter in God's hands.

But as this article arises daily and troubles the conscience we have not wanted to leave the pastors without any guidance at all. We have therefore recommended that the following method and instruction, based on God's counsel, be tried until the Holy Spirit leads us to a better understanding.

First, as indicated above, in every way and manner the doctrine itself shall be firmly held and positively preached and made known that according to the institution of Christ both kinds are to be used in the sacrament. This teaching shall be presented without compromise to everyone, including the weak and the obstinate.

Secondly, where there are weak Christians, who as yet have not heard, or been sufficiently instructed and strengthened by the word of the gospel, and so out of weakness and terror of conscience rather than obstinacy cannot receive both kinds, one may allow these to take communion in one kind for the time being and where they ask for it the pastor or preacher may so administer it. The reason is this: In this way the doctrine of both kinds will not be

---

[18] The following section to "Thirdly . . . ," p. 291, written by Luther for this edition was stricken by him in the second edition, 1538.

weakened or compromised, but only the application or use of the doctrine will be temporarily postponed through Christian patience and love. So Christ was patient with his apostles in many things which were not right, as when they wanted to destroy the Samaritans with fire (Luke 9 [:54ff.]). Or, when they quarrelled about superiority (Matt. 20 [:24ff.]). This and similar things he overlooked, since at that time they were unable to do or know better. They had not yet received the Holy Spirit, they were afraid of death, and for fear of the Jews did not confess Christ when he died. Even nowadays God tolerates much in us and in others which is wrong or insufficient, as a weak faith and other defects, according to Romans 14 and 15.

If despite all this the doctrine nevertheless is maintained and in no wise contradicted, love forgives and endures its inadequate application.

Further, it is uncharitable, even un-Christian, to force these weak ones to receive the sacrament in both kinds or to withhold it in one kind. For thus they feel they are made to sin. We have often experienced that they make confession and do penance for gross heresy when they have taken both kinds against their conscience. Also they think themselves guilty of heresy when they do not receive the one kind as has been their inclination. In both cases the weak faith burdens itself with grievous sin such as heresy, though falsely. This is much worse than for a while not practicing full obedience to the doctrine of both kinds. St. Paul in Rom. 14 [:23] says, "He who judges himself in that he eats is condemned."

So also Paul tolerated circumcision and Jewish food, all the while freely proclaiming freedom in regard to food. To teach and practice this freedom was also God's command and ordinance, and yet the attitude toward the weak was observed as long as nothing contradictory to the doctrine was taught.

Thirdly, as for the obstinate who will neither learn nor practice this doctrine, one should simply offer them neither kind, but let them go. So St. Paul, according to Gal. 2 [:3f.], refused to circumcise Titus when the Jews wanted to insist on it and to condemn liberty. For such obstinate ones are not only imperfect in the practice of the doctrine, but want also to pervert and condemn the doctrine. This we should not suffer nor tolerate. For the doctrine must run straight and clear, even if the deed and practice creep or crawl, run or leap, after it.

The pastor, who knows his people and daily associates with them, must distinguish between the weak and the obstinate. He can easily observe those folk who have a good disposition, who gladly listen to the preaching and gladly want to learn and be rightly guided thereby.

But the rough and the perverse who pay no attention to preaching are under no circumstances to be considered weak, however loudly they claim to be so.

The third article, and the most fundamental, is that one teach the reason for the use of the sacrament and how one shall be properly prepared.

First, the pastor needs to instruct the people how great a sin it is to dishonor the sacrament and to misuse it. For Paul says in I Cor. 11 [:27f.]: "You are guilty of profaning the body and blood of Christ," and "You receive it to judgment upon yourself." Also, "Many of you are ill and many among the Christians have died." For God declared in the second commandment (Exod. 20 [:7]): Whoever dishonors his name, he will not hold guiltless. Undoubtedly also this dishonor to the body and blood of Christ will not go unpunished. This shall be taught the people carefully, so that they may avoid this sin and be urged to reverence, penitence, and improvement. Nor shall such be admitted to the sacrament as are caught in the web of open sin, adultery, gluttony, and the like, and show no contrition.

Secondly, no one shall be admitted to the sacrament unless he has previously been to the pastor who shall inquire if he rightly understands the sacrament, or is in need of further counsel, etc.

Also, it shall be taught that they alone are worthy to receive the sacrament who show true repentance and sorrow for their sins and are terror-stricken in their consciences. Rough, fearless persons will not be admitted. For it is written in I Cor. 11 [:25]: "Do this, as often as ye drink it, in remembrance of me."

Now to remember Christ's death is not only to hear a preacher relate its happening but to feel terrified that God has shown such anger over sin that on its account he has brought death to his only Son, and that no angel or any saint could make satisfaction for sin.

Only Christ, himself God, has had to sacrifice himself, etc. O what severe punishment will fall upon those who regard sin so lightly when they hear how seriously God regards it.

He who rightly remembers the death of Christ shall receive the sacrament and seek comfort. Not that the outward reception will comfort the heart, but it is a sign of the comfort and of the forgiveness of sins. This sign encourages the heart to believe that God forgives a penitent his sins.

Not only by the reception of the sacrament but by the words associated with the sacrament the heart will be encouraged to believe and be quickened. For it is in the words that God promises the forgiveness of sins: "This is my body, given for you." "This is the cup of the new covenant," is the new promise, the promised righteousness, eternal life, "in my blood which is shed for many for the remission of sin."

Thus they obtain the forgiveness of sins not through any outward act but through the faith which is awakened by the word and the sign.

Also the people are to be taught that this sign has been instituted not only to awaken faith but also to instruct us in love, as St. Paul says in I Cor. 10 [:17]: "It is one loaf and it is one body, for we all partake of the same loaf." We are not to harbor envy and hatred, but each is to care for the other, to help the other with alms and every kind of service which God has commanded us.

This teaching shall be repeated often. For what else is it than dishonor of the body of Christ when we harbor envy and hate and want to show no love and yet want to be considered a part of the body of Christ?

True Christian Penance

Penance also is to be reckoned as a sacrament—all sacraments are a kind of penance. There are other reasons, too, for calling it a sacrament, but they need not be recounted here.

Now we have already shown that it is necessary to preach penance, and to punish fearless behavior which is now in the world and has its origin, at least in part, in a wrong understanding of the faith. For many who hear that they should believe, so that all their sins will be forgiven, fashion their own faith and think they are pure. Thus they become secure and arrogant. Such carnal security is worse than all the errors hitherto prevailing. Therefore in preaching the gospel it is necessary in every way to instruct the people where faith may be found and how one attains it. For true faith cannot exist where there is not true contrition and true fear and terror before God.

This is most important in teaching the people. For where there is not contrition and sorrow for sin, there also is no true faith. Thus we read in Ps. 147 [:11]: "The Lord takes pleasure in those who fear him, in those who hope in his steadfast love." God himself also says in Ezek. 3 [:18] that if the preacher does not condemn the error and sin of those whom he teaches, God will lay the loss of their souls to his account. Such a verdict God pronounced upon that kind of preacher who comforts the people and says much about faith and the forgiveness of sins but nothing about penitence or the fear and judgment of God. Jeremiah, too, condemns such preachers in the seventh chapter [Jer. 6:14]: One should not believe those who cry, Peace, Peace, when God is angry and there is no peace.

We need to fear that God will severely punish these preachers and pupils because of such security. For that is the sin which is decried in Jer. 6 [:15], "They did not know how to blush." And St. Paul in Eph. 5 [:5], condemning those who live securely in their perverse ways without sting of conscience, says, "Be sure of this, that no immoral or impure man, or one who is covetous (that is, an idolator) has any inheritance in the kingdom of Christ and of God. Let no one deceive you with empty words, for it is because of these things that the wrath of God comes upon the sons of disobedience. Therefore do not associate with them."

Now penance in reality is sincere contrition and sorrow over one's sins and sincere fear of the wrath and judgment of God. This is contrition and the acknowledgment of sin. "Mortification of the flesh" is also, properly, penance. So in the Scriptures contrition has many names.

Some, in speaking of mortification, mean only holding the carnal nature in check, though this is rather a work of a new life, and is a work that depends on the putting to death of the flesh. So this is nothing else than true contrition.

Some talk this way: We must admit to ourselves that our whole nature is evil, etc. When the people think they thereby acknowledge their sin, they only show their wantonness.

It is one thing "to know oneself," and another, "through the law comes the knowledge of sin." For to know one's sin is to have contrition and sorrow over it and sincere fear of the wrath and judgment of God. So David confessed his sin, when the prophet Nathan came to him and condemned him in II Sam. 12 [:13]. For David knew well enough before that he had sinned, but he still knew no contrition. So he did not have the right knowledge of his sin.

That there is nothing in us without sin is too lofty a truth for laymen to grasp who are just beginning to understand. For we do not easily reach the point where a person fears for all his good works and understands that he sins even in good works. So Solomon says in Eccles. 7 [:20]: "Surely there is not a righteous man on earth who does good and never sins."

Children need to be taught gradually. Similarly, we are to teach penance and contrition on the basis of the gross sins we all know. We are to condemn drunkenness, unchastity, envy and hatred, greed, falsehood, and the like. We are to awaken the people to contrition, and hold before them the judgment of God, his condemnation, and the scriptural examples of God's punishment for sin.

As for hypocrites, when it is necessary let us not forget the wrath and judgment of God upon the false servants of God or hypocrites who slander his name by their seeming holiness.

Some hold that since God creates true contrition in our hearts one ought not to exhort the people to it. It is true that God works true contrition, but he works it through the Word and preaching. We exhort the people to faith and through such preaching God works faith. So we are to exhort and urge to contrition and leave to God in whom he will work contrition. For he works through preaching, as Moses says in Deut. 4 [:24], "God is a devouring fire." The preaching of God's judgment and wrath works contrition in us.

So, the first part of penance is contrition and sorrow. The

second part is faith that the sins will be forgiven on Christ's account. This faith effects good resolution. So with faith we receive the forgiveness of sins, as Paul has said in Rom. 3 [:35]. But, as we have often said, this faith cannot be until there has been contrition and sorrow. For contrition without faith is the contrition of Judas and of Saul; it is despair. So faith without contrition, as we shall show, is presumption and carnal security.

Formerly it has been taught that penance consists of three parts: contrition, confession, and satisfaction. We have said of the first part that contrition and sorrow shall always be preached and that contrition and sorrow imply the acknowledgment of sin and mortification of the flesh. It is well we use these words, contrition and sorrow, for they are clear and easily understood.

True Christian Confession

The papal kind of confession is not commanded, namely, the recounting of all sins. This, furthermore, is impossible, as we read in Ps. 19 [:13], "But who can discern his errors? Clear thou me from hidden faults." Yet there are many reasons why we should exhort the people to confession, especially in those cases where they need counsel and wherein they are most troubled.

No one should be allowed to go to communion who has not been individually examined by his pastor to see if he is prepared to go to the holy sacrament. For Paul says in I Cor. 11 [:27], that they are guilty of profaning the body and blood of Christ who receive it unworthily.

Not only do they who receive it unworthily dishonor the sacrament, but also those who carelessly give it to the unworthy. For the common people run by custom to the sacrament and do not know why they should use the sacrament.

Whoever, thus, does not know why he should receive the sacrament is not to be admitted to it. In examination before the sacrament the people are to be exhorted to make confession, so that they may be instructed where cases of doubt arise in conscience, and may be comforted, when true contrition is in their hearts, as they hear the words of absolution.

True Christian Satisfaction for Sin

It is not in us to make satisfaction for our sins, for Christ alone has made satisfaction for our sins. This part of penance belongs to the forgiveness of sins and faith—we know and believe that our sins are forgiven us on account of Christ. This is the way we ought to teach this article. For it is not enough to know that God will punish sin, and to be contrite for sin, but also we must know that God on account of Christ will forgive sin and that we attain to this forgiveness through faith, if we believe that God will forgive sin on Christ's account. For contrition and faith go together. For contrition without faith produces despair as in Judas [Matt. 27:5] and Saul [I Sam. 31:4]. One cannot have true faith without contrition.

Thus we should instruct the people: First, we should awaken the people to fear. Surely it must be a great wrath that God feels over sin, since no one except Christ the Son of God can make satisfaction for sin. This ought certainly to frighten us, that God has such anger over sin. We should consider well the word of Christ in Luke 23 [:31]: "For if they do this when the wood is green, what will happen when it is dry?" If Christ has had to suffer so much on account of our sins, how much shall we have to suffer if we will have no part of contrition, but rather despise God?

Secondly, we should awaken the people to faith, even if we have deserved nothing else than condemnation. For God forgives us on Christ's account without our having deserved it. That is satisfaction. For by faith we attain to the forgiveness of sins, if we believe that Christ has made satisfaction for us, as John says in I John 2 [:2]: "He is the expiation for our sins, and not for ours only but also for the sins of the whole world."

The Human Order of the Church

It is obvious that much confusion has resulted from an unrestrained preaching about church order. Therefore the pastors have been admonished to give greater attention to important subjects, such as Christian repentance, as treated above, faith, good works, the fear of God, prayer, the honoring of God, regard for parents, the education of children, respect for government, not to envy, not to bear hate, not to injure or kill any one, chastity, living virtuously in marriage, not to be greedy, not to steal, not to drink intemperately, not to lie, to slander no one. These subjects are of greater importance than the eating of meat on Friday and the like, however correct such may be before God and conscience.

But the people are to be taught to speak with restraint about such matters as church order. For some church ordinances have been instituted for the sake of good order and harmony, as St. Paul says in I Cor. 14 [:40]: "All things shall be done in order in the churches." [19]

Holy days such as Sunday shall be observed and as many others as the respective pastors have been accustomed to observe. For the people must have certain set times to come together to hear the Word of God.

Pastors should not make an issue of the fact that one observes a holy day and another does not. Let each one peacefully keep to his custom. Only do not do away with all holy days. It would be well if there were some uniformity. The days of Annunciation, Purification, Visitation of the Virgin Mary, St. John the Baptist, St. Michael's, Apostles' Day, Magdalene—these have already been discarded and could not conveniently be restored. We should keep especially Christmas, Circumcision, Epiphany, Easter, Ascension, Pentecost, though leaving out the un-Christian legends and songs associated with them. These days have been instituted because it is not possible to teach all parts of the gospel at one time. So the teaching of it is divided into various parts of the year, just as in school one arranges to read Virgil one day and Homer on another. Also we should retain the usual holy days in the week before Easter when we preach on the Passion. It is not necessary to change so old a custom and order, just as it is not necessary to emphasize the suffering of Christ only at this one particular time.

Yet the people are to be taught that the only reason for keeping these festivals is to learn the Word of God. If one wishes to do manual labor, he may do so in his own way. For God requires observance of these church ordinances by us only on account of the teaching, as Paul says in Col. 2 [:16]: "Therefore let no one pass judgment on you in questions of food and drink or with regard to a festival or new moon or sabbath."

---

[19] "All things should be done decently and in order."

Beyond such regulations, which were made for the sake of good order, are others, such as regular fasts and abstaining from meat on Fridays, which were instituted in the thought that they would be a special service to God, to appease God and secure his grace. Now Christ teaches in Matt. 15 [:9] that it is futile to appease God by the observance of such regulations, for he says: "In vain do they worship me, teaching as doctrines the precepts of men." In I Tim. 4 [:1] Paul teaches that ordinances made with the intention of appeasing God are "doctrines of demons."

Paul also says in Col. 2 [:20] that no one shall submit to such regulations. We should not make such regulations and should not teach that it is sin to break them. Nor should one teach that it is a service to God [Gottesdienst] to keep these rules.

Even the apostles broke rules of this kind (Matt. 15 [:1ff.]). Yet we should teach the people not to break these regulations among persons not yet instructed, lest these be offended. For one should not employ faith to the injury of love but for its increase. For Paul says in I Cor. 13 [:2]: "And if I have (all) faith, so as to remove mountains, but have not love, I am nothing."

The people should be taught the difference between church order and secular government. Every secular authority is to be obeyed not because it sets up a new service to God but because it makes for orderly life in peace and love. Therefore it is to be obeyed in everything except when it commands what is contrary to the law of God, for example, if the government ordered us to disregard the gospel or some of its parts. In such cases we are to follow the rule of Acts 5 [:29]: "We must obey God rather than men."

Memorial masses and other paid masses shall no longer be held. For if there were any value in memorial masses, vigils, and the like, it would be possible to atone for sin through works. But as St. John the Baptist testified (John 1 [:29]), Christ alone is the Lamb of God that takes away the sin of the world. Furthermore, the mass in which we receive the body and blood of Christ and remember his death, is for the living, not the dead. Only the living can make remembrance of the death of Christ.

What the priests are to use of the canon [of the mass] is clearly explained in other writings. It is not necessary to preach much about this to the laity.

Some sing the mass in German, some in Latin, either of which is permissible. It would be reasonable and useful if we used German where most of the people do not understand Latin. Then the people would better understand what is sung or read. St. Paul speaks thus in I Cor. 14 [:16f.]: "If you bless with the spirit, how can anyone in the position of a layman[20] say the 'Amen' to your thanksgiving when he does not know what you are saying? For you may give thanks well enough, but the other man is not edified." And Paul says in the same place [1 Cor. 14:26]: "Let all things be done for edification."

On high festivals such as Christmas, Easter, Ascension, Pentecost, or the like, it would be well to use some Latin hymns in the mass, if they are in accordance with Scripture. For it is in poor taste to sing only one thing. If anyone wishes to compose German hymns let no one presume to do this unless he is endowed with grace for it.

But though we have said that a number of holy days may and should be kept (in order that the people might hear and learn the Word of God), this is not to be interpreted to mean that we establish or approve of prayer to the saints, for their intercession. For Christ Jesus alone is our mediator who represents us, as John in I John 2 [:1] and Paul in Rom. 8 [:34] show.

We rightly honor the saints when we recognize that they are held up before us as a mirror of the grace and mercy of God. For just as Peter, Paul, and other saints like us in body, blood, and infirmity, were made blessed by the grace of God through faith, so we are comforted by their example that God will look in mercy and grace on our infirmity, if we, as they did, put our trust in him, believe in, and call upon him in our infirmity.

Honoring the saints, also, consists in exercising ourselves and increasing in faith and good works in a manner similar to what we see and hear they have done.

Thus the people are to be aroused to faith and good works by the example of the saints, as it is written in Heb. 13 [:7]: "Remember those who have gone before you who spoke to you the word of God; consider the outcome of their life, and follow their faith."

So St. Peter exhorts the women in I Pet. 3 [:5f.] to imitate their

---

[20] ". . . in the position of an outsider. . . ."

mother Sarah in adorning the heart by a kind and gentle spirit. He writes: "So once the holy women who hoped in God used to adorn themselves and were submissive to their husbands, as Sarah obeyed Abraham, calling him lord. And you are now her children if you do right and let nothing terrify you."

Marriage

The pastors are to teach the people diligently that marriage is instituted by God. Therefore we should go to God with prayer and hopefulness in all the difficulties of marriage. For since God has ordained and blessed marriage (Gen. 2 [:18ff.]) married persons may look to God and be confident that he will give grace and help in all their needs. Thus Solomon says in Prov. 18 [:22]: "He who finds a wife finds a good thing, and obtains favor from the Lord." Discipline is to be maintained in marriage, and patience and love are to be shown and practiced by the one to the other, as enjoined in Eph. 5 [:22ff.]. And they should be taught that they may not be divorced or desert each other, as Christ himself commands in Matt. 19 [:6, 9].

Since it happens that in many cases Christian liberty is carelessly and perversely abused, needlessly giving rise to offense and unhappiness, the pastors should teach and act sympathetically and reasonably in such matters as forbidden degrees of relationship in marriage.[21] So St. Paul teaches in Gal. [5:13]: Christian liberty is not given in order that each one might seek or satisfy his own feelings or notions, but that with clear conscience he might live and act as a servant to his neighbor. "For you were called to freedom, brethren; only do not use your freedom as an opportunity for the flesh." In cases where the pastors are confused or uncertain, they should ask counsel of other learned men, or, if so ordered, they should let the case go to the officers or chancellery of the prince.

Free Will

Many talk improperly about the freedom of the will, wherefore we have composed here this brief statement.

Man has in his own power a freedom of the will to do or not to do external works, regulated by law and punishment. There are

---

[21] Cf. *What Persons Are Forbidden to Marry* (1522), WA 10^{II}, 263-266.

good works he can do and there is a secular goodness he can achieve through a power of his own which he has and receives from God for this purpose. Paul speaks of it as a righteousness of the flesh, that is, a righteousness which the flesh or man of himself can effect. If man thus of himself effects a righteousness he must have a certain freedom and choice to refuse evil and do good. God also requires such external or secular righteousness, as we read in Gal. 3 [:24]: The law is given to guard against trespasses in outward things. And in I Tim. 1 [:9]: "The law is not laid down for the just but for the lawless and disobedient, for the ungodly and sinners," as if St. Paul wanted to say: We cannot change the heart by our own power, but we can prevent outward transgression. We should teach that God has no pleasure in an immoral, heathen life. God requires of every man this righteousness, and punishes such immorality with all kinds of severe temporal consequences and an eternal suffering.

But this freedom is hindered by the devil. For if man is not protected and ruled by God, the devil drives him to sin so that he has not even this external goodness. It is important that the people be taught and learn how weak and miserable man is when he does not seek help from God. This we should acknowledge, and pray God for help that he might guard and keep us from the devil and give us true godly gifts.

On the other hand man cannot by his own power purify his heart and bring forth godly gifts, such as true repentance of sins, a true, as over against an artificial, fear of God, true faith, sincere love, chastity, a spirit without vengefulness, true long-suffering, longing prayer, not to be miserly, etc.

In Rom. 8 [:7] Paul writes: The natural mind cannot do anything godly. It does not perceive the wrath of God, therefore cannot rightly fear him. It does not see the goodness of God, therefore cannot trust or believe in him either. Therefore we should constantly pray that God will bring forth his gifts in us. This we call Christian goodness.

Christian Freedom

Others talk equally improperly about Christian freedom. Consequently some people think they are free in the sense that they need no government and even that they need pay no taxes. Others interpret Christian freedom to mean that they can eat meat, refrain from confession and fasting, and the like.

Such wild illusions of the people the preachers should condemn and their teaching should lead to improvement and not to wickedness.

In the first place Christian freedom is the forgiveness of sins through Christ by the Holy Spirit without our merit or aid.

If this freedom is properly explained it can be of great comfort to sincere souls and inspire them to the love of God and Christian works. Therefore this subject should be treated often. The devil has those in his power who are not preserved by the Holy Spirit, prodding them into vice and crime. Of one he makes an adulterer, of another a thief, of a third a murderer. We see how many who have fallen into such disgrace do not know how it happened. It is the devil who has driven them to it. This we call the bondage of humanity. For the devil does not relax. He is a murderer who lies in wait to destroy body and soul and has his delight and joy in our destruction.

Christian freedom, on the other hand, means that Christ has promised us the Holy Spirit, to rule over us and protect us against such power of the devil.

This is the word of Christ himself in John 8 [:36]: "If the Son makes you free, you will be free indeed."

The people are to be admonished to fear so they may realize in what great peril they are if God does not keep them, since no one is secure from sin and disgrace. They are also to be comforted and exhorted to faith and prayer, so that they may be protected from the devil by the Holy Spirit. So Christ has bidden us to pray, in Luke 22 [:40]: "Pray that you may not enter into temptation." For the devil is no mean and weak foe, but the prince of the world, as Christ himself terms him in John 12 [:31], 14 [:30], and 16 [:11], and a god of this world, as Paul calls him in II Cor. 4 [:4]. Therefore we have to contend, as Paul writes in Eph. 6 [:12], not against flesh and blood, but against the principalities and powers, against the world rulers of darkness, against the spiritual hosts of wickedness in the heavenly places. Yet St. John says in his epistle [I John 4:4] that he who is in us is greater than he who is in the world.

This subject of Christian freedom should be treated often so that the people may be constrained to fear and faith. For there is no point of Christian doctrine which can make or bring greater joy to sincere souls than this by which we know that God wishes to rule over and protect us, as Christ has promised in Matt. 16 [:18]: "The gates of hell shall not prevail against it."

The second part of Christian freedom is that Christ does not impose on us the ceremonies and judicial ordinances of the law of Moses, but Christians may follow the laws of all lands—Saxons the Saxon law, others the Roman law. God approves of and confirms all such laws, if they be not against his law or against reason, as we have already explained. It is written in Rom. 13 [:1]: "For there is no authority except from God." This applies not only to Jewish law, but the law of all lands, as St. Peter says in I Pet. 2 [:13]: "Be subject to every human institution."

The third part of Christian freedom concerns human church regulations such as fasts, holy days, and the like. Here it is necessary to know that the observance of such regulations is of no help in attaining goodness before God, as Christ says in Matt. 15 [:9]: "In vain do they worship me . . . with precepts of men." On this point we have already indicated that church regulations are of three kinds.[22]

Some ordinances may not be kept without sinning, namely, such a one as the forbidding of marriage. Such we should not obey, for, "We must obey God rather than men" (Acts 15 [:29]). St. Paul calls this prohibition in I Tim. 4 [:1-3], "a doctrine of the devil." In addition Christ himself describes these ordinances as commandments to sin (Matt. 15 [:3ff.]).

Other ordinances have been made, not in order to earn grace or to make satisfaction for sin, or even because it is necessary to observe them, but because they serve a useful purpose. Such is the observance of Sunday, Easter, Pentecost, and Christmas, which have been fixed in time so that the people may know when to come together and learn the Word of God. Not that it is necessary even to keep these days or that it is sinful to do manual labor on them, but it is well to keep them so that every man may know the time at which to assemble and to learn.

---

[22] Cf. pp. 299-300.

A third kind of regulations has been made with the intention of earning grace for our sins, such as fixed seasons of fasting, abstinence from meat on Fridays, observing the seven hours of prayer, and the like. Such are contrary to the will of God and may well be abandoned. Paul gives the name of "doctrine of the devil" to regulations which give or encourage the idea that thereby one earns grace or that they are necessary to secure God's grace.

The Turks[23]

Some preachers clamor recklessly about the Turks, saying we should not oppose the Turks since Christians may not avenge themselves. This is seditious talk which should not be permitted or tolerated. For the government is given the power of the sword and commanded to punish all murder and pillage. Therefore it is obligated to wage war against those who start an unjust war and are responsible for pillage and murder. This vengeance is not forbidden. For Paul says in Rom. 13 [:4] that government executes the vengeance of God, which means that it is instituted and commanded of God and given help by God in time of need.

But the Christian is forbidden to avenge what is not undertaken by the government or authorized by it. Scripture forbids Christians to exercise personal and individual vengeance, but commands government to execute it and calls it a service of God when done by the government. Indeed the best way of giving alms is to employ the sword against murder. So God has commanded, as we read in Gen. 9 [:6]: "Whoever sheds the blood of man, by man shall his blood be shed."

Some say that we should not defend the faith with the sword, but should suffer like Christ, or the apostles, etc. Undoubtedly it is true that they who do not bear rule should each in his place be willing to suffer and not defend himself, as Christ did not defend himself. For he had no worldly authority or rule, and did not wish any, as in John 6 [:15] he would not allow the Jews to make him a king.

---

[23] The Lutherans had been charged with lack of loyalty to their country and of obedience to the Emperor. To meet this criticism Luther felt compelled to issue special treatises against the Turks in which he developed the ideas here mentioned. Cf. Luther's *On War Against the Turks* (1529), PE 5, p. 79ff.; WA 30I, 81ff.

The government, however, must protect its subjects against unjust powers whether such unjust power be exercised on account of faith or for some other reason.

Since the authorities are to honor good and punish evil works according to Rom. 13 [:4] and I Pet. 2 [:14], it is their duty to make defense against those who would destroy the worship of God, the peaceful order of the country, law, and justice. On this account we are to defend ourselves against the Turks, who not only seek to destroy countries, to violate and murder women and children, but also to obliterate justice and divine worship and all forms of good order, so that the survivors afterward may have no security and the children may not be brought up in discipline and virtue.

For this reason a government may wage war, so that justice and honor may be established in the land and the coming generation may not lead a life without virtue. For a devout man would much rather see his children dead than have to adopt Turkish customs. For honor is unknown to and not respected by the Turks. Those who have power rob others of possessions, wife, and children as they please. The common man observes no marriage vows, takes and rejects wives as he wills, sells the children. Are such customs anything but plain murder? This the Hungarians have surely experienced and they bear witness to it as they encourage the people in fighting against the Turks, saying, Brothers, even if there were no Christian faith we would yet need to war against the Turks for the sake of our wives and children. For we would rather choose death than to see and tolerate such shame and vice among our own. For the Turks drive the people to market, buy and sell and use them as animals, be they man or woman, young or old, married or unmarried—so evil is the Turkish nature.

Therefore the preachers should exhort the people to pray God that he would protect us from this destructive nation, and explain to them what a rightful service it is before God to fight against the Turks when the authorities so command.

Daily Worship in the Church

Since the old ceremonies have been discarded altogether in many places of the land and little is read or sung in the churches, we have made the following arrangements as to what the procedure in churches and schools should henceforth be, especially in cities and places where there are many people.

First, in the daily matins in the churches three Latin or German psalms may be sung. On days when there is no sermon a lesson may be read by the preacher, for instance from Matthew, Luke, the first epistle of St. John, the two epistles of Peter, St. James, some of the epistles of St. Paul, as well as both the epistles to Timothy, the epistle to Titus, to the Ephesians and Colossians. When these have been read through, one should start again from the beginning. He who reads the lesson shall then exhort the people to pray the Lord's Prayer for some common need appropriate at the time, such as peace, the needful fruits of the earth, and especially for the grace of God, that he may protect and rule over us. Then the whole congregation may sing a German hymn and the preacher read a collect.

At vespers it would be excellent to sing three evening hymns in Latin, not German, on account of the school youth, to accustom them to the Latin. Then follow the simple antiphons, hymns, and responses, and a lesson in German from Genesis, Judges, or Kings. After the lesson the Lord's Prayer should be said. Then one might sing the *Magnificat* or *Te Deum Laudamus* or *Benedictus* or *Quicumque vult salus esse* or simple preces[24] so that the youth remain close to the Scriptures. Thereupon the whole congregation may sing a German hymn and the priest conclude with a collect.

In small communities where there are no students it is not necessary to sing the daily offices. But it would be well to sing something when there is preaching.

During the week there should be preaching on Wednesdays and Fridays.

A pastor shall give serious attention to the choice of books [of the Bible] on which to preach, that they be useful and not too difficult, and that faith be preached, so that true Christian repentance, the judgment of God, the fear of God, and good works (in the sense we have already indicated and explained) be not forgotten. For one cannot have or understand faith without repentance.

---

[24] Prayers in the form of versicles and responses.

On festival days there should be preaching at matins and vespers, on the gospel at matins. Since the servants and young people come to church in the afternoon we recommend that on Sunday afternoons there be constant repetition, through preaching and exposition, of the Ten Commandments, the articles of the Creed and the Lord's Prayer.

The Ten Commandments are to be used so that the people be exhorted to fear God.

The Lord's Prayer is to be used so that the people know what to pray.

The articles of the Creed are to be proclaimed and the people taught carefully these three most important articles comprehended in the Creed: creation, redemption, and sanctification. For we consider it useful for the people to learn that God still creates, daily renews us, gives growth, etc. Thus the people are to be exhorted to faith and to prayer for food, life, health, and similar temporal needs.

Then the people are to be instructed concerning redemption, how our sins are forgiven through Christ. This should include all the articles on Christ, his birth, his death, his resurrection.

The third article, sanctification, deals with the work of the Holy Spirit. The people are to be taught to pray that God rule and protect us by his Holy Spirit, and are to be shown how weak we are and how miserably we fail if God does not draw us to himself and keep us through the Holy Spirit.

If on Sundays we preach on the Ten Commandments, the Lord's Prayer, and the Creed, one after the other, we should also diligently preach about marriage and the sacraments of baptism and of the altar.

In such preaching we should spell out, word for word, the Ten Commandments, the Lord's Prayer and the articles of the Creed, for the sake of the children and other simple unschooled folk.

The preachers are to refrain from all libelous utterance and, without becoming personal, condemn the vices of which they are personally aware, and not preach about those of which they are not personally aware, e.g., those of the pope, bishops, or the like, except where it is necessary to warn the people by example. For those have not yet triumphed over the pope who imagine that they have done so.

On festival days such as Christmas, Circumcision, Epiphany, Easter, Ascension, Pentecost, or others, the pastor may preach at vespers on the festival, if that has been the custom in the parish.

As mentioned, these festivals are to be observed: Christmas, Circumcision, Epiphany, Easter, Ascension, and Pentecost.

As mentioned also, we should observe Maundy Thursday and Good Friday in Holy Week when portions of the Passion are subjects of preaching.

The people are, however, to be instructed not to go to the sacrament merely on account of custom, but should go to communion at any time of the year when God exhorts them to attend.

Some there are who out of crude ignorance clamor against all holy days, but they are not to be heeded. For such holy days have been instituted because it is not possible to instruct the people in all of the Scriptures in one day. So the different portions of the teaching are distributed over certain seasons, just as the schools might arrange to read Virgil on one day, Cicero on another.

But a competent preacher ought to be able to show how to celebrate the festivals without superstition.

The festivals are to be observed peacefully so that one should not raise a quarrel over improper practices which may have been discarded.

Since it is not fitting that singing should be uniform at all festivals, it would be well on high festivals to sing the Latin Introits, the *Gloria in Excelsis*, the *Hallelujah*, the simple sequences, the *Sanctus*, and *Agnus Dei*.

Otherwise, on Sundays, we allow whatever practice each individual pastor follows in Christian ceremonies. It were well to exhort the people to partake of the sacrament.

No one is to be permitted to receive the holy sacrament who has not, as indicated already, been examined and questioned, so that the body of Christ be not dishonored.

The many different forms of the mass should not greatly agitate or disturb us, until we can (as far as possible) achieve uniformity. Even under the papacy there were many differences and variations in all the institutions. Furthermore, at times three or four masses might be going on at one time, so that a great hubbub resulted. Yet no one either then or since has been disturbed.

At time of death the corpse is to be fittingly treated. A chaplain and a sexton should accompany it [to the place of burial]. The people should be urged from the pulpit to follow and at the burial sing in German the hymn, *Mitten in dem Leben*.[25]

We have heard reports of unseemly preaching about the six weeks which the women observe following childbirth, so that women have been forced to go to work, without consideration of their weakness, with the result that some have become ill and are supposed to have died.

Therefore we have deemed it necessary to advise the pastors to speak cautiously about these and similar customs, for the six weeks are ordained in the law of Moses Lev. 12 [:4ff.]. Though that law is superseded, still those things that not only the law but nature itself teaches are not superseded, namely, the natural and ethical truths that belong to the realm of nature and ethics. So Paul in I Cor. [11:14ff.], as indeed nature itself, teaches and shows that we are obligated to keep the law which nature teaches. Consequently the women are to be spared for so long a time as needed for the return of their normal strength, which is not apt to happen in a shorter time than the six-week period. It is not sinful to go out before this period expires, but it is sin to cause injury to the body. So it is not sin to drink wine, though one should not give wine to someone sick of a fever, because of his sick condition. In this case, too, one should consider the need of the body and maintain self-discipline, not using Christian liberty for the injury of the body or looseness of life. For when Christian liberty is abused it is like a herd of swine being invited to the table of a prince. They understand not such an honor, but only ravage what is set before them, even soiling the prince. So when the masses hear of freedom they do not understand the meaning of it. Imagining that they need observe no discipline or proper behavior they even blaspheme God.

---

[25] The Latin hymn *Media vita in morte sumus*, erroneously attributed to Balbulus Notker (d. 912), librarian and guest master at St. Gall, was freely rendered in German by Luther in 1524: *Mitten wir im Leben sind*. Cf. *PE* 6, 301f.

The True Christian Ban

It were well, too, if we did not entirely do away with the penalty of the ban in the true Christian sense described in Matt. 18 [:17f.]. It consists in not admitting to the Lord's Table those who, unwilling to mend their ways, live in open sin, such as adultery, habitual drunkenness, and the like. However, before taking such action, they are to be warned several times to mend their ways. Then, if they refuse, the ban may be proclaimed. This punishment is not to be despised. Since it is a curse commanded by God to be pronounced upon the sinner, it is not to be minimized, for such a curse is not without effect. Thus Paul in I Cor. 5 [:5] delivered the man who was living in sin with his stepmother to Satan for the destruction of the flesh, that his spirit might be saved in the day of the Lord.

The banned person is to be allowed to attend the preaching service, for even Jews and heathen are permitted to attend.

Many pastors[26] quarrel with their people over unnecessary and childish things, as pealing of bells (Pacem ringing) and the like. In such matters the pastors may well show themselves as sensible and for the sake of peace yield to the people, instructing them wherein the bells have been improperly used and how they may henceforth be rightly used. Although in some places the custom of ringing the bells against bad weather is retained, undoubtedly the custom had its origin in a good intention, probably of arousing the people thereby to pray God that he would protect the fruits of the earth, and us against other harm.

Since, however, the people afterwards became superstitious and it was believed that bad weather was driven away by the bells and especially by the consecration of the bells, which had become a custom of long standing, it would not be amiss if in summertime the preacher explained to the people when storms threatened and the bells were rung, that the reason for the custom was not that the sound of the bells or the consecration of the bells drove away the storm or the frost, as had been taught and believed hitherto, but that thereby each one should be reminded to pray to God for

---

* The remaining part of this section was omitted from the second edition of the *Instructions* in 1538.

his protection of the fruits of the earth. Also that our life and nourishment are truly gifts of God, which without the help of God would not be preserved. Unfavorable weather is a punishment from God, as is indicated in many places in the books of Moses, and favorable weather is a good gift of God, as Moses told the people. If they obeyed God and heeded his word, God would give them rain in due season (Lev. 26 [:4] and Deut. 28 [:12]); [Deut. 11:44].

If now the ringing is done away with the people will probably be less often reminded that God determines the weather, and will that much less call on God.

Also the people will become the more barbarous if they are not exhorted to pray to God for life and food.

But the preacher must accomplish this much better than the bells else the result will be a devil's farce, as mentioned above.

Ringing the *Pacem* is in many places meant to let the people know the time of morning, or of evening when it is time to leave the fields for home.

Because some erroneously think it is a service rendered the Virgin Mary the people are to be taught that the purpose is rather to call them to prayer against the devil and threatening death and all the perils that might befall, day or night, as is seen in the ancient hymns and songs of compline and prime.[27] But especially that we might pray God for peace. Peace is a gift of God, as Ps. 127 [:1] shows: "Unless the Lord builds the house, those who build it labor in vain. Unless the Lord watches over the city, the watchman stays awake in vain." And Ps. 68 [:30], "God has scattered the peoples, those who delight in war."

Also we should instruct the people what a good and precious thing peace is. For in war time the poor cannot seek food, children cannot be reared, virgins and married women are violated, all kinds of wanton acts are committed both by friend and foe, law and justice and every virtue and service of God are overthrown in war. Therefore we should daily and sincerely pray that God would not punish us with such sharp lashes. It is necessary to preach often

---

[27] The day's office in the breviary begins with prime (normally at 6 A.M.) and concludes with vespers (normally at 6 P.M.) of which compline is usually considered a part.

on these themes, for they are really good works to which Scripture everywhere directs us.

But this is written so that the pastors will not quarrel about these things. It is not necessary to observe such ringing of bells; where the custom has fallen into disuse, it is not necessary to revive it again.

The Office of Superintendent

This pastor (*Pfarrherr*) shall be superintendent of all the other priests who have their parish or benefice in the region, whether they live in monasteries or foundations of nobles or of others. He shall make sure that in these parishes there is correct Christian teaching, that the Word of God and the holy gospel are truly and purely proclaimed, and that the holy sacraments according to the institution of Christ are provided to the blessing of the people. The preachers are to exemplify a good life so that the people take no offense but better their own lives. They are not to teach or preach anything that is contrary to the Word of God or that contributes to rebellion against the government.

If one or more of the pastors or preachers is guilty of error in this or that respect, the superintendent shall call to himself those concerned and have them abstain from it, but also carefully instruct them wherein they are guilty and have erred either in commission or omission, either in doctrine or in life.

But if such a one will not then leave off or desist, especially if it leads to false teaching and sedition, then the superintendent shall report this immediately to the proper official who will then bring it to the knowledge of our gracious lord, the Elector. His Electoral grace will then be able in good time to give this proper attention.

We have also considered it wise to ordain that in the future when a pastor or preacher either by death or otherwise leaves his benefice and some one is accepted in his place by the patron, such a one shall be presented to the superintendent before he is given the benefice or received as a preacher. The superintendent shall question and examine him as to his life and teaching and whether he will satisfactorily serve the people, so that by God's help we may carefully prevent any ignorant or incompetent person from being accepted and unlearned folk being misled. For time and again and especially in recent years experience has shown how much good or evil may be expected from competent or incompetent preachers. So there is good reason to keep this point under sharp surveillance in order by God's grace to guard against and prevent further irregularity and trouble, so that the name of God and his Word be not blasphemed among us. Of this St. Paul has faithfully warned us in many passages.

Schools

The preachers are to exhort the people to send their children to school so that persons are educated for competent service both in church and state.[28] For some suppose it is sufficient if the preacher can read German, but this is a dangerous delusion. For whoever would teach another must have long practice and special ability which are achieved only after long study from youth on. As St. Paul says in I Tim. 3 [:2]: A bishop must be capable to instruct and to teach others. Thereby he shows that preachers must be better qualified than laymen. He praises Timothy in I Tim. 4 [:6] because he has been instructed from his youth, nourished on the words of the faith and of good doctrine. For it is not an insignificant art to teach others clearly and correctly, and it is not within the power of such folk as have no learning.

Able people of this kind are needed not only in the churches but God also desires them in secular government.

Because it is God's will, then, parents should send their children to school, and prepare them for the Lord God so that he may use them for the service of others.

Hitherto one has run off to school for the stomach's sake, and for the most part learned how to secure a prebend where he has concerned himself with income from holding sinful masses. Why do we not do God the honor of learning on account of his commandment? For undoubtedly he would also provide food for the stomach.

---

[*] Cf. *To the Councilmen of All Cities in Germany That They Establish and Maintain Christian Schools* (1524), *PE* 4, 103ff.; *WA* 15, 9-53. *A Sermon on Keeping Children in School* (1530), *PE* 4, 135ff.; *WA* 30, 508-588.

For he speaks in Matt. 6 [:33] thus: "Seek first the kingdom of God, and all these things shall be yours as well." [29]

In the law of Moses God provided the Levites with the tithe. The gospel does not command us to give tithes to the priests, but does command us to provide for their needs. So Christ himself commanded in Matt. 10 [:10] and in Luke 10 [:7]: Every day laborer is worthy of his hire and of his food.

Therefore even if the world despises the commandment of God and does not give the priests their due, God will still not forget those priests who teach the truth, and will provide for them as he has promised.

How richly other professions are rewarded by God's will can be seen daily. In Ecclus. 38 [:2] we read: "From the most High cometh healing, and he shall receive honor of the king."

At present many faults exist in the schools. We have set up the following syllabus of study so that the youth may be rightly instructed.

In the first place the schoolmasters are to be concerned about teaching the children Latin only, not German or Greek or Hebrew as some have done hitherto and troubled the poor children with so many languages. This is not only useless but even injurious. It is evident that these teachers undertake so many languages not because they are thinking of their value to the children but of their own reputation.

Secondly, they are also not to burden the children with a great many books, but avoid multiplicity in every way possible.

Thirdly, it is necessary to divide the children into groups.

The First Division

The first division consists of children who are beginning to read. Here this order should be followed.

They shall first learn to read the primer in which are found the alphabet, the Lord's Prayer, the Creed, and other prayers.

When they have learned this they shall be given Donatus[30] and

---

[29] Matt. 6:33: "Seek first his kingdom and his righteousness. . . ."
[30] Aelius Donatus, a Roman grammarian and teacher of rhetoric about 350 B.C. His Ars grammatica was a popular textbook of medieval schools.

Cato,[31] to read Donatus and to expound Cato. The schoolmaster is to expound one or two verses at a time, and the children are to repeat these at a later time, so that they thereby build up a vocabulary of Latin words and get a supply of words for speaking.

They shall practice this until they can read well. We would consider it not unfruitful if the weaker children who do not have especially quick minds, went through Cato and Donatus not only once but also a second time.

The children are to be taught to write and be obliged to show their lessons daily to the schoolmaster.

In order that they may learn a greater number of Latin words, the children may be assigned a few words for memorization each evening, as wise teachers formerly have done in the schools.

These children shall also be taught music and shall sing with the others, as we hope by God's help to show later.

The Second Division

The second division consists of those children who can read and should now learn grammar. With these we should proceed in the following manner.

All the children, large and small, should practice music daily, the first hour in the afternoon.

Then the schoolmaster shall first expound the fables of Aesop[32] to the second division.

After vespers the *Paedagogia* of Mosselanus[33] should be explained and, these books learned, selections should be made from

---

[31] Publius Valerius Cato (b. *ca.* 100 B.C.) was a Roman poet but known in the Middle Ages especially as a teacher of grammar. Medieval education inherited the seven liberal arts from Roman teaching. The seven were divided into the trivium: grammar, dialectic, rhetoric, and the quadrivium: geometry, arithmetic, music, astronomy. Grammar was largely the study of parts of speech, and was intended to enable the student to read Latin.

[32] Aesop is supposed to have lived about 600 B.C. To him has been attributed a collection of stories of animals which has been translated into many languages. The stories have a moral, and in the Middle Ages were often used as texts in the schools.

[33] Peter Mosselanus (1493-1524), a humanist scholar, who became professor at Leipzig. His grammar, *Paedagogia*, was widely acclaimed.

the *Colloquies* of Erasmus,[34] such as are useful and edifying for the children.

This may be repeated on the following evening.

When the children go home in the evening a sentence from a poet or other writer may be prescribed which is to be repeated the next morning, such as *Amicus certus in re incerta cernitur:* A friend in need is a friend in deed. Or, *Fortuna quem nimium fovet, stultum facit:* Of him on whom fortune smiles too much it makes a fool. Also Ovid:[35] *Vulgus amicitias utilitate probat:* The crowd praises friendship for its usefulness.

In the morning the children shall again explain Aesop.

The preceptor shall decline a number of nouns and [conjugate] verbs, many or few, easy or hard, according to the ability of the pupils, and have them give the rule or explanation of these forms.

When the children have learned the rules of syntax they should be required in this period to identify parts of speech or to construe, as it is called, which is a very useful practice, though employed by few.

When now the children have learned Aesop in this way, they are to be given Terence[36] to be learned by heart. For they have now matured and can carry more work. But the schoolmaster shall exercise care so that the children are not overtaxed.

After Terence the children shall be given some of the fables of Plautus,[37] such as are not objectionable: *Aulularia, Trinummus, Pseudolus,* and the like.

The hours before noon shall always and everywhere be so ordered that only grammar be taught. First, etymology. Then, syntax. Next, prosody.[38] When this is finished, the teacher should

---

[34] Erasmus (1466-1563) was the leader in the great revival of learning, known as the Renaissance, in northern Europe. His *Colloquies* were a collection of dialogues in which he caricatured superstitious practices of his day.

[35] Ovid (43 B.C.-A.D. 17), last of the great Roman poets, is known especially for his *Ars amatoria*, the art of love, and the *Metamorphoses*, a narrative poem recounting legendary transformations.

[36] Terence (*ca.* 190—*ca.* 159 B.C.), a Roman comic poet, whose plays were printed in Strassburg about 1470.

[37] Plautus (d. 184 B.C.), a popular Roman comic dramatist who adapted Greek plays to the Roman stage, with original additions. He has had much influence on modern European drama.

[38] Allen and Greenough's *Latin Grammar* in our own century is divided into these sections: Words and Forms, Syntax, Prosody.

start over again from the beginning, giving the children a good training in grammar. For if this is not done all learning is lost labor and fruitless.

The children are to recite these grammatical rules from memory, so that they are compelled and driven to learn grammar well.

Where the schoolmaster shuns this kind of work, as is often the case, he should be dismissed and another teacher found for the children, who will take on this work of holding the children to grammar. For no greater harm can be done to all the arts than where the children are not well trained in grammar.

This is to be done all through the week, and the children are not to be assigned a new book every day.

But one day, for instance Saturday or Wednesday, shall be appointed on which the children are given Christian instruction.

For some are taught nothing out of holy Scripture. Some teach their children nothing but holy Scripture. We should yield to neither of these practices.

It is essential that the children learn the beginning of a Christian and blessed life. But there are many reasons why also other books beside Scripture should be given the children from which they may learn to speak.

This order should be followed: The schoolmaster shall have the whole division come up for recitation, asking each pupil in turn to repeat the Lord's Prayer, the Creed, and the Ten Commandments.

If the group is too large one part may come up for recitation one week, another the following.

In one period the schoolmaster should explain simply and correctly the meaning of the Lord's Prayer, at another time, the Creed, at another, the Ten Commandments. He should emphasize what is necessary for living a good life, namely, the fear of God, faith, good works. He should not touch on points of dissension. He also should not accustom the children to lampoon monks or others, as many incompetent teachers do.

Furthermore the teachers should ask the pupils to memorize a number of easy Psalms that contain in themselves a summary of the Christian life and speak about the fear of God, faith and good works, e.g.:

Psalm 112 [:1]: "Blessed is the man who fears the Lord."

Psalm 34 [:1]: "I will bless the Lord at all times."

Psalm 128 [:1]: "Blessed is every one who fears the Lord, who walks in his ways!"

Psalm 125 [:1]: "Those who trust in the Lord are like Mount Zion, which cannot be moved, but abides for ever."

Psalm 127 [:1]: "Unless the Lord builds the house, those who build it labor in vain."

Psalm 133 [:1]: "Behold, how good and pleasant it is when brothers dwell in unity!" And other similar Psalms which are easy and clear. They are to be explained briefly and correctly so that the children understand what they are to learn and seek in these Psalms.

On these days, too, St. Matthew is to be expounded grammatically. When one has completed it, one should begin again from the beginning.

Or, if the boys are a little older, one may expound the two epistles of Paul to Timothy, or the first epistle of John, or the Book of Proverbs.

The schoolmaster should not undertake to read other books than these. For it is fruitless to burden the youth with hard and deep books. It is for their own reputation that some have assayed to read Isaiah, the Epistle of Paul to the Romans, the Gospel of St. John, and the like.

The Third Division

When now the children have been well drilled in grammar the more excellent ones may be chosen for a third group.

Along with the others these shall rehearse music the hour after noon.

Then one should expound Virgil[39] to them, and when this is finished one may read Ovid's *Metamorphoses* with them.

In the evening: Cicero's[40] *Officia* or *Familiar Letters*.

---

[39] Virgil (70–19 B.C.), best known of Roman poets, author of *Eclogues, Georgics,* and the *Aeneid.* He was the most popular of all poets in the Middle Ages.

[40] The writings of Cicero (106–43 B.C.), Roman orator, politician, and philosopher, were admired in the Middle Ages as a model of Latin rhetoric.

In the morning: Virgil is to be repeated, and in grammar the pupils are to be required to explain, decline, and indicate the various forms of discourse.

One should keep to grammar the hours before noon, so that the pupils may be well drilled in this.

When they have mastered etymology and syntax the pupils shall go on to prosody, wherein they become accustomed to composing verses. For this practice is very useful in learning to understand other writings. Also it gives the pupils a rich vocabulary and makes them apt in many ways.

When they have sufficiently studied grammar they may use these hours for dialectic and rhetoric.

Of the second and third divisions should be required each week a written exercise such as a letter or a poem.

The pupils shall also be required to speak Latin. The schoolmaster himself, as far as possible, should speak only Latin with the pupils so that they become accustomed to and are encouraged in this practice.

THE KEYS

1530

Translated by Earl Beyer and Conrad Bergendoff

INTRODUCTION

The medieval church had built an imposing system of doctrine on the Christian affirmation of the forgiveness of sins. Whereas the gospel had spoken of a confession and absolution by members of the congregation, the Roman church connected the practice with its doctrine of the church. Out of monastic development came a system of penance with carefully defined steps and helps for the priest. The priest would hear confession but to test the sincerity of the penitent would enjoin certain deeds as satisfaction before absolution could be proclaimed. The sacrament of baptism gave grace for original sin. The sacrament of penance was directed toward mortal sins. The Christian who possessed the grace which the church dispensed through the sacraments would evidence such grace in contrition for sin, but would win added grace through confession and absolution. The satisfaction imposed would win exemption from temporal punishment, whereas the priests' absolution forgave guilt and eternal punishment. In time the practice afforded opportunity for abuses such as payment of money as satisfaction, and the sale of indulgences, at least in the popular mind, was an easy way to escape punishment for sin, even hereafter.

In the Roman doctrine the power of the priest to forgive sins and give absolution was a result of his ordination, which also gave him the power to administer the sacraments. His ordination was by a bishop who stood in relation to the pope, from whom came the apostolic power through Peter. Thus the central doctrine of the forgiveness of sins was woven into the system of the hierarchy, or priesthood, as explained by Rome. The pope was supposed to have the power of the keys. He could open and close the doors of the kingdom of Christ. Hence the immense authority of the medieval church over the minds of the common people, the priests of the church, and even the kings and emperors who were dependent on the favor of the church in keeping open the doors of the parish churches.

When Luther saw in the gospel the message of a God who

323

freely forgives sins because of the ministry of Christ, he returned to the original concept of confession and absolution centering in the proclamation of the Word in the congregation. The whole elaborate scheme of sacramental penance, insofar as it depended on a supposed power of the pope to bind and to loose, fell apart, and the proclamation of the forgiveness of sins by faith alone in the justifying power of Christ became the main message of the Reformation church.

Because of the almost universal ignorance of the true meaning of the keys Luther undertook to expound the abuses and the truth of the doctrine. This he did early in the summer of 1530. His first draft* was, in his own estimation, too verbose. Even the rewritten form has much of repetition and in it the argument moves slowly. But Luther was emphasizing fundamental truths and he knew how ingrained were the abuses. The treatise contains some of Luther's clearest statements, in simple language, of the nature of Christian faith. The text reminds us of the catechism, and it is well to recall that Luther never rejected confession and absolution. He retained it as a part of the teaching and practice of the church, though freeing it from all hierarchical and sacramental connections. The book stems from the time of the Augsburg Confession and indicates Luther's concern for the thought of the common man as well as for the relationship of the church to princes.

The translation is prepared from the text as contained in WA 30^{II}, 465-507. A small part of the rewritten text, differing only in minor details from the one which has been translated, is found in WA 30^{III}, 584-588.

---

* Cf. WA 30^{II}, 435-464.

THE KEYS

The horrible abuse and misunderstanding of the precious keys is one of the greatest plagues which God's wrath has spread over the ungrateful world. It has increased so greatly in Christendom that almost nowhere in the world do we find a true use and understanding of the keys. Yet the abuses are so gross and obvious that even a child with a rudimentary education could discern them. So soundly have all of the clergy and scholars slept and snored, indeed they have become completely blind. For this reason I want to point out, with God's help and grace, some of these abuses, and, as Christ says, to help in plucking out such offenses from his kingdom [Matt. 13:41]. Then our descendants may see how conditions were in Christendom; henceforth they will know how to guard themselves against such a calamity and will recognize and learn to use the keys rightly. For this knowledge has much to do with overcoming and avoiding innumerable abominations.

The First Abuse

The noble saying of Christ to Peter in Matt. 16 [:19] and 18 [:18], "Whatever you bind on earth shall be bound in heaven," etc., has been cited.[1] From this quotation they took the word "to bind" and twisted its interpretation so as to make it mean "to command" and "to forbid," or to make a law and commandment for Christendom. By this kind of reasoning they give power to the pope and boast that he has the authority to bind with laws the soul and conscience of a Christian so that one must obey him in this matter, on penalty of the loss of everlasting bliss and under the threat of eternal damnation. On the other hand, he who is obedient to the pope in this matter shall be saved. To this end they have perverted

---

[1] For aspects related to Luther's interpretation of these scriptural passages, cf. LW 31, 93, 229, 230, 280, 281.

all quotations of Scripture about obedience and disobedience. By such insolent interpretations of Christ's word the whole world has been frightened and bullied until everybody has been cornered and made the victim of human doctrine. Well, then, we want to examine and place such an interpretation before the judgment seat of Christ, that is, before his own Word, comparing the one with the other.

In the first place, dear friend, is one doing the right thing if one thus takes one little word of a quotation of Christ out of its proper context and gives it an interpretation and meaning that pleases us, without taking into account whether or not it is in harmony with the text or quotation? Should one not honor Christ and his Word at least to such an extent that one should consider faithfully and diligently the entire quotation, word by word, examining it closely in order to see whether the quotation would allow for one little word to be interpreted in a certain way? If they had looked at the text with slumbering and only half-open eyes, the clear bright light would have struck them so that they would have had to open their eyes wide and awaken to the fact that "to bind" here could not be interpreted to mean the making of a law. But now since they did not do that, but only heard the word, "to bind," as if in a dream, they also speak of it like a sleepy toper when one asks him whether he would not like to go home and he replies, "Bring me another," and really believes that one brings him another drink.

Just tell me one thing: In what schools does one learn the kind of Latin or German which makes "to bind" mean to command or to decree? What mother teaches her child to talk in such a fashion? Whence do our "key-explainers" get the interpretation that "to bind" is supposed to mean to command or to decree? What else can one say here, except that it originates in their own wanton concoctions, or in a drunken dream? That is as much as to say that they want to falsify God's Word and truth with their lies, and thereby endeavor to lead astray Christian people and serve the devil. But suppose, there is a school where one learns that "to bind" means to command. Or perchance there be a new "gypsy" language which talks that way, how can we be certain that here in Christ's own saying words are used that way, and that "to bind" means to command, and that this is Christ's own understanding? One must prove, indeed, by plain Scripture, that it is clearly to be understood that way, always keeping in mind that this quotation is their [i.e. the key-explainers] only foundation and cornerstone upon which the papacy rests. Therefore it must be proved with certainty that "to bind" could mean nothing else but to command.

If that cannot be proven with certainty then everybody must assuredly recognize upon what basis the papacy with its vast power rests, namely, upon an uncertain foundation. It stands and walks in darkness and not in the light; it cannot even itself know where it really stands or goes. It rests upon nothing but lies, that much is certain. For he who teaches doubtful matters as true and certain, he denies and leads astray in the same way as he who proclaims obvious lies. What's more, to teach uncertainly is a worse and more dangerous falsehood than an obvious lie. This is especially true of such important matters as concern eternal life and death. But how and when are they going to make their interpretation reliable? Only when the devil himself goes to heaven. Meanwhile the papacy with its binding keys (I rather should say its blinding keys) is founded on vain lies.

In the second place, it is certain that Christ in the above-mentioned quotation speaks of the kind of "binding" in which sin is bound or retained, just as he speaks of a loosing in which sin is loosed or forgiven. The binding here must mean to bind sin, and to loose must mean to forgive sin. For he teaches in that passage how we should admonish, punish, and accuse a brother if he sin. "And if he refuses to listen, let him be to you as a Gentile," etc. [Matt. 18:15-17], as we shall see later. Now it is also certain that to bind sin cannot mean the same as to command and decree, as the papists interpret it. For commandment and law are not sin themselves, but sin is something done against the law and commandment. Of this there can be no doubt, and everyone must recognize it. Therefore it cannot be that one and the same word such as "binding" should mean at the same time to command and to retain sin. One must be wrong and incorrect. Law binds no sin, but it commands to avoid future sin and to do good. It naturally precedes sins not yet committed. But the key binds sin already committed against the law, and it comes of necessity, after the law and follows

327

sins. Clearly, then, the pope's binding and Christ's binding are contrary to each other and are irreconcilable. Unquestionably one of the two must be wrong.

In the third place, the purpose of Christ's binding is to redeem the sinner from his sins. With his "binding" Christ attempts nothing else but to free and rid the sinner's conscience of sins. It is for this reason that he "binds" and punishes the sinner so that he might let go of his sin, repent of it, and avoid it. One may call such "binding" a saving of his conscience and an aid in getting rid of his sins. But the pope's sort of "binding," aimed at catching innocent consciences, does not want them to be free, but bound; the pope has no other purpose than to ensnare and to deprive of their liberty the consciences of men. Such binding may well be called an imprisonment and a cause for sinning, as St. Paul says to the Romans (Rom. 7 [:8]), that all laws are the cause of sinning. Therefore, I believe, an important, great and mighty difference exists between Christ's and the pope's binding. They cannot be the same, nor can the same passage be interpreted to contain both meanings. Christ's binding only deals with sins and sinners in order that they may be pious and without sin; the pope's binding only deals with holy and righteous persons and causes them to fall and become sinners, for his laws are laid on all pious and innocent Christians. But Christ's keys apply only to sinners among Christians; so well does the pope's key harmonize with Christ's!

In the fourth place, Christ's keys help in the attainment of heaven and eternal life, for he himself calls them keys to the kingdom of heaven, because they close heaven to the hardened sinner and open it to the repentant one. Consequently, there must lie hidden in the keys of Christ his blood, death, and resurrection, by which he has opened to us heaven, and thus imparts through the keys to poor sinners what he has wrought through his blood. The office of the keys is a high and divine office, aiding our souls to pass from sin and death to grace and life; it grants them righteousness without any merit of works, solely through forgiveness of sins. By way of contrast, what do the pope's keys accomplish? They command and set up external laws. Dear friend, what good do they accomplish against sin, death, and hell? How can they lead a soul to grace and life? How do they open heaven to poor sinners?

In no way! Indeed, even the fulfilment of the Ten Commandments does not save us nor make us holy, but only the grace of Christ accomplishes this. How then could external laws do this, or humanly contrived papal decrees, which are nothing but rubbish in comparison with the Ten Commandments?

In the fifth place, the keys of Christ demand no work on our part but faith only. For "the key which binds," indeed, is nothing else and can be nothing but a divine threat with which God threatens the hardened sinner with hell. And "the key which looses" is nothing else and can be nothing but a divine promise with which he promises to the humble sinner the kingdom of heaven. As is known to everyone, a divine threat or promise cannot be fulfilled by works but must be comprehended by faith alone, without any works on our part. Threats and promises are not commandments, nor do they indicate what we shall do for God, but they announce to us what God will do for us. They tell us of God's works and not our own. On the other hand, the pope's keys teach us concerning our own works, what we must do. For his binding lays down laws, according to which we must act, as we have heard already. Now do not Christ's keys and the pope's keys agree in a wonderful way? The former teach about what God and not man has done; the latter tell us about human accomplishments and nothing concerning what God has done. Why does the pope call his keys the keys of heaven, since they help one neither to believe or to become a Christian, but only deal with outward and earthly observances? They ought to be called earthly keys, and perhaps not even that.

In the sixth place, as the writer to the Hebrews says [Heb. 13:9], outward earthly laws and observance are unprofitable. The heart (he says) shall be strengthened by grace, not by food, which does not benefit those who want to serve God. So also St. Paul everywhere forbids and condemns such teachings and laws. And Christ himself speaks in Luke 17 [:20-21], "The kingdom of God is not coming with signs to be observed . . . for behold, the kingdom of God is in the midst of you." Would it not be absurd of God to give keys for the purpose of locking his kingdom with outward observances? Would God condemn and banish from his kingdom all outward observances and at the same time provide keys for the same and command that it be governed by such outward observances? For, after all, he calls them keys of heaven, in the service of the kingdom of God. For this no outward work or law can be of any avail, as Christ himself says. Again, the pope's keys can only bind, that is to say, can only command outward human works. To express it in a different way, they may be the pope's keys, but they are of no value in attaining heaven or in the practice of the Christian religion, but are condemned by Christ and his apostles, forbidden and banished from his kingdom. They are indeed strange keys to his heavenly kingdom.

But all such rubbish stems from denying Christ and wanting to attain salvation by one's own works so that Christ died to no purpose (as Paul says) [Gal. 2:21]. We want to become holy by our own righteousness, beyond and outside of divine grace. For that reason the pope must lay upon us laws which, if we keep and obey them, will admit us to heaven, but if we do not, we go to hell. Hence, they prove here out of their own mouth that they are apostate Christians. Thereby they deny both Christ and his death, placing themselves above Christ. Since their keys can do nothing but bind and make laws, while pretending to be keys to heaven, it is clear that they desire to attain salvation through law and works and not through their office of the keys. Such, indeed, is the work of the Antichrist who bases our salvation on his keys, upon our own works, and not upon the grace of God. And the net result of their expert tricks is to make the words "to bind" mean to give laws. Thereby they deny Christ and raise up and preserve the greatest abomination, namely, our own righteousness.

However, in discussing this matter, we also desire to be of service to the papists with an interpretation. Let it be this: As Christ and the pope have two different kinds of keys, so there exist two kinds of heavenly kingdoms with their respective keys. The first heavenly kingdom is eternal life. We poor sinners obtain the heavenly kingdom through Christ's keys, by the forgiveness of sins, given to us through Christ's death, and not through the merit of our own works. This is God's kingdom of heaven. The other realm is in the air where the devils rule, as St. Paul says [Eph. 2:2]. The pope's keys open this kingdom to all his saints who observe his restrictions and laws. Saints of this kind belong to that kind of heaven which one merits by human laws and works. There are thus heavenly keys for each realm but, with the important difference just mentioned. That's why the pope roars like a lion in all his bulls, warning that one should not endanger the salvation of souls by disobedience to his keys; he also threatens with the fire of hell. But he who is obedient to his keys is safe in the bosom of the holy church, being in need neither of Christ nor his keys.

In the seventh place, if Christ had not wanted to give us more in the keys than the power to set up outward laws and commandments, he might just as well have withheld them; Christianity could have gotten along without them. For secular authorities such as father, mother, master, wife, relatives, elders, and others provide us outwardly with enough laws, discipline, morals, and customs, so that there is no need for Christ giving us keys for more of them. For can the pope and his keys accomplish anything with binding and giving of laws, which human reason by itself cannot contrive, comprehend, and create, including his keys? If Christ with his keys had given to his church nothing higher and better than he had given previously to all the world through reason, then our faith and even the church would not stand on the rock of the divine word but on human reasoning. It would indeed be well founded! And that is the firm foundation of the pope's church! For just as his keys are a fictitious interpretation by men, so is also the church which he binds therewith. Like priest, like people.

In the eighth place, Christendom itself is also harmed by such popish keys. It suffers major damage and ruin by the denial and blasphemy of Christ's grace and mercy and the assertion of nothing but self-righteousness. But also by the pope's keys Christians are being daily overwhelmed and crushed by new, innumerable, and unbearable ordinances and the consciences of men are thereby greatly afflicted and disturbed. As a result no people under the sun has been or can be more miserable. Christ has not given his keys to harm or ruin his church; neither for her burdening or suppression, but for her profit and salvation. They should not be called either keys of the church or the keys of heaven, but the pope's keys. For the pope and his adherents by their doings have assumed authority over body and soul, property and honor. The church has suffered nothing but bodily and spiritual loss and become subject moreover to such raging tyrants of souls.

331

All this they cannot deny. From their decrees, books, writings, and works, it is as clear as day that they never taught the precious faith along with the keys, but kept silent. And with such pronouncements they have neither praised nor taught the blood of Christ nor the grace of God, but have only blown up thereby the pope's power. They boasted how he could bind, and how one had to be obedient to his laws. This they have drubbed into people's heads and plotted and pursued without ceasing until they have raised the pope's power not only over all Christians but also above all secular emperors, kings, and princes everywhere in this world. They have also claimed the pope has power under the earth, over the dead in purgatory, and at last over the angels in heaven. But most shameful of all, since they could go no further, they made the pope a god on earth, half god, half man, not only man. But about this we shall speak further at another time,[2] and then we will give these shouters something to rant and rave about.[3] For such hellish and devilish horrors—if God will—shall not remain concealed, contrary to their hope and belief.

So here we see how faithfully these pious people have dealt with Christendom. They have made the office of the keys into a law. They have interpreted the words which speak of God's work and grace to mean our own works and merit. However, our natural reason must confess, no matter how blind and without faith it is, that grace and law [Recht] are not one and the same thing, and that one passage cannot speak of grace and the law at one and the same time, nor can it be so interpreted. Even the world would consider whoever tried to do so a rogue or a madman. Now the papists speak in that manner, to be sure, not in secular affairs, where

---

[2] Probably Luther is referring to his Widerruf vom Fegefeuer (A Revocation Concerning Purgatory) (1530), WA 30II, 367ff., and to the second part of his treatise Sendbrief vom Dolmetschen und Fürbitte der Heiligen (A Circular Letter Concerning Translating and Interpreting, and Intercession of Saints) (1530), WA 30II, 632ff.

[3] Through his Propositiones adversus totam synagogam Sathanae et universas portas inferorum (Theses Against the Whole School of Satan and All the Gates of Hell) (1530), WA 30II, 420ff., Luther intended to infuriate and give his enemies something to rant and rave about (furendi et vociferandi in Luther's letter to Wenzeslaus Link in Nuremberg, July 20, 1530, WA, Br 5, 488). Cf. also his treatise, Auf das Schreien etlicher Papisten über die siebenzehen Artikel, Antwort Martini Luthers (A Reply of Martin Luther to the Ranting of Several Papists at the Seventeen Articles) (1530), WA 30II, 186ff.

it would not be tolerated, but in dealing with matters concerning the Word of God and Christ. They do it in such a way as to make their decrees articles of faith. He who does not believe them must be a heretic whose body is burned in this world and whose soul is condemned forever. How would these jabberers rage and rant if they could catch us in such an execrable, hellish, and blasphemous lie, as we now have caught them here!

In the ninth place, if we grant that to bind means the same as to make a law, then to loose, on the other hand, must signify to annul and abolish a law. For here two powers of equal character are placed side by side. Both are given by Christ in the same Scripture passage, and both keys are of equal power. Now, if the pope and his church has the power to make laws, he must also have the authority to annul them. For if the law is applicable to the process of binding, it is equally applicable to the process of loosing. Well then, under such conditions the pope might annul the Ten Commandments of God as well as the Gospels and all of Scripture and release and free the whole world from them. But if he cannot do that, neither can he bind and give laws. For he must be able to do the one as well as the other. If he cannot abrogate or annul one letter of sacred Scripture, neither can he establish one single letter of a law.

And most certainly, he has done this very thing. By his actions he has eradicated and denied Christ—as stated above—and put in his place his own laws and works. So there are also many people who teach that the pope is above Scripture, that he may interpret and change it according to his will. This he has also done. He boasts of a sacred spiritual privilege whereby sacred Scripture derives from himself the characteristic to be called sacred Scripture and to be considered by Christians to be so. For if he had not confirmed them, they would be worth nothing, nor could they be called sacred Scriptures. But the devil shall bless him for that, and I hope that these slanderous tongues will somehow be stopped, although some still grumble and belch. For it is written, "The Word of our God will stand for ever" [Isa. 40:8]. And Christ says in Matt. 5 [:18], "Not an iota, not a dot, will pass from the law until all is accomplished," and again in John 10 [:35], "And Scripture cannot be broken," and in Luke 21 [:33], "Heaven and earth will pass away, but my words will not pass away." This is the One who has put a stop to the pope's doings, so that he can neither annul nor abrogate one single letter or dot in the Scriptures. Therefore he shall neither bind Christians to one single letter nor lord it over them.

Yes, you might say, he ought to be able to annul his own laws. That is true, but it is not enough, for the key which looses, that is, the power to forgive sins, would not be equal to the key which binds, the power to retain sins. But just as the pope can bind, when God as yet had bound no one and all are free and unbound, so he must also be able to loose, when as yet God has loosed no one and all are bound; otherwise the two powers would not be equally great. I would call that a poor loosing if I could only loose that which I had bound, but could not loose what another might have bound. What good then would the key which looses be? Then the act of loosing would be nothing else than that I would discontinue and cease to bind. In this manner I could loose no soul which the devil had bound, and the key which looses would be worthless. But Christ declares here that what is loosed in heaven the key which looses, looses on earth. Thus he grants the power to loose even that which another has bound, that is to say, even God in heaven. And this is what Christ's keys accomplish. For they loose on earth what is bound before God in heaven. How plainly the words are written and witness, "Whatever you loose on earth shall be loosed in heaven" [Matt. 18:18]. To bind and to loose must both be nothing but God's words, as we shall hear later.

In short, the pope must be able to loose God's commandment and his Word which no man as a human being has bound. Or, otherwise, he cannot bind what God has not bound. Or, indeed, he does not have the right keys. So one of the two must go—either God or the pope. Either the pope annuls and makes the Word of God of no effect or God keeps him in check so that he cannot bind at all and all his laws perish. For the two powers are equal and are given at the same time. He who has not one of them, has none. What happens to the power or key which binds? It has turned out to mean nothing. Quite clearly, all those who say that to bind means to make laws are forgers of Scripture. The same applies to those who assert that when Christ gave the power of the keys, he gave the pope and his bishops also the power to make laws. For the pope cannot abrogate one letter of the law of God—as we have demonstrated above—and by the same token cannot establish a single one.

In the tenth place, let us hear of the marvelous feats which result from such binding. Now, because binding means to make laws, a bond or fetter must be called a law, and he who allows himself to be fettered with such a bond, that is, he who keeps the pope's laws and bonds, is to be called a pious Christian. Now compare their statements with those of Christ. Christ calls him bound who has been banished [from God's presence] and whose sins are retained and not forgiven, as he commands in Matt. 22 [:13], "Bind him hand and foot, and cast him into outer darkness." Christ calls him loosed who is free and rid of his sins, and whose sins are forgiven. But on the other hand the pope speaks as follows: He who is obedient to my bonds is bound—he shall be saved. Loosed is he who is rid and free of all of God's commandments—he must be considered disobedient and condemned. Where to now? Christ says to be bound is to be condemned. The pope asserts to be bound is to be saved. And both of them speak of one and the same word and passage in the gospel. Is it not tenderly sweet to so interpret a passage in Scripture that it denies exactly what in reality it affirms, and results in contradiction and controversy! Our thanks to these noble gentlemen for having interpreted for us what binding means in such masterly fashion.

And while we are talking about the pope's ability to annul his own laws, I must ask, friend, when has the pope ever annulled his own laws with which he has been tormenting all of Christendom in such a wretched way? When has the pope ever used the key which looses? The act of binding he has continuously performed, and he has used the key which binds to such an extent that it has become bright and shining, but he has left the key which looses lying idle, ruined and rusted. Why does the pope show two keys in his escutcheon if he never uses the one key? After all, the one should be in use as much as the other. For Christ has given them both to be used in aiding his Christians. So one knows full well that the pope and his followers have not the least intention to abolish or abrogate either their laws or customs, but they persist in their binding and daily multiply their laws. We wonder why.

Well, my friend, if the key which looses should be employed to

335

annul the pope's bonds or laws on the one hand, that might be only a forceful beginning and have the bad result of abolishing all his other laws. Then a vigorous reformation would threaten these ecclesiastical tyrants. For that reason it is better always to bind and never to loose. And yet the pope carries two keys to hoodwink the people. But he uses only the key which binds. The key which looses would work too great havoc. It would deprive the papists of as much power, honors, and possessions as the key which binds brings to them. We see clearly enough how firmly and tenaciously they hold on so as to loose or remit nothing, since they well know that they bind unjustly and contrary to God's will. So now they cannot find the key which looses. Dear friend, they say that if we yield and give way in one respect, we shall have to yield in more. And we cannot do that. The deuce! That is clever advice and an excellent scheme of these important and very learned gentlemen. It certainly will help them a lot, as was to be expected! They certainly cannot snuff out the light. But what will Christ say to the fact that you have deprived his Christians forever of the key which looses? My goodness! Always Christ, Christ, they say! These are Lutheran tricks. Well then, if you cannot find the key which looses, I will seek and find it with this little book. And I will find it in such a way that you will keep neither the keys which bind nor loose. What do you bet? For I hear they are both tied to each other. If we obtain the one, we have both. If you can bind, then we can loose.

Yes, they say, the pope also has need of the key which looses when he makes dispensations or allows people to do certain things. When, for instance, he relaxes his bonds and laws—I almost said, sells them for money. What should we say? Does it mean to loose when one sells the bonds of the key which binds for money? Why does he not also loose for the Lord's sake, or for the sake of distressed souls? Well, these are purely Lutheran ideas. They have no application here. Furthermore, why is not the key which looses as powerful as the key which binds? Why doesn't its power to loose reach as far as that of the key which binds? For the key which binds holds sway over all of Christendom. Through its entire realm it never sets anything free. It always binds and holds everything fast in its bonds. But the key which looses might free one or perhaps two from such bonds. But not through the free exercise of its function to loose, but through the intercession, means, and power of the great god Mammon without which its power to loose would be dead and nonexistent. Why then does the pope have in his coat of arms two keys of equal size, since he does not want them to be equally effective? He really should only have the key which binds in his escutcheon. The little key which looses should hardly occupy the space of a poppy seed. He really should have in the place of it the image of the god Mammon and with it a devil's head. So the poor little key which looses serves no other purpose but to help the key which binds increase its money and power, as if the key which binds is not equal by itself to the task.

The Second Abuse

So now they turn their attention to the beloved keys. In their interpretation they torture even worse the keys themselves which were given to us through the words of Scripture. They set out and treat the keys in such a way that the one is sometimes called *clavis errans*, that is to say, a wrong or erring key. As for example, when the pope binds or excommunicates someone who after all is not bound before God, or looses someone who is not loosed before God, then the key errs and accomplishes nothing, for it fails and misses the mark. And especially the key which looses is in danger of erring. For the key which binds, especially in the making of laws, never errs and cannot err. For the Holy Spirit guides the pope in the use of the key which binds so well that he cannot err. But the Spirit does not know the key which looses and so he allows the pope to get along with it as well as he can, and perhaps for the simple reason that Christ has given us the key which looses without the will and knowledge of the Holy Spirit. That grieves the Holy Spirit and he will not use it with such assurance as he does the key which binds. Believe this or you are a heretic.

For all this is so certain that even the key which binds, when it does not make laws (as mentioned above) but when it excommunicates, can still not err. For they have a quotation (I believe) by St. Gregory, *Sententiae, etiam injustae, metuendae sunt,*[4] that is to

---

[4] It has not been possible to establish the source for this reference.

say, even when we excommunicate someone unjustly such excommunication is nevertheless to be feared. If one has to fear the unjust and erroneous excommunication then indeed you can well grant that it did not fail its purpose. Why should one otherwise be afraid of an erroneous excommunication, if it did not strike home but missed the mark? For you must know that the pope is so important in heaven that God himself must be afraid of him. And if the pope excommunicates someone unjustly then God with all his heavenly host trembles before such papal lightning and thundering on earth. And God must condemn the excommunicated one and affirm and execute the erroneous excommunication. Thus he must abandon his divine inerrancy and become a rogue for the pope's sake in order that the key which binds may never fail. But I would rather lay a curse on this abomination than write about it if I dared to do so. But later on we shall examine the passage from St. Gregory.

Well then, greeting to you, dear Sirs; I would like to talk to you about something if it did not annoy you. "You say that you have a wrong key: But rather tell us, what have you sold us so far in German lands, indeed in the whole world, with your indulgences? In exchange for them you have robbed us of an immense amount of money. Was it the wrong key or the right one? I would like to know."

"Well, have you not read in the papal bull: Who has repented of his sin and confessed, he is certain of having received indulgence. But whether or not you will receive it is your worry, for we cannot know whether you have rightly repented and confessed. For that reason we too cannot know whether the key has hit or missed the mark. It is possible that it can err and fail."

"Do I hear correctly? There is nothing uncertain, however, about the money you have taken in exchange for it. You have not given it into the care and keeping of the wrong key, have you?"

"How could that be? You fool, who would entrust money to the wrong key?"

"Would it not be better to commend to the keeping of the true key the souls which live forever and cannot return to this life, and assign to the wrong key the money which one can recover at any time?"

338

"Friend, that is Lutheran talk, we now act in the popish manner."

"Many thanks, and the good Lord reward you for the fine comforting instruction! For I now well realize that the key connected with the indulgence is not founded on God's Word but based upon my own repentance and confession. For if I repent and confess properly the key will aid me to obtain indulgence. If I do not, all is lost, both the indulgence and the money I have paid for it. Friend, but how can I get the assurance that I have repented and confessed properly in order that the wrong key may become the correct one and God may look with satisfaction on me?"

"Friend, that is your own worry; that I cannot know!"

"Is this after all permissible, and can't one consider the money as stolen from me for such uncertain merchandise? For now you have my money, and you give me an indulgence in exchange for it. And yet you say it is not certain whether I have it (the indulgence). And I feel no different after the purchase than I did before. For I possess now as much as I possessed before, that is to say, an uncertain indulgence which means no indulgence."

"How is that? Do you think I stole the money from you? You gave it to me willingly. And the money is now entrusted to the right key which cannot err."

"Well spoken!"

"Furthermore, what do you give us in the annual confession with which you have conquered and probed the world, at the continual expense of our body and soul, our possessions and honor?"

"What should we give you?"

"Absolution."

"But is absolution really certain? In case you repent and if our absolution is valid in heaven, then you are absolved; if not, you are not absolved. For the key can miss."

"Here I am again told that the key depends upon my repentance and worthiness before God. And I can become such a skilful locksmith with my repentance that I can manufacture for my Lord God from his (selection of) keys both right and wrong keys. If I repent I make his key the right one; if I do not repent I make of it the wrong one. That is to say, if I repent then God is truthful, if I do not he lies. Things are going along real well! But how do I know whether my repentance and worthiness before God are sufficient? Shall I stand there, open-mouthed, gaping toward heaven and wait until I learn and become convinced that my repentance is sufficient? When will I really get to know?"

"You have to worry about that."

"Well said! The money I paid the confessor which was worth something in this world's goods you also have. In return for it you give me anxiety and doubt?"

"Let that be my concern."

"To continue, why do you fraudulently sell us your letters of indulgence with all kinds of so-called privileges? As, for example, that one may marry a close relative and the like?"

"If it is the right key, you buy with it God's approval and with honor. But if it is displeasing to God and if there were insufficient reasons for what you did, then the key errs and you possess what you have illegally."

"But how do I know that it is pleasing before God and my cause is just in his sight?"

"Let that be my worry."

"But what of those who put their trust and confidence in such an uncertain bargain and then died?"

"That is their concern."

"Furthermore, if popes, bishops, provosts, and other clerical officials place someone under the ban, even without God's Word and command, is such a ban valid?"

"There is no doubt about it. It is the work of the key which binds. It can neither fail nor err, as you have heard."

"But how can you be certain that it does not fail in this respect?"

"Let that be my worry."

"I understand all right that if it concerns your power, possessions, and honor, then there exist only true keys, and none can err nor fail. But if you are to help and counsel our souls, then you have nothing but wrong keys."

"Excellent idea, you are absolutely right."

"Furthermore, if the pope anathematizes kings and princes to the ninth generation (as it is reported), is such an anathema valid since God in Exod. 20 [:5] only threatens, 'To visit the iniquities of the fathers upon the children to the third and fourth generation, and does not call any one accursed?"

"Yes, the anathema is certainly valid, for that is the work of the key which binds, and cannot fail."

"How do you know that God confirms such anathemas?"

"Let that be my concern."

"To go on, when the pope, on the other hand, blesses such princes and kings, do the keys prove equally correct?"

"When the princes are worthy of God's blessing the keys are effective to that extent, but if not, they fail. For here only the key which looses acts, and the latter can possibly fail or err."

"But how do I know whether the princes are worthy of God's blessing?"

"I let them worry about that."

"Again, regarding the papal bull of anathema which is published annually in Rome on Maundy Thursday,[5] does that curse strike everything it anathematizes?"

"Why should not the papal bull be effective since it is the chief work of the key which binds? You know that the key which binds cannot fail since the Holy Spirit guides it."

"How can I become certain that the Holy Spirit guides it?"

"Let that be my worry."

"Furthermore, what are you doing in purgatory when you release souls by means of your indulgences? Is this really certain?"

"If God in heaven considers such release as justified, then it is certain."

"But how do I know that God considers it justified?"

"That is your worry."

"But where is all that money you have stolen and robbed (I intended to say) gained through the use of that wrong key in purgatory?"

"Let that be my concern. The right key will guard it well."

"Correct."

---

[5] On January 3, 1521, while in hiding at the Wartburg, Luther was excommunicated and condemned as a heretic in the papal bull *Decet Romanum Pontificum ex tradita sibi.* Following its publication Luther's name appeared among the heretics listed in the bull *Coena Domini* which was read in the churches according to established custom on Maundy Thursday in each year. Cf. WA 8, 688ff.

"Again, when the pope commands the angels to lead the souls of those pilgrims directly to heaven because they died on a pilgrimage to Rome during the Year of Jubilee[6] is it certain to happen? After all Christ's keys are only valid on earth and angels do not dwell on earth"

"If it is a fact that God bids the angels to do what the pope commands then it is true."

"But how do I know for certain that God commands such things to angels?"

"That is your worry."

"To continue, how certain is the ordination of priests, the appointment of bishops, crowning of popes, anointing of emperors and kings, consecration of monks and nuns, blessing of bells and churches, salt and water, and the like?"

"Why so many questions? Just listen, all that the key which binds does is certain. But what the key which looses performs is not so sure. Therefore, what the key which binds performs in the above-mentioned matters that stands and is certain. But whatever pertains to the (work of) the key which looses may fail and remains uncertain."

"But how do I know that all the things are the way you say?"

"To be sure! The work of the key which binds is my concern, that of the key which looses is yours."

"Dear friend, if that is your understanding why do you not withhold the wrong key until you are sure that repentance for sin is sufficient before God so that you do not have to err and act with uncertainty regarding remission and absolution? Likewise, why do you not wait with your 'butter letters' [7] and all such matters until you arrive at a greater degree of certainty in all these things? One should not deal so lightly with God's commandments. This is a great sin."

"Yes, my dear fellow, if we should wait that long we would

---

[6] When thousands of pilgrims died of the plague while passing through Italy in the Year of Jubilee in 1500, Clement VI, according to rumor, is supposed to have ordered the angels to bear the souls of those who died in the course of the pilgrimage directly to paradise. *WA* 30[II], 282. Cf. also Luther's *Warnung an seine lieben Deutschen* (1531), *WA* 30[III], 252ff.

[7] "Butter letters" was a popular term applied to dispensations from the observance of fasting regulations regarding milk products.

never get a cent, neither honor nor power. And the keys would long since have gotten rusty. And we would be poorer and more miserable than were the apostles, prophets, and even Christ himself. We act neither fruitlessly nor frivolously with the keys, for they certainly yield us sufficient well-filled, important, weighty money bags and treasure chests. The apostles handled the keys carelessly and were therefore unable to raise any money with them."

"One more thing. For heaven's sake, do tell me how you got hold of the wrong key? The entire Bible knows nothing at all of wrong keys. It speaks of nothing but true and genuine keys."

"Well, our source is this: God is silent. He tells us nothing as to the genuineness of your repentance, or whether the causes for granting relaxations and dispensations are sufficient. And so we cannot guess it either. If now the keys are not to get rusty we have to use them even in doubtful cases. Whether the key hits or misses the mark is a matter of chance. It is similar to a game of blindman's bluff."

"What shall I say to that? So you play blindman's bluff with our souls, bodies, and possessions. You pilfer and steal in the dark! I did not know that before. Now I see how you divide the spoils with us in a brotherly fashion. You keep the right key to our treasure chests, money, and possessions, and you leave us the wrong key to heaven. As far as your interests are concerned, you have the right key, as far as our welfare is concerned, you have the doubtful key."

"Let that be your worry."

"Can you say nothing else about these matters than, 'Let that be your concern'?"

"Should I say nothing more about it? I do say this, 'As to the right and the wrong key, you should let that be my concern.' Is that not enough?"

"Oh, more than enough, unfortunately too much. You are very learned doctors and people of great experience. I can say that for you. To be sure, I now notice, why the keys are made of silver and why they rest on red silk. I now see that by means of these keys Christ has made you masters of the world. I now see why he wanted to deliver all of Christendom into your hands as a poor, captive, miserable servant girl. And he has given you the keys not for Christendom's sake but solely for your own sake. Indeed, how else could it be?"

How do you like these people, my dear brother? My opinion is that you are gambling with God's Word, like a rogue. You play with Christendom and poor sinners as if they were an old worn-out deck of cards, though God himself has redeemed them so dearly by his dear Son's blood and death. Indeed, such wickedness cannot be overcome by complaining, cursing, and words of anger. If I or one of our persuasion had said and taught that the pope's key was ineffective in its working and that it might possibly fail, heaven help us! What an outcry we would have heard. Heaven and earth would have been in danger of caving in. First of all they would have made heretics out of us. Then they would have threatened us with the (papal) ban, with anathemas and damnation, as if we intended to weaken the power of the church. For they never could endure that one would say that the pope can err and be mistaken in matters of belief. But now they say, teach, and confess openly that absolution in confession is uncertain. And if repentance before God is insufficient, absolution is not effective. The papists can never tell us what kind of repentance is sufficient or when. In so doing they plant doubt into the pitiable conscience of poor people so that they never know where they stand, or what they have or do not possess. Nevertheless they take all their money and possessions in exchange for uncertain words and works.

As a consequence, as long as the pope has been in possession of the wrong key he never absolved any human being in his entire papal realm. He never was in possession of the key nor could he use it but rather populated hell by means of this wrong key and his uncertain absolutions. For an uncertain absolution is none at all. Indeed it is equivalent to lying and deception. That is a fine way of governing the church of Christ and feeding Christ's lambs. The same holds true for indulgences. Based on the uncertain foundation of man's repentance, the pope has never granted one day or hour of indulgence as long as this doctrine existed. Hence, his papal bulls and Years of Jubilee were the greatest robbery and scandal ever visited upon this earth. For uncertain absolution is none at all, but rather deceit and knavery. But such indulgence must be uncertain since the kind of repentance is uncertain upon which it is based. For who can say that his repentance is sufficient before God? Not our own repentance; but Christ himself with his suffering must be our repentance and satisfaction before God.

The same applies to dispensations and "butter letters" [8] and such things, for they have a dubious justification both before God and man. In all his life the pope has never given a genuine indulgence or "butter letter." For an uncertain dispensation is no dispensation at all. It is nothing but a lie and deceit. God is unerring and true. He does not deal with doubtful things. Anything he does and which is to be valid in his eyes must be altogether certain, as James 1 [:6f.] says, "One should not waver . . . or doubt . . . for he who wavers or doubts . . . must not suppose . . . that he will receive anything from the Lord." Do the wrong keys teach anything other than to waver, doubt, and be uncertain? That is, they teach us to despair, deny Christ, and be uncertain. "For he who does not believe shall be condemned" [Mark 16:16], for, "Whatever does not proceed from faith is sin" [Rom. 14:23]. Now they do not believe because the key and its power depend on our own uncertain works and repentance. For who can have faith in one's own works and repentance? No one except he who is unbelieving and who denies Christ, since our works are not God's Word.

Now go to Rome and fetch all kinds of indulgences and "butter letters." Pay money and obtain dispensations. Get yourself consecrated or become a bishop. Go on pilgrimages and call on the saints. Secure release from purgatory and confess to the priests and so forth. Then you get to the point of not even realizing what you do, have, or are before God. You are indeed cheated and deceived by falsehood, and that is what all like you deserve. Why do we despise God's Word, and why are we so ungrateful to our Lord, Christ? To be sure, the papists like to have people believe firmly that they loose and deliver by means of the true key. And they defy anyone who says differently. But privately they say that the key might fail. They do this for the following reason: If the people believe in their ability, then the papists obtain thereby the right key to the treasure chest of the whole world. But if people realize that

---

[8] Cf. p. 342, n. 7.

their endeavors are uncertain, vain, and fraudulent, they help the devil to fill his hell with Christian souls and to lay waste the kingdom of Christ. For what other purpose, after all, should the devil have given them the keys?

Let us see what results the teaching of the wrong key has produced. First of all, God must be lying in their favor. For God has promised firmly and faithfully through Jesus Christ, "Whatever you bind on earth shall be bound in heaven, and whatever you loose on earth shall be loosed in heaven" [Matt. 18:18]. These are clear, lucid, and plain words which admit of no *clavem errantem*, of no wrong key. God says it shall be certain and it shall not err. What they bind and loose shall be bound and loosed. What does master pope say to that? I really do not know (he says). I will loose on earth, but whether it is therefore loosed in heaven, that will be your worry. Thereby he flatly flies in the face of what God says. God says, if it is loosed on earth it must be loosed in heaven. The pope says, it must not necessarily be loosed in heaven, although it is loosed on earth. It is possible for the key to err.

Does that not mean as much as if he said to God: Lord, you are a liar. What we loose is done with certainty, but do you not see that we also have the *clavem errantem*, the wrong key? For because we do not believe nor know that the person we loose is assuredly loosed, you should not know it either. Much less should you say it so openly and with such assurance. With that you make the people so sure of it and so joyful. What would you know that we ought not to know? What promises can you offer to people which we cannot offer? If the one loosed is God-fearing and worthy, he will be freed by our loosening. If he is not God-fearing, although we loose him, he is not freed after all. But because we do not know whether he is God-fearing or not, both the key and the loosing are uncertain. Both the key and its power are based not on your word, but upon our knowledge concerning a man's piety or lack of it. But since such knowledge is forever uncertain our loosing must also be so. You are apt to lie if you assert so boldly that our loosing must be certain and beyond the shadow of a doubt.

They honor in like manner our Lord Jesus Christ, asserting that he has purchased with his precious blood nothing but the wrong key and an uncertain power of loosing. They also assert that our Lord made a fool of his dear Christendom. They maintain that Christ, like a common cheat, gives his Christendom uncertain keys. He commands it to bind and loose. Yet, as the pope says, it must remain uncertain whether men are bound or loosed, because one can neither see nor fathom the hearts of men.

But as to the key which binds there is no doubt. With it they ensnare all of Christendom through their abominable lies. In this instance, they are sure of God's action and use his name and Word to confirm their own tyrannies and rascalities. This, we have to hear, is God's doing. So God is horribly profaned and blasphemed from either side. On the one hand he is supposed to be a liar in the exercise of the key which looses; on the other hand he is made out to be a rogue in the use of the key which binds. Such words they attempt to put into God's mouth.

From all this we can easily conclude that these people do not consider the keys a divine institution, work, order, or office. But like Turks and the heathen, they consider them a man-made order or office, subject as any other temporal order to their control. For they base their doctrines not on God's Word but on human action and concern. The papists maintain that if people are pious, the key will loose them. If they are not pious, it will not do so. The key is valid and performs its functions, depending on man's worthiness, otherwise it does not do so. Likewise, the key which binds in its function is not based on God's Word, but on the pope's good pleasure. When the people have been prepared, the pope is ready with his laws and binds them. Whether this is against God's Word or not, he holds them bound. For there it is: *Sic volo, sic jubeo, sit pro ratione voluntas*,[9] "This I will, this I command; let this my will be the reason." God has to approve, whether he wants to do so or not, for what else can the poor fellow do?

Even if the papists considered the keys a divine institution and office, it would be impossible for them to make the wrong key of it. For God's orders are true and cannot fail, just as his Word can neither lie nor deceive. So baptism, the sacrament of the Lord's Supper, and the office of the ministry are God's order and therefore can neither err nor fail. It would be intolerable to speak of

---

[9] Cited frequently by Luther, from Juvenal's *Satires*, vi., 223.

two kinds of baptism, a right and a wrong one or of two kinds of gospels or two kinds of sacraments, a genuine and a spurious one. For what God speaks and does is pure truth. Otherwise one would also have to assert that God himself was twofold, the One who is genuine and the other who is spurious. And one would have to divide all of God's creatures into these two categories. Hence, even if they considered the key which binds as belonging to God's order they would never be able to say and teach that it was therefore lawful to make ordinances and issue bans unjustly. For the key which binds does not do any of these things, but they themselves do them under the semblance or pretext of the key and in the name of God in order that they may cover up their tyranny and rascality with such blasphemous abuse.

In the second place, the result and fruit of such teaching is the destruction of Christendom and the Christian faith. For when a Christian hears and is convinced that the keys may err and fail, it is not possible for him to ground his hopes and belief on what the key promises. For one should believe only that of which one can say or hold that it is certainly God's Word and the truth without any kind of doubt. Otherwise, there is nothing left but an erroneous and unstable belief. Indeed, genuine unbelief is sure to follow. Because the pope and his followers confess and boast freely that their keys can err and fail, so also everything the papacy does must be considered altogether uncertain. For the pope does not know whether he binds or looses rightly. Hence, his subjects must also be in doubt, whether they are loosed or bound, whether they live or act rightly or wrongly, that is to say, they must be unstable believers, even unbelievers, infidels, Turks and heathen. Thus one blind man leads the other, and both fall into the pit [Matt. 15:14].

What kind of a church is the pope's church? It is an uncertain, vacillating and tottering church. Indeed, it is a deceitful, lying church, doubting and unbelieving, without God's Word. For the pope with his wrong keys teaches his church to doubt and to be uncertain. If it is a vacillating church, then it is not the church of faith, for the latter is founded upon a rock, and the gates of hell cannot prevail against it [Matt. 16:18]. If it is not the church of faith, then it is not the Christian church, but it must be an un-christian, antichristian, and faithless church which destroys and ruins the real, holy, Christian church. So they testify here with their own mouth that the pope must be the Antichrist who takes his seat in the temple of God, being a corrupter and master in sinning, as St. Paul says in II Thess. 2 [:4]. Good heavens, one dare not make the keys uncertain and questionable. One should preach most intensely and urgently that they most certainly proclaim God's Word which is to be believed without any doubt whatsoever. It is difficult enough for a wretched conscience to believe. How can one believe at all if, to begin with, doubt is cast upon the object of one's belief? Thereby doubt and despair are only strengthened and confirmed.

The third result of such teaching is the establishment of human endeavor and self-righteousness in opposition to the righteousness of Christ, given to us by grace through faith. In this matter one can forcefully convict them because of their abomination. For with their spurious keys they not only destroy God's Word, but also distract people from God's Word, referring them to their own works and merits, saying, if you are repentant and pious and upright the keys will benefit you, otherwise not. Is not this to say, you must earn grace and become worthy of the same through your own works before God, and then the keys also will benefit you? Tell me how could one more thoroughly leave a Christian to his own works and entice him to a reliance upon his own merits, thus driving him farther away from God's mercy and Christ's blood, than with such teaching? Further, they teach us how to turn God into a false judge who is a respecter of persons and is bound to look upon our works favorably, thereby selling his grace instead of giving it freely through his mercy. If I am first to earn grace before God with my own endeavors, of what use, in the devil's name, are the keys to me, since they cannot give me grace unless I have earned it first before God? But if I first obtain grace I need heed neither keys nor pope. For, "If God is for us, who is against us?" [Rom 8:31].

From this you can gather that the keys of the pope are not keys but husks and shells of the keys. Or, as he shows in his deeds and exhibits them in his escutcheon, they are painted and useless keys, which might please the eye, but give nothing to the soul.

For here you learn that they themselves confess that the keys impart no grace. They contain nothing of God's grace. But man has to obtain grace first without the keys by his own endeavors. Now if they are such useless and empty keys which do not bring grace but make demands, then they cannot be genuine keys, for the real keys are full of grace. They bring and give grace—as we shall learn later on—also to the unworthy and undeserving, indeed, to the unworthy and undeserving only. Now because their keys are so void and empty you can well see how thoroughly they have destroyed, denied, and rejected the Lord Jesus Christ by their use. And their keys give to their people nothing but the grace of the pope, or as they say, the grace of the church in order that the sinner may be reconciled with pope or church. But the grace of God man must earn himself without the keys. It is turning things upside down to suppose that Christ has given his keys so that we might thereby obtain human grace, whereas the grace of God is to be acquired by ourselves without keys and without Christ. That must be heinous abomination since Christ has surely given the keys to obtain God's grace alone through them. For men and churches to obtain grace, God has prepared other ways and means.

Beyond all this they still have a higher power which gives them such great control over the keys. When they so wish, it becomes the wrong key, when they wish otherwise, it becomes the right key. In this connection, I want to give a good illustration. At a recent meeting of the German Diet the papal legate, Cardinal Campeggius[10] made a statement. The pope might possibly give a dispensation and allow the celebration of the sacrament in both kinds, as well as the marriage of priests. However, to allow the monks and nuns to marry, that he cannot do, for the key would fail and err. Now, as is common knowledge, the pope has frequently allowed this, but then it was no error nor did he use the wrong key. And he who would have called it an error would have

---

[10] Lorenzo Campeggius (1474-1539) served as papal adviser to Charles V during the Diet of Augsburg (1530). In a letter written in Augsburg on July 8, 1530, to Veit Dietrich, Melanchthon reports Campeggio as having stated at the meeting of the Diet: "He could grant the observance [of the sacrament of the Lord's Supper] in both kinds and the marriage of priests; with reference to monks he said he could not grant a dispensation without erring in the use of the key." CR 2, 174.

been condemned to the nethermost hell. But because a cardinal, his legate, calls this an error, it becomes an article of faith. So this is the way they treat us poor Christians. Today they say "yes," tomorrow "no"; today it is the wrong key, tomorrow it is the right one. And yet both of them are supposed to be articles of faith. It is all the same; the Germans must believe them whether they want to or not. But what became of those whom the pope has allowed to leave their cloisters to contract marriage because they believed this was right and now the cardinal says it was wrong? What does a pope and a cardinal care? It is enough if people believe it to be right, when they so decide, and again to believe it is wrong, if they desire otherwise.

Well, we pretty well know that the Romans do not consider us Germans to be human beings, but empty shells and shadows. They are so proud and overbearing that they think when a cardinal lets wind, the Germans believe a new article of faith is born. This is our own doing, and it is our own fault that we are such idiots and allow ourselves to be so duped and imposed upon. But I hope we idiots have made some impression on them, and foolish Balaam ought to listen for once to his donkey [Num. 22:28]. If they do not want to give dispensations and permission, they do not have to do so. Let the cursed devil ask them for it in my stead. Let them give him a dispensation and hang it around his neck. I will act according to my understanding of God's Word. I will not first ask God's enemies and blasphemers, the fools in Rome, whether they will permit it, but follow the old adage, "act first, ask afterwards." As far as I by God's will can help it, they shall not place their throne above God's Word, and teach him what he should command us.

To sum up, we will not have the word "wrong key" in Christendom. The cursed devil has brought it up from hell in order to destroy our faith, the gospel, and God's kingdom. Neither can a pious Christian heart endure this word. In the Christian church only true, right keys should exist, and no one should argue and ask whether the key might err or fail in its purpose. That would be the same as asking if the Word of God could err or fail. But one ought to inquire diligently and examine carefully whether it is the key or not. If it is the key, you may be sure it does not fail or err, but always accomplishes its purpose in the certain performance of God's tasks. Just as I am not to ask whether the gospel is right or wrong. For the gospel is right and cannot be mistaken. But there is need to inquire and see to it whether it is the gospel or not. If it is the gospel, we may not further question whether it is right. What matters is to believe simply and firmly, and live accordingly.

I once heard of a wise man who said, *Clavis non errat, sed Papa errat;* the key does not err, he said, but the pope can err. And that is well said. Just as I may say that the gospel does not err, but the preacher or pastor can err if he propounds his own dreams under the guise of the gospel. Therefore, the key does not err either, but the pope errs if in the name and under the guise of the keys he pursues his wanton and self-contrived ways. They turn this around and say, *Clavis errat, Papa non errat;* the key errs, but the pope does not. And before they permit a human being to err they would rather say that God errs in his Word and work. To fit their case, the pope's fools, his courtesans, have coined an important adage, *Non est praesumendum, quod tantae celsitudinis Apex erret;* one must not suppose that such a highly-placed majesty can err. It is truly a statement worthy of the Turks, for they say about their imperial realm: One cannot suppose that God will permit such a great people to err and be condemned. If you depend on that, you will find out how badly mistaken you were. Consider that such a supreme majesty is after all not God but man. And a human being sins, errs, lies and deceives, as Scripture says.

But tell me, dear asses, since one cannot suppose that such a supreme majesty can err, why should one presume to think that God's keys and his divine Majesty can be mistaken? Or is the key and God not as on the same plane with the pope? The keys, indeed, are not man's, but God's, Word and work above and for all mankind. It is for this reason that God did not command any human being to rule over his Christian church, but rather reserved this privilege for himself and commanded us to teach nothing but his Word. For he knows that if we teach by our own wisdom without his Word, the results are only error, lies, and sin. We are only to be God's instruments and to lend him our voices so that he himself alone may speak and govern through us. So be it. In opposition to this, these asses teach that the pope shall govern and not God, and that one should believe the pope and not the keys. Since the pope cannot err, one believes him readily. But because God's keys err, one cannot believe him. In this manner the Christian church is to be taught and governed so that it might be turned into a kingdom of Satan, full of lies, unbelief and all kinds of abomination. This is the part played by "men of sin and sons of perdition" [II Thess. 2:3] who corrupt with their sins the whole world.

The Third Abuse

So far we have learned how they separated the keys in a two-fold manner. In the first place, they made of them keys which bind and keys which loose in order to make laws which could be enforced or annulled at will. In the second place, they made out of them spurious and genuine keys. As if this were not enough, they have made a third division, *Clavem Potestatis et Scientiae*, that is, one key is called the key of power and the other the key of knowledge. And these are the real two keys which the pope employs with deadly seriousness. This is what happens when one leaves the right path. Then there is no end to straying or possibility of stopping. And one lie needs seven other lies to cover it up, and yet to no avail.

The key of power signifies the pope's right to issue commands and prohibitions in heaven and on earth concerning anything and in any way he pleases. He can enthrone and dethrone emperors, kings and princes. He can rule and control all authority. He can command the angels in heaven. He can empty purgatory. And what more can one say? They haggle and quarrel at length over whether the pope is a man or God. Finally, they have decided that he is God's vicar on earth and an earthly god, a fusion of divine and human elements, *mixtus deus et homo*.[11] Such is the work of the key of power.

Hence they roar and thunder forth in the terrible decrees of canon law that God gave to St. Peter, *Jura simul coelestis et terreni imperii*, as Pope Nicholas III writes,[12] that is to say, the pope is emperor in heaven and on earth. This power Christ is supposed

---

[11] Cf. *LW* 31, 390.
[12] *Ibid.*, p. 390, Thesis 19.

to have given to St. Peter. And again, in *Canon Pastoralis*,[13] the pope boasts that in case the empire is without an emperor, there is no doubt whatsoever he, the pope, is the rightful emperor. And in the *Canon Solitae*[14] he declares that the pope is as far above the emperor as the sun is above the moon. And there are many more such horrible and abominable, thundering decrees in canon law. As St. John well says in Rev. 10 [:1-3], "The angel, wrapped in a cloud, called out with a loud voice, like a lion roaring, and the seven thunders answered him." They have acted in accordance with this description, to this very day. They have dethroned and enthroned many emperors and kings. They have excommunicated and driven princes into exile. They have made themselves lords above all lords and kings above all kings by virtue of this key of power.

The key of knowledge signifies the pope's power over all law both canon and secular, over all doctrines, both divine and human, over all business and affairs, over all questions and errors. In short, by virtue of this key he is judge over all one can say and think in heaven and on earth. By means of this key, just as by virtue of the key of power, he is lord over all one can do in heaven and on earth. And the pope with his threefold crown is truly an emperor in heaven, on earth, and under the earth. If God possessed anything more the pope would also be emperor over it and would have to wear four crowns. What of life and activity he now permits through the key of power is the life and activity of all kingdoms on earth. But what of life and activity he does not allow does not take place. Therefore, also, whatever he decrees shall be taught, preached, judged and carried out, must be taught, judged, preached, and carried out. Whatever he decrees shall not be taught, preached, judged, carried out, is not taught, preached, judged, carried out; whether it is God's Word or secular law, it must be heresy. For he is lord over all power and doctrine, over all realms and law in

---

[13] *Pastoralis, Clementinarum* ii. tit. XI: *De Sententia et re iudicata*, cap. 2. *Corpus Iuris Canonici*, ed. Aemilius Friedberg (Graz, 1955), II cols. 1151ff. Hereafter referred to as *Corpus Iuris Canonici*. Cf. also *LW* 31, 390, Thesis 21.

[14] *Solitae, Decretalium Gregorii IX* i. tit. XXXIII: *De maioritate et obedientia*, cap 6. *Corpus Iuris Canonici*, II, cols. 196ff. Cf. also *LW* 31, 385, Thesis 1.

heaven and on earth. Friend, who would not like to possess such an empire if he could obtain it?

Therefore, he roars likewise in his canon law, *Judicantium throni*,[15] etc., that all who give judgments from thrones of emperors and kings, must learn the law from him and receive it as a fief is received by a vassal from his lord. And in *Cuncta*,[16] all of Christendom throughout the whole world knows that one can neither teach nor judge the pope, but all without exception must allow themselves to be judged by him. Likewise, the holy Scriptures and God's Word must be received from him in fief, that is, *robur et auctoritatem accipere* (to accept its strength and authority), as he expresses it. And the sum total of it all is, neither God nor man may say to the pope, what are you doing? Or, why are you doing that? But he may do and teach whatever he desires, unpunished, unhindered, and uncontrolled. There is much of such abominable roaring in his canon law and decrees. And all these are the supreme articles of the Christian faith. You could deny God with more impunity than one of these decrees. And many pious people have been burned and tortured on their account.

Well, then here you really have what Christ meant with his words to Peter, "Whatever you bind on earth shall be bound in heaven, and whatever you loose on earth shall be loosed in heaven." That is, Peter, if you trample under foot emperors and kings, you are doing what is right. If you loose my Word, it shall be loosed. You shall be god and I will no longer be God. Is this not a fine interpretation! But there is no need to contend much more about it. It would fill too large a volume since such an interpretation of this passage is recognized to be false and untrue by almost everybody, even by those loyal to the pope. For Christ has given to Peter no such power to rule either in heaven or on earth. On the contrary, he distinguished between his kingdom and the kingdom of this world. Before Pilate he confesses that his kingship is not of this world, but of a kingdom of truth [John 18:36]. And he declared to his disciples, "You know that those who are supposed to rule over

---

[15] Cf., *LW* 31, 386, Thesis 10.
[16] *Decreti Secunda Pars*, causa IX, ques. III, cap. 17: *Cuncta per mundum novit ecclesia. Corpus Iuris Canonici*, I, col. 611. Cf. also *LW* 31, 387, Thesis 10.

the Gentiles lord it over them, and their great men exercise authority over them. But it shall not be so among you" [Mark 10:42-43]. With these and similar clear words Christ forbade Peter and the other disciples to exercise any worldly rule. He admonishes them to exercise their office and service to which he has called them, allowing the worldly princes to take care of their own rule.

Since this shameful abuse and misinterpretation is not as abominable as either of the first two, souls have not suffered as the result of it in such a murderous fashion. For if only God's Word is present, one may remain a Christian and be saved, whether or not his bishop or clergyman be secular, especially since secular rule need not harm his faith. A Christian may even suffer popes and bishops to be and remain his rulers, since they set aside and steer clear of the exercise of the episcopal office anyway, provided they assist in carrying forward and encouraging the spiritual office. Yet such misinterpretation has done great bodily harm. For the pope and his followers have naturally thereby caused much war, bloodshed, murder, and misery among emperors, kings, princes, lands and people. He who is a liar must also become a murderer, even as his father, the devil, also is [John 8:44]. To be sure, through this interpretation the pope has long since lost St. Peter's inheritance. He could no longer be St. Peter's successor, but the emperor's or rather the devil's.

Christ has given the keys to his church for the kingdom of heaven and not for an earthly kingdom. As he says, "It shall be loosed in heaven." But in which way does the kingdom of this world aid a Christian in obtaining the kingdom of heaven? Indeed, if it could help one in obtaining heaven, then Christ should not have come down from heaven. There have, indeed, existed many such excellent kingdoms before and after, armed with power and equipped with laws. So Christ himself could have become an earthly king if it had been useful and necessary for the gaining of heaven. But since he has not done this, it is easy to understand that he has not lent his keys for the exercise of worldly power. And the pope and his followers fraudulently and maliciously interpreted this wonderful saying of Christ as applying to worldly power. Nor do they repent or make amends for it but persist in hardening their hearts until they suffer shipwreck.

But I cannot let this pass unnoticed that they add the *Clavem Scientiae,* the key of knowledge, to the keys given to St. Peter and the apostles, in Matt. 16 [:19] and 18 [:18]. And although some teachers do interpret the words that way, it is nevertheless wrong. One should never snatch up the word of a teacher without forethought and take one's stand without the dependable testimony of Scripture. For the detestable abomination of the spurious key has partly come from such a misinterpretation. It has been taught that the key could not bind or loose unless one knew exactly how things stood before God, something that is after all impossible. Just as if Christ had commanded to bind and loose nothing with the key of knowledge unless the papists knew beforehand how man stood before God. They themselves did not keep such an imaginary commandment, but they bound and loosed like blind men. And afterwards they have tried to excuse themselves with the spurious key as if it had not been their fault that they erred and made a mistake. Now it is hardly consistent to believe that one must know, and yet in blind chance bind without knowledge. Hence, one lie must always bring forth another one, betraying each other.

But we assert, that the key of knowledge is not one of the keys of which we were treating in reference to Matt. 16 [:19] and 18 [:18] but an altogether different key. The two keys are the ones which bind and loose according to the words of Christ, "What you bind, what you loose," etc. But regarding the key of knowledge, Christ in Luke 11:52 speaks to the Pharisees as follows, "Woe to you lawyers! for you have taken away the key of knowledge; you did not enter yourselves, and you hindered those who were entering." Here Christ does not offer keys, but he says they have them. And they must be old keys, already in existence before Christ opened heaven. Therefore he calls it also the key of knowledge or to knowledge, in order that it might serve in the obtaining of knowledge. And he adds, "They do not themselves enter." Enter where? To knowledge, they have the key to it. And they hinder those who would like to obtain knowledge.

From this I draw the conclusion that Christ speaks here neither of binding nor loosing, but of preaching and teaching. And this key is nothing else but the key to teaching, that is to say, the key to the office of the teacher, preacher, and pastor. Through it, people are to be brought to knowledge so they may learn how to serve God and to know the way of salvation. That is the knowledge of which he speaks here. Many a pious heart would like to acquire and possess this knowledge being hindered and led astray by the very ones from whom such knowledge should be learned and acquired, namely those who are in possession of the key and office. This was true also of the Pharisees who were to bring people to a knowledge of Christ and of the truth. Instead they attacked, forbade, fought, and taught against it. And they called it heresy in order to prevent many from arriving at the truth. As so often happens the most pious who were eager for the truth were also led farthest astray. For those who are infamous and despise the truth, the devil cannot lead astray—they are his already.

Therefore St. Matthew in Matt. 23 [:13] also calls their hindering and preventing an abuse of a key whereby they close heaven. He says, "But woe to you scribes and Pharisees, hypocrites! because you shut the kingdom of heaven against men; for you neither enter yourselves, nor allow those who would enter to go in." Now the Pharisees, of course, did not have St. Peter's keys. This is certain. So Christ does not say anything here of binding and loosing. But he speaks of pious people who would like to enter heaven, and who are prevented from doing so by force, injustice, lies, and deceit. Therefore Christ's words refer to the office of preaching which is to proclaim the opening of the gates of heaven to all. But the keys of St. Peter only apply to some, namely to sinners. Therefore, we should not jumble the keys as lazy and sleepy theologians are in the habit of doing. We should make a proper and precise distinction. Thus we can adhere to the pure and clear truth, avoiding all misunderstanding.

To be sure, it is true that we must know and be certain whom and what we should bind or loose. For we must not play blindman's buff with God's order, as we shall hear later on. But the knowledge which they claim we should have in order to use the key, namely, how a man stands in the sight of God, is impossible and therefore the key becomes a wrong key. For this reason we do not want to possess or demand such a knowledge-key, as little as we want a wrong key; neither ought to exist in Christendom. Neither should we endure the power-key, the key of secular rule. It has no place in

Christendom. Neither do we care for the key which binds in order to make laws or the loosing key in order to give dispensations or sell them for money. We want only the common teaching-key. For those who sin we want to have and keep the true keys that bind or loose.

The Fourth Abuse

We need to re-establish the old, true meaning of this biblical passage, handed down to us from the apostles' time, but of which now hardly anything remains. Otherwise they will leave nothing of this passage except in a tortured and twisted form. They have invented six sorts of keys and interpreted the words as they desired. Now they also go to work on the genuine keys and their true significance, dealing with them as we shall see. The true interpretation of the real keys and their function does not consist in the making of laws or the selling of dispensations. Neither does it mean to bind or loose wrongly nor to acquire power and find out things that are secret. But its true significance consists only in binding and loosing from sin. It means to ban and to absolve from the same, to excommunicate and to release from excommunication. For thus Christ speaks of it, and he gives the keys for that purpose. But as far as these people are concerned, there is plenty of excommunication and absolving. But how do they go about it?

In the first place, they pay no attention to, nor take any interest in, the real sins which should be punished by excommunication. The keys which were given to bind and loose from sin lie idle and gather rust. For if they would use the keys, dear friend, how many popes, cardinals, bishops, priests, monks, princes, noblemen, burghers, and peasants would remain free of the ban and the key which binds? For there exists everywhere such a free and easy, impudent way of living, which goes unpunished, especially among the clergy, and such a deluge of all kinds of shameful vices, avarice, robbing, stealing, ostentation, immorality, etc., that God and the world can hardly endure it any longer. I will not even mention the abominable sin that they all bear the name of Christ and yet despise his Word so thoroughly that the clergy do not even want to read or teach it, and the others do not want to hear or learn it. All these are the real cardinal sins which one should bind, punish, and ban by means of the key. In the performance of this work the key would be busy beyond all measure. But how can the clergy bind when they are worse and more guilty than all the rest?

They exercise their rule by confidently using the binding key in the making of laws, and employing the key which looses in the remitting of sins, as if to say by their deeds: Christ has granted us power through the keys to bind the rest of the people everywhere by torturing them with laws, but made us free to live unrestrained and unchecked with impunity, shamelessly and most infamously, and knowing all our sins freely forgiven. As St. Peter in II Pet. 2:14 describes them, "*Incessabiles delicto*," they cannot be made to cease from sin. In this way they harmonize the binding and the loosing nicely, making their new interpretation agree with the old one! The binding is to entangle other people with laws, the process of loosing should be applicable to themselves in order that they might live untrammelled and free.

Is not this a wonderfully exact interpretation of Christ's saying, "What you bind is to be bound," that is to say, the whole world; and what you loose is to be loosed, namely ourselves, the clergy! This interpretation would be superb and very useful and comforting to the Christian church. For according to the first interpretation, they would improve the church through their sacred laws. And according to their second interpretation, they would improve the church through their nice living. That would mean they had helped the church with words and works, with doctrine and example. How disgracefully spoken, but also how seriously! All the same, that is the way it is. This was the devil's intention of binding, and he has put it into practice.

In the second place, instead of applying the key to real sins, they use it in the fashion of jugglers on imaginary sins, practicing deceit with the command and Word of God, proving themselves thorough fools and knaves. For their binding and loosing extends only to sins against their own laws where money and monks are concerned. These they call the cardinal sins. Murder, adultery, blasphemy, and all sodomy are nothing. But just touch the church's avarice and love of luxury and see how the key which binds flashes and thunders. But on him who leaves his avarice and love for luxury untouched, the loosing key smiles and beams. Now, as we have heard above, they have no power to make laws for Christendom. Hence, there can be no real sin when these laws are not kept. For no one ought to comply in practice with the laws of the clergy, as if it were necessary to observe them. One should not become party to their sacrilegious and unjust exercise of power.

Since there is no sinning involved here, their binding and loosing turn out to be nothing but jugglers' work and plain tom foolery. Through them the keys of God are desecrated, and Christians have been troubled without cause and, indeed, deceived. They are in terror when there is no need of terror, as Psalm 14 [Ps. 53:5] states. And they have been led "to serve God in vain," as Christ says in Matt. 15 [:9]. What is more, in turning from faith and God's command to live according to imaginary and spurious laws and works, they have been forced to serve God falsely to their own harm. For this ban or binding strengthens and preserves that binding by which they make laws. Knowing and recognizing such binding and loosing is a spider web the Christian is to avoid and despise. Indeed, he is to condemn it as blasphemy and say with Ps. 109 [:28], "Let them curse, but do thou bless"; let them excommunicate, but do thou loose; let them be angry, but do thou laugh. And as are their laws, so is their ban. And as their laws and ban, so is also their church. And as is their church, so is also their God—nothing but pure fantasy, yet [all of it] in the name of the holy key of God. God's name must be as a juggler's bag of tricks by which dear Christendom is led astray so as to destroy sacrament and faith, to deny Christ, and forget God. Truly a horrid abomination!

Thirdly. Aware of the presence of right and truth and the absence of sin, they bend and ban, murder and burn holy men of Christ, thus carrying on in a manner worse than ever. They ban the gospel knowingly since they admit that the administration of the sacrament in both kinds is correct. They also acknowledge that marriage and food are matters of free choice and the teachings of the Gospels are the truth. But as they have not taught this themselves, they call it heresy. So the key which binds must extend over both body and soul. Furthermore, he who whistles and howls with them, aiding in the exercise of such blasphemy, excommunicating, binding, and murdering, is not only rid and free of all sins and heresy, but is their darling and greatest saint. He is on the way of becoming a bishop and cardinal, a canon and prelate. That is their understanding of the right use of the keys, binding real sins and loosing those who truly repent when they set Barabbas free and crucify the Son of God. For the Jews well knew that Barabbas was a notorious murderer and Christ a holy person. Yet, Barabbas had to be set free as a holy man and Christ had to die as a murderer. Hence, one should search, find, and invent sin that the key which binds might be kept busy and not gather rust but punish and condemn pious Christians everywhere. Likewise one should be on the alert for virtue and good works, to reward and crown murderers, seducers, blasphemers, and heretics everywhere. That is indeed a praiseworthy use of the keys. From all this one can gather that the pope really never bound or loosed any person, neither excommunicated nor freed from excommunication anyone. All his actions are nothing but beating the air and shadowboxing. And it is evident that nobody has so little claim to the keys as he who boasts the most about possessing them. All along he has been exhibiting them in his escutcheon, and painted them upon the wall. And, tell me, how can he possess the keys since he neither possesses nor tolerates the Word of God? Truly where the Word of God is not found the keys do not remain either. The keys want to be where God's Word and the church are, or else they are no keys. Christ has shared the keys with the pope in a truly fine fashion. He retains the true keys, and leaves to the pope the painted ones. The latter he may place in his escutcheon or hang on the wall. They have no place or space in the church of Christ.

But what do I think of Gregory's quotation mentioned above,[17] which says, "Our ban is to be feared even if it is an unjust one"? This is my answer: Whether the quotation is Gregory's or his mother's it is nonetheless of the devil. I would gladly come face to face with that doctor who would teach that I ought to fear injustice and lies. Even if it were from an angel from heaven I would take his horrible ban, and, after having used it as toilet paper, wipe its nose. What is the purpose of such vile blasphemy which shamelessly dares to command us Christians to fear public

---

[17] Cf. pp. 337-338.

injustice and well-known lies and to give them divine adoration? If St. Gregory had said and maintained such a thing without properly repenting of the same, his place would have to be in the abyss of hell. There is no argument about that. However, I do not want to condemn St. Gregory. But it has always been a great annoyance that the Roman asses and sophists have plagued us both in the universities and monastaries by always making the sayings of the dear church fathers articles of faith. They do not listen to St. Paul [I Thess. 5:21] who says, "To test everything and hold fast what is good." Neither do they take into consideration the fact that the more saintly the church fathers were, the more they were subject to continuous temptations of evil thoughts and secret treacherous attacks by the devil. Having to suffer and wait without respite, some of them at times said or wrote things impetuously. Such was the hasty accusation uttered by Job against God while he was undergoing severe trials. They were human as we are, and they also had to pray: Forgive us our debts and lead us not into temptation, etc. For the rubbish into which they have turned this quotation, I do not blame so much St. Gregory, as I blame the asses and sophists who like swine devour indiscriminately everything they find in the writings of the dear church fathers. There can be no other reason for them to prefer to devour those things in the church fathers which are nasty and evil, rather than those which are good, pure, and holy, if only they can thereby satisfy their belly.

What I have said of the abuse of the keys I have said in the simplest manner possible. Otherwise, if I had wanted to be angry and seek revenge, it would have sounded quite differently. Let him who desires to be a Christian make up his mind to think nothing of the pope's keys. Let him be loyal to the first two real keys of Christ and his church which do not make laws and sell for money as do the first two keys of the pope. And these keys do not involve us in doubt as to whether they hit or miss the mark in their binding and loosing as is the case with the two others, the wrong key and the right key. Neither have the two real keys anything to do with secular rule nor with the delving into secret matters, as do the third pair of keys. The real keys do not concern themselves either with imaginary sins and virtues as do the last two keys. All these eight, six, four, and two keys, or whatever number there may be—let the pope have them in his escutcheon. For they destroy our faith in Christ and deprive our conscience of all comfort and counsel. They point to our own righteousness based on works, which is opposed to God. These wrong keys teach people to forget and to deny Christ, as we have learned. For our soul must indeed be very certain of those things on which it can rely to be comforted in the face of sin and eternal death. Hence, the judgment of the keys must be based solely upon the certain Word of God, otherwise they are not the right keys.

Remember that the keys or the forgiveness of sins are not based on our own repentance or worthiness, as they wrongly teach. Such teachings are entirely Pelagian, Mohammedan (*Türkisch*), pagan, Jewish, like those of the Anabaptists, fanatic, and anti-Christian. On the contrary our repentance and work, our disposition and all we are, should be built on the keys. We are to depend on them with as daring confidence as on God's Word itself. You must never doubt what the keys say and give you, at the risk of losing both body and soul. It is as certain as if God himself were saying so, which indeed he does. It is his own Word and command. But if you doubt the same you make God a liar. You pervert his order and base his keys on your own repentance and worthiness. You should, indeed, repent. But to make repentance the basis of the forgiveness of your sins and of corroborating the work of the keys, is to abandon faith and deny Christ. By means of the key, he will forgive your sins, not for your own sake but for his own name's sake, out of pure grace.

Now let us talk a little about the real basis and true nature of the keys. Christ says, "Truly, I say to you, whatever you bind on earth shall be bound in heaven and whatever you loose on earth shall be loosed in heaven" [Matt. 18:18]. Notice that assuredly, yes assuredly, it shall be bound and loosed what we bind and loose on earth. There is no suggestion of any wrong key. He does not say: what I bind and loose in heaven, you shall also bind and loose on earth, as the teachers of the wrong key so foolishly say. How could we find out what God binds and looses in heaven? Never. And the keys would be without purpose and to no avail. Neither does Christ say, you should know what I bind and loose in heaven. Who would and could know that? But he speaks in this fashion, If you bind and loose on earth, I will also bind and loose right along with you in heaven. When you use the keys, I will also. Indeed, if you do it, it shall be done, and it is not necessary that I do it after you. What you bind and loose (I say) I will neither bind nor loose, but it shall be bound and loosed without my doing so. It shall be one single action, mine and yours, not a twofold one. It shall be one and the same key, mine and yours, not a twofold one. While you do your work, mine is already done. When you bind and loose, I have already bound and loosed.

He binds and joins himself to our work. Indeed, he himself commands us to do his own work. Why then, should we make it uncertain or reverse it, pretending he must first bind and loose in heaven? Just as if his binding and loosing in heaven were different from our binding and loosing on earth. Or, as if he had different keys in heaven above from those we have below on earth. He distinctly and clearly states that they are heaven's keys and not those of the earth. You shall have my keys (he says), and no others. And you shall have them here on earth. Clearly above and besides these keys of heaven, he can have no others which are not to be used in heaven, but above and outside of heaven. What would they bind there? If now they are the keys of heaven, then they are not of two kinds but of one kind only, binding and loosing here on earth and in heaven above.

But such ideas regarding two kinds of keys originate in the mistaken notion that God's Word is not his Word. Because it is spoken through men it is regarded as the word of men. And God is thought of as 'way up there in heaven, very, very far removed from his Word here below. So we stand there and with open mouth stare heavenward and invent still other keys. Yet Christ says very clearly in Matt. 16:19 that he will give the keys to Peter. He does not say he has two kinds of keys, but he gives to Peter the keys he himself has and no others. It is as if he were saying: Why are you staring heavenward in search of my keys? Do you not understand I gave them to Peter? They are indeed the keys of heaven, but they are not found in heaven. I left them on earth. Don't look for them in heaven or anywhere else except in Peter's mouth where I have placed them. Peter's mouth is my mouth, and his tongue is my key case. His office is my office, his binding and loosing are my binding and loosing. His keys are my keys, and I have no others, nor do I know of any others. What they bind that is bound, what they loose is free, just as if there were no other to bind or to loose in heaven or on earth. If there are any other keys in heaven, on earth, or in hell, they do not concern me. I know nothing of them. Whatever they might bind or loose is not my affair. Therefore, don't concern yourself about it either, and don't be led astray. I pay attention only to what my Peter binds and looses. I rely on that, and you should do likewise. In so doing you are already bound and loosed as far as I am concerned. For Peter binds and looses in heaven, and nobody else. This is the right way of thinking and speaking of the keys.

Here we have the true significance of the keys. They are an office, a power or command given by God through Christ to all of Christendom for the retaining and remitting of the sins of men. For so Christ says in Matt. 9 [:6], "But that you may know that the Son of Man has authority to forgive sins," and he says to the paralytic, "arise," etc. And soon thereafter, "When the crowd saw it . . . they praised God who had given such authority to men" [Matt. 9:8]. Do not allow yourself to be led astray by this Pharisaic babbling by which some deceive themselves, saying, "How can a man forgive sins when he can bestow neither grace nor the Holy Spirit?" Rely on the words of Christ and be assured that God has no other way to forgive sins than through the spoken Word, as he has commanded us. If you do not look for forgiveness through the Word, you will gape toward heaven in vain for grace, or (as they say), for a sense of inner forgiveness.

But if you speak as the factious spirits and sophists do: "After all, many hear of the binding and loosing of the keys, yet it makes no impression on them and they remain unbound and without being loosed. Hence, there must exist something else beside the Word and the keys. It is the spirit, the spirit, yes, the spirit that does it!" Do you believe he is not bound who does not believe in the key which binds? Indeed, he shall learn, in due time, that his unbelief did not make the binding vain, nor did it fail in its purpose. Even he who does not believe that he is free and his sins forgiven shall also learn, in due time, how assuredly his sins were forgiven, even though he did not believe it. St. Paul says in Rom. 3 [:3]: "Their faithlessness nullify the faithfulness of God." We are not talking here either about people's belief or disbelief regarding the efficacy of the keys. We realize that few believe. We are speaking of what the keys accomplish and give. He who does not accept what the keys give receives, of course, nothing. But this is not the key's fault. Many do not believe the gospel, but this does not mean that the gospel is not true or effective. A king gives you a castle. If you do not accept it, then it is not the king's fault, nor is he guilty of a lie. But you have deceived yourself and the fault is yours. The king certainly gave it.

Well, you say, here you yourself teach that the key fails. For the keys do not accomplish their purpose when some do not believe nor accept. Well, friend, if you call this failing, then God fails in all his words and works. For few accept what he constantly speaks and does for all. This means doing violence to the proper meaning of words. I do not call it a failure or a mistake if I say or do something, and somebody else despises or ignores it. But so they understand, teach, and observe concerning the pope's wrong key: The key itself can err, even though a person would like to accept and rely on it. For it is a *conditionalis clavis*, a conditional, a vacillating key which does not direct us to God's Word, but to our own repentance. It does not say candidly and boldly that you are to believe that I most certainly loose you. But it says that if you are repentant and pious, I loose you, if not, then I fail. That is the *clavis errans*, the erring key. It cannot with any assurance say that I know for certain that I have loosed you before God, whether you believe it or not, as St. Peter's key can say. But it must say something like this, that I loose you on earth, but I really and truly do not know whether you are loosed before God. For faith has not been taught in connection with the keys, as one clearly sees in the bulls of indulgence wherein repentance and confession and money are required but nothing is ever said of faith.

This is quite evident, for they neither repent of nor punish such deceitful uncertainties, among themselves or in others. They proceed confidently as if such doubting were no sin at all, reasoning thus: It makes no difference whether I have hit the mark; if I have missed the mark, I have missed it. They display no compunction of conscience or worry on account of such unbelief. Yet it is an abominable unbelief on the part of both him who binds and looses as well as on the part of him who is being bound and loosed. For it is God's Word and command that the former speaks and the latter listens. Both are bound, on peril of losing their soul's salvation, to believe this article as truly and firmly as all other articles of faith. For he who binds and looses without faith, and doubts whether he succeeds in binding and loosing rightly, or thinks to himself quite unconcernedly, well, if the key hits the mark, it hits the mark, that man blasphemes God and denies Christ, tramples the keys underfoot, and is worse than a heathen, Turk, or Jew. He also who is bound or loosed, blasphemes God, and denies Christ if he does not believe but doubts and despises what is done. For one ought and must believe God's Word with all seriousness and confidence. He who does not believe should leave the keys alone. He should rather dwell with Judas and Herod in hell, for God does not want to be reviled by our unbelief. It is truly not everybody's business to use the keys rightly.

Again, he who believes or would gladly believe that the keys are doing their work effectively, let him rejoice and use them with confidence. The greatest honor you can bestow on God and his keys is to trust in them. It is for that reason we teach our people that he who is bound or loosed by means of the key, let him rather die ten deaths than doubt their efficacy. No greater dishonor can be done to God's Word and judgment than lack of faith in the same. For this means as much as to say: God, you are a liar. It is not true what you say. I do not believe it. Hence God must be a prevaricator. He who binds and looses must be equally as certain, otherwise he is guilty of similar abominations. But where has one ever taught or heard of such a thing under the papacy? Indeed, if it had been taught, the wrong keys and their companions would never have come into being. And these two keys would have been the only ones and would have remained pure and unspotted. How many bishops and their representatives use the keys in this fashion? They do not believe the judgment of the keys is God's Word. They are in the habit of treating them as if they were of an ancient, worldly origin. But if they were to believe that it was the judgment of God in which they themselves should first of all have faith, at the risk of endangering their souls' salvation, they would not treat it so thoughtlessly but rather with fear and trembling. But where would one then secure episcopal representatives? What would then become of the consistories? A radical reformation would then begin to appear. And such a one must and shall come to pass!

But to prevent this, they use an artful dodge. With hearts hardened and eyes blinded, they do not realize the true nature of the keys. They value them only insofar as they produce money. Otherwise they would rather have the most primitive of keys, even if only made of wood,[18] in their pocket than a world full of divine keys which could unlock heaven. The keys are nowhere more dishonored than with those who possess them or rather who boast of possessing them, as may become clear from the following illustration. A Christian is not allowed to touch a consecrated chalice, although he be baptized and redeemed, consecrated, and sanctified through the blood of Christ. No, indeed, Christ's blood counts for nothing in comparison to a consecrated chalice. A corporal[19] is not supposed to be washed by a Christian woman, not even by a nun who is supposed to be Christ's special bride. But flies that are not consecrated are allowed to soil the same. That is the type of noble holiness prevailing here. But the keys, truly sacred objects, and of the holiest and noblest of the jewels of God, of Christ, and the church, sanctified by the blood of Christ, and which daily distributes the blood of Christ—these the most frivolous and wicked fellows in all the world may not only touch but abuse in the most shameful manner. And to such people they entrust the keys, thus showing how valuable and sacred they consider them, while trying to make themselves lords of the earth.

But how shall we proceed to use the keys rightly so that what is done is valid in God's eyes? In Matt. 18 [:15-17], you have a definite text in which Christ himself describes the office of the keys. You cannot go wrong if you follow his instructions. But if you do not, and instead take a novel and peculiar path of your own, you

---

[18] "Made of wood" is a descriptive phrase employed by Luther in his first draft of this treatise. WA 30II, 461.
[19] A corporal is a square linen cloth, about as wide as the altar, which is placed under the sacramental vessels.

can be sure that you will err and that you are not in possession of the true keys. These are the words of the passage: "If your brother sins against you, go and tell him his fault, between you and him alone. If he listens to you, you have gained your brother. But if he does not listen, take one or two others along with you, that every word may be confirmed by the evidence of two or three witnesses. If he refuses to listen to them, tell it to the church; and if he refuses to listen to the church, let him be to you as a Gentile and a tax collector." Here you have a sure rule and way, comprehended in God's Word, which will not let you err. And you can use the keys effectively and according to God's intent without anxiety and fear. For this is the context of the words about the keys, "Whatever you bind on earth," etc.

But when you do not hold yourself to this rule, you become uncertain and your heart cannot say, I know that I do not err. But your heart will accuse you and say something like this: You have bound and loosed without God's Word. Your own arrogance and not God has commanded you to do so. Therefore, you did not have the keys but only dreamed of having them. Because of this your own conscience will condemn you and say: You have blasphemed God's name and dishonored the keys, and, in addition, you have done an injustice and violence to your neighbor. You have disturbed his conscience with lies and led him astray, leaving him in error as to his understanding of the keys and causing his spiritual death. What will you then do? Indeed (you say) this is not the way they look at it at the courts of the bishops and of the pope. That I know well, but it is the way it happens at Christ's court. And if it is not the practice at the courts of the bishops then these are not Christian bishops. A bishop is not God; neither is his court God's Word. If they can improve on the commands of the Son of God, let them lead on. Then we will ask the Son of God to pull in his horns and be silent. But if they cannot improve on it, let them end their abuse, and re-establish the right usage, for God will not change his Word on account of the episcopal courts and their abuses.

In the biblical passage you hear that we must deal with certain public sins, committed by persons who are known, and with cases where one brother sees another commit sin. Furthermore such sins are supposed to have been punished first in a brotherly manner, and finally established as such by the whole congregation. Therefore the bulls and papal bans which read, "We excommunicate after sentence has been passed, though only after three admonitions," [20] and "out of the fulness of our power," [21] we call in our own language an execrable ban. I call it a devil's and not God's ban, contrary to Christ's command, when people are cursed with the ban sacrilegiously, before they have been convicted in the presence of the assembled congregation. Such are all the bans with which the episcopal representatives and spiritual courts practice their illusions when, with a slip of paper, they excommunicate people before a congregation ten, twenty, or thirty miles distant, although these people have never been condemned, accused, or convicted in their own congregation and before their own pastor. Instead, a bat comes flying out of a corner of episcopal officialdom, without witnesses and without divine command! But you must not be afraid of such an execrable ban. If a bishop or his representative desires to excommunicate someone, let him or his representative go to the pastor of the congregation where the person is to be excommunicated. Justice must be done to him according to these words of Christ.

I am saying all this for the sake of the congregation. In dealing with one of its members who is under the ban it should be sure of the reason it thinks him to be deserving of excommunication as the words of Christ in our text direct. Otherwise the congregation might be deceived in imposing a ban which is false, thereby dealing with a neighbor unjustly. By such action it would blaspheme the keys, dishonor God, and be uncharitable toward the neighbor. This is not fitting for a Christian congregation. For it should be consulted if one of its members is to be excommunicated, as Christ commands. A congregation is not bound to put any faith in a slip of paper issued by an episcopal representative, nor need it be concerned about any bishop's letters. Indeed, it is bound not to give it credence. One should not believe the word of men if it concerns the affairs of God. Consequently a Christian congregation is not to play the part of a servant girl in the court of the bishop's deputy, or of the jailer to the bishop, so that either one of them can say: "Hey there, Gretel and Hans, keep this or that person under the ban." The congrega-

---

[20] *Excommunicamus ipso facto, lata sententia, trina tamen monitione praemissa.*
[21] *De plenitudine potestatis.*

tion need not respond, "At your service, dear deputy." This perhaps might make sense in secular government, but in this case, where souls are at stake, the congregation shall have a place as judge and helper. Paul was an apostle, yet he was not willing to excommunicate a person who was living in adultery with his stepmother [I Cor. 5:1]. But he called on the congregation to act. And when the congregation did not take any action, he did not either, because he was satisfied with whatever punishment the congregation meted out to him.

But how about a person who confesses his sins in public or in private? He has not yet been convicted and his confession may be false. In his case would the keys fail in their purpose? Answer: Christ says in Matt. 12 [:37], "By your words you will be justified, and by your words you will be condemned." Therefore, he who confesses of his own free will, and does it humbly, should be believed and forgiven. If he does it defiantly and with lying lips, he should also be believed. To him we say, Let it be to you as you say. Even if he confesses an imaginary sin, it is nonetheless a double sin, by which he intends to lie and to deceive. Hence he gets what he deserves and the key does not fail in its purpose. Just as David's sword did not fail in its purpose when he had the youth put to death who boasted in the king's presence of having killed Saul, although it was a lie (II Kings 1 [II Sam. 1:16]). For David said, "Your blood be on your head; for your own mouth has testified against you, saying, 'I have slain the Lord's anointed.'" And all law codes agree that confession against one's own self is the surest conviction.

In conclusion, we possess these two keys through Christ's command. The key which binds is the power or office to punish the sinner who refuses to repent by means of a public condemnation to eternal death and separation from the rest of Christendom. And when such a judgment is pronounced, it is as a judgment of Christ himself. And if the sinner perseveres in his sin, he is certainly eternally damned. The loosing key is the power or office to absolve the sinner who makes confession and is converted from sins, promising again eternal life. And it has the same significance as if Christ himself passed judgment. And if he believes and continues in this faith he is certainly saved forever. For the key which binds carries forward the work of the law. It is profitable to the sinner inasmuch as it reveals to him his sins, admonishes him to fear God, causes him to tremble, and moves him to repentance, and not to destruction. The loosing key carries forward the work of the gospel. It invites to grace and mercy. It comforts and promises life and salvation through the forgiveness of sins. In short, the two keys advance and foster the gospel by simply proclaiming these two things: repentance and forgiveness of sins [Luke 24:47].

Both of these keys are extremely necessary in Christendom, so that we never can thank God enough for them. For no human being can console a truly frightened sinful conscience. It takes a good deal of effort on the part of the key which looses to accomplish this task. A feeble and fearful conscience is like a severe illness so that faith in the judgment of the key must be stressed forcefully by preachers, pastors, and other Christians. Of such a faith nothing has ever been heard under the papal regime. Again, there are among Christians some uncouth and rude people with arrogant hearts who would grant to pious persons no rest or peace unless the key which binds is present with its rod, reprimanding the former and granting grace and safety to the latter. Despite the sharpness and severity of the key which binds, the achievement of its effect requires a good deal of effort. Therefore, the strong key which binds is for the pious Christians a great consolation, protection, defense, and fortress against evil people. Also, it serves as a wholesome medicine and has a beneficial effect on evil persons, although it is terrifying and annoying to the flesh. For this reason we should value dearly from the depth of our heart these two keys as indescribably precious treasures and jewels for our souls.

For the dear Man, the faithful Bishop of our souls, Jesus Christ, is well aware that his beloved Christians are frail, that the devil, the flesh, and the world would tempt them unceasingly and in many ways, and that at times they would fall into sin. Therefore, he has given us this remedy, the key which binds, so that we might not remain too confident in our sins, arrogant, barbarous, and without God, and in the key which looses, that we should not despair in our sins. Thus aided we should stay on a middle road, between arrogance and faint-heartedness, in genuine humility and confidence, being provided for richly in every way. For he who does not sin (but who does not?), or insofar as he does not sin, has the common gospel. But he who does sin also has the keys beside the gospel.

By the gift of these keys God also wanted to guard effectively against future Novatians[22] who taught that after baptism no mortal sin could be forgiven on earth. But here we recognize that Christ does not give the keys to heathen and unbaptized persons, but to his disciples, and to those who have been baptized. Such a gift would be altogether useless, if sins were not forgiven to those baptized. It is written, "If your brother sins" [Matt. 18:15]. Surely, a brother is a baptized Christian. Yet he says, "If he sins." He does not say, "If he sins once," but simply, "If he sins." He does not set limits for the effectiveness of the key as to numbers or time. Rather, Christ clearly declares the keys' work to be limited by neither measure, number, nor time when he says, "Whatever you bind and loose." He does not refer to several things but to all, comprehended in the word "whatever." So the office of the keys covers every quantity, size, length, and form of sins, whatever their names may be. For he who says "whatever" makes no exception.

However, the word "whatever" should not be interpreted in the sense employed by the pope, as though the keys bind and loose all that is in heaven or on earth. By this interpretation we might usurp the claim to omnipotence. But, as already stated, it should only refer to sin and to nothing else. For we must understand the words of Christ, *secundum materiam subjectam,* that is, we must observe closely of what Christ is speaking in any given passage, and treat the words accordingly, so as not to stretch them beyond their meaning. In attempting to teach everything on the basis of one passage or to make one passage apply to all sorts of things we would become like the factious spirits who simply apply all passages of Scripture to the sacrament of the altar even though they do not have the slightest reference to it. Clearly, Christ does not speak in this connection of any power in heaven or on earth, but of the sins of our brethren, and how we can help them to make amends. Therefore, we may not stretch the words of Christ nor interpret them in

---

[22] The teaching of the Novatians to which Luther refers became the center of controversy in the middle of the third century. Under the pressure of persecution during the reign of the Roman emperor, Decius (249-251), many Christians fell from the faith. Since they had committed the mortal sin of idolatry, Novatus and his adherents in North Africa doubted whether this sin could be forgiven by the church.

any other sense. And the words "whatever" and "binding and loosing" cannot be applied except to these sins.

For Christ's intention is to comfort us poor sinners in the most loving and effective manner. His purpose is not to give the pope power over the angels in heaven nor over emperors on earth. For our consolation all sins, none excepted, are subject to Peter or to the keys. All sins which he binds and looses shall be bound and loosed, despite the resistance of all devils, the whole world, and of all angels, and all despairing thoughts of our heart, even in the presence of death and evil omens. A simple, trusting heart can boldly rely on God's action. And in times of deep distress, with our conscience accusing us, we may say: Well then! I have been absolved of my sins, however many and great they may be, by means of the key, on which I may rely. Let no one remind me of my sins any longer. All are gone, forgiven, forgotten. He who promises me, "Whatever you loose shall be loosed," does not lie; this I know. If my repentance is not sufficient, his Word is; if I am not worthy, his keys are: He is faithful and true. My sins shall not make a liar of him.

Behold, such faith should have been fostered and taught along with the keys. For they demand faith in our hearts, and without faith you cannot use them with profit. But if you believe in their judgment they recover for you the innocence you received in baptism. You will be born anew as a real saint, for God's Word and the keys are holy. They sanctify all who believe in them. It is a very absurd and blasphemous thing to have made the keys depend so exclusively and vigorously on repentance and works. Instead, one should separate the work of the keys from human endeavor as far as the heavens are removed from the earth. Any reasonable person must admit that in the text the keys are not associated with the performance of any works. They enjoin and command nothing, but threaten and promise. Now, to threaten and promise are not the same as to command. The intention of the key which binds is that we heed its threatening and thereby come to fear God. He who believes the key which threatens has satisfied it before and without performing any works. The key does not demand any other work. Afterward such faith will indeed perform works. The intention of the key which looses is to make us believe its consolation and promise, and so learn to love God and receive a joyful, confident, and peaceful heart. He who has faith in the key, has satisfied it by means of such faith, before and without performing any works. This key demands no other works. Afterward such faith will indeed perform works.

We should also be very careful not to foster or teach the one key without the other, according to the example and words of Christ, who always connected the two. Under the papacy the key which binds was used so abominably and tyranically, while the key which looses with its power was stifled altogether, so that everybody had come to hate both keys, and no one experienced sincere contrition or penitence. According to papal teaching, a man should catalogue all his sins and recall them and as a result of the fear of hell create the experience of contrition. Thus through human endeavor he would earn grace before having had recourse to the keys, although it naturally was impossible to recall all one's sins. In addition, the papists taught one should reflect only on the dragon's scaly and coarse sins. But they did not discern the powerful and real abominations, the head and tail of the dragon-like devil with his spiritual poison—that is to say, unbelief, grumbling against God, hatred of God, doubt, blasphemy, despising God, and the like. Much less were they able to teach repentance concerning them. Therefore, their penance was a mere pretense, and it lasted only half the length of Holy Week. Their penance was not thorough, nor was their understanding of it adequate. Instead of attacking real abominations they only taught about imaginary sins committed against their dishonest laws. Of what value could such penance be?

They gave no thorough instruction about sin, nor did they teach anything about Christ, our Mediator, or the consolation attained by the keys. Teaching nothing about faith but only about the unbearable and futile torments of penance, confession, satisfaction, and our own human endeavor, they represented Christ as a cruel judge whom we had to appease, not only with our penance, confession, and works of satisfaction, but with the intercession of his mother and of all the saints. We had to placate Christ with every priest's mass and with every monk's and nun's merit, yet without avail. Nothing remained but a troubled conscience, a fearful heart, despair, and the beginning of the pangs of hell. Is it not so? Who can deny it? Are not the bulls and documents at hand? When I tried to rebuke such manner of penance, I merited the distinction of being condemned as a heretic through Pope Leo [X] and his jackasses. Their harmful and blasphemous abominations had to stand as true articles of faith.

But Christ teaches here [i.e., Matt. 16:19; 18:18] that one should point a sinful conscience to the consolation of the other key and not only the fear produced by the first key. For repentance should also arise from joy and love. To repent out of fear of everlasting punishment without love and devotion to righteousness is to hate God secretly, to blaspheme, and add to one's sins. Such a repentance is no more than that of Judas. But who can repent gladly and joyfully without having the certain consolation and promise of grace which is not the product of our own mind (for this will not last or hold), but must be offered and presented through a definite promise of God's Word? This same consolation mellows and alleviates the terror of the key which binds, enabling our heart to bear and endure it. This is the sort of repentance which does not curse God nor secretly hate him but loves and praises him. It stems from a joyful fear and trembling (Ps. 2 [:1]). This fear pleases God and is of lasting value, bringing forth a new and different man and imparting a true hatred for sin. This can never be achieved by reflection on one's own trespasses, by the fear of hell, or by papal penance.

I maintain one should restore and exalt the teaching about the two keys. Many believe they are experts on this matter, yet they do not understand it. The papists pay little attention to it, for although they hear and read about it, they do not, in the last analysis, care to understand it. For their hearts are set on other thoughts, and they have the veil of Moses covering their eyes.

For the time being let this be enough regarding the keys. May God in grace grant that the ban again come into its right and the doctrine of repentance and of the keys again be rightly known. May the Father of all wisdom and consolation so help us through the Holy Spirit in Jesus Christ our Lord to whom be praise and thanks in all eternity. Amen.

INFILTRATING AND
CLANDESTINE PREACHERS

1532

Translated by Conrad Bergendoff

INTRODUCTION

This letter appeared in January 1532. It was occasioned by the spread of Anabaptist teaching in and around Eisenach. Luther had written against Anabaptist doctrine in 1528,* though he admitted it was difficult for him to ascertain what the teachings were since there were many contradictions among those in the group itself. He said then that he was unaware of Anabaptist preachers in his region, but it was not long before they appeared, and by 1532 they had caused much disturbance, especially among peasants and villagers. Luther is not inclined in this letter to argue their peculiar tenets and falls back rather on the necessity of order in the church— the Anabaptist preachers are not called, and their preaching is done covertly and stealthily instead of openly and properly.

To us it seems a harsh treatise and we are less impressed than Luther's followers by his argument for order. We need, however, to judge the letter from the viewpoint of Luther's century rather than ours. For then it was taken almost for granted that there could be only one ecclesiastical authority in a given region, and challenging the spiritual order was as criminal an offense as rebellion against the temporal. Luther realizes that his argument can be turned against himself. He defends himself with his call and protests that his actions were within his duty. He could not grant the same justification to those who were not interested in the kind of a church organization he himself considered essential. A later generation, in a new world, removed the foundations of Luther's arguments when it separated church and state, and took from all churches their ancient privileges. And a clearer view of the character of the Anabaptists has revealed that Luther's judgment of them was a result of his presuppositions. Luther's verdict is understandable but is not the verdict of history, which has discovered saints and martyrs among them and found that they were used of God for momentous consequences.

The translation follows the 1532 text in WA 30^{III}, 518-527.

---

* Cf. pp. 226-262.

INFILTRATING AND
CLANDESTINE PREACHERS

A Letter of Doctor Martin Luther

To the Honorable and worthy Eberhard von der Tannen,[1] magistrate at the Wartburg, my gracious lord and friend.

Grace and peace in Christ, our Lord and Savior, Amen. I have learned, my dear lord and friend, how the Anabaptists are seeking to infiltrate also in your vicinity and to infect our people with their poison. I know you have been well informed and advised by the book of Justus Menius.[2] You have discharged your office in a proper and praiseworthy manner against these emissaries of the devil. But the devil does not gladly refrain from his activities, and the majority only read a book hastily and then throw it in a corner, forgetting what they were told, so that they need a daily and incessant reminder. Therefore I have wanted, by this letter to you, to also ask and advise all other magistrates, cities, and princes to be on the alert against these infiltrators, so that we do our duty.

There is a way of convicting them easily and effectively. If

---

[1] Appointed as counselor to the elector of Saxony in 1527 and as chief magistrate of the Wartburg and the nearby town of Eisenach, Eberhard von und zu der Tann (or Tannen) (1495-1574) served as representative and diplomat-at-large of the electors of Saxony in dealing with the Anabaptist movement, the Zwinglian party at Marburg (1529), the bigamy of Philip of Hesse (1540), and the complex problems arising from and following the Smalcald War (1547).
[2] Upon his participation in the visitation of congregations in Thuringia in 1527, Justus Menius (1499-1558) was appointed as pastor and superintendent of Gotha in 1529. Active in opposing the Anabaptist movement in association with von der Tannen and his colleague in Eisenach, Friedrich Myconius, he published the book *Der Wiedertäufer Lehre und Geheimnis widerlegt* (1530) *(Refutation of the Doctrine and Stealth of the Anabaptists),* of which Luther approved and to which he wrote a preface. Cf. WA 30^{II}, 211f.

you ask them about their call, who has commanded them to come hither stealthily and to preach secretly, they will be unable to answer or to produce their authorization. Even if these infiltrators were otherwise faultless and saintly through and through, still this one fact (that they sneak about unbidden and uncommissioned) sufficiently proves that they are the devil's messengers and teachers. For the Holy Spirit does not come with stealth. He descends in full view from heaven. The serpents glide unnoticed. The doves fly. You can be sure that this secretiveness is characteristic of the devil.

I have been told how these infiltrators worm their way to harvesters and preach to them in the field during their work, as well as to the solitary workers at charcoal kilns or in the woods. Everywhere they sow their seed and spread their poison, turning the people from their parish churches. There you see the true print and touch of the devil, how he shuns the light and works in the dark. Who is so dull as not to be able to discern that these are messengers of the devil? If they came from God and were honest, they would first of all repair to the parish pastor and deal with him, making clear their call and telling what they believed and asking for his permission to preach publicly. If then the parish pastor would not permit it, they would be blameless before God and could then wipe the dust off their feet, etc. [cf. Luke 10:11]. For to the pastor is committed the pulpit, baptism, the sacrament [of the altar], and he is charged with the care of souls. But now these want to dislodge the pastor secretly, together with all of his authority, without revealing their secret commission. They are indeed regular thieves and murderers of souls, blasphemers, and enemies of Christ and his churches.

There is no other solution than that both offices, the spiritual and temporal, concern themselves diligently with these matters. Through the spiritual office, the people must be constantly instructed, emphasizing what has been mentioned previously, so that they admit no infiltrators, considering them truly as sent of the devil, and learning to ask of them, whence do you come? Who has sent you? Who has bidden you to preach to me? Where are your seals and letters of authorization from persons who have sent you? What signs do you perform to show that God has sent you? Why do you not go to our pastor? Why do you come so furtively to me and crouch as in a corner? Why don't you appear publicly? If you are a child of light, why do you shun the light? With such questions I think you can guard against them easily, for they cannot prove their calling. If we can bring the people to so understand a call, one could control such infiltrators.

Also we should teach and urge the people to report such intruders to their pastors, for they are duty bound to do so, if they are Christians and seek salvation. When they do not do so, they abet the emissaries of the devil and these infiltrators in secretly robbing the pastor (indeed God himself) of his ministry, baptism, sacrament of the altar, the care of souls, and his parishioners. Thus they destroy and bring to naught the parish system (ordained of God). If the people hear such instruction and know the meaning of the call, some devoted members will undoubtedly report these furtive preachers and conspirators. For, as said, if we emphasize the matter of the call, we can worry the devil. A parish pastor can claim that he possesses the office of the ministry, baptism, the sacrament, the care of souls, and is commissioned, publicly and legally. Therefore the people should go to him for these things. But the alien interlopers and plotters can make no such claim and must confess that they are strangers and graspingly seek what is not theirs. This cannot be of the Holy Spirit, but of an exasperating devil.

Also the temporal authorities must heed the situation. For since these infiltrators are sent by the devil to preach nothing but poison and lies, and the devil is not only a liar but a murderer [John 8:44], it can only be that he intends through these emissaries to create rebellion and murder (even if for a while he carries on peacefully), and to overthrow both spiritual and temporal government against the will of God. He cannot do otherwise, for it is his nature to lie and kill. Nor can those possessed by him control themselves, but must do what he urges them on to do.

It is proper for officials, judges, and those concerned with government to be certain of their right to suspect these infiltrators not only of false teaching, but also of violence and revolt, realizing that the devil occupies the driver's seat in these people. Through their lieutenants they should assemble their subjects and call attention to and warn against such villains. They should sternly command their people to inform on these intruders on peril of heavy penalty, and make clear their duties as subjects if they do not wish to be regarded as accomplices in murder and revolt, which is the devil's purpose. Like the church officials they should press the matter of the call, questioning the infiltrator or his host, as mentioned previously, whence do you come? Who sent you? And the host should be asked, who has bidden you to give this intruder lodging, or to listen to his clandestine preaching? How do you know that he is authorized to teach you or you to learn of him? Why have you not notified the parish pastor or us? Why do you slouch in dark corners and forsake the church where you were baptized, instructed, went to communion and where you belong, in the order of God? Why, secretly and without commission, do you start something new? Who has given you right to divide this parish and cause dissensions among us? Who has commanded you to despise your pastor, to judge and condemn him behind his back without a charge or a fair hearing? Since when are you a judge of your pastor, or for that matter, your own judge?

Of such misdeeds and worse each one is guilty who joins these infiltrators, and is justly called to give an account of his actions. Wherever authorities are diligent, I have every reason to hope, great advantages would accrue to all concerned. Many pious people would be on the alert and therefore lend a helping hand in expelling these knaves, were they made aware of the great danger posed by infiltrators and the importance attached to a proper call and commission. If we did not hold fast to and emphasize the call and commission, there would finally be no church. For just as the infiltrators come among us and want to split and devastate our churches, so afterwards other intruders would invade their churches and divide and devastate them. And there would be no end to the process of intrusion and division, until soon nothing would be left of the church on earth. So indeed is the devil's purpose with such spirits of dissension and intrusion.

So we say, either demand proof of a call and commission to preach, or immediately enjoin silence and forbid to preach, for an office is involved—the office of the ministry. One cannot hold an office without a commission or a call. In Christ's parable in Matt. 25 [:14], the lord did not give the servants the talents with which they were to trade before he called them in and commanded them to trade. "He called his servants," the text says, and "entrusted to them his property." Let the interloper bring such a call and authorization with him, or else let the Lord's money alone. Otherwise he will be found a thief and a rogue. According to Matt. 20 [:2], the laborers did not go into the vineyard until the householder hired them and sent them. Some stood idle the whole day until they were called and sent.

God speaks of infiltrators of this kind in Jer. 23 [:21]: "They run and I have not sent them. They preach, and I have not commanded them." There is worry and work enough to maintain the right kind of preaching and true doctrine in the case of those who have an undoubted call and commission from God himself or from those acting on his behalf. What then is preaching without the commandment of God, indeed against his will and prohibition, in consequence of the prodding and agitation of the devil? Such preaching can indeed be nothing but an inspiration of the evil one and be merely the teaching of the devil no matter how it glistens.

Who has ever had a greater and more certain call than Aaron, the first high priest? Yet he fell into idolatry and permitted the Jews to make a golden calf [Exod. 32:1ff.]. Later the whole Levitical priesthood for the most part became guilty of idolatry, even persecuting the Word of God and the true prophets [Cf. I Sam. 2:12ff.]. King Solomon had a good enough call and confirmation of it, but in his old age he fell and committed much idolatry [Cf. I Kings 11:4ff.]. What a splendid call and commission the bishops and popes have had! Do they not sit in the chair of the apostles and in Christ's stead? Still, they are altogether the worst enemies of the gospel, unless they teach correctly and preserve the true worship and service of God.

If then teachers who are called, ordained, and consecrated of God himself can be misled by the devil to engage in false teaching and persecute the truth, how shall he accomplish anything good through those whom he inspires and ordains, without and contrary to the bidding of God? Will he not through them bring forth more truly devilish lies? I have often said and still say, I would not exchange my doctor's degree for all the world's gold. For I would surely in the long run lose courage and fall into despair if, as these infiltrators, I had undertaken these great and serious matters without call or commission. But God and the whole world bears me testimony that I entered into this work publicly and by virtue of my office as teacher and preacher, and have carried it on hitherto by the grace and help of God.

Undoubtedly some maintain that in I Cor. 14, St. Paul gave anyone liberty to preach in the congregation, even to bark against the established preacher. For he says, "If a revelation is made to another sitting by, let the first be silent" [I Cor. 14:30]. The interlopers take this to mean that to whatever church they come they have the right and power to judge the preacher and to proclaim otherwise. But this is far wide of the mark. The interlopers do not rightly regard the text, but read out of it—rather, smuggle into it— what they wish. In this passage Paul is speaking of the prophets, who are to teach, not of the people, who are to listen.[3] For prophets are teachers who have the office of preaching in the churches. Otherwise why should they be called prophets? If the interloper can prove that he is a prophet or a teacher of the church to which he comes, and can show who has authorized him, then let him be heard as St. Paul prescribes. Failing this let him return to the devil who sent him to steal the preacher's office belonging to another in a church to which he belongs neither as a listener nor a pupil, let alone as a prophet and master.

What a fine model I imagine that would be, for anyone to have the right to interrupt the preacher and begin to argue with him! Soon another would join in and tell the other two to hush up. Perchance a drunk from the tavern would come in and join the trio calling on the third to be silent. At last the women too would claim the right of "sitting by," telling the men to be silent [I Cor. 14:34]. Then one woman silencing the other—oh, what a beautiful holiday, auction, and carnival that would be! What pig sties could compare in goings-on with such churches? There the devil may have my place as preacher. But the blind interlopers do not realize this. They think they alone "sit by," and do not see that any one else has just as much right to hush them up. Neither do they know

---

[3] Cf., however, Luther's interpretation of this passage in *Concerning the Ministry*, pp. 32, 37.

what they say, nor get the meaning of what St. Paul says here about sitting or speaking, about prophets or people.

Whoever reads the entire chapter will see clearly that St. Paul is concerned about speaking with tongues, about teaching and preaching in the churches or congregations. He is not commanding the congregation to preach, but is dealing with those who are preachers in the congregations or assemblies. Otherwise he would not be forbidding women to preach since they also are a part of the Christian congregation [I Cor. 14:34f.]. The text shows how it was customary for the prophets to be seated among the people in the churches as the regular parish pastors and preachers, and how the lesson was sung or read by one or two, just as in our days on high festivals it is the custom in some churches for two to sing the Gospel together.

Then one of the prophets whose turn it was spoke and interpreted the lesson, much in the way a homily[4] used to be delivered in the Roman church. When one was through, another might have something to add in confirmation or clarification, just as in Acts 15 [:13ff.], St. James commented on the sermon of St. Peter, confirming and explaining it. St. Luke records that St. Paul followed a similar practice in the synagogues, especially in Antioch of Pisidia, where the ruler of the synagogue permitted him to speak after the reading of the lesson from the Law [Acts 13:14f.]. Then St. Paul rose and spoke, but as a commissioned apostle and on that prescribed by the master, and not as an interloper. From this it is clear that "sitting by" refers only to authorized prophets or preachers. It was a question of who among them was to speak, who to rise, and who to sit.

The practice is similar to that of a prince seated in council with his councilors or of a mayor with his councilmen. One rises to speak, then another, and finally they harmoniously follow him who gives the best advice. They counsel one another and so everything proceeds in a decent and dignified way. Thus the

---

The homily is a verse by verse interpretation of a given section of the Scriptures. Usually considered the earliest sermon form in the history of preaching, it was simple and informal in style. Under the influence of medieval scholasticism it was gradually replaced by a more ornate and rhetorical form of preaching.

prophets served as a church council, teaching the Scriptures, caring for and governing the congregation. Should one tolerate a tramp who intrudes or a citizen who comes without authorization to the council, to rebuke or control the mayor? There wouldn't be much question of his being taken by the neck and put in stocks so that he would learn where to sit and be put in his proper place.

Still less should one tolerate in a spiritual council, that is in a council of preachers or prophets, a stranger intruding himself or an unauthorized layman presuming to preach in his parish church. It is and remains the duty of the prophets to care for the teaching in proper succession, faithfully helping each other, so that everything is done decently and in order, as St. Paul commands [I Cor. 14:40]. But how can there be decency and order when one attacks another in a ministry not committed to him, and any layman whatsoever wants to get up in church and preach?

But I am astonished that in their spiritual wisdom they haven't learned to adduce examples of how women have prophesied and thereby attained rule over men, land, and people. There was Deborah (Judg. 4 [:1f.]), who caused the death of King Jabin and Sisera and ruled Israel. There was the wise woman in Abel, in David's days of whom we read in II Sam. 20 [:13ff.], and the prophetess Huldah, in the days of Josiah (II Kings 22 [:14ff.]). Long before, there was Sarah, who directed her husband and lord, Abraham, to cast out Ishmael and his mother Hagar, and God commanded Abraham to obey her. Furthermore, the widow Hannah (Luke 2 [:36ff.]), and the Virgin Mary (Luke 1 [:46ff.]). Here they might deck themselves out and find authority for women to preach in the churches. How much greater the reason for men to preach, where and when they please.

We shall for the present not be concerned about the right of these women of the Old Testament to teach and to rule. But surely they did not act as the infiltrators do, unauthorized, and out of superior piety and wisdom. For then God would not have confirmed their ministry and worked by miracles and great deeds. But in the New Testament the Holy Spirit, speaking through St. Paul, ordained that women should be silent in the churches and assemblies [I Cor. 14:34], and said that this is the Lord's commandment.[5] Yet he knew that previously Joel [2:28f.] had proclaimed that God would pour out his Spirit also on handmaidens. Furthermore, the four daughters of Philip prophesied (Acts 21 [:9]). But in the congregations or churches where there is a ministry women are to be silent and not preach [I Tim. 2:12]. Otherwise they may pray, sing, praise, and say "Amen," and read at home, teach each other, exhort, comfort, and interpret the Scriptures as best they can.

In sum, St. Paul would not tolerate the wickedness and arrogance of someone interfering with the office of another. Each one should pay attention to his own commission and call, allowing another to discharge his office unmolested and in peace. As for the rest, he may be wise, teach, sing, read, interpret to his heart's content, in matters of his concern. If God wants to accomplish something over and beyond this order of offices and calling and raise up someone who is above the prophets, he will demonstrate this with signs and deeds, just as he made the ass to speak and chastise his lord, the prophet Balaam [Num. 22:21ff.]. When God does not do so we are to remain obedient to the office and authority already ordained. If the incumbents of the office teach wrongly, what affair is that of yours? You are not called to give account for it.

In this chapter [I Cor. 14] St. Paul, thus, often refers to the "congregation," clearly distinguishing between prophets and people. The prophets speak, the congregation listens. For so he says, "He who prophesies builds up the church." And again, "Strive to excel in building up the church" [I Cor. 14:4, 12]. Who then are those who are to build up the church? Is it not the prophets, and (as he says) those speaking with tongues, that is who read or sing the lesson, to whom the congregation listens, and the prophets whose duty it is to interpret the lesson for the building up of the congregation? It should be clear that he is commanding the congregation to listen and build itself up, and is not commissioning it to teach or preach. He makes an even clearer distinction when he speaks of the congregation as the laity, and says, "If you bless with the spirit, how can anyone in the place of the laity say the 'Amen,' when he does not know what you are saying? For you may

---

[5] Apparently, Luther is thinking of I Cor. 7:10.

give thanks well enough, but the other man is not edified" [I Cor. 14:16f.]. This again points to a difference between preacher and layman. But what need is there for further discussion? The text is plain, and reason tells us that we are not to interfere with an office not our own.

Thus we read in St. Paul: "Let two or three prophets speak, and let the others weigh what is said," etc. [I Cor. 14:29]. This of course is said only of the prophets, and of which ones should speak and which should weigh what was said. What is meant by "others"? The people? Of course not. It means the other prophets or those speaking with tongues who should help in the church with preaching and building up of the congregation, those who should judge and assist in seeing to it that the preaching is right. Should it happen that one of the prophets or preachers came upon the best interpretation, the other should yield and say, yes, you are right. I did not understand it as well. Just as at table or in other circumstances, even in temporal affairs, one gives in to the other. In matters such as these one ought to yield much more readily to the other.

From this we can see how beautifully and carefully the infiltrators have considered St. Paul! They think they can use him to prove that in all churches they have the right to "sit by," to attack any preacher anywhere in Christendom, judging and condemning, and to arrogate to themselves a call and power to pass sentence on pulpits not theirs. It is indeed nothing but thievery and murder to interfere in another's office with wantonness and violence. Against such St. Peter warns in I Pet. 4 [:15]: "Let none of you suffer . . . as a wrongdoer, or as a meddler in other men's matters."

Though it is no longer the custom for prophets or preachers to sit in the church and take turns in speaking (as St. Paul describes it), some indication and vestige of it does remain. For we do sing alternately in the choir and read one lesson after the other and then together sing an antiphon, hymn, or response. And when one preacher interprets what another reads, and another explains or preaches thereon, then indeed we follow the right method in the churches, according to St. Paul. For then one sings or speaks with tongues, the second translates, the third expounds, and still another confirms or illustrates with maxims and examples, as St. James in Acts 15 [:13ff.] and Paul in Acts 13 [:14f.]. This certainly is better than merely reading or singing the lesson in Latin, an unfamiliar language, as the nuns read the Psalter. St. Paul indeed does not condemn such speaking in tongues in itself, but he neither commands nor praises it in the churches when unaccompanied by explanation.

But I would not be in favor of restoring this custom and doing away with the pulpit. Rather I would oppose it, for the people are at present too untamed and forward. And a devil might easily worm his way in among parish pastors, preachers, and chaplains. One would want to be above and better than the other, quarreling and snapping at each other in the presence of the people. Therefore it is better to retain the pulpit, for then at least things are done decently and in order, as St. Paul admonishes. It is sufficient that in one parish the preachers take daily turns in preaching or, if they wish, preach in different places in turn. One might expound in the afternoon or forenoon what the other has sung or read in matins or in the mass, as now and then it happens with the Gospel and the Epistle. For St. Paul is not so rigidly concerned about the one method, but he is concerned about order and decent procedure, and gives this method as an example. We had better keep our custom in preaching since it more than the other will keep order among our stupid folk.

In the days of the Apostle the custom of prophets sitting alongside each other was possible. For it was a habit of long standing and practiced daily among a well-disciplined people who had inherited it from Moses through the Levitical priesthood. It would hardly do to restore the practice among such uncouth, undisciplined, shameless people as ours.

So much for the words of St. Paul. To sum it all up, the infiltrating and clandestine preachers are apostles of the devil. St. Paul everywhere complains of those who run in and out of houses upsetting whole families, always teaching yet not knowing what they say or direct [Tit. 1:11]. Therefore the spiritual office is to be warned and admonished, and the temporal office is to be warned and admonished. Let each one who is a Christian and a subject be warned to be on guard against these interlopers and not to heed them. Whoever tolerates and listens to them should know that he is listening to the devil himself, incarnate and abominable, as he speaks out of the mouth of a possessed person. I have done my duty. I am innocent, as I said in my commentary on Psalm 82.[6] Let the blood of anyone who does not follow good and honest advice be upon himself.

I commend you, my dear lord and friend, and yours to the grace and mercy of God. To him be thanks and praise, honor and glory forever in Christ Jesus, our Lord and Savior. Amen.

---

[6] *WA* 31^I, 189ff.; *LW* 13, 39ff.; *PE* 4, 287ff.

INDEXES

INDEX OF NAMES AND SUBJECTS

sacrament dispoiled, 206
expelled from Saxony, 63, 75, 102
spiritualist leader, xi, 75, 113 n. 82
Strassburg disturbance, 67
studies at Erfurt, Cologne, Wittenberg, 75
unstable, 133
unworthy participation denied, 179 n. 139
and Word of God, 91, 100
works:
  Anzeig etlicher Hauptartikel christlicher Lehre, 149 n. 105
  Auhslegung dieser Wort Christi Das ist mein Leib, 131 n. 77, 201 n. 157
  Dialogus oder ein Gesprächbüchlein von dem grevlichen und abgöttischen Missbrauch des hochwürdigen Sakraments Jesu Christi, 145 n. 99, 154 n. 114, 158 n. 120, 195 n. 151, 211 n. 160
  Von dem alten und neuen Testament, 102 n. 25, 166 n. 130
  Wider die alten und neuen papistischen Messen, 127 n. 75, 132 n. 81
Keys, office of
  believer and Christ use, 365
  both keys together, 376
  belongs to all Christians, 26
  Christ's Word certain, 346
  cannot fail, 368
  not a command, 327
  proclaim forgiveness, 28, 328, 373
  frees, not binds, 335
  looses in heaven, 334
  heavenly kingdom, 328, 330
  not human ordinance, 330
  key of knowledge, 357
  pope's keys not Christ's, 330
    binding not in error, 333 ff.
    loosing may err, 333 ff.
    bring no grace, 350
  Scripture misinterpreted, 325 ff., 374
  secular different, 331
  sins to be stressed, 359
  treasure of church, 373
  true use, 370, 372, 375
  uncertain, 344
  where Word is, 362

demand no work, but produce works, 375-376
Knebel, Victus, 211
Knowledge
  ardent, 204, 205-206, 208, 212-213
Kolb, Franz, 68 n. 2
Kolkryb, 199 n. 155

Latin
  on festivals, 309
  hymns permissible, 300, 307
  in schools, 315-320
Law
  Ten Commandments, 276, 308, 318, 329, 333
  right use, 82, 83
Leipzig, 53
Leo X, pope, 377
Lord's Prayer, 161, 307, 308, 315, 318
Love
  works of, 83
Luther
  and Agricola, 266
  use of allegory, 190
  nature of Church, ix
  confessional retained, 323-324
  defends himself, 54-55
  doctor's degree, 387
  doctrine all-important, 57
  dogmas not morals attacked, 200
  and Elector, 102
  freedom of Christian, 129
  and images, 84, 85, 91
  at Jena and Orlamünde, 69 n. 3, 100, 107 ns. 40, 43
  and Karlstadt, 75, 103, 107 n. 42, 129, 136, 186
  wrong key rejected, 351
  one kind in communion, 290-291
  mass, 122-123, 141
  and Münzer, 48, 53-54
  accused of being papist, 231
  accused of fawning before princes, 90, 110
  duty of princes, 57
  beginning of reform, 53
  defends term sacrament, 151
  wanted easier explanation of sacrament, 68
  allows term sacrifice, 124 ff.
  Spirit's fruits, 52, 55
  unworthy participation, 183
  visitation commended, 272-273

INDEX TO SCRIPTURE PASSAGES